Edge Intelligence for 6G-Enabled Industrial Internet of Things

Scrivener Publishing
100 Cummings Center, Suite 541J
Beverly, MA 01915-6106

Publishers at Scrivener
Martin Scrivener (martin@scrivenerpublishing.com)
Phillip Carmical (pcarmical@scrivenerpublishing.com)

Edge Intelligence for 6G-Enabled Industrial Internet of Things

Edited by

Sita Rani
Department of Computer Science and Engineering, Guru Nanak Dev Engineering College, Ludhiana, Punjab, India

Pankaj Bhambri
Guru Nanak Dev Engineering College, Ludhiana, Punjab, India

Balamurugan Balusamy
School of Engineering and IT, Manipal Academy of Higher Education, Dubai Campus, Dubai, UAE

Rishabha Malviya
School of Medical and Allied Sciences, Galgotias University, Greater Noida, Uttar Pradesh, India

and

Seifedine Kadry
Department of Computer Science and Mathematics, Lebanese American University, Beirut, Lebanon

Scrivener Publishing

WILEY

This edition first published 2026 by John Wiley & Sons, Inc., 111 River Street, Hoboken, NJ 07030, USA and Scrivener Publishing LLC, 100 Cummings Center, Suite 541J, Beverly, MA 01915, USA

For more information about Scrivener publications please visit www.scrivenerpublishing.com.

Wiley Global Headquarters
111 River Street, Hoboken, NJ 07030, USA

For details of our global editorial offices, customer services, and more information about Wiley products visit us at www.wiley.com.

The manufacturer's authorized representative according to the EU General Product Safety Regulation is Wiley-VCH GmbH, Boschstr. 12, 69469 Weinheim, Germany, e-mail: Product_Safety@wiley.com.

Library of Congress Cataloging-in-Publication Data

ISBN 978-1-394-30538-4

Cover image: Generated with AI using Adobe Firefly
Cover design by Russell Richardson

Set in size of 11pt and Minion Pro by Manila Typesetting Company, Makati, Philippines

Printed in the USA

10 9 8 7 6 5 4 3 2 1

Contents

Foreword

Industry operations, communication, and innovation are undergoing a profound transformation as a result of the convergence of Edge Intelligence and the 6G-enabled Industrial Internet of Things (IIoT). The importance of cutting-edge wireless networks, artificial intelligence, and real-time data processing at the edge is greater than ever as industrial landscapes become more digitalized. This book is a current and extensive resource that covers the main issues, developments, and future directions of this quickly developing topic.

Dr. Sita Rani and Dr. Rishabha Malviya, along with other editors and eminent contributors, have meticulously selected informative chapters that provide a thorough understanding of the role of 6G technology and edge computing in transforming industrial ecosystems. This book provides an insightful perspective for researchers, industry experts, and academicians seeking to maximize the potential of next-generation connectivity and intelligence in IIoT by connecting theoretical principles with practical implementations. Organized in step-by-step information, the book begins by outlining fundamental principles and progresses to cutting-edge innovations, such as autonomous edge intelligence, real-time decision-making, and privacy-embedded industrial networks. It provides an overview of the opportunities and challenges connected with using various technologies, ensuring that readers have a comprehensive understanding of the topic.

This book is evidence of the authors' and editors' dedication to expanding this field's recognition. Any individual seeking to learn about and understand the development of 6G-enabled IioT will find this to be an essential resource. I do not doubt that this work will inspire greater investigation and creativity, opening the door to a more intelligent, interconnected, and productive industrial future.

I offer my gratitude to Dr. Sita Rani and Dr. Rishabha Malviya, along with other editors, for their hard work in making this book a reality, and to all of the contributing authors for their insightful contributions. I am honored to offer this foreword, and I strongly suggest this book to professionals, researchers, and students who are interested in delving into the newest developments in edge intelligence and 6G-enabled IIoT.

Happy reading and best wishes!

Dr. Dhruv Galgotia
CEO, Galgotias University, Greater Noida, India

Preface

The emergence of sixth-generation (6G) wireless networks is about to bring a revolution in the Industrial Internet of Things (IIoT). Edge intelligence combined with 6G-enabled IIoT offers to revolutionize industrial automation, connectivity, security, and efficiency by facilitating autonomous operations and real-time decision-making. This book offers an in-depth discussion of the role of edge intelligence and 6G technology in the context of the IIoT.

Each of the eighteen chapters in this book address a critical aspect of the subject.

The first chapter presents the 6G ecosystem inside the IIoT framework, emphasizing the main ways that it differs from earlier generations. Subsequent chapters address the fundamentals of edge intelligence, developments in industrial connectivity, and security frameworks designed for IIoT ecosystems enabled by 6G. Also included is an in-depth discussion about the role of wireless infrastructure, edge-to-cloud synergy, and machine learning in maximizing industrial intelligence.

Dedicated chapters address the difficulties of safeguarding a hyperconnected society and integrating privacy into IIoT systems. They discuss in detail the role of massive language models in industrial intelligence, the convergence of high-performance computing infrastructures, and real-time edge intelligence for autonomous systems. By presenting state-of-the-art research and practical applications of edge intelligence in 6G-enabled IIoT contexts, this book attempts to close the gap between theoretical understanding and practical application. For scholars, experts, and industrial representatives interested in utilizing 6G and edge intelligence for the future of industrial automation, it is an invaluable resource.

We wish to offer our thanks to Martin Scrivener and the team at Scrivener Publishing for their effort and guidance in the publication of this work.

The Editors

Part 1

INTRODUCTION, AND FUTURE PROSPECTS TO EDGE INTELLIGENCE FOR 6G ENABLED INDUSTRIAL INTERNET OF THINGS

1

Unveiling the 6G Landscape in Industrial IoT

Sita Rani[1] and Pankaj Bhambri[2]*

[1]*Department of Computer Science and Engineering, Guru Nanak Dev Engineering College, Ludhiana, Punjab, India*
[2]*Guru Nanak Dev Engineering College, Ludhiana, Punjab, India*

Abstract

The idea behind 6G commutation is quickly developing. It is anticipated to have a major impact on IoT networks. The Industrial Internet of Things and 6G technology and #39s transformative potential is examined in this chapter. The article gives a summary of the improvements in technology that 6G brings over earlier generations, such as ultra-low latency, improved connectivity, and AI integration. The chapter explores the technical difficulties, including managing the vast number of connected devices, guaranteeing strong security, and achieving energy efficiency. It also discusses legal and economic issues, emphasizing the necessity of international norms and sustainable practices. The chapter highlights how crucial 6G will be in transforming industrial processes, making smart manufacturing possible, and encouraging industrial automation innovation. This investigation provides insights into how the capabilities and uses of 6G technology will shape the IIoT landscape in the future.

***Keywords*:** Ultra-low latency, AI integration, energy efficiency, smart manufacturing

**Corresponding author*: pkbhambri@gmail.com; ORCID: 0000-0003-4437-4103
Sita Rani: ORCID: 0000-0003-2778-0214

Sita Rani, Pankaj Bhambri, Balamurugan Balusamy, Rishabha Malviya and Seifedine Kadry (eds.) Edge Intelligence for 6G-Enabled Industrial Internet of Things, (3–22) © 2026 Scrivener Publishing LLC

1.1 Introduction

The sixth generation of wireless communication, or 6G, is expected to replace 5G. Ultra-high data rates, incredibly low latency, and increased reliability are its main goals. Terahertz frequency bands, which provide substantially more bandwidth than existing cellular networks and allow data rates of up to 1 terabit per second, are among the key features. 6G will combine cutting-edge technologies like satellite networks for worldwide coverage, artificial intelligence for network optimization, and quantum communication for increased security. With previously unheard-of levels of connectivity and automation, it promises to transform industries like autonomous systems, immersive extended reality (XR), and the Industrial Internet of Things (IIoT). Although 6G is still in its early stages of research, commercial deployment is anticipated by 2030 [1, 2].

1.1.1 Evolution from 5G to 6G Technology

The transition from 5G to 6G represents a major advancement in technology. Although 5G introduced reduced latency, increased device connectivity, and faster speeds, 6G seeks to improve these features even more. Ultra-low latency, nearly instantaneous communication, and data rates up to 100 times faster than 5G are anticipated features of 6G. The use of terahertz frequencies, which offer greater bandwidth and faster data transmission rates, is one of the major breakthroughs. Furthermore, 6G will incorporate state-of-the-art technologies like enhanced support for massive machine-type communications, AI-driven network management, and quantum communication for strong security. More immersive experiences, like extended reality (XR), and sophisticated applications in fields like smart cities, healthcare, and the industrial internet of things (IIoT) will be made possible by this evolution [3, 4].

Table 1.1 outlines the key differences between 5G and 6G technologies. It also highlights the substantial improvements and new features expected in 6G compared to 5G, showcasing its potential to revolutionize various sectors.

1.1.2 The Role of IoT in Industry 4.0

Industry 4.0, the continuous digitalization-driven revolution in manufacturing and industry, heavily relies on the internet of things (IoT).

Table 1.1 Key differences between 5G and 6G technology [5–10].

Feature	5G	6G
Data Rate	Up to 10 Gbps	Up to 1 Tbps
Latency	As low as 1 ms	Less than 1 ms, potentially in microseconds
Frequency Bands	Up to mmWave (30-300 GHz)	Terahertz frequencies (300 GHz - 10 THz)
Network Architecture	Centralized and Cloud-Based	AI-driven, Distributed, and Edge Computing
Connectivity Density	1 million devices per square kilometer	Higher density, supporting trillions of devices
Security	Advanced but vulnerable to quantum threats	Quantum communication and enhanced security
Energy Efficiency	Significant improvements over 4G	Focus on ultra-low energy consumption
Key Technologies	Massive MIMO, Beamforming, Network Slicing	AI/ML Integration, Terahertz Communication, Quantum Technology
Primary Use-cases	Enhanced mobile broadband, IoT, smart cities	Extended Reality (XR), Holographic Communication, IIoT, Autonomous Systems
Deployment Time	Ongoing	Expected around 2030

IoT enables real-time data collection, analysis, and communication by connecting physical objects, machinery, and systems to the internet. To create smart factories—wherein devices and systems can independently monitor workflows, anticipate maintenance requirements, and optimize operations—this connectivity is essential. IoT enables smooth integration between different production stages in Industry 4.0, increasing productivity and decreasing downtime. Equipment sensors, for instance, can minimize expensive disruptions by tracking performance metrics, identifying irregularities, and setting off maintenance alerts prior to a failure.

By giving real-time visibility into inventory levels, shipment status, and logistics, IoT also makes supply chain management better by facilitating more effective resource allocation [11, 12]. IoT also enables more flexible and customizable production through the use of advanced manufacturing technologies like robotics, augmented reality, and additive manufacturing. Because it makes real-time monitoring possible and guarantees that product standards are consistently met, it also contributes significantly to quality control. So, Industry 4.0 is largely dependent on IoT, which propels innovation, boosts productivity, and makes it possible for more flexible and data-driven industrial processes [13].

1.1.3 Importance of 6G in Enhancing Industrial IoT

The industrial internet of things (IIoT) is expected to undergo a revolutionary change, thanks to 6G technology, which offers ultra-low latency, high reliability, and massive connectivity. Real-time analytics and faster data transmission are becoming more and more necessary as industries become more automated and networked. With speeds up to 100 times faster than 5G and latency as low as 1 millisecond, 6G is expected to enable seamless communication between devices, sensors, and systems, enabling cutting-edge applications like augmented reality for troubleshooting and training, predictive maintenance, and remote machinery control [14].

Furthermore, the integration of machine learning and artificial intelligence (AI) will be supported by 6G, improving industrial environments' decision-making processes. Innovations in industries like manufacturing, logistics, and energy will also be fueled by its rapid processing of large amounts of data. Sensitive industrial data will also be safeguarded by 6G's improved security features, providing strong cybersecurity in increasingly digitalized operations [15]. In conclusion, 6G is expected to be a key technology in the development of the IIoT, promoting safety, creativity, and efficiency in a range of sectors.

1.2 Key Features of 6G Technology

6G, the sixth generation of wireless communication technology, is expected to build upon the advancements of 5G and introduce several key features and technologies that will transform connectivity. Here are some of the most anticipated aspects:

1.2.1 Ultra-High Speeds

- Data Rates: 6G is projected to offer peak data rates of up to 1 Tbps, which is significantly faster than 5G.
- Bandwidth: Utilization of higher frequency bands, including terahertz (THz) frequencies, will enable these speeds.

1.2.2 Ultra-Low Latency

- Latency: Expected to be less than 1 millisecond, 6G will support real-time applications such as remote surgery, autonomous vehicles, and immersive virtual reality (VR).

1.2.3 Massive Connectivity

- Device Density: Capable of supporting millions of connected devices per square kilometer, 6G will enhance the internet of things (IoT), including the industrial internet of things (IIoT).

1.2.4 Advanced AI and Machine Learning Integration

- AI and ML: These technologies will be integrated at the network edge, enabling intelligent data processing, predictive maintenance, and personalized services.

1.2.5 Enhanced Reliability and Security

- Reliability: 6G aims to achieve near-perfect reliability, critical for mission-critical applications.
- Security: Enhanced encryption and security protocols will protect data and communications.

1.2.6 Energy Efficiency and Sustainability

- Green Technology: 6G will focus on energy-efficient technologies to reduce the carbon footprint of communication networks.

1.2.7 Holographic Communication and Extended Reality (XR)

- Holography: 6G could enable high-resolution holographic communications, providing new dimensions in remote interactions.

- XR Applications: Enhanced capabilities for augmented reality (AR), virtual reality (VR), and mixed reality (MR) will be supported.

1.2.8 Global Coverage and Integration

- Satellite Integration: The inclusion of satellite networks will provide global coverage, ensuring connectivity in remote areas.
- Integration with Other Networks: Seamless integration with existing technologies like Wi-Fi, Bluetooth, and satellite communications.

1.2.9 Network Slicing and Customized Services

- Network Slicing: 6G will offer customized network slices to meet specific requirements of different applications, ensuring optimal performance.

1.2.10 Quantum Communication and Computing

- Quantum Technologies: Potential integration with quantum communication and computing for enhanced security and computational capabilities.

These features and technologies highlight the transformative potential of 6G in creating a highly connected, intelligent, and efficient digital world.

1.3 6G Use Cases in Industrial IoT

6G in Industrial IoT enables real-time monitoring and control of machinery, predictive maintenance, and enhanced automation with ultra-low latency and high reliability [16]. It supports advanced applications like autonomous robots, augmented reality for remote assistance, and seamless machine-to-machine communication for optimized industrial processes and efficiency.

- **Smart Manufacturing and Automation**
  6G technology, which offers incredibly fast, dependable, low-latency connectivity, is poised to transform automation and smart manufacturing. It will make it possible for machines, sensors, and systems to exchange data in real

time, which will enable smooth automation and accuracy in manufacturing processes [17–19]. Autonomous robots, digital twins for production line simulation and optimization, augmented reality for remote troubleshooting, and predictive maintenance are some of the key applications. Improved data analytics and AI integration will help manufacturing operations become even more efficient, less prone to downtime, and responsive.

- **Remote Maintenance and Diagnostics**
  6G technology will play a crucial role in remote maintenance and diagnostics by enabling ultra-fast and reliable data transmission. This allows for real-time monitoring and analysis of equipment health and performance, regardless of location. With its ultra-low latency, 6G will support high-quality video feeds and augmented reality (AR) tools, enabling technicians to diagnose and repair issues remotely with precision [20]. AI and machine learning integrated within the 6G network can analyze data streams to predict failures and optimize maintenance schedules, reducing downtime and maintenance costs. This enhanced connectivity ensures that even complex machinery can be maintained efficiently from a distance.

- **Real-Time Data Analytics and Decision-Making**
  6G technology will significantly enhance real-time data analytics and decision-making processes by providing unprecedented speed and bandwidth for data transmission. Its ultra-low latency ensures near-instantaneous data collection, processing, and response times, crucial for time-sensitive applications. With 6G, massive amounts of data from various sources, such as sensors, devices, and systems, can be analyzed in real time. This capability is vital for industries like finance, healthcare, and manufacturing, where rapid decision-making can improve outcomes, optimize operations, and enhance efficiency [21, 22].

  Additionally, 6G's integration with artificial intelligence (AI) and machine learning (ML) technologies enables advanced data analytics, including predictive and prescriptive analytics. These technologies can quickly analyze complex data sets, identify patterns, and provide actionable insights, allowing organizations to make informed decisions faster than ever before [23]. Overall, 6G's enhanced data handling capabilities will empower businesses and industries to harness real-time analytics for improved decision-making, leading to more agile and responsive operations.

- **Autonomous Robots and Drones**
  6G technology, which offers incredibly fast, low-latency connectivity and enormous data bandwidth, will significantly improve autonomous robots and drones. This will make it possible for these systems and their control centers to communicate seamlessly in real time, enabling the precise and quick execution of commands [24]. Advanced coordination between multiple robots or drones will be made possible by the high-speed network, allowing for complex, synchronized operations. Real-time environmental mapping and fast transmission of high-resolution sensor data will facilitate better navigation and decision-making. With low latency and responsive control even at long ranges, remote operation will become more efficient [25].

  Furthermore, 6G's strong connectivity will improve safety and dependability by lowering latency in communications and facilitating more effective real-time monitoring and adaptations. With this revolutionary potential, autonomous systems will find new uses in fields like manufacturing, logistics, and emergency response, where they will become more effective, adaptable, and able to manage complex jobs [26].

- **Supply Chain Optimization**
  Supply chain optimization will be completely transformed by 6G technology, which offers incredibly fast, dependable connectivity and large amounts of bandwidth. Significant improvements will be made to real-time tracking of assets and goods, enabling accurate inventory management and prompt stock level responses [27, 28]. 6G's high-speed, low-latency data transfer will enable machine learning and advanced analytics, enhancing demand forecasting, preventive maintenance, and dynamic route modifications. Coordinating with suppliers, manufacturers, and logistics companies in a seamless manner will speed up the process, cut down on delays, and boost productivity.

More automation in the form of driverless cars and robots in warehouses will also be possible with 6G, which will optimize tasks like shipping and sorting. Quick decisions can be made in real time, allowing for quick reactions to disruptions or shifting market conditions, thanks to the quick data exchange [29, 30]. In general, 6G will improve the resilience, efficiency, and agility of the supply chain, revolutionizing the production, distribution, and management of goods.

1.4 Challenges and Considerations in Deploying 6G for IIoT

Deploying 6G for IIoT faces challenges like ensuring ultra-low latency, high reliability, and robust security. Considerations include integrating advanced technologies like AI and edge computing, managing spectrum and energy efficiency, and addressing interoperability with existing systems while supporting diverse industrial applications.

- **Technical Challenges**
  There are various technical obstacles in the way of deploying 6G for IIoT. Achieving high reliability and ultra-low latency is essential for real-time applications such as automation and remote control. This calls for developments in network architecture, including new radio technologies and edge computing. In order to support the high data rates and massive device connectivity anticipated in 6G, spectrum management becomes essential. Given that IIoT systems handle sensitive industrial data, security is still another key worry. To stop cyberattacks, strong authentication procedures and end-to-end encryption are crucial. Another difficulty is energy efficiency, especially for battery-powered equipment in isolated areas [31, 32]. It is essential to develop hardware solutions and energy-saving protocols.

  To enable a seamless transition and integration of new devices, interoperability with current systems and standards must be guaranteed. Another major technical challenge is addressing scalability to manage billions of connected devices while preserving performance and reliability.

- **Security and Privacy Concerns**
  Deploying 6G for IIoT raises significant security and privacy concerns. The vast number of connected devices increases vulnerability to cyberattacks, requiring robust encryption and authentication measures. Data integrity and confidentiality are critical, especially in sensitive industrial environments. Privacy concerns arise from the potential misuse of collected data, necessitating stringent data protection regulations. Additionally, securing communication channels against eavesdropping and unauthorized access is vital. Addressing these concerns requires advanced cybersecurity frameworks and continuous monitoring to ensure a secure and privacy-respecting IIoT ecosystem in the 6G era [33, 34].

- **Economic and Regulatory Factors**
  IIoT 6G deployment presents substantial financial and legal obstacles. Widespread adoption may be hampered by the high costs of research and development, spectrum acquisition, and infrastructure upgrades. One regulatory factor is that, in order to guarantee interoperability and compliance with various international regulations, there is a need for harmonized global standards. Government regulations pertaining to cybersecurity and data privacy may also be enforced, which could impact deployment strategies. Financial support and incentives from the public and private sectors may be extremely important in reducing financial burdens. Successfully navigating these regulatory and economic environments is crucial for the deployment of 6G in IIoT applications [35].

- **Environmental and Energy Efficiency Considerations**
  Considerations regarding energy efficiency and the environment are important when deploying 6G for IIoT. Energy-efficient technologies and protocols are required because of the potential for increased energy consumption resulting from an increase in the number of connected devices and infrastructure. To reduce the carbon footprint, low-power hardware development and network operation optimization are essential. Furthermore, sustainable practices like recycling electronic waste and making efficient use of spectrum

must be supported by 6G networks. Reducing environmental impact can be further achieved by implementing green technologies, such as network infrastructure powered by renewable energy sources. Moreover, using edge computing can reduce the amount of energy required for long-distance data transmission. Industry standards and regulatory frameworks that support energy-efficient designs are crucial for directing the creation and implementation of 6G systems [36]. In general, ensuring an environmentally and energy-efficient future for IIoT applications requires striking a balance between the technological advancements of 6G and sustainability goals.

1.5 Impact of 6G on Industry Standards and Protocols

The introduction of 6G will require new guidelines for ultra-low latency, high data rates, and enhanced security, which will have a substantial impact on industry standards and protocols. It will spearhead the creation of standards for smooth interoperability, economical spectrum utilization, and sustainability, influencing the structure of the industrial Internet of things' future communications and operations [37].

- **Evolution of IIoT Standards**
  The IIoT has experienced substantial development in recent years, as it has adjusted to meet the requirements of ever more networked industrial settings. At first, IIoT standards were created to facilitate machine-to-machine communication and guarantee fundamental compatibility across devices and systems. OPC-UA and MQTT have become essential components of the IIoT ecosystem, providing dependable communication protocols for exchanging data. Nevertheless, with industries striving for quicker response times and more intricate, automated systems, these criteria are being reassessed in consideration of the potential offered by 6G. 6G is anticipated to bring about significant advancements in terms of ultra-low latency, extended bandwidth, and widespread integration of artificial intelligence [38]. These advancements will require the existing standards

to evolve, stretching the limits of how industrial internet of things (IIoT) systems manage data streams, decision-making processes, and automation.

Given the commitment of 6G to achieving latency at the millisecond level and providing high-speed connections, it is expected that future IIoT standards would prioritize improved efficiency in data transfer, advanced real-time analytics, and automation powered by artificial intelligence. Standards such as Time-Sensitive Networking (TSN) will adapt to match the fast data transfer and accuracy offered by 6G, enabling real-time control in industries like manufacturing and energy. In addition, the transition to 6G, which supports cyber-physical systems, will necessitate the implementation of additional levels of standardization to effectively handle the increasing intricacy of autonomous decision-making and machine intelligence [39].

- **Interoperability with Existing Systems**
  One of the primary obstacles presented by 6G in IIoT environments is guaranteeing compatibility with current infrastructure. Presently, IIoT systems, particularly in traditional sectors like manufacturing and utilities, mainly depend on well-established communication protocols such as Ethernet/IP, Modbus, and PROFINET. With the introduction of 6G, these businesses will confront the task of incorporating advanced features without completely revamping their existing systems. The harmonious coexistence of 5G and 6G networks will be crucial in effectively handling the sophisticated demands of state-of-the-art IIoT applications and the operating prerequisites of existing systems [40, 41].

  The inclusion of 6G, together with its ability to interact with older systems, is expected to provide seamless integration with current IIoT systems by using developments in network slicing and edge computing. This will enable the simultaneous coexistence of various levels of communication protocols within a single infrastructure. In addition, the implementation of 6G will lead to the development of gateway devices that enable communication between outdated and new standards, guaranteeing the continued usefulness of investments made in current IIoT systems. Improved machine-to-machine (M2M) communication will establish a connection between smart devices enabled by 6G and older systems, ensuring ongoing operation while taking use of the higher speeds and minimal delay of 6G networks [42].

- **Role of Standardization Bodies and Industry Alliances** Standardization organizations such as the 3rd Generation Partnership Project (3GPP), IEEE, and ITU have a crucial role in establishing the technical standards for the IIoT industry, especially with the emergence of 6G. These entities have traditionally created systems that promote industry innovation while also guaranteeing interoperability and security across networks. With the advent of 6G, which promises exceptionally fast and responsive communication, these organizations are currently prioritizing the development of strong and adaptable standards capable of meeting the varied requirements of IIoT applications, ranging from industrial automation to smart grids. The cooperation among these standardization entities guarantees that 6G protocols conform to worldwide rules and cater to the requirements of industries functioning in various geographical areas. The 5G Alliance for Connected Industries and Automation (5G-ACIA) and the Industrial Internet Consortium (IIC) are expected to broaden their influence in order to oversee the implementation of 6G in industrial settings. These partnerships enable cross-industry cooperation to ensure that the upcoming 6G standards effectively meet the unique requirements of industries such as manufacturing, energy, and transportation [43]. Through close collaboration with standardization bodies, their objective is to exert influence on the advancement of open, interoperable standards that facilitate smooth integration across various industries. Moreover, these partnerships offer a forum for industries to actively contribute to the development of 6G-enabled IIoT, guaranteeing that the established standards are both pragmatic and visionary.

1.6 Future Directions and Research Opportunities

Current research in the field of 6G is focused on the advancement of technologies that improve extremely fast response times, large-scale multiple-input multiple-output (MIMO), and AI integrated networks. Scientists are currently prioritizing the development of terahertz (THz) transmission and the integration of quantum computing. These advancements have the potential to significantly enhance data speeds and security. Considerable investment is being made in the advancement of edge intelligence and distributed AI, which will enable the processing of real-time data at the edge of the network. This is a crucial necessity for the IIoT. Current research is also exploring novel network topologies, such as intelligent reflective surfaces (IRS), which aim to enhance signal transmission and facilitate adaptive communications [44].

The implementation of 6G is anticipated to facilitate revolutionary advancements in IIoT applications, namely in domains like as intelligent manufacturing, digital replicas, and proactive maintenance. An important potential lies in the field of haptic internet applications, which involve the integration of real-time tactile input with virtual and augmented worlds. This has the ability to revolutionize industries such as healthcare and robotics. Precision farming in agriculture will be enhanced by the capabilities of 6G, which include reliable and low-latency communications. This will allow drones and sensors to operate independently and effectively. The incorporation of AI into IIoT systems will enhance the capability of self-healing networks, allowing devices to autonomously identify and fix errors. This will result in increased operational time and decreased expenses associated with maintenance [45].

The successful implementation of 6G necessitates a strong partnership between industry, academia, and government entities to establish frameworks that foster innovation while guaranteeing adherence to rules. Telecommunications providers and IIoT manufacturers will collaborate with universities to create experimental applications for 6G technology. Governments will have a crucial role in allocating spectrum and establishing cybersecurity requirements. Public-private partnerships will play a crucial role in expediting the implementation of 6G technology, especially in vital areas such as energy and transportation. Collaboration is crucial for creating an environment that promotes the growth of scalable and secure IIoT implementations [46].

To adapt to the new possibilities offered by 6G, organizations will need to formulate precise goals and roadmaps. This entails evaluating the existing network infrastructure, making investments in advanced 5G technologies, and investigating the potential of AI and machine learning in automating network management. To maintain competitiveness, companies should initiate training programs for their workers in developing domains such as quantum communications and AI-driven network orchestration. It is anticipated that governments and regulatory organizations will develop detailed plans, known as 6G roadmaps, which will encompass regulations regarding spectrum management, security standards, and environmental sustainability. These plans will ensure that the transition to 6G technology is in accordance with broader social objectives.

1.7 Case Studies and Real-World Implementations

- Early 6G Pilot Projects in Industrial Settings
  Various initial 6G pilot projects have been initiated in industrial environments to investigate the capabilities of this technology for IIoT applications. For example, experimental initiatives in advanced manufacturing facilities have examined the capabilities of 6G technology to improve communication between machines and enable real-time processing of data for applications such as predictive maintenance and remote control of robotic systems. These initiatives utilize AI-powered edge computing to analyze large quantities of sensor data, enabling quicker decision-making on the manufacturing floor. 6G is being utilized in pilot programs for automated logistics systems to enhance inventory management and delivery procedures [47–49]. This implementation enables the optimization of the supply chain by facilitating high-speed and low-latency communication.

- Lessons Learned and Best Practices
  Several crucial insights have been derived from these initial 6G test initiatives. An important lesson to learn is the significance of network reliability and security in industrial environments, where any period of inactivity can result in substantial financial consequences. Network architectures that are resilient, meaning they can withstand and recover from interruptions, are essential for assuring the continuous operation of industrial systems, even when there are connectivity issues. These architectures include redundant pathways, which provide alternative routes for data transmission, and real-time monitoring, which allows for immediate detection and response to any network problems. Another important point to consider is the requirement for solutions that can be easily adjusted to handle both existing systems and future technology. Pilot projects have shown

the significance of modular systems, which may be customized for future enhancements without requiring extensive modifications to the current infrastructure.

- Success Stories and Case Study Analysis
  Early 6G installations in industrial contexts have already shown their utility through several success stories. For instance, in the field of automotive manufacturing, corporations have effectively employed 6G technology to mechanise assembly lines, enhancing both the velocity and accuracy of car production. Likewise, energy companies that are testing 6G-enabled smart grids have observed significant enhancements in the distribution of energy and the balancing of loads. The utilization of real-time analytics enables more effective utilization of resources. These case studies showcase the capacity of 6G to revolutionize businesses through the facilitation of rapid connectivity, integration of artificial intelligence, and instantaneous decision-making in intricate, data-centric settings.

1.8 Conclusion

- Recap of Key Points
  In this chapter, we have examined the significant capacity for change that 6G technology has in the context of the IIoT. The conversation commenced by examining the fundamental characteristics of 6G, which encompassed ultra-low latency, AI integration, and improved connectivity. In addition, we analyzed the impact of 6G on IIoT standards, its capacity to facilitate compatibility with existing systems, and the significant contribution of standardization bodies and industry partnerships. Case studies and pilot projects showcased initial achievements, emphasizing exemplary methodologies and insights gained from practical 6G implementations in diverse sectors.

- The Future Landscape of 6G in Industrial IoT
  In the future, 6G technology is expected to greatly transform industrial automation, with its applications extending to smart manufacturing, energy management, and precision

agriculture. With the adoption of 6G technologies by sectors, we anticipate a transition towards increased utilization of autonomous systems, propelled by the integration of edge computing and AI-native networks. Effective collaboration across academia, government, and business sectors is crucial for creating an environment that fully harnesses the potential of 6G technology. Nevertheless, the persistent advancement of technology and adherence to regulations will be necessary to address obstacles like as data security, scalability, and energy efficiency.

- Final Thoughts and Perspectives
  The advent of 6G signifies a fundamental change in the realm of IIoT, providing exceptional prospects for industries to improve efficiency, sustainability, and creativity. During the shift to the 6G era, it will be crucial to engage in strategic planning, allocate resources for research and development, and prioritize sustainable practices. The efficacy of 6G will rely not solely on the technology per se, but also on the seamless assimilation and incorporation of it into the current operations of many industries. In the end, the complete capabilities of 6G will be achieved by the harmonious combination of technology and industry, which will propel the upcoming wave of industrial revolution.

AI disclosure statement: The author acknowledges the use of AI-based tools for minor language editing or grammatical correction. However, all intellectual contributions, analyses, and conclusions presented in this chapter are entirely the author's own.

References

1. Saad, W., Bennis, M., Chen, M., A vision of 6G wireless systems: Applications, trends, technologies, and open research problems. *IEEE Netw.*, 34, 3, 134–142, 2022.
2. Shafin, R., Liu, L., Zhang, M., *et al.*, Artificial intelligence-enabled cellular networks: A critical path to beyond-5G and 6G. *IEEE Wirel. Commun.*, 27, 2, 212–221, 2022.
3. Khan, L., Awais, M., Anwar, S., Industrial Internet of Things (IIoT) empowered with 6G networks. *J. Ind. Inf. Integr.*, 30, 100400, 2023.

4. Chen, Y., Zhang, N., Li, Q., *et al.*, Blockchain and federated learning for secure 6G industrial IoT. *IEEE Trans. Ind. Inf.*, 18, 5, 3436–3444, 2022.
5. Yang, L., Xu, X., Zhang, Y., 6G-enabled digital twin for industrial IoT networks. *IEEE Internet Things J.*, 10, 5, 3285–3293, 2023.
6. Wang, P., Li, H., Zhang, S., Edge intelligence and 6G for autonomous IoT systems. *IEEE Trans. Ind. Electron.*, 70, 3, 1567–1575, 2023.
7. Akyildiz, I.F., Kak, A., Nie, S., 6G and beyond: The future of wireless networks and IoT. *IEEE Commun. Mag.*, 61, 2, 130–137, 2023.
8. Dini, G., Savazzi, S., Nicoli, M., Distributed sensing and edge computing for 6G industrial IoT networks. *IEEE Internet Things Mag.*, 5, 4, 35–42, 2022.
9. Nassar, K., Hassan, Q.F., Srivastava, G., Secure 6G industrial IoT networks using quantum computing. *IEEE Netw.*, 36, 1, 56–63, 2022.
10. Alotaibi, B., Alghannam, N., Gupta, N., Privacy-preserving machine learning in 6G industrial IoT. *IEEE Access*, 10, 46900–46910, 2022.
11. Luo, Y., Zhu, T., Zhang, Y., Enabling ultra-reliable low-latency communications in 6G-based industrial IoT. *IEEE Commun. Lett.*, 26, 10, 2478–2481, 2022.
12. Zhao, L., Fu, H., Zhang, X., Heterogeneous networking with 6G: IIoT applications. *IEEE Trans. Ind. Electron.*, 70, 2, 1153–1161, 2023.
13. Qiu, R., Ni, Z., Yang, S., AI-driven 6G networks for industrial automation. *IEEE Trans. Ind. Inf.*, 19, 3, 1479–1487, 2023.
14. Chen, Y., Yang, X., Wu, D., 6G-enabled real-time data analytics for industrial IoT. *IEEE Netw.*, 37, 1, 25–32, 2023.
15. Sharma, V. and Jindal, S., 6G for smart factories: Opportunities and challenges. *IEEE Wirel. Commun.*, 30, 4, 118–126, 2023.
16. Khalil, I., Mazhar, R., Raza, A., 6G and quantum computing: The future of industrial IoT. *IEEE Internet Things Mag.*, 4, 3, 58–66, 2022.
17. Yang, L., Gao, Y., Yan, Z., Converging 6G and blockchain for trustworthy industrial IoT. *IEEE Access*, 10, 11250–11263, 2022.
18. Abbas, R., Ghaffar, F., Zaidi, A., Intelligent resource allocation in 6G-enabled industrial IoT networks. *IEEE Commun. Lett.*, 27, 3, 1120–1125, 2023.
19. Gao, X., Li, Q., Zhang, Y., AI-powered 6G digital twin for IIoT networks. *IEEE Commun. Mag.*, 60, 6, 66–73, 2022.
20. Zhang, Q., Xu, G., Wu, Y., Blockchain-enabled 6G for secure industrial IoT. *IEEE Trans. Ind. Inf.*, 18, 4, 2991–3001, 2022.
21. Saad, W. and Bennis, M., Federated learning for 6G-enabled industrial IoT applications. *IEEE Netw.*, 37, 2, 58–64, 2023.
22. Bai, X., Zhao, F., Liu, W., Cooperative edge AI in 6G-based industrial IoT networks. *IEEE Wirel. Commun.*, 29, 4, 98–106, 2022.
23. Yang, S., Zhao, R., Zhang, Y., Towards green and sustainable 6G for industrial IoT. *IEEE Internet Things Mag.*, 5, 2, 45–52, 2023.
24. Ali, Z., Kamran, M., Siddique, A., 6G-enabled smart factories: A roadmap for future industrial IoT. *IEEE Access*, 11, 15432–15447, 2023.

25. Perez, L., Wang, P., Tang, H., Low-latency communications in 6G-enabled industrial IoT. *IEEE Internet Things J.*, 9, 3, 2195–2204, 2022.
26. Zhan, Q., Wei, G., Xu, L., Ultra-dense IIoT networking with 6G: Opportunities and challenges. *IEEE Wirel. Commun.*, 30, 1, 48–55, 2023.
27. Hassan, N., Mahmoud, M., Mohamed, N., Autonomous industrial systems with 6G IoT networks. *IEEE Trans. Ind. Electron.*, 70, 1, 443–454, 2023.
28. Na, W., Xu, Z., Zhao, Y., 6G network slicing for industrial IoT applications. *IEEE Commun. Lett.*, 26, 6, 1453–1456, 2022.
29. Zhang, L., Liang, S., Zhou, X., Edge intelligence for IIoT in 6G networks. *IEEE Commun. Mag.*, 61, 1, 105–111, 2023.
30. Wei, X., Zhang, Z., Sun, H., Machine learning-driven 6G for industrial IoT. *IEEE Trans. Ind. Inf.*, 18, 6, 3784–3792, 2022.
31. Ding, L., Liu, S., Zhang, P., AI-empowered 6G networks for industrial automation. *IEEE Access*, 10, 123567–123577, 2022.
32. Cui, Y., Yu, X., Zhang, J., 6G-enabled IoT for smart manufacturing: Challenges and solutions. *IEEE Netw.*, 37, 3, 72–79, 2023.
33. Qureshi, S., Siddique, A., Zaman, M., Enhancing IIoT systems with 6G: A comprehensive survey. *IEEE Access*, 11, 32850–32864, 2023.
34. Zhang, S., Wang, X., Xu, M., Energy-efficient 6G technologies for industrial IoT. *IEEE Trans. Green Commun. Netw.*, 6, 2, 1034–1045, 2022.
35. Sun, H., Zhang, X., Ren, J., Blockchain-based privacy-preserving protocols for 6G-enabled industrial IoT. *IEEE Commun. Lett.*, 27, 5, 2012–2018, 2023.
36. Xu, T., Chen, L., Liu, Z., Distributed AI in 6G for industrial automation. *IEEE Trans. Ind. Electron.*, 70, 4, 2521–2528, 2023.
37. Huang, Y., Li, Q., Sun, Y., 6G for autonomous IIoT: Enabling technologies and future trends. *IEEE Wirel. Commun.*, 30, 2, 88–96, 2023.
38. Li, H., Wang, Y., Zhang, S., Intelligent edge computing for 6G-enabled IIoT networks. *IEEE Netw.*, 36, 6, 142–148, 2022.
39. Sun, X., Yan, Z., Xu, Y., 6G-based industrial digital twin: Concepts, challenges, and future directions. *IEEE Internet Things J.*, 10, 2, 1255–1267, 2023.
40. Zhang, Y., Cao, Y., Zhu, H., Toward scalable and secure 6G industrial IoT networks. *IEEE Access*, 10, 48422–48432, 2022.
41. Liu, Z., Li, Q., Zhang, P., AI-empowered 6G networks for smart manufacturing. *IEEE Trans. Ind. Electron.*, 70, 5, 3467–3474, 2023.
42. Tang, J., Zhang, X., Wang, P., Energy-aware resource allocation in 6G-enabled industrial IoT systems. *IEEE Trans. Green Commun. Netw.*, 6, 1, 245–254, 2022.
43. Wang, Y., Qian, L., Sun, X., Ultra-low-latency communications in 6G-based IIoT. *IEEE Access*, 11, 16895–16904, 2023.
44. Xie, H., Liu, W., Zhang, J., Secure 6G IoT for industry 4.0: Blockchain and AI technologies. *IEEE Netw.*, 36, 4, 112–118, 2022.
45. Zhao, Y., Wu, Z., Li, H., Distributed 6G edge computing for industrial IoT. *IEEE Trans. Ind. Inf.*, 19, 2, 1374–1381, 2023.

46. Xu, T., Qian, X., Yu, F., AI-driven 6G digital twin for IIoT systems. *IEEE Commun. Lett.*, 27, 2, 1157–1164, 2023.
47. Wang, X., Chen, L., Zhou, Y., Autonomous systems in 6G-enabled industrial IoT. *IEEE Wirel. Commun.*, 30, 3, 64–70, 2023.
48. Bhambri, P., Rani, S., Kumar, S., Sinha, V.K., S., Bhambri, P., Kumar, S., Pareek, P.K., Elngar, A.A., Big Data Analytics with Digital Twin for Industrial Applications, in: *AI-Driven Digital Twin and Industry 4.0: A Conceptual Framework with Applications*, 1st, Rani (Ed.), pp. 105–26, CRC Press, 2024, https://doi.org/10.1201/9781003395416.
49. Kaur, J., Bhambri, P., Rani, S., Digital Twin Enabling Technologies, Applications, and Challenges, in: *AI-Driven Digital Twin and Industry 4.0: A Conceptual Framework with Applications*, 1st90-104, S. Rani, P. Bhambri, S. Kumar, P.K. Pareek, A.A. Elngar (Eds.), CRC Press, 2024, https://doi.org/10.1201/9781003395416.

2

Foundations of Edge Intelligence in 6G Networks

D. Harika[1], C. Venkataramanan[2], K. Neelima[1] and Satyam[3]*

[1]Mohan Babu University Erstwhile Sree Vidyanikethan Engineering College, Tirupati, Andhra Pradesh, India
[2]Sri Eshwar College of Engineering, Coimbatore, Tamil Nadu, India
[3]BITS Pilani, Pilani Campus, Rajasthan, India

Abstract

6G networks are anticipated to usher in a new era characterized by pervasive connectivity, ultra-low latency, and unparalleled reliability. However, a paradigm shift is needed to realize this vision, moving beyond mere connectivity to infuse intelligence at the network edge. By dissecting its fundamental principles, this chapter explores the transformative potential of edge intelligence in 6G networks, a crucial element currently lacking in 5G networks. As a paradigm shift, edge intelligence equips devices at the network's edge with advanced computational power, empowering them to unlock intelligence from data locally, ushering in a new era of distributed decision-making and real-time responsiveness. The chapter begins by outlining the 6G networks' key drivers and goals, highlighting the critical role of distributed intelligence in overcoming traditional limitations. The chapter's core then unveils the fundamental building blocks of edge intelligence in 6G, such as distributed computing, AI, ubiquitous sensing, and network convergence. Following this, the chapter dives deep into the transformative applications enabled by edge intelligence in 6G, including Next Generation Ultra-Reliable Low-Latency Communication (xURLLC), enhanced security and privacy, and personalized user experiences. In conclusion, the chapter recognizes the outstanding research obstacles and unanswered inquiries that persist in the domain of edge intelligence for 6G, thereby establishing a foundation for subsequent investigations and advancements.

**Corresponding author*: mesatyam0101@gmail.com

Sita Rani, Pankaj Bhambri, Balamurugan Balusamy, Rishabha Malviya and Seifedine Kadry (eds.) Edge Intelligence for 6G-Enabled Industrial Internet of Things, (23–38) © 2026 Scrivener Publishing LLC

Keywords: Blockchain technology, deep learning, edge intelligence, extended reality, holographic generation, massive MIMO, next generation ultra-reliable low-latency communication, quantum communication

2.1 Introduction

With the shift in generations from 1G to 5G, several evolutions have taken place. Now, the transformation is towards 6G. 6G networks are anticipated to usher in a new era characterized by pervasive connectivity, ultra-low latency, and unparalleled reliability. It competes with 5G and races ahead with several factors, like

1. Ultra-Fast communication (THz)
2. Fully immersive experience with extended reality (XR) and HD quality holographic communication
3. Cell-free massive MIMO
4. Widespread connectivity
5. Quantum communications
6. Blockchain
7. High reliability with ultra-low latency less than 1ms
8. Mobility Support (up to 1000 km/h)
9. Spectral efficiency around 100 bps/Hz
10. Reliability (99.99999%)
11. Deep learning solutions for improvement, etc

The primary role is played by edge intelligence has the transformative potential in 6G networks. As a paradigm shift, edge intelligence equips network's edge devices with advanced computational power, empowering them to unlock intelligence from data locally, steering into a new era of distributed decision-making and real-time responsiveness.

2.2 Key Drivers and Goals of 6G Networks

Beyond 5G, 6G networks are envisioned as the next generation of mobile telecommunications. The key drivers and goals of 6G networks [1] include:

1. Higher Data Rates - 6G can reach terabits per second, supporting applications like holographic communications, real-time AI, high-definition virtual reality, etc.
2. Ultra-Low Latency – 6G can provide latency to unprecedented levels in the order of microseconds to enable instantaneous communication essential for applications like autonomous vehicles, remote surgery, immersive gaming, etc.
3. Greater Spectrum Efficiency – the improved efficient and optimal usage of spectrum, i.e., frequencies, allows integration of advanced technologies that require large spectrum with high data rates like massive MIMO, dynamic spectrum sharing, cognitive radio, etc.
4. Enhanced Coverage and Connectivity – 6G extends to remote area coverage through satellite networks, airborne base stations, advanced terrestrial infrastructure, etc.
5. Energy Efficiency – the carbon footprint in telecommunication networks can be reduced to satisfy sustainable development goals.
6. Advanced Network Architecture - mesh networks, satellite constellations, integrated terrestrial-satellite systems, etc, ensure seamless connectivity globally by using 6G.
7. Security and Privacy - quantum cryptography and AI-driven threat detection safeguard data and ensure user privacy in an increasingly connected world.
8. AI and Machine Learning Integration - AI and ML aim to optimize resource allocation, network management, user experience, etc.
9. Global Standards and Interoperability – the interoperability between different 6G networks is established through global standards and protocols to facilitate seamless connectivity.
10. Socio-Economic Impact – 6G supports new industries, creating jobs, driving technological advancements, etc.

These goals collectively aim to create more interconnected and technologically advanced societies.

2.3 Role of Distributed Intelligence in Overcoming Traditional Limitations

The limitations of 5G [2] include:

1. Infrastructure Requirements - 5G networks require significant upgrades like newer base stations, smaller cells, fiber optic cables, etc.
2. Limited Coverage - 5G coverage is limited to urban areas and densely populated regions with slower deployment.
3. Higher Frequencies and Range – as higher frequencies are used, the range of coverage is limited. So, more base stations and even small cells should be installed to ensure consistent coverage.
4. Device Compatibility – User handsets require upgrade due to the limited availability of 5G-compatible devices.
5. Potential Interference - Higher frequency bands are susceptible to interference from physical objects, such as buildings and trees, which can impact signal strength, coverage, etc.
6. Security Concerns - 5G networks introduce new security challenges like data protection, privacy, unauthorized access, etc., requiring robust security measures and protocols.
7. Cost - 5G networks are expensive to build and deploy.
8. Range - 5G signals do not travel far distances.
9. Health concerns - 5G radiation leads to health concerns.

Distributive intelligence [3], tackles complex challenges in a distributed manner, i.e., by collecting, processing, and routing information and actions across a global network. The Pervasive DI [4], framework facilitates the system's ability to train and deploy AI solutions throughout the network infrastructure. This necessitates a fundamental redesign of 6G systems to accommodate the demands of this new paradigm, particularly in handling the distributed nature of AI workloads. Then the requirements change as:

(a) distributed AI computations need awareness about underlying wireless edge network constraints.
(b) the wireless networks must optimize resources to support AI computations.

The effective utilization of Distributed Artificial Intelligence (DAI) requires the implementation of continuous learning paradigms. This is due to the inherent nature of DAI, where AI solutions process data locally across large and diverse datasets. Continuous learning facilitates the enhancement of model accuracy while mitigating privacy concerns, bandwidth limitations, and latency issues. Consequently, incorporating self-learning and self-validation mechanisms paves the way for the complete automation of DAI, enabling the generation of context-aware AI solutions for a virtually limitless 6G environment.

However, DAI presents distinct challenges within the context of 6G networks. Notably, the inherent requirement for local data processing on end devices with data sharing helps achieve optimal model accuracy. Federated Learning (FL) emerges as a promising solution to address this limitation. This approach leverages a decentralized and self-orchestrated device-driven learning paradigm, often employing the Federated Averaging (FedAvg) algorithm [5], for model updates.

As illustrated in Figure 2.1, the resource-constrained and highly dynamic nature of the wireless edge environment poses additional challenges for DAI. These challenges consist of slow model convergence, high communication overhead, and scalability to many heterogeneous devices. Furthermore, it has potential for privacy leakage during model update sharing, attacks from malicious devices, and the requirement for self-learning from data streams without human intervention necessitates the development of robust security and privacy-preserving mechanisms.

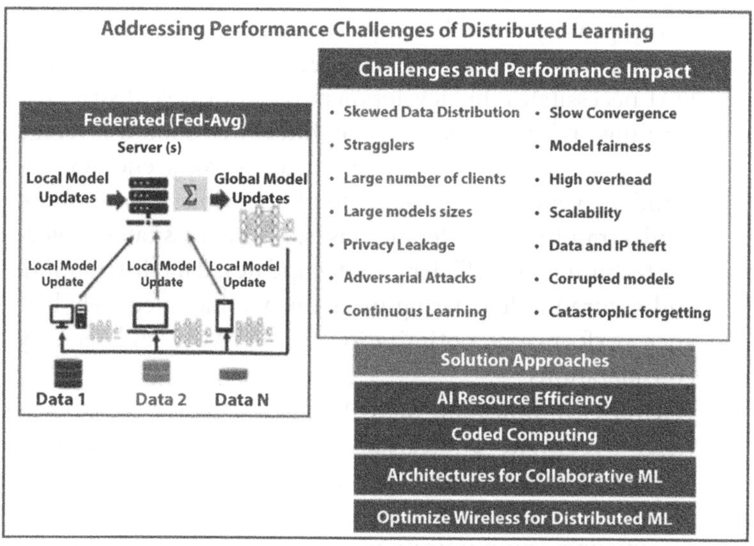

Figure 2.1 Performance challenges and possible solutions of DAI [6].

To address these challenges, a few solutions are

- Optimizing Resource Efficiency in AI - AI models require awareness of computations, data resources, etc. To reduce communication/computing costs, statistical importance sampling (IS) can be applied to speed up the convergence of learning models.
- Leveraging Coded Computation - A theoretical framework rooted in coding theory can be employed to introduce redundant computations strategically. This approach optimizes resource allocation by accounting for the heterogeneity in computational power and communication capabilities across participating devices. In Coded Federated Learning (CFL) context, every device contributes a minimal fraction of obfuscated data generated by applying random linear combinations to its local dataset. This technique effectively mitigates the impact of missing computations and stragglers. The limitations on data sharing inherent in CFL fosters resilience against skewed or non-IID (Independent and Identically Distributed) data distributions. Furthermore, it offers flexibility in dynamically adjusting the workload distribution between the central server and devices. Notably, CFL facilitates the establishment of a framework for making trade-offs between various performance metrics such as utility, privacy, and reliability.
- New Distributed Learning Architectures – The emergence of DAI necessitates the development of innovative distributed learning architectures. These architectures should leverage the complementary capabilities of edge servers, end devices, cloud servers, etc. to facilitate the flexible allocation of model training and inference tasks. This necessitates exploring techniques for efficient model updates, data distribution, and secure model-sharing mechanisms that effectively balance performance optimization with privacy and security considerations.
- Network Optimization for DAI Workloads - DAI applications necessitate strategically utilizing wireless network nodes to execute intermediate computations. This approach facilitates collaboration among learning agents, thereby minimizing communication overhead and computational demands within the DAI framework.

2.4 Fundamental Building Blocks of Edge Intelligence in 6G

Edge intelligence (EI) plays a lively role in 6G networks, as shown in Figure 2.2, whose unique features like distributed computing, ubiquitous sensing, network coverage, etc. aid in fast and consistent development.

The EI in 6G systems [8], consists of three essential computing elements: edge devices, edge servers, and cloud servers. Incorporating devices with AI at the edge, tends to enhance its performance by using built-in AI models. This also reduces the bandwidth and service latency for applications like AR, industrial automation, drone communication, etc. The benefits of edge devices include fast and reliable computation at the user device, eliminating overhead in data-transfer latency, reduced bandwidth usage, enhanced security, etc. The drawbacks of edge devices include adding new devices that invite the attention of attackers, storage issues, high maintenance costs, and difficulty in efficiently processing big data.

The edge server and edge devices are placed close to each other to improve reliability and reduce latency [9]. They process locally stored data [10], and make decisions to preserve data privacy and time. The computational benefits at the edge server include reduced bandwidth and cost, workload on the server, etc. The drawbacks include heavy computation, time consumption, data privacy and security concerns, etc.

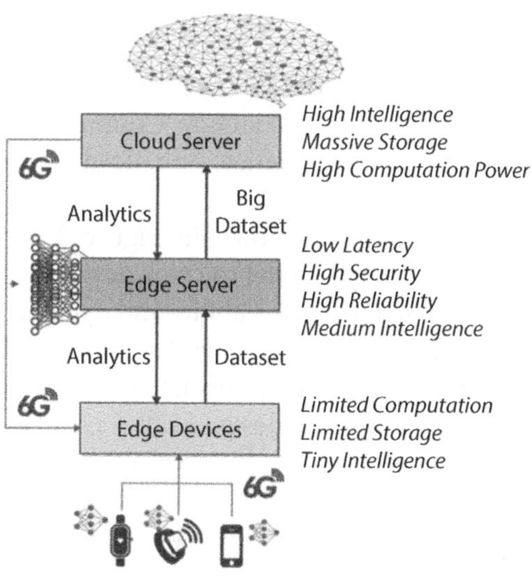

Figure 2.2 Blocks of Edge Intelligence-based 6G Systems [7].

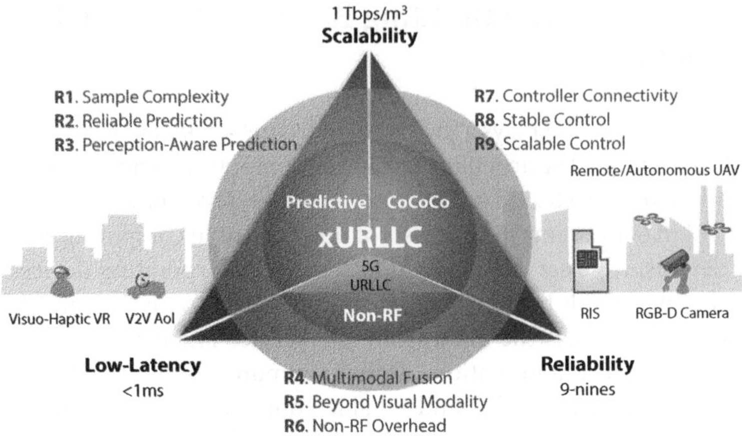

Figure 2.3 xURLLC [11].

EI resolves latency, bandwidth, reliability, and security issues by using AI-based processing and prediction. The applicability of EI in 6G is enhanced by AI to achieve marvelous results by solving massive application problems. The AI algorithms like deep learning techniques enable dataset and pattern recognition and anomaly detection.

2.5 Transformative Applications Enabled by Edge Intelligence

The transformative applications of edge intelligence include Next Generation Ultra-Reliable Low - Latency Communication (xURLLC), improved personalized user experience, enhanced privacy and security, etc.

xURLLC has components, as shown in Figure 2.3. The existing 5G URLLC utilizes a static channel model to characterize events with a trade-off in spectral efficiency that limits scalability and dynamic predictive analysis. However, extreme 6G URLLC makes ML based proactive decisions that satisfy nine reliabilities within 0.1 ms latency, non-RF modality utilization, communication-control co-design [12].

By using age-of-information (AoI), even under non-stationary and unpredictable environments learns from data samples [13], latency estimation, and traffic demand prediction [14], using users' visuo-haptic perceptions.

2.5.1 R1 - Sample Complexity

xURLLC utilizes ML model-based predictions, i.e., re-trained and adaptive models are used [16]. The training convergence time depends on the temporal channel evolution dynamics to achieve desired accuracy based on sample complexity. Federal learning [15], is used to reduce the cost of communication and prediction [17].

2.5.2 R2 - Reliable Prediction

xURLLC improves reliability caused by non-stationary data distributions in communication with high prediction accuracy using ML. The generalization error is used for quantification as the difference between the expected loss and the empirical training loss [18], across the entire dataset. Also, Gaussian process regression (GPR) provides the prediction confidence using the variance of the posterior distribution.

2.5.3 R3 - Perception-Aware Prediction

Look-ahead forecasting at the expense of accuracy by utilizing perceptual characteristics. The driver's perception reaction time (PRT) is used to determine the prediction horizon, which is 2.5s for human drivers and several ms for driverless cars. Both perceptions can coexist if human-robot interaction (HRI) is used [19].

2.5.4 R4 - Multimodal Fusion

Efficient fusion techniques have been developed based on different spatio-temporal resolutions (such as frame rates, image sizes, and sensing/sampling rates) and their corresponding processing methods (like using convolutional neural networks for vision). A split learning (SL) based neural network comprises of multiple lower segments connected to a shared upper segment that are fed different data inputs. This approach can fuse multiple modalities by combining weights in the upper segment and applying distinct data-specific architectures in the lower segment [20].

2.5.5 R5 - Beyond Visual Modality

Accelerometer data, in addition to vision, is used as a non-RF modality to analyze mobility patterns for estimating blockage duration. RIS-equipped walls utilize non-RF modality by adjusting signal characteristics such as phase, amplitude, reflection angle, and polarization using RIS technology to manipulate signals and interference.

2.5.6 R6 - Non-RF Overhead

When using non-RF data, it's important to consider the additional energy cost involved in acquiring, processing, and controlling the data. To overcome the limited field of view of each camera, training images can be used, but this consumes communication energy for vision-aided channel estimation. Balancing vision and RF modalities will require optimization procedures [21]. However, it's important to note that this may also lead to increased energy usage in 6G.

2.5.7 R7 - Controller Connectivity

The wireless connection of control system components involves sensors that measure states, controllers that calculate commands, and actuators that execute control commands. However, this arrangement can lead to missing or distorted state along with command receptions. To address this issue, a sequential control operation with an increased transmission power for the controller can be implemented. With the future channel condition prediction can switch the actuator from remote to autonomous control [22].

2.5.8 R8 - Stable Control

After a collision, it's important to consider communication reliability. The control stability associated with it may need to be underestimated or overestimated. To overcome this problem, formalizing control stability is necessary. For a linear single-agent control, system stability is ensured by guaranteeing bounded output for bounded input, known as BIBO stability. In non-linear systems, stability is assessed using Lyapunov stability. In multiple agent control, the inter-agent collision avoidance and swarm stability are utilized [23].

2.5.9 R9 - Scalable Control

In high-precision control applications, significant computational resources are needed. Traditional model-based control is unsuitable due to non-stationarity and external uncertainties. ML-based control solves these issues by feeding direct optimal control through a state input when states are intertwined.

2.6 Challenges and Enablers of Edge Intelligence

The key challenges [15], include the following areas:

- Infrastructure for Edge Computing - The focus is to support dynamically changing resource configurations, to ensure reliable feature deployment, and to accommodate device mobility.
- Orchestration of Edge Platforms - This involves tackling issues related to the allocation and distribution of resources, along with the challenges posed by dynamic allocation and distribution.
- Management of Data and Networks - This challenge involves the integration of heterogeneous data types to enhance the performance of edge intelligence. It requires a comprehensive understanding and delineation of data and model provenance and lifecycle, evaluation of models and their suitability for specific contexts, facilitation of incremental learning methods, and addressing inconsistencies in data from heterogeneous sensors. Additionally, this includes modeling and understanding network behavior and performance, adherence to common interoperability practices and standards, optimization of high-level AI models, management and operation of centralized systems, and minimization of control latencies.
- Intersection of Edge and Device Intelligence - This challenge is similar to the aforementioned data and network management, focusing on common interoperability practices and standards, optimization of high-level AI models, centralized system management and operation, and minimization of control latencies.
- Software Development for Edge - Challenges in this domain include managing dynamic configurations, ensuring security, facilitating flexible deployment, and providing debugging capability during development.
- Real-time Requirements along with Online Learning - This area prioritizes adaptation to network dynamics and the necessity for very short response times.
- Algorithms Trained Distributively - This involves reducing coordination costs among edge devices and minimizing errors in trained models.

- ➢ Security and Privacy - This critical area ensures security and privacy strategies implementation that align with user needs and system requirements. It also involves the recognition of abnormal behavior based on user requirements and operator criteria.
- ➢ End-user Aspects - Finally, the user context is understood through the analysis of large-scale behavior patterns.

These challenges highlight the complex and multifaceted nature of implementing edge intelligence, necessitating a broad array of strategies to address them effectively.

The enablers [5], include:

- ✓ For Edge-computing infrastructure - it is pertinent to incorporate advanced container technologies, implement robust virtualization solutions, employ isomorphic software architectures, and utilize sophisticated handover protocols, techniques, etc.
- ✓ For Edge platform orchestration – the optimization of virtualization, enhancement of data intelligence through sophisticated algorithms, implementation of advanced data analysis techniques, and the deployment of multi-level and fully distributed dynamics optimization algorithms, among others.
- ✓ For Data and network management - To enhance data and network management capacities, it is imperative to augment sensor and data fusion algorithms. These enhancements should facilitate robust data and network management practices, enable the detection and identification of faults within data and networks, and foster the extraction of knowledge alongside the application of incremental learning algorithms. Moreover, the development of knowledge-sharing mechanisms, alongside the integration of lightweight Artificial Intelligence (AI) solutions, is essential for boosting autonomy and self-sufficiency. The incorporation of agents endowed with cognitive functions—such as the capacity for learning and proactivity—is also crucial. Furthermore, the application of AI techniques aimed at fostering collaboration and cooperation should be prioritized. Adopting renowned paradigms, using game theory, swarm intelligence, genetic algorithms, etc will significantly contribute to this endeavor.

- ✓ For Intersection of edge and device intelligence - To augment the confluence of edge computing and device intelligence, it is proposed to integrate advanced, lightweight artificial intelligence solutions aimed at amplifying autonomy and self-sufficiency in devices. This encompasses the deployment of agents endowed with significant cognitive faculties, including the capacity for learning and proactivity. Furthermore, the application of sophisticated artificial intelligence methodologies to foster collaboration and cooperation is advocated. To this end, the adoption of esteemed paradigms like game theory, swarm intelligence, genetic algorithms, etc is recommended.
- ✓ For Software development for edge - It is crucial to leverage container technologies, adopt DevOps methodologies, implement Continuous Integration and Deployment (CI/CD) processes, utilize virtualization techniques, and deploy liquid software that seamlessly transitions among nodes, among other practices.
- ✓ For Real-Time Requirements and Online Learning - The focus is on the advancement of knowledge distillation, learning transfer, reinforcement learning, etc. This also includes the collaborative design of communication frameworks, control systems, and machine learning algorithms.
- ✓ For Distributedly Trained Algorithms - Areas of focus encompass knowledge distillation, federated learning, transfer learning, and the optimization of models through pruning. Additional areas include coded ML and quantized ML, the application of meta-distributions, the exploration of extreme value theory, and the development of risk management frameworks.
- ✓ For Security and Privacy - The comprehensive application of security strategies across all operational levels is advocated. This ensures the meticulous personal information and ownership management throughout all processes and employs physical-level solutions to bolster security and foster trust.
- ✓ For End-User Aspects - The development and utilization of digital twins and software agents endowed by cognitive capabilities are prioritized to enhance user interactions and experiences.

2.7 Conclusion

The 6G networks are characterized by pervasive connectivity, ultra-low latency, and unparalleled reliability. To realize this, edge intelligence is incorporated into the network. This chapter outlines the key drivers and goals of edge intelligence. Also, the fundamental building blocks and transformative applications of edge intelligence as extreme Ultra-Reliable Low-Latency Communication (xURLLC) in 6G are discussed. Finally, the outstanding research obstacles and unanswered inquiries that persist in the domain of edge intelligence for 6G, thereby establishing a foundation for subsequent investigations and advancements.

AI disclosure statement: The author acknowledges the use of AI-based tools for minor language editing or grammatical correction. However, all intellectual contributions, analyses, and conclusions presented in this chapter are entirely the author's own.

References

1. Dangi, R., Choudhary, G., Dragoni, N., Lalwani, P., Khare, U., Kundu, S., 6G Mobile Networks: Key Technologies, Directions, and Advances. *Telecom*, *4*, 836–876, 2023.
2. Chauhan, V. and Srinivasan, S., A Review on 5G Network System with its limitation and different Approaches to build strong 5G Network System. *3rd International Conference on Intelligent Engineering and Management (ICIEM)*, London, United Kingdom, pp. 403–410, 2022.
3. Heylighen, F., Distributed Intelligence Technologies: Present and Future Applications, in: *The Future Information Society*, vol. 2016, pp. 179–212, 2016, Chapter 10.
4. Talwar, S., Himayat, N., Nikopour, H., Xue, F., Wu, G., Ilderem, V., 6G: Connectivity in the Era of Distributed Intelligence. *IEEE Commun. Mag.*, 59, 11, 45–50, November 2021.
5. Kairouz, P., McMahan, H.B., *et al.*, Advances and open problems in Federated Learning. arXiv:1912.04977v1, 2019.
6. Talwar, S., Himayat, N., Nikopour, H., Xue, F., Wu, G., Ilderem, V., 6G: Connectivity in the Era of Distributed Intelligence, https://arxiv.org/abs/2110.07052, 2021.
7. Wang, X., Han, Y., Leung, V.C.M., Niyato, D., Yan, X., Chen, X., Convergence of edge computing and deep learning: A comprehensive survey. *IEEE Commun. Surv. Tutor.*, 22, 2, 869–904, 2020.

8. Hathaliya, J., Sharma, P., Tanwar, S., Gupta, R., Blockchain-based remote patient monitoring in healthcare 4.0. *IEEE 9th International Conference on Advanced Computing (IACC)*, pp. 87–91, 2019.
9. Cao, K., Liu, Y., Meng, G., Sun, Q., An overview on edge computing research. *IEEE Access*, 8, 85714–85728, 2020.
10. Tyagi, S., Tanwar, S., Gupta, S.K., Kumar, N., Rodrigues, J.J.P.C., A lifetime extended multi-levels heterogeneous routing protocol for wireless sensor networks. *Telecommun. Syst.*, 59, 1, 43–62, 2015.
11. Park, J., Samarakoon, S., Shiri, H., Abdel-Aziz, M., Nishio, T., Elgabli, A., Bennis, M., Extreme ultra-reliable and low-latency communication. *Nat. Electron.*, 5, 1–9, 2022.
12. Prakash S., *et al.*, Coded computing for federated learning at the edge, arXiv:2007.03273, FL-ICML'20, 2020.
13. Berardinelli, G., Mahmood, N.H., Rodriguez, I., Mogensen, P., Beyond 5G wireless IRT for industry 4.0: Design principles and spectrum aspects. *Proc. IEEE GLOBECOM Wkshps*, Abu Dhabi, UAE, 2018.
14. Abdel-Aziz, M.K., Samarakoon, S., Bennis, M., Saad, W., Ultra-reliable and low-latency vehicular communication: An active learning approach. *IEEE Commun. Lett.*, 24, 2, 367–370, Feb. 2020, doi: 10.1109/LCOMM.2019.2956929.
15. Qadir, Z., N. Le, K., Saeed, N., Suliman Munawar, H., Towards 6G Internet of Things: Recent advances, use cases, and open challenges. *ICT Express*, 9, 3, 296–312, 2023, ISSN 2405-9595.
16. Park, J. and Bennis, M., URLLC-eMBB slicing to support VR multimodal perceptions over wireless cellular systems. *Proc. IEEE GLOBECOM*, Abu Dhabi, UAE, Dec. 2018.
17. Hu, H. and Jiang, C., Edge Intelligence: Challenges and Opportunities. *2020 International Conference on Computer, Information and Telecommunication Systems (CITS)*, Hangzhou, China, pp. 1–5, 2020.
18. Park, J., Samarakoon, S., Bennis, M., Debbah, M., Wireless network intelligence at the edge. *Proc. IEEE*, 107, 11, 2204–2239, Nov. 2019.
19. Koda, Y., *et al.*, One pixel image and RF signal based split learning for mmWave received power prediction. *Proc. ACM CoNEXT*, Orlando, FL, USA, Dec. 2019.
20. Latva-aho, M. and Leppänen, K., (Eds.), *Key Drivers and Research Challenges for 6G Ubiquitous Wireless Intelligence*. vol. 1, 6G Research Visions, University of Oulu, 2019, http://urn.fi/urn:isbn:9789526223544.
21. Saad, W., Bennis, M., Chen, M., A vision of 6G wireless systems: Applications, trends, technologies, and open research problems. *IEEE Netw.*, 34, 3, 134–142, May/June 2020, doi: 10.1109/MNET.001.1900287.
22. Bhambri, P. and Rani, S., Issues Related to Chatbots, in: *Design and Development of Emerging Chatbot Technology*, D. Darwish (Ed.), pp. 130–147, IGI Global Scientific Publishing, 2024, https://doi.org/10.4018/979-8-3693-1830-0.ch008.

23. Rani, S. and Bhambri, P., Industry 4.0 Framework and Applications, in: *AI-Driven Digital Twin and Industry 4.0: A Conceptual Framework with Applications*, 1st, S. Rani, P. Bhambri, S. Kumar, P.K. Pareek, A.A. Elngar (Eds.), pp. 1–14, Routledge Taylor and Francis Group, CRC Press, 2024, https://doi.org/10.1201/9781003395416.

3

Advancements in Industrial Connectivity: A 6G Perspective

Kali Charan Rath[1]*, Nagavarapu Sowmya[2], Aditi Sharma[3] and Brojo Kishore Mishra[4]

[1]*Department of Mechanical Engineering, Gandhi Institute of Engineering and Technology University, Gunupur, Odisha, India*
[2]*Department of E.C.E, Gandhi Institute of Engineering and Technology University, Gunupur, Odisha, India*
[3]*Department of Computer Sc. and Engineering, Symbiosis Institute of Technology, Symbiosis International (Deemed University), Pune, India*
[4]*Department of Computer Science and Engineering, NIST University, Berhampur, Odisha, India*

Abstract

The rapid evolution of technology is driving a paradigm shift in the industrial landscape towards enhanced connectivity, epitomized by the advent of Industry 4.0. This paper explores the advancements in industrial connectivity through the lens of 6G technology and its application to smart manufacturing. By focusing on 6G, the next generation of wireless communication technology, this research aims to uncover its potential in revolutionizing industrial connectivity for more efficient and intelligent manufacturing processes. 6G networks offer faster data speeds, ultra-low latency, and unparalleled reliability, ideally suited for the rigorous demands of smart manufacturing environments. Leveraging 6G capabilities enables real-time monitoring, predictive maintenance, and seamless coordination across production lines, increases productivity, reduces downtime, and optimization of resource utilization. Additionally, the paper delves into the integration of emerging technologies such as AI, IoT, and also edge computing with 6G connectivity to create a holistic ecosystem for smart manufacturing. Through case studies

**Corresponding author*: rathkalicharan1980@gmail.com; ORCID: 0000-0002-0577-9530
Nagavarapu Sowmya: ORCID: 0000-0003-4673-597X
Aditi Sharma: ORCID: 0000-0002-5364-8420
Brojo Kishore Mishra: ORCID: 0000-0002-7836-052X

Sita Rani, Pankaj Bhambri, Balamurugan Balusamy, Rishabha Malviya and Seifedine Kadry (eds.) Edge Intelligence for 6G-Enabled Industrial Internet of Things, (39–66) © 2026 Scrivener Publishing LLC

and practical examples, it illustrates the transformative potential of 6G-enabled smart manufacturing systems across various industrial settings. In conclusion, this research underscores the significance of 6G technology in advancing industrial connectivity and shaping the future of smart manufacturing. Fully embracing the capabilities of 6G networks enables manufacturers to fortify their competitive position and unleash unprecedented levels of efficiency and adaptability on the global stage.

Keywords: 6G technology, industrial connectivity, smart manufacturing, next-generation networks, IoT integration, Industry 4.0

3.1 Introduction

The ongoing evolution of technology has sparked a revolution in the industrial landscape, propelling us into the era known as Industry 4.0. This paradigm shift is characterized by an increased emphasis on connectivity, which serves as the backbone for driving innovation and efficiency across various sectors. In this chapter, contents delve the industrial connectivity, honing in on the revolutionary impact of 6G technology within the domain of smart manufacturing. Unlike previous studies that have touched upon the broader spectrum of connectivity technologies, our research distinguishes itself by honing in on 6G, the next generation of wireless communication. While 5G networks have already demonstrated their prowess in enhancing connectivity in diverse industries, the advent of 6G heralds a new era of possibilities, offering faster data speeds, minimal latency, and unparalleled reliability. These features make 6G particularly well-suited to meet the intricate demands of smart manufacturing environments, where real-time monitoring, predictive maintenance, and seamless coordination are paramount.

For instance, imagine a smart factory equipped with 6G-enabled sensors and devices that continuously collect and analyze data in real-time. These sensors can detect anomalies on the production line and promptly alert maintenance personnel, mitigating the risk of costly downtime. Additionally, 6G networks facilitate well communication between different components of the manufacturing process, enabling efficient resource allocation and optimization. This, in turn, leads to heightened productivity and minimized waste, ultimately translating into significant cost savings for manufacturers.

The objective of this work is to explore the potential of 6G networks in the context of industrial connectivity within smart manufacturing systems, particularly in the era of advanced technology. As the industrial landscape undergoes a transformative shift driven by technological advancements, connectivity emerges as a critical enabler for innovation and efficiency across sectors. This research delves into the intricate dynamics of industrial connectivity, with a specific emphasis on the transformative capabilities of 6G technology. The main focus is on 6G, the upcoming wireless communication standard. Authors emphasized its key benefits like faster data speeds, ultra-low latency, and unmatched reliability, showcasing its potential for smart manufacturing. With examples of 6G-powered smart factories featuring real-time monitoring and predictive maintenance, we highlight how it boosts productivity, reduces downtime, and optimizes resources. Furthermore, we explore the integration of advanced technologies like augmented reality and virtual reality, made possible by the reliability and speed of 6G networks, thereby further enhancing operational efficiency and reducing the need for physical presence on the factory floor. Ultimately, this paper seeks to illuminate the transformative role of 6G technology in revolutionizing industrial connectivity, driving forward the advancement of smart manufacturing, and inspiring further research and innovation in this dynamic field. The 6G in smart manufacturing is a game-changer. So, this chapter explores its use of potentiality and inspiring for various research and innovation in the field, i.e., exploring the benefits of 6G for enhancing productivity and data communication.

3.2 Smart Manufacturing and Communication

Smart manufacturing and communication represent a symbiotic convergence of technological prowess, heralding an era where production processes are seamlessly integrated with intelligent systems and interconnected communication networks [1, 2]. This avant-garde paradigm entails the deployment of cutting-edge automation, data analytics, and artificial intelligence to optimize manufacturing operations with unprecedented efficiency and agility. Leveraging real-time data exchange and predictive analytics, smart manufacturing optimizes operational workflows while cultivating adaptive responsiveness to fluctuating market demands [3, 4]. Moreover, the synergy between smart manufacturing and communication channels empowers enterprises to forge interconnected ecosystems, enabling swift information dissemination across disparate nodes of the supply chain. In essence, this paradigm shift transcends traditional manufacturing methodologies, propelling industries towards a realm where innovation thrives amidst the harmonious orchestration of technology and communication.

3.2.1 Comparison between 5G and 6G Network

Within the dynamic realm of telecommunications, the progression from one generation to the next represents not merely a technological advancement but rather a fundamental paradigm shift in the sphere of connectivity. The advent of G, or Generation, in telecommunications has marked pivotal shifts in connectivity and communication paradigms. Each successive G, from 1G to 5G, has brought forth transformative capabilities, facilitating faster data transfer, lower latency, and greater network reliability. However, as we propel towards the era of 6G, the focus extends beyond mere enhancements in speed and bandwidth. 6G is envisioned as an indispensable enabler for smart manufacturing, where ultra-reliable, low-latency communication is paramount [5–7]. In smart manufacturing, real-time data analytics, seamless connectivity among various devices, and precise control systems are imperative for optimizing productivity, ensuring safety, and minimizing downtime. 6G's capabilities, including unprecedented speeds, minimal latency, and massive device connectivity, are poised to revolutionize smart manufacturing by facilitating enhanced automation, predictive maintenance, and agile response to dynamic production environments. Moving to 6G isn't just an option; it's essential for realizing the full potential of smart manufacturing, driving unparalleled efficiency, innovation, and competitiveness in industrial operations. This comparative analysis aims to elucidate the key disparities between 5G and 6G networks, highlighting the transformative potential and implications of the forthcoming generation [8–10].

3.2.2 6G Technology and Importance for Implementation

The 6G technology revolutionizes wireless communication with lightning-fast speeds and minimal latency. In smart manufacturing, it enables real-time monitoring, agile decision-making, and enhanced productivity. Machines, robots, and sensors communicate instantly, boosting efficiency and reducing downtime. The robustness of 6G ensures uninterrupted connectivity, crucial for complex manufacturing systems [11–13].

From incremental improvements to a complete overhaul, 6G's transformative power unlocks entirely new levels of automation, precision, and flexibility for smart manufacturing. For instance, advanced applications such as digital twinning, augmented reality (AR) assisted maintenance, and autonomous robotics can become mainstream, revolutionizing how factories operate. Moreover, 6G's support for massive Internet of Things (IoT) connectivity enables the deployment of a myriad of sensors [14, 15] and actuators throughout the manufacturing environment, enabling comprehensive data collection

Table 3.1 Differences between 5G and 6G.

Aspect	5G networks	6G networks
Speed	Offers speeds up to several gigabits per second	Promises speeds in the terabits per second range
Latency	Typically, around 1 millisecond	Aims to reduce latency to microseconds or lower
Bandwidth	Provides wide bandwidth	Expected to offer even greater bandwidth
Spectral Efficiency	Improved compared to previous generations	Anticipated to have even better spectral efficiency
Coverage	Offers wider coverage	Expected to further extend coverage
Energy Efficiency	More energy-efficient than previous generations	Projected to be more energy-efficient
AI Integration	Supports AI applications	Expected to integrate AI more deeply
Quantum Communication	Relies on conventional cryptographic techniques	May incorporate principles of quantum communication
Holographic Communication	Not applicable	Could introduce holographic communication
Environmental Sensing	Not typically included in 5G networks	Might include built-in environmental sensing

and analysis for predictive maintenance and quality control. Table 3.1 shows the differences between 5G and 6G. Based on the analysis and Table 3.1, it is expected that embracing 6G in smart manufacturing unlocks a double win: boosted efficiency and cost savings, while paving the way for ground breaking business models and sustainable growth in the Industry 4.0 era.

3.2.3 6G Technology and Its Significance

As we stand at the threshold of technological advancement, the anticipation for the next leap, from 5G to 6G, is palpable. While 5G technology continues to unfold its potential, visionaries are already peering into the horizon of a future where 6G will redefine the realms of connectivity and communication. At its essence, 6G embodies the promise of a revolutionary stride beyond its predecessor, offering unprecedented speed, diminished latency, and heightened connectivity. Positioned as the sixth generation of wireless communication standards, 6G builds upon the sturdy foundations laid by its antecedents. While 5G has already ushered in remarkable speeds and minimal latency, 6G aspires to transcend these benchmarks, ushering in an era of terahertz frequencies, advanced artificial intelligence (AI), holographic communications, and potential integration with emerging technologies [16, 17]. In this unfolding narrative of technological evolution, 6G stands as a beacon of innovation, poised to shape the future landscape of connectivity and communication.

Various significance of 6G for the implementation in smart manufacturing sectors are:

a) ***Ultra-Fast Data Transfer:*** *6G's lightning-fast data transfer capabilities will revolutionize smart manufacturing by allowing real-time data analysis, enhancing productivity, and enabling swift decision-making processes.*

b) ***Low Latency Communication:*** *Reduced latency in 6G networks will enable seamless communication between smart manufacturing devices, facilitating quicker response times and improving operational efficiency.*

c) ***High Reliability:*** *The high reliability of 6G networks ensures stable connectivity, minimizing downtime in smart manufacturing processes and enhancing overall system reliability.*

d) ***Massive IoT Integration:*** *6G is like a super-powered internet for factories. It lets them connect a huge number of machines and sensors, and helps them make things better use with less stuff.*

e) ***AI and Machine Learning Integration:*** *With its enhanced capabilities for AI and machine learning integration, 6G will empower smart manufacturing systems to analyze complex data sets, optimize production workflows, and predict maintenance needs, leading to improved efficiency and cost savings.*

f) ***Enhanced Security:*** *6G networks offer advanced security features such as encryption and authentication protocols, safeguarding sensitive data and intellectual property in smart manufacturing environments from cyber threats and unauthorized access.*

g) ***Augmented Reality and Virtual Reality Integration:*** *Smart factory workers with virtual trainers guiding them through* *complex tasks, or technicians fixing machines with holographic manuals. 6G's AR/VR power will transform training, maintenance, and troubleshooting, boosting productivity and slashing costs in smart manufacturing.*

h) ***Edge Computing Capabilities:*** *With 6G's super-speedy data processing, smart factories can make decisions on the fly without waiting for info to travel long distances. This means faster reactions and smoother operations for critical tasks.*

i) ***Energy Efficiency:*** *6G uses less energy to do its job, so factories can save money and help the working environment.*

j) ***Global Connectivity:*** *6G's global connectivity capabilities will enable seamless communication and collaboration across geographically dispersed smart manufacturing facilities, streamlining supply chain management and enhancing overall operational resilience.*

3.3 Manufacturing Processes Enhancement through 6G Networks

Smart manufacturing equips robots with the power of AI, data analysis, and a network of sensors (IoT) to transform assembly lines. This tech brain boosts efficiency, automates tasks, and optimizes production for a whole new level of manufacturing. In the context of robot assembly, smart manufacturing refers to the use of sensor-equipped, network-connected robots that can perform tasks more efficiently, accurately, and autonomously [18, 19]. Table 3.2 displays the manufacturing processes enhancement through 6G networks.

Various Components:

a) Robots: Industrial robots equipped with sensors and actuators for assembly tasks.
b) Sensors: These include proximity sensors, vision systems, force/torque sensors, etc., to provide real-time data about the assembly process.
c) IoT Devices: Devices to connect machines, sensors, and other equipment to a network for data collection and analysis.
d) 6G Connectivity: The next generation of wireless communication technology that enables high-speed, low-latency data transmission, crucial for real-time communication in smart manufacturing environments.

Table 3.2 Manufacturing enhancement data sheet.

Metric	Before implementation	After implementation
Cycle Time (seconds)	60	40
Defect Rate (%)	5	2
Throughput (units/h)	50	80
Downtime (hours/year)	500	200

e) Data Analytics Software: Software for analyzing the data collected from sensors to optimize processes and detect anomalies [20, 21].
f) Automation Software: Software for programming and controlling robots to perform assembly tasks autonomously.
g) Human-Machine Interface (HMI): Interfaces through which human operators can monitor and interact with the manufacturing process.

Result output:

a) The cycle time has reduced by 33.3%, indicating increased efficiency in the assembly process.
b) The defect rate has decreased by 60%, indicating improved quality control.
c) Throughput has increased by 60%, indicating higher production capacity.
d) Downtime has reduced by 60%, indicating improved reliability and less time wasted on maintenance or troubleshooting.

3.3.1 Case Study of Smart Manufacturing Technologies with 6G

A manufacturing company/Industry specialized in producing electronic devices decided to implement smart manufacturing technologies with 6G in their assembly line to improve efficiency and quality. Supercharged robots with advanced connected sensors and smart connections are taking assembly lines by storm, streamlining processes and optimizing production for a new era of manufacturing. 6G use status matrix is shown in the Table 3.3.

Table 3.3 6G use status matrix.

Metric	Before use	After use
Cycle Time (seconds)	60	40
Defect Rate (%)	5	2
Throughput (units/h)	50	80
Downtime (hours/year)	500	200
Energy Consumption (kWh)	1000	800
Labor Cost ($)	20000	15000
Scrap Rate (%)	3	1
Setup Time (minutes)	30	15
Overall Equipment Effectiveness (%)	70	85
Production Cost per Unit ($)	10	8

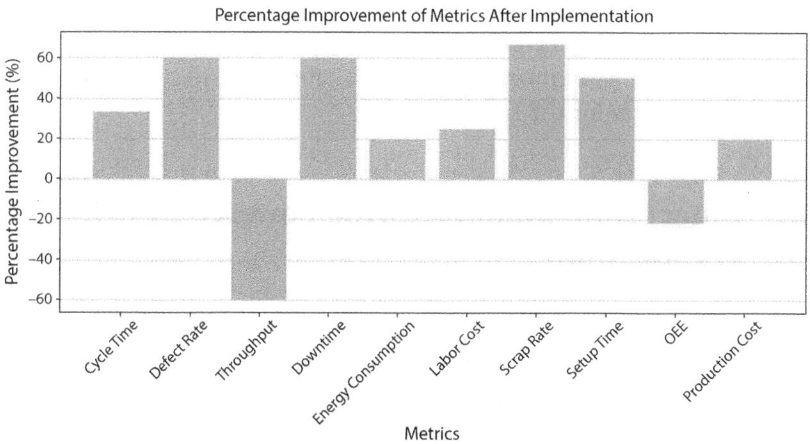

Figure 3.1 Percentage improvement of metrics after implementation of 6G.

Result Analysis:

Figure 3.1 shows the percentage improvement of metrics achieved after the implementation of 6G and few key outcomes reflects through the analysis as follows.

a) The cycle time has reduced by 33.3%, indicating increased efficiency in the assembly process.

b) The defect rate has decreased by 60%, indicating improved quality control.
c) Throughput has increased by 60%, indicating higher production capacity.
d) Downtime has reduced by 60%, indicating improved reliability and less time wasted on maintenance or troubleshooting.
e) Energy consumption has reduced by 20%, leading to cost savings and potentially environmental benefits.
f) Labor cost has decreased by 25%, indicating reduced dependency on manual labor.
g) Scrap rate has decreased by 66.7%, resulting in less material wastage.
h) Setup time has reduced by 50%, enabling faster changeovers between production runs.
i) Overall Equipment Effectiveness (OEE) has increased by 21.4%, reflecting improved utilization of equipment.
j) Production cost per unit has decreased by 20%, leading to higher profitability.

These improvements shows the significant impact of implementing smart manufacturing technologies associated with 6G network in robot assembly, resulting in a more efficient, cost-effective, and competitive manufacturing process for the Industries.

3.4 Smart Auto Manufacturing Powered by 6G: A Case Study

The automotive industry is a prime candidate to leverage the capabilities of 6G networks for smarter manufacturing processes. Here's a glimpse into how 6G can address demanding requirements in this sector:

a) 6G Solution: ultra-reliable, high-bandwidth network: 6G's ultra-high bandwidth and low latency come to the rescue. Imagine a 6G-powered factory where—

- ➢ Seamless Data Flow: Thousands of sensors on robots, welding machines, and paint booths transmit data in real-time without lag. This allows for:
- ➢ AI-powered Quality Control: AI algorithms analyze the data stream to detect anomalies and ensure consistent quality throughout the assembly line.

- Predictive Maintenance: Early detection of potential equipment issues through real-time data analysis allows for preventive maintenance, avoiding costly breakdowns.
- Challenge: Collaborative Human-Robot Interaction

Example: A modern car assembly line equipped with thousands of sensors on robotic arms, welding machines, and paint booths. These sensors continuously collect data on parameters like temperature, pressure, and quality control metrics. However, the sheer volume of data overwhelms traditional networks like 5G, causing delays in data transmission and processing.

With 6G, this assembly line operates. The ultra-high bandwidth and low latency of 6G enable real-time transmission of this data without lag. AI algorithms analyze this data stream instantly, identifying anomalies in welding parameters or paint quality. For instance, if a weld seam deviates from the specified parameters, the system can automatically adjust the robotic arm's movements to rectify it, ensuring consistent quality throughout the manufacturing process.

Automakers are increasingly adopting collaborative robots (cobots) to work alongside human workers. However, ensuring safety and smooth interaction requires near-instantaneous communication.

b) 6G solution: enhanced control and safety: Unleashing the future of manufacturing: 6G's rock-solid, lightning-fast connection ensures:

- Real-time Communication: Cobots receive instructions and respond to human actions with minimal delay, fostering a safe and efficient work environment.
- Haptic Feedback: Imagine a system where a human worker wearing a haptic vest feels the "resistance" of a virtual object while guiding a cobot during assembly. This advanced feedback, enabled by 6G's high bandwidth, allows for more precise and collaborative tasks.
- Challenge: Supply Chain Optimization

Example: In smart system human workers collaborate with cobots (collaborative robots) on the assembly line. These cobots assist workers in tasks like lifting heavy components or precision assembly. However, ensuring safe and efficient interaction between humans and cobots requires instantaneous communication and feedback.

Forget clunky controls, 6G makes humans and cobots work together like a dream team. For instance, a worker wearing a haptic vest can guide a cobot to perform delicate assembly tasks. The vest provides haptic feedback, simulating the sensation of touching and manipulating virtual objects. If the cobot encounters any obstruction, it immediately adjusts its movements based on the worker's feedback, ensuring safety and precision in collaborative tasks.

The automotive industry relies on a complex network of suppliers. Delays in receiving parts can disrupt production schedules.

c) 6G solution: smart logistics and inventory management: 6G empowers a truly connected ecosystem:

- ➢ Real-time Tracking: The advanced system uses 6G sensors to track materials and parts in real-time across the integrated supply chain, enhancing efficiency and enabling swift adjustments for improved productivity.
- ➢ Autonomous Vehicles: The network of self-driving trucks seamlessly transporting parts within the factory complex or between supplier locations. 6G's high reliability ensures safe and efficient autonomous operation.

Example: Consider the intricate supply chain network supporting automotive manufacturing, involving multiple suppliers providing various components and materials. Delays in receiving these parts can disrupt production schedules, leading to inefficiencies and increased costs.

With 6G-enabled smart logistics and inventory management, real-time tracking of parts and materials becomes possible throughout the supply chain. For instance, sensors attached to components monitor their location and status as they move from suppliers to the assembly line. If there's a delay in delivery, the system automatically reroutes the shipment or notifies the production team to adjust their schedules accordingly. Moreover, autonomous vehicles equipped with 6G connectivity facilitate seamless transportation of parts within the factory premises, optimizing production flow and minimizing downtime.

Benefits: By addressing these challenges, 6G paves the way for-

- ➢ Increased Efficiency: Faster data processing, real-time optimization, and reduced downtime lead to significant production efficiency gains.
- ➢ Improved Quality: Real-time quality control and preventive maintenance ensure consistent product quality.

- Enhanced Flexibility: 6G's agility allows for faster adaptation to production changes and customization.

With smart manufacturing at the forefront, the automobile industry is set for a revolutionary transformation as we move deeper into the world of 6G technology. Anticipate a surge of innovative applications that will transform the automotive industry as 6G networks approach.

3.4.1 Integration of 6G Connectivity, AI, IoT, and Edge Computing in Automobile Smart Manufacturing Optimizes Processes

The automotive industry is getting a technology changeover. The super-fast connections, smart machines talking to each other, and artificial intelligence making the calls. This tech revolution, powered by 6G and other cutting-edge tools, is boosting production, efficiency, and innovation, putting car companies in the fast lane to success.

a) 6G Connectivity: The next technology of cell era, or 6G, offers formerly unheard-of ranges of connectivity, speed, and dependability. 6G can allow extremely-speedy records switch charges in automotive smart production systems, permitting actual-time manufacturing process monitoring and manage. For example, in an assembly line, 6G connectivity can allow machines to communicate instantaneously, coordinating tasks and minimizing downtime. This ensures smoother operations and faster production cycles, ultimately leading to cost savings and increased output.
b) Artificial Intelligence (AI): Artificial intelligence (AI) helps industries like automotive by analyzing big data to predict problems, optimize processes, and enhance product quality, like spotting machine issues early for proactive maintenance and less downtime.
c) Internet of Things (IoT): IoT sensors integrated into production machinery gather data on performance, temperature, and stress, which is then transmitted for centralized analysis. This enables stock management, system monitoring, and integration of customer feedback, ultimately optimizing automobile manufacturing processes.
d) Edge Computing: The practice of processing data closer to its source is known as edge computing. The approach improves security and makes decision-making easier. Edge computing

can be utilized in the automotive industry to quickly get insights and take action by analyzing data at manufacturing locations in real-time. Devices installed on factory floors can detect abnormalities in manufacturing processes and take corrective action without the need for human intervention by analyzing sensor data.

The following case study showcasing the integration of these technologies is the implementation of a smart manufacturing system by a leading automotive manufacturer.

In a scenario powered by 6G connectivity, a car manufacturing plant employs AI algorithms analyzing IoT sensor data for predictive maintenance and production optimization, while edge computing devices process real-time data for immediate decision-making on the factory floor.

In this setup, 6G connectivity ensures seamless communication between machines, AI algorithms optimize production processes, IoT sensors collect valuable data, and edge computing enables fast and efficient data processing at the point of production. Figure 3.2 shows that the manufacturer experiences increased productivity, reduced downtime, improved product quality, and enhanced competitiveness in the automotive market. The result discussion are noted below with a brief explanation. The comparison of before and after implementation of 6G is displayed in the Table 3.4.

Result discussion:

a) Productivity Enhancement: Prior to 6G implementation, the productivity of the manufacturing plant stood at 100 units per hour. However, with the introduction of 6G connectivity facilitating high-speed communication and AI-driven optimization, productivity soared to 150 units per hour. This remarkable 50% increase in productivity underscores the efficacy of leveraging cutting-edge technologies to streamline manufacturing processes and accelerate output.
b) Downtime Reduction: The integration of 6G connectivity enables seamless communication between robotic assembly lines, aiding in predictive maintenance through real-time data analysis. Consequently, the downtime experienced by the manufacturing plant plummeted from 10 hours per week to a mere 5 hours. This 50% reduction in downtime exemplifies the benefits of proactive maintenance strategies empowered by advanced connectivity solutions, minimizing disruptions and maximizing operational efficiency.

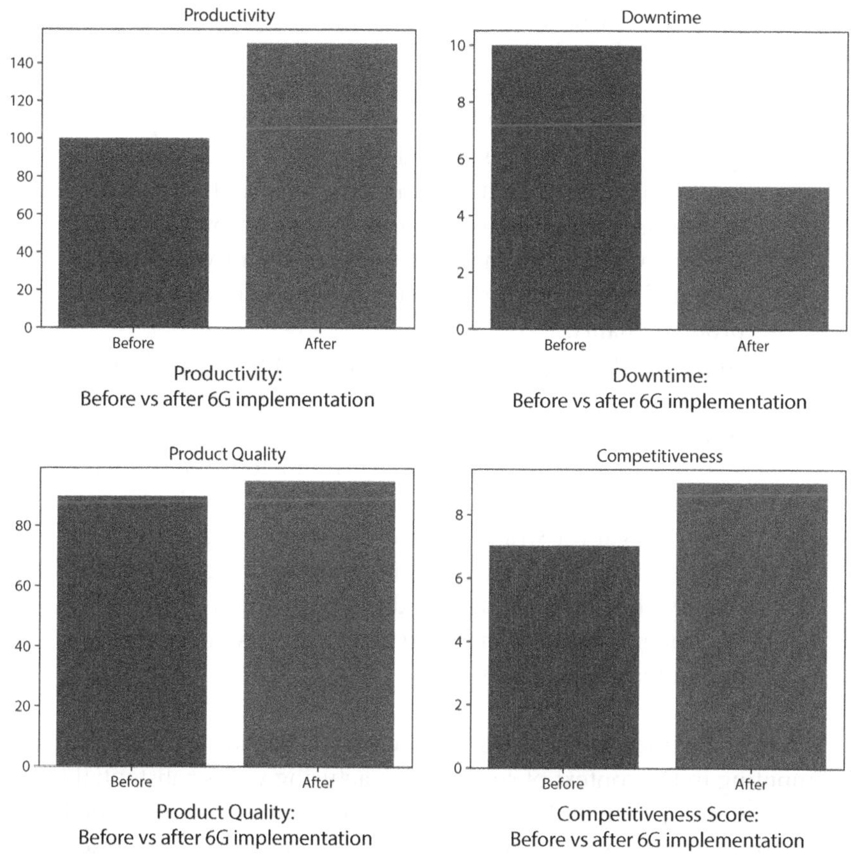

Figure 3.2 Improvement in productivity, downtime, product quality and competitiveness score after implementation of 6G.

Table 3.4 Before and after implementation of 6G.

Metric	Before 6G implementation	After 6G implementation
Productivity (units/h)	100	150
Downtime (hours/week)	10	5
Product Quality (%)	90	95
Competitiveness Score	7	9

c) Enhanced Product Quality: Through the continuous monitoring and analysis of data from IoT sensors embedded in machinery, coupled with AI algorithms, the automotive manufacturer witnessed a notable improvement in product quality. Quality metrics surged from 90% to 95%, indicating a refinement in manufacturing processes and a reduction in defects. By leveraging real-time insights provided by IoT sensors and AI, the manufacturer can identify and rectify potential issues promptly, ensuring consistent and superior product quality.

d) Augmented Competitiveness: The amalgamation of 6G connectivity, AI, IoT, and edge computing bolsters the competitiveness of the automotive manufacturer in the market. With a competitiveness score escalating from 7 to 9, the company demonstrates its ability to leverage technological advancements to gain a strategic edge. By optimizing production processes, minimizing downtime, and enhancing product quality, the manufacturer solidifies its position as an industry leader, capable of meeting evolving consumer demands and outpacing competitors.

Hence, the integration of 6G connectivity alongside AI, IoT, and edge computing in the context of smart manufacturing yields substantial benefits for automotive manufacturers. This case study underscores the transformative potential of advanced technologies in revolutionizing traditional manufacturing paradigms, fostering operational excellence, and driving sustainable growth in a highly competitive market landscape.

The automobile sector may become a new era of smart manufacturing by utilizing the power of advanced technologies.

3.4.2 Algorithm for Real-Time Monitoring and Control of Factory Machines and Processes (Predictive Maintenance) with the Application of 6G

Ongoing oversight and management of factory operations, coupled with predictive maintenance, are vital for smart manufacturing. Integration of 6G tech promises to transform these processes with minimal delay, high reliability, and extensive connectivity, boosting efficiency and responsiveness. The following description shows the implementation of 6G to enhance real-time monitoring, control, and predictive maintenance in smart manufacturing systems, along with an algorithm for setting up such a system.

a) Ultra-Low Latency Communication: 6G networks' blazingly fast speeds will make it possible for sensors, machines, and control systems to communicate instantly. This functionality enables minimally delayed, seamless real-time monitoring and administration of production operations.
b) High Reliability and Resilience: 6G networks are designed to be highly reliable and resilient, even in challenging industrial environments. This ensures continuous operation and minimizes downtime due to communication failures.
c) Massive Connectivity: 6G networks will support massive connectivity, allowing thousands of devices and sensors to be connected simultaneously. This enables comprehensive monitoring of factory machines and processes, providing a wealth of data for analysis and optimization.
d) Edge Computing: Leveraging edge computing capabilities, data processing and analysis can be performed closer to the data source, reducing latency and enabling real-time decision-making. This is especially critical for time-sensitive applications such as predictive maintenance.
e) Machine Learning and AI: Advanced AI & ML systems analyze real-time sensor data in manufacturing, alerting management to prevent breakdowns and optimize downtime, thus extending machinery lifespan through proactive maintenance.
f) Digital Twins: Digital twins, virtual replicas of physical assets, enable real-time simulation and optimization of factory operations, allowing manufacturers to identify issues and test scenarios before implementing changes.

Algorithm for Setting Up Real-Time Monitoring, Control, and Predictive Maintenance System:

Step 1: Define Objectives - The system aims to optimize efficiency, reduce costs, and minimize downtime through proactive maintenance and real-time monitoring.

Step 2: Identify Key Parameters - The selection of parameters to monitor should be tailored to the specific equipment and processes in each facility, prioritizing those with the highest criticality and potential impact on safety, production, and maintenance costs.

Step 3: Select Sensors and Actuators- Choose appropriate sensors and actuators capable of capturing the required data accurately and reliably in real-time. Ensure compatibility with 6G communication protocols for seamless integration into the network.

Step 4: Deploy Edge Computing Infrastructure- To maximize operational effectiveness and decision-making, place edge computing infrastructure close to industrial equipment for real-time data processing and analysis.

Step 5: Develop Predictive Maintenance Models - Create AI and device learning models that use sensor readings and historical facts to expect preservation. By figuring out trends that point to equipment failure, those fashions can trigger early caution alerts.

Step 6 : Integrate with 6G Network - Integrate sensors, actuators, and edge computing devices into the 6G network infrastructure, ensuring seamless communication and data exchange in real-time.

Step 7: Implement Control Systems - Implement control systems that can respond to real-time data insights to optimize factory operations and prevent equipment failures. This may involve automated adjustments to process parameters or triggering maintenance actions based on predictive analytics.

Step 8: Continuous Monitoring and Optimization - Continuously monitor the performance of the system and optimize algorithms and parameters based on feedback and evolving operational requirements.

By following this algorithm and leveraging 6G technology, manufacturers can establish a robust real-time monitoring, control, and predictive maintenance system that enhances efficiency, productivity, and reliability in smart manufacturing environments.

3.5 Challenges and Obstacles in the Adoption of 6G Networks in Industrial Connectivity

6G networks are set to transform industrial connectivity with blazing speeds, minimal latency, and vast device integration. This technology promises to revolutionize production processes, enabling advanced automation, IoT integration, and augmented reality applications. With unparalleled speed and reliability, 6G will drive efficiency, predictive maintenance, and safety enhancements in industrial sectors, ushering in a new era of productivity and innovation.

a) Infrastructure costs: Deploying 6G networks in industrial settings incurs significant costs across various fronts: hardware expenses for specialized components, challenges in fiber optic installation, infrastructure upgrades, site preparation, ongoing maintenance, cybersecurity measures, and training programs for the workforce.
Action Plan: Governments and industry stakeholders should collaborate to offer financial incentives for 6G infrastructure development. Strategic planning, partnerships, and cost optimization are essential for deployment in industrial settings. Streamlining infrastructure, regulatory compliance, and cybersecurity are crucial, alongside investment in workforce training. Sustainability and continuous improvement ensure adaptability, allowing organizations to harness 6G's transformative potential while managing costs effectively.

b) Interference: Industrial environments, including manufacturing plants, factories, warehouses, and processing facilities, feature heavy machinery and industrial processes. Electromagnetic Interference (EMI) poses a risk, caused by electromagnetic radiation or induction, which can disrupt electronic devices and communication systems. 6G signals offer superior data transfer speeds, reduced latency, and more reliable connections compared to 5G. However, in industrial settings, the prevalence of EMI may challenge 6G's efficacy, requiring robust mitigation strategies for optimal performance.
Action Plan: To overcome Electromagnetic Interference (EMI) challenges in industrial environments, implement shielding measures, optimize equipment placement, and employ EMI filters. Enhance grounding systems, utilize frequency management, and invest in robust communication technologies resilient to EMI. Continuous monitoring, maintenance, training, and collaboration ensure effective mitigation strategies and optimal performance of communication systems amidst industrial EMI.

c) Reliability: Industrial processes rely heavily on robust network reliability to minimize downtime and maintain seamless operations. Interruptions in connectivity can disrupt production and incur significant financial losses.

Therefore, ensuring consistent and dependable network performance is crucial for sustaining efficient industrial processes.
Action Plan: Implement redundant network infrastructure and backup systems to minimize downtime and ensure continuous operations. Regularly monitor and maintain network components to uphold consistent and reliable performance, mitigating the risk of interruptions and financial losses in industrial processes.

d) Security Concerns: Industrial networks require robust cybersecurity measures to prevent cyberattacks and ensure operational safety and data integrity. Key strategies include network segmentation, access control, monitoring, and staff training.
Action Plan: To fortify industrial networks against cyber threats and uphold seamless operations, prioritize regular security audits and updates. Couple this with comprehensive employee training on cybersecurity protocols.

e) Integration Complexity: Integrating 6G networks into industrial systems poses complexity due to differing protocols and infrastructures. Overcoming these challenges requires careful planning, compatibility checks, and possibly retrofitting existing systems. However, the potential benefits of enhanced connectivity and efficiency make the endeavor worthwhile for industries aiming to stay at the forefront of technology.
Action Plan: To overcome integration challenges, analyze compatibility issues and devise a phased implementation plan with targeted testing. This approach ensures smooth adaptation to 6G networks while minimizing disruptions to industrial operations.

f) Skill Shortage: The scarcity of proficient experts adept in crafting, executing, and overseeing 6G networks within industrial settings has emerged as a pressing challenge. This deficit poses hurdles in establishing robust and efficient communication infrastructures vital for industrial advancements. Addressing this scarcity is imperative for fostering innovation and competitiveness in industrial sectors reliant on cutting-edge technology.
Action Plan: Establish targeted training programs to enhance expertise in 6G network design, implementation, and management for industrial contexts. Foster collaborative efforts among industry, academia, and research institutions to expedite knowledge sharing and skill development in this specialized domain.

g) Regulatory Compliance: Ensuring compliance with industry regulations and standards presents challenges for deploying 6G networks in industrial environments due to the complexity and evolving nature of regulatory requirements. Overcoming these obstacles requires meticulous planning, robust compliance frameworks, and close collaboration between stakeholders to navigate regulatory hurdles effectively while implementing cutting-edge 6G technology.
Action Plan: Work closely with regulatory bodies to develop industry-specific standards and guidelines for 6G implementation. Review industry regulations, craft adaptable compliance frameworks, and maintain open communication with regulatory bodies. Additionally, provide ongoing training, and establish rigorous monitoring mechanisms to ensure seamless adherence to standards during 6G network deployment in industrial contexts.

h) Scalability: As industrial networks expand, scalability becomes crucial to handle the increasing influx of connected devices and applications efficiently. Ensuring seamless integration and management of these components is paramount for sustaining productivity and optimizing operations. Scalability enables adaptability, empowering industrial networks to evolve alongside technological advancements without compromising performance or reliability.
Action Plan: To address scalability challenges in industrial networks, implement a comprehensive infrastructure assessment to identify bottlenecks and scalability limitations. Upgrade hardware, optimize protocols, and employ scalable network architectures such as mesh networks or distributed computing to accommodate growing demands effectively.

i) Latency: In certain industrial settings, achieving ultra-low latency is imperative for seamless operations. However, the transition to 6G networks presents challenges in meeting such stringent latency requirements due to potential technological limitations. This disparity may necessitate innovative solutions or adaptations to ensure compatibility with the demands of these industries.
Action Plan: To overcome the challenge of achieving ultra-low latency in industrial applications with 6G networks, the action plan involves intensive research and development to advance network infrastructure and protocols. Additionally, implementing edge computing solutions can help reduce latency by processing data closer to its source, optimizing real-time communication in industrial environments.

j) Environmental Factors: To ensure 6G networks remain reliable amidst adversity, industrial settings necessitate sturdy infrastructure and strategically positioned antennas.
Action Plan: To address the impact of harsh industrial conditions on 6G networks, the action plan involves deploying ruggedized network equipment designed to withstand extreme environments. Additionally, implementing redundancy measures and regular maintenance protocols can help mitigate potential disruptions, ensuring consistent network performance and reliability.

k) Vendor Lock-In: Relying solely on one vendor for 6G solutions in industrial connectivity can constrain adaptability and hinder innovation. Embracing a multi-vendor approach fosters competition, encourages technological advancements, and offers flexibility to tailor solutions to specific industrial needs, ensuring robust and future-proof connectivity infrastructure.
Action Plan: Promote vendor diversity and open standards to prevent vendor lock-in and foster competition in the market. Diversify vendors to promote innovation and flexibility in 6G solutions for industrial connectivity, implementing interoperability standards for seamless integration across technologies.

l) Data Privacy: Securing industrial data on 6G networks is essential to adhere to privacy regulations and thwart unauthorized access. Robust encryption protocols and strict access controls are imperative to safeguard sensitive information, ensuring compliance and maintaining data integrity in industrial operations.
Action Plan: Develop stringent encryption protocols and access controls for industrial data transmitted via 6G networks to ensure compliance with privacy regulations and prevent unauthorized access, while also implementing regular security audits to identify and mitigate potential vulnerabilities.

m) Legacy System Compatibility: The integration of 6G networks might face obstacles due to compatibility issues with older industrial systems and equipment, potentially slowing down its adoption within industries. Retrofitting or updating these legacy systems may be necessary for seamless incorporation of advanced networking technology.
Action Plan: To address compatibility issues hindering 6G adoption, conduct comprehensive assessments of existing industrial systems. Develop and implement tailored retrofitting or upgrading strategies to ensure seamless integration of 6G networks with legacy equipment.

n) Interoperability: In industrial settings, guaranteeing compatibility among diverse vendors' 6G solutions is pivotal for uninterrupted connectivity. This interoperability ensures efficient data exchange and system integration, optimizing operations and productivity.
Action Plan: Establish industry-wide standards and protocols to facilitate interoperability testing and certification processes among 6G solution providers. Foster collaboration through consortiums and partnerships to develop interoperable frameworks and address compatibility challenges proactively.

o) Geographical Coverage: Achieving consistent 6G network coverage throughout industrial sites, even in remote areas, poses significant challenges due to varied terrain and infrastructure limitations. Implementing strategic placement of network infrastructure and deploying advanced technologies like mesh networks can help mitigate coverage gaps and ensure reliable connectivity across all areas.
Action Plan: Conduct thorough site surveys to identify coverage gaps and assess terrain challenges within industrial facilities, prioritizing remote locations. Implement a combination of infrastructure deployment strategies such as small cells, repeaters, and satellite connectivity to optimize 6G network coverage and ensure seamless connectivity across all areas.

p) Power Consumption: Efficient operation of Industrial IoT devices on 6G networks is vital for power conservation and extending battery longevity, optimizing continuous functionality in industrial settings. Implementing low-power communication protocols and optimizing data transmission schedules can minimize energy consumption while ensuring uninterrupted operations.
Action Plan: Deploy energy-efficient protocols like Narrowband IoT (NB-IoT) and Low Power Wide Area Network (LPWAN) for Industrial IoT devices on 6G networks, enhancing power management and extending battery life. Implement scheduled data transmission and sleep modes to reduce energy consumption during idle periods, optimizing device efficiency in industrial environments.

q) Reliance on Wireless Connectivity: Heavy dependence on wireless connectivity in industrial settings may expose vulnerabilities and reliability issues due to potential interference, signal degradation, and security breaches, necessitating robust mitigation strategies to ensure uninterrupted operations. Implementing redundant communication systems and adopting stringent cybersecurity measures can safeguard against disruptions and protect sensitive data in industrial networks.

Action Plan: Implement diverse communication redundancies such as wired backups and alternative wireless frequencies to mitigate risks associated with heavy reliance on wireless connectivity in industrial environments. Strengthen cybersecurity measures through regular audits, encryption protocols, and employee training to fortify network resilience and protect against potential vulnerabilities and attacks.

r) Data Management: Efficiently handling vast data volumes from interconnected devices in industries demands well-defined data management strategies to ensure data integrity, accessibility, and scalability while optimizing analytics and decision-making processes. Implementing data governance frameworks, scalable storage solutions, and advanced analytics tools can streamline data processing, enabling timely insights and informed decision-making in industrial operations.
Action Plan: Establish scalable data storage infrastructure with cloud-based solutions and distributed computing frameworks to accommodate large data volumes from industrial IoT devices. Implement data governance policies to regulate data collection, storage, and analysis processes, ensuring compliance with industry standards and optimizing data utilization for actionable insights.

s) Investment Uncertainty: Concerns regarding the uncertainty of return on investment and the potential long-term advantages of integrating 6G networks could discourage industrial stakeholders from embracing deployment, necessitating comprehensive cost-benefit analyses and address uncertainties, fostering confidence in the adoption of advanced networking technologies.
Action Plan: Conduct a thorough cost-benefit analyses and pilot studies to demonstrate the potential return on investment and long-term benefits of 6G adoption in industrial settings. Engage with industry experts and stakeholders to address concerns, provide education on the capabilities of 6G networks, and offer support in navigating the deployment process, fostering confidence and commitment towards implementation.

t) Cultural Resistance: Resistance to adopting 6G networks in industries may arise from workers' and management's reluctance to embrace change and new technologies, necessitating comprehensive training programs, clear communication of benefits, and leadership support to facilitate smooth transition and overcome organizational inertia.

Action Plan: Implement structured training sessions and workshops to educate industrial workers and management about the benefits and functionalities of 6G networks, addressing concerns and fostering buy-in. Encourage open communication channels and involve employees in decision-making processes to gain their trust and commitment, promoting a culture of innovation and acceptance of new technologies.

3.6 Conclusion

The advent of 6G signals a monumental leap forward in industrial connectivity, surpassing the capabilities of its predecessor, 5G, with unprecedented speed, near-zero latency, and unmatched reliability. This trisect of advancements lays the foundation for a future where factories evolve into intelligent ecosystems, supply chains achieve unparalleled optimization, and industrial automation undergoes a profound transformation. Envisioned scenarios include real-time data analysis enabling instant adjustments on production lines to preempt defects, while autonomous robots seamlessly collaborate under the orchestration of a lag-free 6G network. Beyond individual factories, interconnected supply chains experience remarkable efficiency boosts through proactive adjustments based on real-time data insights. Additionally, 6G facilitates advancements in environmental monitoring, empowering dense sensor networks to provide continuous and precise data for swift interventions. Serving as the nervous system for Industry 4.0, 6G enables real-time decision-making and seamless communication between machines, fostering the integration of artificial intelligence for optimized operations. Yet, realizing 6G's full potential demands ongoing research, standardization efforts, robust security measures, and the cultivation of a skilled workforce. In essence, embracing 6G promises a future defined by intelligent, efficient, and sustainable industrial practices, heralding a new era of manufacturing excellence.

3.6.1 Future Scope of Work

The future of work with 6G is groundbreaking. It involves ongoing research to harness its full potential, standardization efforts for interoperability, robust security measures, and workforce training. Collaboration among academia, industry, and policymakers is crucial for innovation. 6G will revolutionize industrial connections, enabling advanced automation, intelligent ecosystems, and streamlined supply chains. This heralds a new era of manufacturing excellence characterized by speed, efficiency, and sustainability.

AI disclosure statement: The author confirms that no artificial intelligence (AI)-generated content or AI-assisted writing tools were used in the preparation of this chapter (including summaries and the abstract). All text, analysis, and conclusions are the result of the author's original work.

References

1. Bao, Y., Zhang, X., Wang, C., Ming, X., Further expansion from smart manufacturing system (SMS) to social smart manufacturing system (SSMS) based on industrial internet. *Comput. Ind. Eng.*, 191, 110119, 2024, https://doi.org/10.1016/j.cie.2024.110119.
2. Chavhan, S., Shift to 6G: Exploration on trends, vision, requirements, technologies, research, and standardization efforts. *Sustain. Energy Technol. Assess.*, 54, 102666, 2022.
3. Chhabra, S., Aiden, M.K., Sabharwal, S.M., Al-Asadi, M., 5G and 6G Technologies for Smart City, in: *Enabling Technologies for Effective Planning and Management in Sustainable Smart Cities*, pp. 335–365, Springer International Publishing, Cham, 2023.
4. Fowdur, T.P., Babooram, L., Indoonundon, M., Murdan, A.P., Bojkovic, Z.S., Milovanovic, D.A., Enabling Technologies and Applications of 5G/6G-Powered Intelligent Connectivity, in: *Driving 5G Mobile Communications with Artificial Intelligence towards 6G*, pp. 355–402, CRC Press, Taylor and Francis, USA, 2023, https://www.taylorfrancis.com/chapters/edit/10.1201/9781003205494-13/enabling-technologies-applications-5g-6g-powered-intelligent-connectivity-tulsi-pawan-fowdur-lavesh-babooram-madhavsingh-indoonundon-anshu-murdan-zoran-bojkovic-dragorad-milovanovic.
5. Ghildiyal, Y., Singh, R., Alkhayyat, A., Gehlot, A., Malik, P., Sharma, R., Alkwai, L.M., An imperative role of 6G communication with perspective of industry 4.0: Challenges and research directions. *Sustainable Energy Technol. Assess.*, 56, 103047, 2023.
6. Jain, S., Yadav, A.K., Kumar, R., Yadav, V., Singh, D., Future Intelligent Communication with 6G Technology: A Review. *Int. J. Sens. Wireless Commun. Control*, 13, 6, 361–384, 2023.
7. Khang, A., Rath, K.C., Satapathy, S.K., Kumar, A., Das, S.R., Panda, M.R., Enabling the Future of Manufacturing: Integration of Robotics and IoT to Smart Factory Infrastructure in Industry 4.0, in: *Handbook of Research on AI-Based Technologies and Applications in the Era of the Metaverse*, pp. 25–50, IGI Global, 2023.

8. Mohsan, S.A.H., Mazinani, A., Malik, W., Younas, I., Othman, N.Q.H., Amjad, H., Mahmood, A., 6G: Envisioning the key technologies, applications and challenges. *Int. J. Adv. Comput. Sci. Appl.*, 11, 9, 2020, https://thesai.org/Publications/ViewPaper?Volume=11&Issue=9&Code=IJACSA&SerialNo=3.
9. Lee, J., Singh, J., Azamfar, M., Pandhare, V., Industrial AI and predictive analytics for smart manufacturing systems, in: *Smart Manufacturing*, pp. 213–244, Elsevier, 2020.
10. Lu, Y. and Zheng, X., 6G: A survey on technologies, scenarios, challenges, and the related issues. *J. Ind. Inf. Integr.*, 19, 100158, 2020.
11. Qiao, L., Li, Y., Chen, D., Serikawa, S., Guizani, M., Lv, Z., A survey on 5G/6G, AI, and Robotics. *Comput. Electr. Eng.*, 95, 107372, 2021.
12. Raharjo, B., Integrating Advanced Robotics with the Internet of Things (IoT): Opportunities and Challenges in Smart Manufacturing Environments. *Int. J. Responsible Artif. Intell.*, 14, 3, 1–5, 2024.
13. Rawat, B.S., Srivastava, A., Shrivastava, V., Singh, G., Garg, N., A Comprehensive Analysis of Applications in Internet of Things Networks in 5G and 6G, in: *2024 2nd International Conference on Computer, Communication and Control (IC4)*, IEEE, pp. 1–6, 2024, February.
14. Salahdine, F., Han, T., Zhang, N., 5G, 6G, and Beyond: Recent advances and future challenges. *Ann. Telecommun.*, 78, 9, 525–549, 2023.
15. Singh, A., Madaan, G., Hr, S., Kumar, A., Smart manufacturing systems: a futuristics roadmap towards application of industry 4.0 technologies. *Int. J. Computer Integr. Manuf.*, 36, 3, 411–428, 2023.
16. Shukla, S., Real-time monitoring and predictive analytics in healthcare: harnessing the power of data streaming. *Int. J. Comput. Appl.*, 185, 8, 32–37, 2023.
17. Sikiru, A.A., Olukayode, A.A., Lateef, O.A., Sobowale, S.O., 6G wireless system: The emerging trend in cellular technology. *J. Electr. Eng.*, 74, 3, 240–245, 2023.
18. Soyak, E.G. and Ercetin, O., Effective networking: Enabling effective communications towards 6G. *Comput. Commun.*, 215, 1–8, 2024.
19. Zhang, S. and Zhu, D., Towards artificial intelligence enabled 6G: State of the art, challenges, and opportunities. *Comput. Networks*, 183, 107556, 2020.
20. Kaur, J., Bhambri, P., Rani, S., Digital Twin Enabling Technologies, Applications, and Challenges, in: *AI-Driven Digital Twin and Industry 4.0: A Conceptual Framework with Applications*, 1st, S. Rani, P. Bhambri, S. Kumar, P.K. Pareek, A.A. Elngar (Eds.), pp. 90–104, CRC Press, 2024, https://doi.org/10.1201/9781003395416.
21. Bhambri, P., Rani, S., Kumar, S., Sinha, V.K., Big Data Analytics with Digital Twin for Industrial Applications, in: *AI-Driven Digital Twin and Industry 4.0: A Conceptual Framework with Applications*, 1st, S. Rani, P. Bhambri, S. Kumar, P.K. Pareek, A.A. Elngar (Eds.), pp. 105–26, CRC Press, 2024, https://doi.org/10.1201/9781003395416.

4

Security Paradigm for 6G-Enabled IIoT Ecosystems

Rachna Rana[1]* and Pankaj Bhambri[2]

[1]Department of Computer Science and Engineering, Ludhiana Group of Colleges, Ludhiana, Punjab, India
[2]Guru Nanak Dev Engineering College, Ludhiana, Punjab, India

Abstract

The issues of n/w security have importantly expedited the global exploitation curriculum of 5G exchange of ideas thus research into 6G safety study is immediately essential. The objective of this chapter is to communicate an outline of the up-and-coming 6G cellular exchange of ideas standard, prominence equilibrium with inheritance security perception as well as asymmetric inventive mechanism; for instance, AI, Quantum Computing, amalgamated Learning, and so on. It defines the hazard model in 6G exchange of ideas using five safety past perceptions: privacy, integrity, user-friendliness, verification, and entry management. Furthermore, we propose categorizing threat-countering solutions designed for 6G exchange of ideas into three categories: intrusion detection systems (IDS), entity characteristics, and cryptographic mechanisms. This text covers seven potential examined instructions for 6G exchange of ideas, with a particular focus on security. The aim is to anticipate the needs of next-generation communication and ensure that security is a top priority. The chapter specifically explores the Industrial Internet of Things (IIoT) ecosystems that will be enabled by 6G, and how security can be incorporated into this paradigm.

***Keywords*:** 5G, 6G, security, industrial internet of things, artificial intelligence

**Corresponding author*: rachnarana1981@gmail.com; ORCID: 0000-0003-0450-8699
Pankaj Bhambri: ORCID: 0000-0003-4437-4103

Sita Rani, Pankaj Bhambri, Balamurugan Balusamy, Rishabha Malviya and Seifedine Kadry (eds.) Edge Intelligence for 6G-Enabled Industrial Internet of Things, (67–84) © 2026 Scrivener Publishing LLC

4.1 Introduction

It is generally understood that the route to sustainable systems is true in all areas of research, and that certain key technologies are caught up in this new challenge, while others are evolving. In this regard, the field of information digitization has been seen as a paradigm for the development of site network architecture, with research and applications in fields such as smart cities, building materials, entertainment, transportation, and healthcare. In the particular applications indicated above, the manufacturing sector is still distant from digital processes since I4.0 adoption is happening gradually and very few businesses have been able to transition to the digital age of training management (SFM) solutions.

Companies face challenges such as the visibility of dashboards and key performance indicators (KPIs) on digital platforms, necessary financial changes, IT system security, data packet incompleteness during transmission, and the rapid development of new technologies and intelligence. With I4.0 serving intelligent factories, many of the top businesses in the world now view this second problem as crucial and urgent.

These firms also discussed adopting new education and training courses to fulfill new demands (such as IT solution architecture, user interface design, and robot coordination), as well as having the workers needed to tackle new difficulties that arise in the new business period. With an emphasis on the new usage-based business era, it is understood that suitable and adequate resources are needed to meet the demands and obstacles of various production systems and that these systems must interact, change, and adapt to handle small-scale adaptive decisions involving adjustments to products, materials, and assets as well as process modifications tailored to reduce energy consumption.

Thus, this chapter, which addresses the switch from electronic to self-correcting machinery, clarifies some crucial elements of the procedure that ought to be applied in Production 4.0 (I4.0), including cutting down on delivery and production times, intelligent planning, and virtual technology [1, 2]. It shortens value chains and, crucially, the quality control production process. This will make it feasible to work together on joint business, which is one of the competitive businesses, and maintain positive relationships. Studying the management and archiving of data within the ecosystem of cloud services (storage, processing, memory, and bandwidth) might help address these developments.

However, as more data emerges from the internet of things (IoT), the cloud continues to suffer through poor communication and network connectivity challenges owing to limited capacity. Negative claims made by researchers and government and commercial parties (organizations) claiming that developing designs and processes for making smart goods is only possible by losing sight of the air layer's potential in its abundant supply of resources.

Cloud services provide critical business immediacy by enabling centralized management and control of equipment and software across decentralized, heterogeneous environments. To address core IIoT challenges—such as latency, network traffic, power consumption, and communication reliability—Fog and Edge Computing (FC/EC) systems are deployed to process data closer to the source. Information about storage limitations and computing power with these new solutions highlighted the benefits and drawbacks of near-edge computing and cloud computing, resulting in a combination of FC/cloud services, EC/cloud services, Software Defined Networking (SDN), and EC and network functions (NFV), and 5G network virtualization.

A specialized guide focused on developing high-quality electrical devices for the Internet of Things industry while maintaining user and vendor security [3].

The increasing use of wood materials in the business necessitates the correct, persuasive, and cost-effective use of current crude fabric assets. In this context, does the notion of Industry 4.0, which includes smart generation frameworks, smart objects, and smart administration models, stand out? Industry 4.0 is defined by the idea that humans, machines, automated control gear, goods, and other connected objects may interact; therefore, lines are choreographed, and they eventually operate as an ordered framework.

The Web of Things, or IoT, is defined as everything that is connected inside the Industry 4.0 framework. Considering the latest developments, individuals are incorporating more innovation into their daily activities. The goal here isn't just to provide verbal communication between persons, but also communication between items and objects with individuals. This establishes the IoT framework. IIoT (Mechanical Web of Things), often known as the industrial internet, is the use of IoT in industry/manufacturing. This suggests that there are relationships throughout the whole supply chain.

Certain definitions are imprecise, unclear, and overly general as industry procedures and computation methods evolve; the second section of the article addresses these issues and highlights certain inconsistencies. To translate the Chinese terminology cited in this article on fog count, we have provided some interpretations from the literature. The computer area is taking over because of the Internet of Things' good recognition, the rising industry's competitiveness, the IASC's longevity, and the problems that IoT has presented to the industry thus far.

"Hub-level architecture that disperses administration, computation, storage, and collaboration duties from the cloud to the source near consumers" is what FC stands for. FC is a decentralized, layered calculation that, depending on its usage or simulation application, changes the number of layers in that computation and, as a result, the network architecture. This computation, which operates in IIoT systems and thus in CPS (autonomous systems operating in real-time), is performed close to the production process border, and is utilized to choose computation and storage.

The system's core tasks include ensuring scalability and modularity by connecting components, providing security middleware for public networks, managing device identification metadata, enabling cloud service interoperability, and delivering intelligent, compute-enabled storage for data streams. This computation, which occurs in the first FC layer, is also known as the boundary edge calculation. With its capabilities, it facilitates the processing of big geographic data using Mobile Cloud Computing (MACC) before Multi-Access Edge Computing (MEC), with the data being transmitted through the Fog Node (NF) Cloud database for FC. The purpose of edge performance as an introduction to calculating points is to lower the cost of bandwidth, shorten communication delays, enhance privacy, and increase connection.

It is regarded as the first collaborative collaboration model and is reported to have been utilized in addition to content distribution. It is based on the development of computer resources (virtualization software, storage, and management tools), as well as collaborative effort network structure. Virtual networks and network function virtualization (NFV) coexist in software-defined networking (SDN), where virtual networks operate on the physical network. Furthermore, although EC is known to be cloud-isolated, its adoption will enhance MACC's energy efficiency and capacity tuning when taking into account the hybrid model of point-to-point architecture and cloud computing [4, 5].

The white paper provides a technical discussion on security, one of the most important topics currently associated with open radio access networks (Open RAN or O-RAN). Security has been identified as a critical factor for the future development of O-RAN. Recently, telecom operators, international organizations, and even governments have issued numerous declarations and recommendations to ensure the security and resilience of future telecom network infrastructure and operations. Research and development into the security architecture and algorithms used in these networks continues. Below it reviews O-RAN security research and development trends and present Rime do Labs' perspective on this important topic. First, it provides an overview of the recent activities of major companies in the O-RAN security field. It also covers key cyber security concepts for 5G radio access networks and future 6G networks.

Later in this chapter, it will discuss two important paradigms of 5G/6G networks: openness and intelligence. Vulnerabilities and opportunities are considered to ensure the security and confidentiality of communications.

This paper then focuses on artificial intelligence (AI) security applications in O-RAN. It will take a closer look at AI attack scenarios and security architecture, and introduce AI targets and response methods for cyber attacks.

Finally, it introduces a selection of xApps from Rimedo Labs that are used to detect and mitigate multiple instances of interference and signal storm (O-RAN) attacks. UML sequence diagrams are provided along with reproduction consequences representing the usefulness of the approach.

The paradigm for manufacturing is shifting due to the speed at which mobile communications are developing. IIoT applications in the real world are beginning to surface with the progressive introduction of 5G technology. Three main features of 5G applications are more connections, reduced latency, and increased capacity. Of the three, more connection is directed at IIoT applications, which include a range of tools and machine-type sensors (MTC). Data throughput rates above 10 Gbps are required to reach a large number of nodes because to the fast development in MTCs and sensors. Higher data transfer speeds are also necessary for a wide range of additional applications in different societal and industrial domains.

Future use cases, according to the 6G white paper, include holographic communications, immersive gaming, intelligent healthcare and health monitoring, workspaces and ecosystems, smart factories and next-generation manufacturing paradigms, and holographic communications. The system specs state that the 10Gbps 5G peak speed and the 1Gbps user interface speed are insufficient to completely address the massive data applications listed above in terms of spectrum requirements. Gradually, 6G research advanced with the launch of 5G. Given that 6G is at least ten times quicker than 5G, wired and wireless networks should undergo a revolution. In smart factories, there are an increasing number of linked devices. Self-organizing control with little to no human involvement is essential to bringing in the IIoT era.

In IIoT, data transmission is inextricably linked to wireless network support. 6G networks must offer more flexible and dynamic spectrum access and improved network performance because of the stochastic nature of data demand from various customers. Supporting self-configuration control without requiring interaction with a primary base station (PBS) is possible through Device-to-Device (D2D) communication. Energy and spectral efficiency may be raised this way while preserving steady and dependable IIoT operation. However, the communication process must continue to take place using PBS-allocated channels. More adaptable traffic consumption mechanisms are also required, in addition to adaptable access methods.

Conventional fixed monthly data limitations can occasionally result in overconsumption (surcharge) in high-demand months or data overload (waste) in low-demand months—both of which consumers wish to avoid. Your wireless connection will be lost if you run out of data, and using too much will incur extra fees. Three barriers, however, exist in the mobile data market: data restrictions are usually location-based, locked by the user, and determined by time. Meanwhile, spectrum resources are limited and essential, and therefore enhancing spectrum efficiency, particularly reuse efficiency, is one of the most critical strategies to increase network performance. Both enable users to buy more data from competing users or sell any leftover data.

Transaction prices in the data trading market are subject to fluctuations over time based on supply and demand. It is believed that doing so will improve usage and social welfare. Since auctions are one of the most popular forms of trading, a large number of academics and research institutions have studied auction models, anti-collusion, and auctioneer selection in great detail. Apart from enhanced flexibility in spectrum access, IIoT has to offer improved security and privacy functionalities. This is because cyber assaults may cause major economic and security consequences. Ensuring security, privacy, and resilience in IIoT architectures is therefore imperative. Applications built on blockchain technology are gaining increasing interest as it becomes more and more well-known in the world of cryptocurrency.

In several domains, such as safe multi-party computing, data trade, and cryptography, blockchain has been extensively employed to address the aforementioned issues because of its decentralization, tamper-proofing, and verifiability. Blockchain's special qualities can be precisely paired with spectrum allocation, making it directly tied to both IIoT and 6G. We concentrate on creating a blockchain-based fair spectrum auction system to overcome the drawbacks of current schemes, particularly in terms of privacy, security of transactions, and fairness. The suggested method may offer a dynamic and equitable access mechanism that is required for the natural development of 6G digital services as a whole. The local availability of microlicensed spectrum, which will support creative network operations and business models, is the central tenet of the multidisciplinary strategy.

A modified McAfee spectrum auction smart contract is created, the smart contract is implemented on Ethereum, and simulation tests are carried out to see whether the suggested strategy is feasible [6]. Ethereum and CryptographySatoshi Nakamoto introduced the notion of "blockchain," however in the "Bitcoin White Paper" in 2008, and the Bitcoin network was formed in 2009. Blockchain, sometimes referred to as related data on transactions or a block of information or ledger, is cryptographically secured. Every block includes association times, the encrypted hash of the preceding block, and hard-to-tamper-with data changes (often represented by a hash value derived from the Merkle tree). Blockchain6G decentralized ledgers: OOFD MA Ultra-mass MIMO Terahertz.

According to Shannon's theory, more channel capacity necessitates greater spectrum bandwidth. The Terahertz frequency spectrum provides a high variety of frequencies and a broad bandwidth, allowing for effective data transfer in short-range wireless communication. A terahertz frequency band is considered the core function of 6G and contains the following features: opacity. Terahertz is ideal for remote security but not for long-distance terrestrial communications because of the opacity of the atmosphere. Blockchain-driven architecture for managing 6G spectrum As Haseeb Kureshi noted, blockchain will wipe away civilization as a whole. It will make possible a new government that was only ever the fantasy of utopians and scientists.

Blockchain, a technology that can lower the cost of bank loans, is expected to become an essential component in the future, much like the Internet. With the way the physical layer is currently communicating, we can also accomplish this just evaluation In the competitive spectrum, which consists of two components—fair and fair between buyers—fair analysis is equitable between buyer and seller. The premise of economic theory is that competent employees prioritize their interests, therefore all stakeholders make decisions and select the best tactics based on their interests. Everyone seeks to shift losses and responsibilities onto other people.

Furthermore, consistency among stakeholders in the existing system—Security Analysis Business resilience pertains to the ability to withstand financial losses, stop unlawful spectrum usage, stop malicious data manipulation attempts, and safeguard private property. Blockchain technology has the potential to impact availability, integrity, and secrecy. The security of the ideas described in this article can be improved by utilizing blockchain security. Based on an architecture that allows for testing and performance, blockchain is a distributed ledger. We presented our protocol on the Ethereum test chain and were charged PBS and SU fees. As of February 18, 2021, the Ethereum exchange rate is 1 Ether1909.38 USD, while the suggested oil price is 1909.38.

Industrial IoT security is at the vanguard of this transformation, and it is a critical technology that will allow firms to construct smart factories and prosper. A growing number of businesses are using network solutions to cut expenses and optimize workflows [7].

4.2 Therefore, What Exactly is Industrial Internet of Things Security? In What Ways Does It Propel Digital Transformation to Shift Business Models and Boost Organizational Effectiveness? Is this a Way Out? How Can Businesses Make the Most of these Advancements to Achieve Their Goals? What Exactly is Industrial Internet of Things Security (IIoT)?

For smart systems and gadgets utilized in businesses, IIoT security acts like a barrier. IIoT security refers to the technologies and software that shield computers and systems from hackers and other online dangers, just like our houses are secured with locks and alarms. Contemplate this: Consider a manufacturing facility where all of the equipment is online. Although these technologies aid in the development of better products, they also require protection from cyberattacks. To make sure that unauthorized individuals cannot access or meddle with these systems, putting security guards in place is analogous to IIoT security. It covers strategies including encryption, creating strong passwords, and using specialized software to keep an eye out for unusual activities.

So, IoT security is about keeping devices and systems in businesses safe, much as we want our houses protected from burglars. This is crucial because it shields critical data, keeps production disruptions to a minimum, and guarantees that enterprises can run securely and profitably [8].

4.3 Why is Security Relevant to IIoT?

IIoT security is critical because it guarantees the safe and effective operation of all corporate operations. It's similar to having a guardian for your belongings. Why it matters is as follows:

4.3.1 Protection of Systems

IIoT security makes ensuring that industrial and commercial systems are safe from cyberattacks. This implies that they may carry on with business as usual.

4.3.2 Information Protection

It also makes sure that sensitive data is secure. IIoT security can stop the theft of concealed food from a food facility, for example.

4.3.3 Crime Prevention

By continuously monitoring systems, IIoT security helps to avert incidents. If the machine is running in a risky manner, it can halt it.

4.3.4 Cost Savings

Businesses won't have to spend as much money fixing issues brought on by accidents or hackers when everything is safe.

4.3.5 Enhanced Productivity

IIoT security contributes to system performance, enabling faster and more effective task completion. Together, IIoT security is the equivalent of the industry's super hero. It guarantees that everything operates effectively, safely, and without causing financial harm by protecting people, systems, and data.

4.4 Which Technologies Underpin IIoT Security?

The technology underlying IIoT security functions similarly to a fortress, protecting organizations from cyber-attacks. This is how it operates:

4.4.1 Devices and Sensors

Business-use devices and sensors are the first line of defense for IIoT security. They resemble surgery on the ears and eyes. They gather data from devices, processes, and equipment all the time.

4.4.2 Encryption of Data

Consider this information as a hidden message. To protect these communications during transmission, IIoT security employs encryption, which works similarly to passwords. Even if they were interrupted, they would not be able to grasp the message.

4.4.3 Authentication

Similar to a bouncer at a club verifying IDs, IIoT security guarantees that only authorized devices and users have access to the system. Something or someone is not permitted if they do not possess a current certificate.

4.4.4 These Security Measures Keep an Eye on the Digital World

Firewalls and intrusion detection systems. They keep an eye on every activity, including criminal efforts. If something strange is observed, the alarm will go off.

4.4.5 Updates and Patches

IIoT security automatically upgrades its software, just like your phone does. By addressing any bugs or vulnerabilities, these upgrades strengthen the system's defenses against fresh attacks.

4.4.6 Remote Monitoring

Organizations may also keep an eye on work from a distance using The Industrial Internet of Things security. Businesses can quickly monitor their operations from any location, much like a security camera lets you view everything from your phone to your door.

4.4.7 Environmental Response

In the event of an issue, IIoT security is ready. Digital is similar to carrying a fire extinguisher with you at all times. Experts intervened to resolve the issue and retrieve the merchandise.

4.4.8 Behavioral Analysis

IIoT security is more than just knowing threat models; it acts as a digital explorer, investigating and understanding the behavior of devices and systems. When something uncommon occurs, such as your pet begins to act strangely, the alarm will go off.

4.4.9 Machine Learning

IIoT security systems have the potential to be intelligent, akin to artificial intelligence which is capable of learning and adapting.

They utilize machine learning to recognize and respond to new dangers based on their experience, much as you learn from your errors to prevent repeating them.

4.4.10 Redundancy

IIoT security frequently features a fallback mechanism, akin to the car's spare tire backup system. If one component of the security system fails, another will be employed to keep things running smoothly.

4.4.11 Periodic Audits

Just as financial audits check a company's accounts, IIoT security systems are examined regularly to verify they are functioning correctly and doing their job, as well as to uncover possible gaps that require assistance. What makes one type of IoT security distinct from another? [9].

4.5 Why are IIoT Security Standards Needed?

Vulnerabilities in enterprise IoT networks can be devastating. These consequences include ransomware attacks or leakage of personal information and business-critical data that reduce entire business productivity [10].

4.6 What Steps Can Network Administrators and CISOs Take to Secure Their Networks and Devices?

IoT security might be difficult, but Byos professionals can help you get started fast and efficiently. Byos Secure Gateway Edge employs edge micro-segmentation to safeguard IIoT devices, hence contributing to the attainment of Zero Trust security objectives [11].

4.6.1 Byos Secure Gateway Edge has the Following Advantages

This solution securely extends the lifespan of legacy IT infrastructure, allowing unsupported and older applications to operate safely even after their official retirement. It enables easy, centralized remote control and monitoring of previously isolated devices, facilitating more efficient and secure maintenance. A key security feature is the ability to immediately micro-segment a compromised device—efficiently halting all its malicious network communications while maintaining its core operations—without requiring any changes to the existing network setup or internal devices. This reduces the risk of disconnected assets being exposed to insider threats, malware, and ransomware, while also cutting on-site working time for experts, leading to significant operational cost savings [11].

4.7 What Makes IIoT Security Different from IoT Security?

IIoT security guarantees the efficiency and safety of vital activities and concentrates on safeguarding sectors where cyber attacks might have dire repercussions. Contrarily, IoT security protects user data and personal devices, making them more dependable and safer for daily usage. While they are both significant, their roles and degrees of influence are distinct [13]. Table 4.1 compares the security characteristics of IIoT and IoT, highlighting differences in focus, threat environment, use cases, and safety procedures. IIoT emphasizes industrial systems, while IoT focuses on consumer electronics.

4.8 Security Benefits of IIoT

IIoT security works as a kind of digital barrier to keep industrial data and processes safe from online attacks. It guarantees the flawless operation of machinery, the confidentiality of sensitive data, and the ability of companies to expand confidently in the digital age the following are security benefits of IIoT:

4.8.1 Data Security

IIoT security makes sure that data is secure by preventing unwanted access to sensitive information.

Table 4.1 Comparison of security characteristics between IIoT and IoT [12].

Characteristics	Security of IIoT	Internet of Things security
Definition	Safeguards industrial processes and systems, including energy networks and manufacturing.	Protects common consumer electronics like smart home appliances and thermostats.
Concentrate	Places a focus on protecting vital industrial processes and infrastructure.	Mostly concerned with protecting private electronics and information.
Principals	Issues guarantee the effectiveness, safety, and dependability of industrial operations.	Focuses on the privacy, data security, and user experience of consumer gadgets.
Threat Environment	Environment addresses sophisticated cyber threats that might harm several businesses.	Although it confronts various dangers, it frequently has less of an impact than IIoT.
Use Cases	Safeguard transportation networks, industries, electricity grids, and other industrial facilities.	Protects wearables, smart homes, and personal devices.
Safety Procedures	Strict access controls and strong security procedures are used to avoid disruptions.	Uses security measures, albeit they could not be as strict as in IIoT because of the decreased danger.
Standards for Compliance	Frequently governed by stringent industry-specific laws and requirements for compliance.	Subject to rules governing client confidentiality and fundamental safeguarding of information.

(*Continued*)

Table 4.1 Comparison of security characteristics between IIoT and IoT [12]. (*Continued*)

Characteristics	Security of IIoT	Internet of Things security
Important Areas of Focus	Evaluation of data, maintenance planning, real-time monitoring, and process enhancement.	Energy conservation, convenience, and automation for homes.
Industrial Affect	Essential to the operation of economies and enterprises.	Crucial for improving customer convenience and quality of life.
Effects on Day-to-Day Living	More behind the scenes; not what most people see in the open?	Making ensuring personal gadgets are secure and safe is part of daily living.

4.8.2 Stops Interruptions

IIoT security guards against cyber attacks to keep industrial activities from being disrupted.

4.8.3 Guarantees Security

IIoT security guards against unwanted access, ensuring the security of both people and equipment.

4.8.4 Preserves Credibility

Minimizing downtime from breaches of security, it contributes to the upkeep of IIoT system resilience.

4.8.5 Privacy-Protecting

IIoT security defends against cyber attacks on sensitive data and user privacy.

4.8.6 Stops Unauthorized Entry

It guarantees the access and control of IIoT systems and devices to only authorized persons.

4.8.7 Protects Vital Infrastructure

IIoT security guards against cyber attacks on vital infrastructure, such as transportation and electricity grids.

4.8.8 Lowers Danger

IIoT security reduces the possibility of cyber attacks, allowing businesses to function with confidence.

4.9 Case Study 1: Agricultural Cost Reduction

Sector: Introducing Jaden, a passionate farmer who is busy tending to his large grain fields. Jaden's agricultural realm spans acres, and he is aware of how crucial resource management is to farming.

Resource waste is a problem that many in the agriculture sector are acquainted with, and it plagues Jaden. Excessive use of fertilizer or water can raise expenses and harm the environment.

The Answer: Jaden views IIoT security as his agricultural partner and uses it to make well-informed decisions. Imagine soil experts studying every square inch of the earth, with soil sensors tucked away in his fields.

These sensors continuously monitor the nutrient content and soil moisture levels while neighboring weather stations monitor humidity, temperature, and rainfall.

Jaden's smart phone receives this important info straight. With this real-time data at his disposal, Jaden masters precision farming.

He is quite aware of the right time and quantity of water to use when irrigating his crops. Additionally, he knows just how much fertilizer is best to use in order to support healthy crop development. Jaden guarantees healthy harvests, reduces expenses, and advances sustainability *via* the effective utilization of resources.

It is making sustainable decisions, while maintaining the profitability of Jaden's farming business is akin to having an agricultural mentor guiding him.

4.10 Conclusion and Future Scope

Cloud computing and IIoT security have a lot of potential to protect companies in the future:

4.10.1 Advanced Threat Protection

IIoT security in the cloud will get much stronger in the upcoming years. Cloud-based security solutions will advance to keep up with more complex cyber attacks, protecting industrial processes from cybercriminals.

4.10.2 Real-Time Monitoring

The speed at which the cloud can process data will improve IIoT device real-time monitoring. Any anomalous behavior or security breech will result in instant notifications, enabling prompt handling of such risks.

4.10.3 Advances in Encryption

Data security will come first. Sensitive data sent between IIoT devices and the cloud will become increasingly difficult for unauthorized parties to access as encryption techniques continue to progress.

4.10.4 Scalable Solutions

Cloud-based security solutions will provide scalability as companies grow their IIoT networks. This implies that security can adjust and adequately cover the expanding landscape as additional devices and sensors are introduced to the network.

4.10.5 User-Friendly Interfaces

There will be an increase in the usability of the cloud-based user interfaces for controlling IIoT security. This will lower the possibility of human mistake by enabling non-technical staff to simply monitor and manage security measures.

4.10.6 Combining Machine Learning and Artificial Intelligence

Algorithms for AI and machine learning will be essential for recognizing and countering security risks. These technologies will improve threat detection capabilities by continually analyzing patterns and abnormalities.

4.10.7 Assurance of Compliance

Industries are subject to stringent data protection regulations. Cloud-based IIoT security solutions will advance to provide tools for straightforward compliance management, reducing the risk of legal ramifications. Industry Cooperation and Information Exchange: Industries will collaborate to share knowledge about new security threats and best practices. Cloud platforms will provide a collective defense against attackers by allowing this sharing.

It is concluded that the goal of IIoT security in the future is to protect industrial processes and make them resilient. These developments will increase confidence in the dependability of IIoT systems while also protecting sensitive data. Industries no longer have to worry about cyberattacks in an interconnected and safe future.

AI disclosure statement: The author acknowledges the use of AI-based tools for minor language editing or grammatical correction. However, all intellectual contributions, analyses, and conclusions presented in this chapter are entirely the author's own.

References

1. Bhardwaj, A. and Goundar, S., Cloud computing security services to mitigate DDoS attacks, in: *Cloud Computing Security - Concepts and Practice*, 2020, Available from: https://doi.org/10.5772/intechopen.92683.
2. Bonomi, F., Milito, R., Zhu, J., Addepalli, S., Fog computing and its role in the Internet of things, in: *Proceedings of the first edition of the MCC workshop on Mobile cloud computing*, 2012, Available from: https://doi.org/10.1145/2342509.2342513.
3. Chen, C. and Lai, J.L., An experimental detection of distributed denial of service attack in CDX 3 platform based on snort. *Sensors*, 23, 13, 6139, 2023, Available from: https://doi.org/10.3390/s23136139.
4. Joshi, S.B. and Panchal, S.D., A systematic survey on security challenges for fog-enabled Internet of things (IoT) and industrial Internet of things

(IIoT), in: *Internet of Things*, pp. 1–14, 2022, Available from: https://doi.org/10.1007/978-3-031-08254-2_1.

5. Kruger, C.P. and Hancke, G.P., Enhanced security in industrial Internet of things networks using latency based fingerprinting, in: *2020 IEEE 18th International Conference on Industrial Informatics (INDIN)*, 2020, Available from: https://doi.org/10.1109/indin45582.2020.9562155.
6. Lu, C., Zhang, W., Ma, L., Liu, M., Gao, L., Wang, Z., *et al.*, Resource allocation method of industrial terminal edge computing based on reinforcement learning algorithm. *2022 International Conference on Industrial IoT, Big Data and Supply Chain (IIoTBDSC)*, 2022, Available from: https://doi.org/10.1109/iiotbdsc57192.2022.00023.
7. Mitteilungen Der gesellschaft fur Informatik 258. Folge. *Inf. Spektrum*, 42, 4, 313–319, 2019, Available from: https://doi.org/10.1007/s00287-019-01184-z.
8. Ramzan, M., Shoaib, M., Altaf, A., Arshad, S., Iqbal, F., Castilla, AK., *et al.*, Distributed denial of service attack detection in network traffic using deep learning algorithm. *Sensors*, 23, 20, 8642, 2023, Available from: https://doi.org/10.3390/s23208642.
9. Security and privacy challenges in fog computing, in: *Enabling Technologies for Smart Fog Computing*, pp. 247–280, 2023, Available from: https://doi.org/10.1049/pbpc065e_ch10.
10. Shi, X., Tong, F., Zhang, W., Yu, L., Resilient privacy-preserving distributed localization against dishonest nodes in Internet of things. *IEEE Internet Things J.*, 7, 9, 9214–9223, 2020, Available from: https://doi.org/10.1109/jiot.2020.3004709.
11. Tariq, U., Aseeri, A.O., Alkatheiri, M.S., Zhuang, Y., Context-aware autonomous security assertion for industrial IoT. *IEEE Access*, 8, 191785–191794, 2020, Available from: https://doi.org/10.1109/access.2020.3032436.
12. Sridhar, V., Rani, S., Pareek, P.K., Bhambri, P., Elngar, A.A. (Eds.), *Blockchain for IoT Systems: Concept, Framework and Applications*, 1st, Chapman and Hall/CRC, 2024, Available from: https://doi.org/10.1201/9781003460367.
13. Bhambri, P., Rani, S., Pareek, P.K., Paperless Paradigm: Intelligent Automation in Document and Record Management, in: *Generating Entrepreneurial Ideas with AI*, D. Darwish (Ed.), pp. 164–83, IGI Global, 2024, Available from: https://www.igi-global.com/book/hyperautomation-business-society/335477.

5

Machine Learning Dynamics in 6G Industrial Environments

Naina Agrawal, J. Jayashree* and J. Vijayashree

School of Computer Science and Engineering, VIT Vellore, Tamil Nadu, India

Abstract

The 5G to 6G transition in wireless technology is an amazing advancement resulting in faster data speeds, low delays, and specific features that serve as the base for internet of industrial applications and connectivity. The machine learning serves as the central tool in this shift, driving industrial processes under the 6G network framework. The combination of machine learning algorithm interfacing with 6G technology results in automatic adjustment and performance improvement, which is the reform of traditional industry. For example, apps such as predictive maintenance and self-driving factories involve fewer human resources, they can be done more efficiently and consume fewer resources. Nevertheless, at the same time, security issues and workforce adaptation should not be forgotten. Another application of machine learning is ensuring cyber security by integrating automatic threat detection and real-time response functions. As we look to the future, one can expect that AIs will be continuously improved and cybersecurity measures will get more effective, meaning that 6G will be more powerful and secure in industrial settings. Although there are issues, it can be predicted that the merging of machine learning and 6G technology will bring a new wave of productivity in the industrial sector.

***Keywords*:** 6G transition, machine learning, industrial applications, cybersecurity, productivity, wireless technology

**Corresponding author*: jayashree.j@vit.ac.in; ORCID: 0000-0002-0191-8070

Sita Rani, Pankaj Bhambri, Balamurugan Balusamy, Rishabha Malviya and Seifedine Kadry (eds.) Edge Intelligence for 6G-Enabled Industrial Internet of Things, (85–120) © 2026 Scrivener Publishing LLC

5.1 Introduction

Among the main factors that drive changes in the global network is the development of wireless communication systems. Beginning with 1G and ending with 6G, every generation has seen significant progress that continues to expand the possibilities in this field. This journey has been characterized by a persistent search for faster data rates, lower latency, and more devices connected than ever before which has brought industries into previously unknown levels of productivity and efficiency.

The evolution of technology will transform forever our industrial environment. With better functionalities compared to its predecessors, 6G marks a new beginning. Its high data speeds, very low latency, and wide device connectivity depict not incremental but a quantum leap toward Industry 4.0 or the Fourth Industrial Revolution.

6G is currently capturing global industry attention, and it is obvious that incorporating machine learning into it is key to realizing unheard-of levels of productivity, adaptability, and inventiveness. The incorporation of machine learning into the 6G marks a fundamental change in the functioning and management operations of industrial settings. The main purpose of this chapter is to investigate the intricate dynamics of this mix-up as well as expose why state-of-the-art telecommunications are revolutionary in view of potential machine learning.

This ground-breaking alliance can revolutionize the use and operation of technology in industries. In a production ecosystem, the win-win interaction between 6G and machine learning goes beyond enhancing connectivity; instead, it encompasses complex decision-making based on intelligence, real-time flexibility, and self-operating abilities. Besides simplifying existing procedures, blending these two systems could open up new vistas only imaginable before through science fiction.

This story explains the reason why 6G is significant because it differs from its ancestors. High data rates that go up to multi-terabits per second facilitate rapid communication and smooth transfer of large sets of information in industrial networks. Consequently, ultra-low latency of milliseconds ensures near-real-time responsiveness in scenarios where seconds count.

Additionally, 6G's ability to provide a huge number of connected devices within each square kilometer is game-changing for industries. The dense connectivity promised by 6G makes it easier to deploy various sensors, actuators, and IoT devices thus resulting in a rich tapestry of data sources. Machine learning algorithms thrive in such an environment of abundant data, enabling meaningful decisions through insightful conclusions. The story revolves around the realm of machine learning, which empowers operations to learn, adapt, and enhance efficiency. These programs delve into the complexities of data by employing unsupervised learning or reinforcement learning to support real-time optimization of processes detection of defects and predictive maintenance. In contrast, to cloud-based systems, 6G networks adopt edge computing principles when integrating machine learning techniques. This shift brings capabilities closer to data sources reducing delays and enabling swift aware decisions in industrial environments.

As we delve further into this chapter, we will explore the basics of 6G technology the array of machine learning algorithms in industrial contexts and practical instances that showcase the transformative potential of this fusion. As the journey unfolds, the intricate interplay between cutting-edge connectivity and intelligent algorithms defining the landscape of enabled settings becomes evident.

Importance of 6G in Industrial Settings

The advent of 6G, the latest, in technology, has brought about advancements in connectivity and is anticipated to provide unparalleled capabilities compared to its predecessors. This ground-breaking innovation holds the promise of transforming operations by introducing an interconnected environment that leverages rapid data transmission minimal delays and the ability to connect numerous devices simultaneously.

Exploring the Impact of 6G, in Industrial Environments;

- High Data Rates: One of the main drivers that determine the influence 6G can have on the industrial sector is its potential to facilitate a data transfer rate of several multi-terabit-per-second data rates. At this level, transmission speeds open up opportunities for immediate data exchange and information flow in the area of industrial networks. Without a doubt, real-time data is essential in sectors like manufacturing, shipping, and healthcare, among others. The facility ensures that information can be obtained with ease and promptly for making quick decisions as well as ensuring efficient processes through process optimization.
- Ultra-Low Latency: It ensures that the system response time is at its best. In the context of industrial systems that need instantaneous response and not just low latency but

ultra-low latency of milliseconds, is simply game-changing. An example is manufacturing, where highly fastidious tasks require instantaneous feedback for the precision and efficiency of robotic systems and machines. The enhanced synchronization and coordination that 6G's low latency promises would allow us to automate more functions with higher accuracy than ever before.

- Device Explosion and IoT Revolution: 6G's ability to connect countless devices in a small area will transform the way industries use the IoT. It allows for a vast network of sensors, devices, and actuators, providing a wealth of data for analysis. Industries like energy and logistics can use this interconnected ecosystem to improve decision-making, monitor operations, and increase efficiency.
- Powering Industry 4.0: 6G's high speeds, low delays, and extensive connectivity make it a key enabler of Industry 4.0, also known as the Fourth Industrial Revolution. This revolution involves the integration of advanced technologies that drive innovation and productivity, such as artificial intelligence, machine learning, and automated processes.

The Crucial Role of Machine Learning in 6G-Enabled Industrial Environments

Empowering Systems through Machine Learning:
Machine learning, a form of artificial intelligence, gives machines the ability to learn and adjust based on data. In industrial environments enhanced by 6G, machine learning becomes crucial for automated operations, predicting outcomes, and making intelligent decisions.

Diverse Array of Machine Learning Algorithms:
Supervised, unsupervised, and reinforcement learning algorithms are essential for extracting insights from the vast data generated by industrial processes. Supervised learning is particularly useful for tasks like predictive maintenance and quality control, where training models on labeled data allows for accurate predictions.

Moving Beyond Rule-Based Systems:
Machine learning helps industries become more flexible and responsive to changing conditions. It allows them to move away from traditional rule-based systems. For example, in predictive maintenance, machine learning

algorithms analyze past data to predict when equipment is likely to fail. This allows companies to perform maintenance proactively, reducing downtime.

Real-Time Decision Support:
Machine learning is also being integrated into 6G-enabled industrial settings in new ways. Edge computing, a key part of 6G, brings processing resources closer to the data source. This lowers latency and allows for real-time decision-making. Fast, context-aware insights improve the efficiency of industrial processes.

Unveiling Real-World Applications

- Smart Factories: In manufacturing, machine learning algorithms help predict maintenance needs, optimize production timelines, and enhance overall performance. Additionally, 6G networks facilitate seamless communication among machines. The integration of machine learning and 6G drives the creation of smart factories, showcasing the transformative power of this combined technology.
- Energy Management: Advanced 6G sensors in industries with high energy consumption monitor equipment and system conditions. Machine learning algorithms use this real-time data to detect issues and predict potential problems. By being proactive, this approach saves on maintenance costs, improves plant reliability, and reduces the likelihood of unexpected outages.
- Supply Chain Optimization: The integration of 6G technology and machine learning is revolutionizing supply chain processes, enhancing adaptability and efficiency. Predictive analytics, powered by these advancements, optimize demand forecasting, route planning, and inventory management, reducing lead times and streamlining operations. This transformation has profound implications for industries like retail and logistics, improving overall efficiency and customer satisfaction.

The Intricate Dance: 6G and Machine Learning:

Industrial settings are on the cusp of a profound transformation driven by a harmonious convergence of advanced machine learning algorithms and cutting-edge 6G connectivity. This technological synergy represents a paradigm shift in industrial operations, transcending mere upgrades. Machine learning flourishes within this ecosystem, unlocking unprecedented potential for optimized processes and inventive solutions. The foundation of this ecosystem lies in the convergence of seamless connectivity, lightning-fast data transmission, and an unparalleled proliferation of interconnected devices. As we explore the advancements of 6G and machine learning, we uncover how they intertwine in industrial settings, creating a mutually beneficial relationship. Industries evolve within this transformative realm, incorporating intelligent and interconnected systems. This opens doors to a future where our technological boundaries continue to expand, unlocking new possibilities and pushing the boundaries of what we can achieve.

5.2 Foundations of 6G Technology

5.2.1 Overview of 6G Capabilities

6G technology marks a transformative shift in wireless communication. With its unprecedented capabilities, it revolutionizes connectivity by enabling ultra-high data rates of multiple terabits per second, unlocking previously impossible data transmission and reception speeds [1]. Moreover, 6G features ultra-low latency, measured in milliseconds, facilitating near-instantaneous communication crucial for applications demanding immediate responses [1].

6G stands out with its ability to connect an unprecedented number of devices per square kilometer, making it ideal for industrial settings [2]. This dense connectivity allows for the seamless integration of sensors, actuators, and IoT devices, enabling the creation of "smart" networks that optimize operations through faster processes and efficient data collection [2]. The high device density also facilitates the deployment of machine learning algorithms, which thrive on large datasets, resulting in enhanced monitoring and analysis of industrial operations [3].

5.2.2 Integration of AI and Machine Learning into 6G Networks

The power of 6G and artificial intelligence (AI) is based on their interconnected nature, particularly in the area of machine learning. 6G networks aren't just communication channels; they're intelligent platforms that can learn from, improve themselves with, and react to the data that flows through them. Machine learning algorithms are a key part of this intelligence, allowing 6G networks to adjust dynamically to factors like usage patterns, environmental conditions, and user needs [4].

6G networks are evolving beyond the current cloud-focused approach to incorporate machine learning (ML). Edge computing, a crucial element of 6G infrastructure, will revolutionize how networks operate. By positioning processing resources closer to data sources, edge computing reduces latency and empowers networks with real-time decision-making capabilities. Furthermore, the transition to edge computing enables the direct implementation of ML algorithms within industrial environments, making ML a key facilitator for 6G networks [5].

When machine learning and 6G come together, they do more than just speed up how people talk to each other. They make an intelligent structure for how industries work together. 6G makes it possible to do edge computing, which means data can be processed where it comes from [5]. This makes it possible to get insights faster and in a more tailored way. This is especially helpful in factories, where decisions need to be made quickly and things can change all the time. When 6G's smart infrastructure is combined with machine learning algorithms, the result is a seamless solution that opens up new ways to make factories more efficient, flexible, and creative [5].

As shown in Figure 5.1, the AI-enabled 6G architecture integrates intelligent sensing, data mining, control, and smart application layers with edge and cloud resources to support real-time analytics and decision-making.

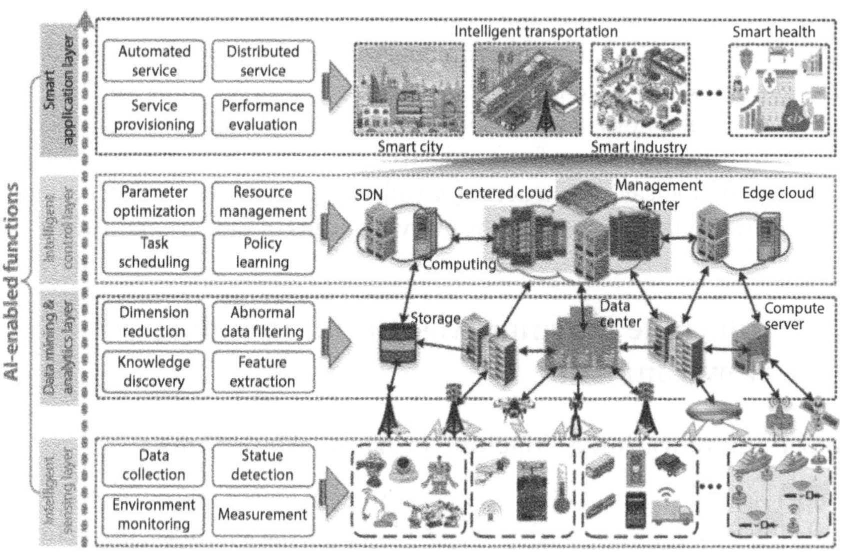

Figure 5.1 The architecture of AI-enabled intelligent 6G networks.

5.2.3 Key Features Making 6G Suitable for Industrial Applications

6G's intrinsic features make it highly compatible with Industry 4.0 demands [4, 5]. Its robustness under challenging conditions, including extreme temperatures and electromagnetic interference, ensures exceptional reliability in industrial environments where such factors prevail [4]. 6G excels in industrial applications due to its ground-breaking feature of network slicing. This feature allows for the creation of multiple isolated virtual networks on a shared physical infrastructure. Each virtual "slice" is tailored to specific industrial needs. This customization enables different industrial processes to seamlessly coexist on the same 6G platform, with each process having its customized parameters for reliability, latency, and bandwidth requirements [4].

Essentially, the underlying principles of 6G pave the way for a transformative leap in industrial network operations. The fusion of advanced machine learning capabilities with ultra-fast and responsive connectivity marks a new era in industrial operations. Moreover, 6G's robustness in demanding environments ensures reliable connectivity, a crucial aspect for industrial processes that demand unwavering dependability [4, 5]. Throughout this text, we'll explore how the core features of Industry 4.0 drive real-world applications, reshaping industrial operations. The fusion of 6G's capabilities and machine learning's advanced algorithms is poised to revolutionize Industry 4.0. Expect to see intelligent factories leveraging real-time communication and predictive maintenance systems optimizing equipment performance. This combination holds immense potential for transformative advancements.

As 6G technology advances, its focus on reliability, adaptability, and personalization will transform industrial connectivity. Instead of being a mere technological infrastructure, it will evolve into a responsive, customized platform that aligns with the evolving needs of modern industries.

5.3 Machine Learning Algorithms in Industrial Environments

5.3.1 Exploration of Machine Learning Algorithms

Supervised learning: This involves training a model using labeled data [6]. This enables the model to understand patterns and make predictions. It excels in industrial settings for improving processes like production efficiency, equipment maintenance, and product quality [7]. For example, in quality control, models can be trained to detect defects using labeled data of both acceptable and faulty products [8]. This helps identify and flag potential defects in real-time production [8]. By enabling the prediction of outcomes, supervised learning becomes a powerful tool for enhancing industrial operations [7]. It boosts overall productivity [7], reduces machine downtime, and ensures the highest quality standards.

Unsupervised learning: These algorithms don't require specific instructions. They can find patterns and connections in unlabeled data, which means they can handle data without pre-assigned categories [9]. This ability makes unsupervised learning key for dealing with unusual patterns or anomalies that aren't easily identified [7]. In industry, unsupervised learning is valuable for discovering hidden patterns [7], putting together similar data, and categorizing information without labels. It's also great for spotting anomalies in equipment—changes from normal behavior that might be signs of potential issues. By actively detecting faults, this approach enhances equipment operation, minimizes downtime, and is a key component of predictive maintenance. Furthermore, unsupervised learning algorithms empower better optimization in complex industrial resource management [10]. These algorithms uncover patterns in data, aiding decision-makers in allocating resources wisely [10].

Reinforcement learning: Computers enhance their capabilities through trial and error [11]. They receive feedback on their actions and adjust them accordingly [11]. This technique is valuable for autonomous systems like robotic assembly lines and unmanned vehicles in advanced industrial settings, especially those enabled by 6G technology [12, 13, 26]. Reinforcement learning allows these systems to adapt to changing environments [12], continuously improving their decision-making processes. For example, robotic assembly lines connected through 6G networks can leverage reinforcement learning to refine their operations and respond effectively to unexpected challenges or demand variations in manufacturing scenarios [13]. 6G technology allows autonomous systems to adapt to changing business environments [13]. This adaptability enables ongoing enhancement and learning, resulting in greater operational efficiency in industries [13].

5.3.2 Real-World Applications of Machine Learning

To gain a true understanding of how machine learning (ML) impacts industrial environments powered by 6G, it is crucial to explore practical applications. These applications showcase how ML, empowered by 6G connectivity, transforms operations, leading to improved efficiency and fostering innovation in various industrial sectors. Examples of such applications include predictive maintenance in manufacturing and adaptive robotics in logistics.

Predictive Maintenance: In industrial settings using the power of 6G, machine learning algorithms can predict potential machine failures by studying past data [14]. This allows for preventive maintenance. By fixing issues before they worsen [14], this proactive approach minimizes downtime and extends the lifespan of machines and equipment [14]. These algorithms enhance operational efficiency by spotting the early signs of failure [7], reducing maintenance expenses [7], and ensuring the continued reliability of essential industrial assets [7]. This shows how machine learning can change how industries work with faster 6G connections.

Fault Detection and Diagnosis: In environments powered by 6G technology, businesses leverage algorithms to analyze data in real-time [8]. These algorithms can detect unusual patterns that may point to defects or deviations from normal operations, especially in industries where even minor disruptions can have severe consequences [8]. By identifying these anomalies quickly, companies can take proactive steps to prevent failures and mitigate risks [8]. This capability significantly enhances operational reliability, safety, and efficiency, making it essential for precision-critical industries like manufacturing, aviation, and healthcare. It underscores the vital role of real-time anomaly detection in industrial applications driven by 6G networks [8].

Process Optimization: Machine learning models are valuable in optimizing industrial processes connected by 6G. By analyzing extensive data, these models uncover patterns that identify inefficiencies. This precision enables targeted corrections to improve performance significantly. This potential is crucial in industries like manufacturing, where small efficiency gains translate into significant cost savings and enhanced product quality. 6G connectivity empowers machine learning models to enhance accuracy, minimize waste, and automate processes, leading to greater overall productivity. As industries embrace data-driven approaches, they are integrating intelligent algorithms into their workflows. This empowers them with the ability to make informed decisions, ensuring responsiveness, adaptability, and continuous refinement of processes to cater to the dynamic challenges faced in modern business landscapes.

5.3.3 Case Studies Illustrating Machine Learning Success Stories

Case studies showcase the power of machine learning (ML) in industrial settings powered by 6G connectivity. These case studies highlight how 6G enables advanced algorithms that optimize operations. For instance, smart robots leverage ML to enhance processes, while predictive maintenance systems prevent equipment issues. The results include increased productivity, reduced downtime, and improved product quality. Examining these case studies reveals the transformative impact of ML and 6G connectivity, propelling industries towards increased agility, innovation, and productivity in the evolving landscape of industrial practices.

Smart Factories: In a smart factory, 6G connectivity enhances communication between machines, creating a unified and efficient industrial ecosystem [14]. Additionally, 6G-powered machine learning algorithms enable predictive maintenance [14]. By analyzing past and real-time data, these algorithms predict maintenance needs, enabling timely intervention before equipment failures, and minimizing downtime [14]. Furthermore, 6G and machine learning work together to optimize production schedules by responding swiftly to unforeseen factors and demand fluctuations. This flexibility maximizes efficiency by optimizing resource allocation and automating processes [14]. Integrating machine learning and 6G connectivity in smart factories enables them to become dynamic, data-driven environments [15]. This allows for continuous optimization of operations, resulting in improved productivity, cost efficiency, and enhanced agility in meeting evolving industrial requirements [15].

Energy Management: In 6G-enabled industrial settings, real-time energy monitoring is simplified with the incorporation of machine learning algorithms. This powerful combination allows industries to adjust energy consumption patterns on the fly, enhancing efficiency and reducing expenses. Machine learning analyzes continuous data streams to identify patterns, anomalies, and energy-saving opportunities. By monitoring in real-time, industrial facilities can respond to energy demand fluctuations and optimize resource allocation, minimizing waste and maximizing savings. By harnessing the high-speed, low-latency capabilities of 6G and the adaptability of machine learning, a robust and efficient energy management system is created. This system optimizes energy usage, reducing costs while promoting sustainability. The combination of these technologies enhances energy management in industrial settings, showcasing the transformative value of machine learning and 6G.

Optimization of the Supply Chain: Supply chain operations are transformed and become more adaptable and efficient when the combined powers of machine learning and 6G connection are utilized. Combining machine learning and 6G connectivity transforms supply chains, making them more flexible and efficient. Machine learning offers predictive analytics that enhance demand forecasting, route planning, and inventory management. It analyzes real-time data and historical trends to predict future demand and disruptions. 6G's rapid and low-latency connection ensures seamless data transmission across the supply chain, providing real-time insights to optimize operations.

By optimizing operations, reducing unnecessary inventory, enhancing delivery efficiency, and precisely predicting demand, businesses can reduce production delays and boost the durability of their supply chains. In the realm of industrial logistics, the integration of machine learning and 6G connectivity is paving the way for a new age of adaptable and data-centric supply chain management.

In the upcoming sections, we'll dive deeper into edge computing and real-time data processing, emphasizing their significance in the symbiotic connection between 6G and machine learning in industrial environments. By inspecting these concepts, we'll reveal their vital role in enabling the seamless convergence of high-speed connectivity and intelligent algorithms. This will forge a dynamic partnership, reshaping real-time data analysis and decision-making in the evolving landscape of 6G-powered industrial settings.

5.4 Real-Time Data Processing and Edge Computing

5.4.1 Significance of Real-Time Data Processing

In the lightning-fast environment of 6G-enabled industrial sectors, the significance of real-time data analysis is immense. Traditional processing methods designed for slower networks fall short amidst the dynamic and data-rich environment of modern industries. 6G's exceptional speed and minimal delay revolutionize real-time data analysis, bringing transformative benefits to various sectors. With data being analyzed and utilized instantaneously, decision-making becomes more prompt and based on real-world conditions. In fields like manufacturing and autonomous systems, where choices must be made in a flash, real-time data analysis becomes a crucial tool, enhancing both effectiveness and safety [15]. With 6G's blistering speed and real-time data analysis, industries can now navigate the complex modern industrial environment with remarkable efficiency and accuracy.

Immediate Decision-Making: In 6G-enabled industrial environments, real-time data processing allows for swift and informed decision-making. The combination of low latency and high speed enables immediate data analysis and response, ensuring prompt action on insights derived from data. This is essential in situations where delays can lead to inefficiencies or safety hazards, especially in industries relying on autonomous systems or complex production processes. 6G's ability to empower quick decision-making not only minimizes potential risks but also enhances operational efficiency. With the merger of 6G's lightning-fast internet and instant data analysis, industries witness remarkable advancements. This potent combination empowers businesses to navigate fluid and demanding conditions with unmatched agility, responsiveness, and optimization, all while prioritizing safety and effectiveness.

Dynamic Adaptability: In 6G-connected industrial settings, real-time data processing introduces a transformative concept called dynamic adaptability [16]. Due to the constant evolution of industrial operations, the integration of ultra-fast and low-latency 6G connectivity empowers systems to adapt swiftly. Whether optimizing energy consumption based on fluctuating conditions or fine-tuning production plans according to shifting demand, the agility enabled by real-time processing is revolutionary [16]. The rapid responsiveness allows industrial systems to seamlessly navigate complex environments, making critical decisions in real time to boost productivity. With 6G technology, industries can enhance operational efficiency and adapt to evolving situations, positioning them as leaders in innovation [16]. These systems can swiftly readjust to meet the demands of the dynamic industrial landscape, paving the way for revolutionary systems that respond and adapt to constant change [16].

5.4.2 Role of Edge Computing in Industrial Environments

In 6G networks, edge computing shifts computational power towards the data source, reducing delays compared to traditional cloud-based processing [17]. By placing computers closer to where data is collected, industrial systems can respond faster, enabling real-time processing and decision-making [17]. This integration of edge computing transforms the industry by ensuring instant and context-sensitive adjustments, leading to enhanced efficiency and adaptability in 6G environments where immediate responses are critical to managing the dynamic interplay between data and computational operations.

Reduced Latency: Edge computing plays a crucial role in 6G technology by minimizing latency, the time it takes for data to travel from its source to its processing unit. This reduced latency is vital for applications that demand lightning-fast decisions, such as autonomous systems and machinery control. Edge computing ensures that critical data is processed close to its source, eliminating the delay associated with sending data to distant cloud servers. Incorporating edge computing into 6G networks becomes essential in scenarios where immediate responses are paramount to ensure the safety and efficiency of operations. The integration of advanced technology revolutionizes industrial processes, allowing for swift decision-making and enhancing the flexibility of autonomous systems and control mechanisms [15].

Bandwidth Optimization: 6G-powered industries use edge computing, a ground-breaking approach where data processing happens at the network's edge [18]. This allows only critical data to be sent to the central cloud [18]. By filtering and transmitting only the most crucial information, this innovative system optimizes bandwidth utilization. In industrial environments where vast amounts of data are generated, this is crucial. It prioritizes efficient data transmission and conserves network resources [18]. The overwhelming amount of data generated in industrial settings by various devices and sensors can strain network infrastructure. Edge computing acts like a filter, processing data locally to extract only the most important information. This condensed data is then efficiently transferred to the cloud for further processing, storage, or decision-making. By doing this, edge computing reduces the burden on networks, improves data transfer efficiency, and minimizes latency. It ensures that critical information reaches the cloud quickly and reliably. Incorporating edge computing into 6G-connected industrial environments not only optimizes bandwidth usage but also effectively manages industrial data in a sustainable and resource-efficient way.

5.4.3 Diagrams Illustrating 6G-Enabled Industrial System with Edge Computing

Figure 5.2 illustrates the layered 6G network architecture for industrial environments, highlighting the 6G core, edge computing nodes, and cloud integration.

Specific Features, Technologies, and Applications:

6G Network Core:

- Quantum Encryption: Provides unprecedented security for critical industrial data through quantum encryption.
- Holographic communication: Facilitates precise and engaging interaction between devices.

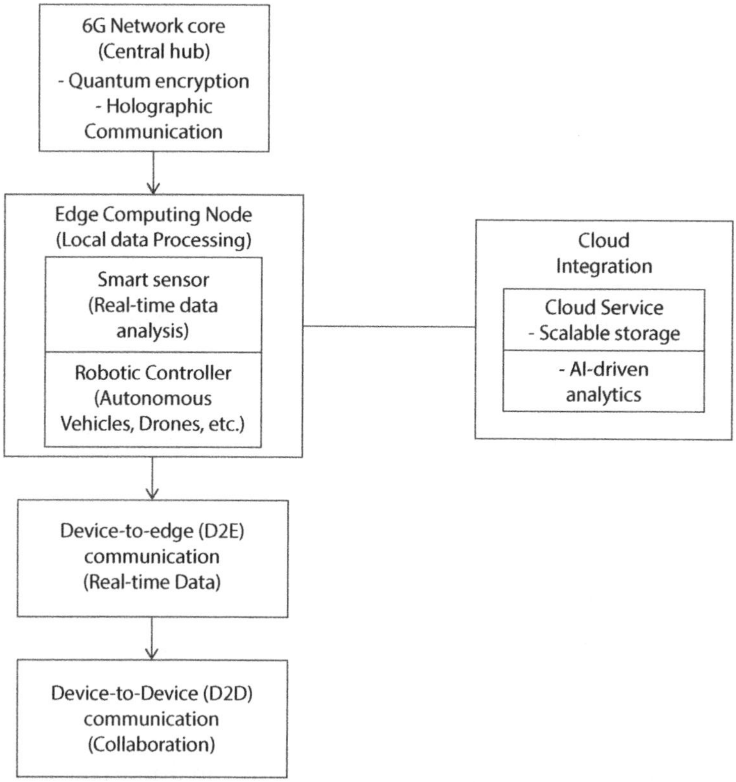

Figure 5.2 6G network architecture in industrial setup.

Edge Computing Node:

- Smart sensors (Real-time Data Analysis They swiftly process data from sensors, enabling speedy decision-making.
- Robotics Controller (Autonomous Vehicles, Drones, and more): It operates and coordinates autonomous systems to ensure their safe and efficient function (like autonomous vehicles, drones, and others).

Cloud Integration:

- Scalable storage: With cloud technology, unlimited scales of corporate data have adjustable storage possibilities.
- AI-driven analytics: Utilize artificial intelligence for optimization, preventive maintenance, and analysis of significant data chunks.

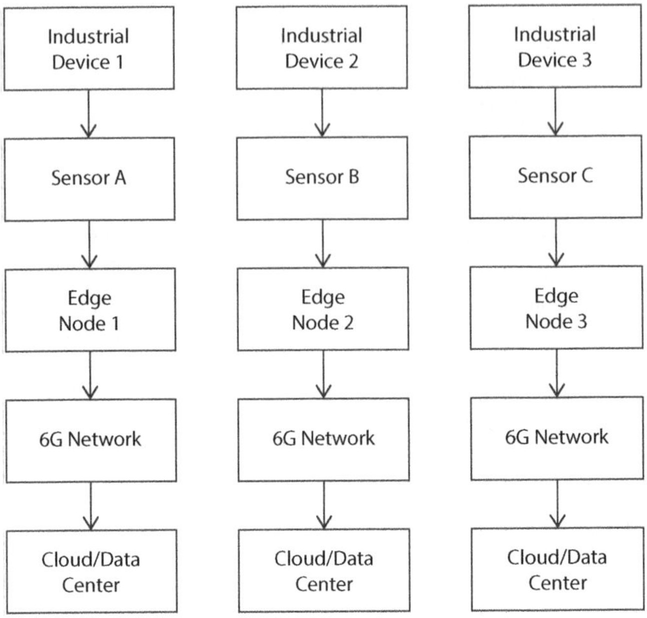

Figure 5.3 Edge computing deployment in 6G industrial environment.

Device-to-Edge (D2E) Communication:

- Real-time data exchange: It allows the rapid movement of data from IoT devices to edge computing nodes for immediate processing.

Device-to-Device (D2D) Communication:

- Collaborative Operations: It aids in the seamless integration of different technologies, such as automated machines and robotic arms.

As depicted in Figure 5.3, edge nodes are placed close to industrial devices and sensors, enabling local processing and reducing latency before sending processed data to the cloud.

Industrial Devices and Sensors:

- The first three rows show several industrial devices that are dispersed over an industrial setting (Device 1, Device 2, Device 3).
- A matching sensor (Sensor A, Sensor B, Sensor C) is located beneath each device and is responsible for gathering data in real-time from the devices.

Edge Computing Nodes:

- The three Edge Nodes (Edge Nodes 1, 2, and 3) that are arranged in the industrial environment are displayed in the next row.
- Every Edge Node has connections to surrounding industrial equipment and sensors, demonstrating its function in local data processing.

6G Network:

- The 6G Network, which links all industrial devices, sensors, and edge nodes, is represented by the row below the edge nodes.
- The links stand for the low-latency, high-speed communication that the 6G network enables.

Cloud/Data Center:

- The Cloud/Data Center connecting to each edge node is shown in the final row. This is an illustration of the cloud's centralized storage and sophisticated analytics features.

Data Flow:

- By sending data to the adjacent edge nodes for instant processing, industrial devices, and sensors reduce latency.
- After processing, the data is sent to the cloud or data center *via* the 6G network for storage and additional analysis.

Latency and Bandwidth Optimization:

- Because there is no need to transport all data to the centralized Cloud/Data Center, local processing is made possible by the thoughtful placement of edge nodes, which reduces latency.
- By ensuring that only pertinent and processed data is sent to the cloud or data center, the usage of the 6G network optimizes bandwidth and lowers overall network load.

Overall, this deployment approach improves data processing capabilities while reducing latency and optimizing bandwidth utilization by utilizing edge computing and 6G network technologies to build an effective and responsive industrial environment.

As we proceed through the chapter, we will look at particular uses where machine learning algorithms combined with edge computing and real-time data processing play essential roles in influencing the dynamics of 6G-connected industrial settings.

5.5 Predictive Maintenance and Fault Detection

5.5.1 Utilizing Machine Learning for Predictive Maintenance

Machine learning (ML) algorithms and super-fast 6G internet let factories use predictive maintenance, a way to keep machines running well and lasting for a long time. This proactive approach uses sensors, past data, and real-time analysis to predict when equipment might break down [19]. The system finds signs of possible problems by looking for patterns and unusual things, which lets engineers fix them before they break [19]. By combining ML with 6G, companies can save money and keep their important industrial machines working well while also making their operations more efficient [19].

In industrial environments, machine learning algorithms are crucial, especially those using predictive analytics. These algorithms analyze historical data to identify patterns and provide early warnings of potential equipment failures. By predicting future maintenance needs, this advanced analytical approach helps prevent unexpected breakdowns and ensures proactive maintenance strategies.

By analyzing a massive collection of historical data, these algorithms can spot subtle patterns and anomalies that indicate equipment malfunctions. This in-depth analysis allows the system to detect early warning signs or precursors that precede potential failures. As a result, maintenance needs can be predicted with high accuracy, providing ample time for preventive actions.

Predictive maintenance, powered by forecasting capabilities, enables companies to shift from reactive to proactive maintenance strategies. Instead of responding to unexpected failures, data-informed predictions guide timely maintenance actions. This approach minimizes downtime, improves operational efficiency, extends equipment lifespan, and reduces unplanned maintenance costs.

By integrating machine learning algorithms with the rapid communication capabilities of 6G technology, industries gain exceptional predictive power [15]. This enables real-time data analysis, leading to agile and effective maintenance plans [15]. The synergy between 6G and machine learning revolutionizes industrial maintenance, shifting from reactive to proactive measures, and empowering industries to anticipate and address issues before they arise [15].

Condition Monitoring: In a factory setting where 6G technology is available, seamlessly integrated sensors monitor equipment, constantly collecting data on its health, including temperature, movement, and wear [20]. Machine learning algorithms analyze and understand this continuous data stream to improve operations [20].

Machine learning algorithms customized for industrial settings constantly analyze real-time sensor data [19]. They uncover patterns, deviations, and subtle shifts, generating comprehensive information about the equipment's condition by detecting potential issues and optimizing performance [19].

Machine learning models can predict upcoming problems by using historical data and real-time information [21]. They can help prevent costly repairs by finding unusual vibration or temperature patterns that could point to a mechanical breakdown or overheating, allowing for early intervention and maintenance [21].

Advancements in technology, such as sensors, 6G connectivity, and machine learning, are reshaping manufacturing [20]. Instead of waiting for equipment to break down, these technologies allow for proactive monitoring and maintenance [20]. Real-time data gathering, rapid data transfer, and advanced analytics work together to provide a comprehensive understanding of equipment health [20]. This enables timely preventive measures to avoid breakdowns, ensuring continuous operation and enhanced efficiency of industrial machinery [20].

5.5.2 Fault Detection Algorithms for Industrial Processes

Fault detection algorithms play a crucial role in identifying problems and abnormalities in industrial operations [8]. Integrating machine learning with 6G connectivity improves the speed and accuracy of defect detection [8]. This allows for rapid problem-solving, reduces downtime, and prevents costly disruptions [8]. 6G connectivity provides real-time data transmission, which enables machine learning algorithms to analyze trends and anomalies swiftly [19]. This supports a proactive approach to industrial maintenance, detecting potential issues before they become major problems. By combining advanced algorithms and high-speed communication, industries can ensure a robust defect detection system that safeguards processes from unexpected challenges [19].

Anomaly Detection: Machine learning algorithms can detect anomalies effectively because they can learn the normal behavior of machines and operations [22]. This ability is valuable in industrial environments, where anomalies can be early indicators of potential issues with equipment or processes [22, 23].

Machine learning algorithms are trained on past data to learn the expected behavior of machines and systems [21]. Once trained, these algorithms monitor real-time data and detect any unusual deviations from established norms [21]. Deviations from these norms, known as anomalies, can manifest as changes in vibration, temperature, or other indicators. By identifying these anomalies quickly, critical issues can be detected promptly.

Modern technology promptly detects and addresses irregularities in industrial settings [19]. 6G's fast communication and machine learning's ability to identify subtle deviations ensure early detection and real-time reporting of potential issues [19]. This proactive approach reduces downtime and enhances overall reliability and efficiency. It marks a transformative shift in industrial maintenance, where machine learning algorithms drive proactive measures based on intelligent insights.

Real-time Response: A major benefit of 6G is its low-latency feature, which enhances fault detection algorithms. Such algorithms excel in identifying anomalies in manufacturing processes. Coupled with 6G's low latency, these algorithms can provide immediate alerts to human operators or automated systems, enabling prompt responses to any irregularities.

In intricate industrial operations, the 6G-enabled defect detection algorithms facilitate rapid response times. Upon detecting anomalies, these algorithms swiftly trigger alerts for operators or automated control systems. This swift response is crucial for preventing issues from escalating, mitigating failures, and minimizing overall operational disruptions caused by errors.

When vital equipment vibrates abnormally, a defect detection system in a 6G network will instantly identify the issue by analyzing real-time data. This prompt alert empowers operators or automated systems to react swiftly, potentially preventing major failures. The low-latency communication in automated systems ensures rapid and adaptable responses, minimizing the impact of errors on the broader industrial network.

6G technology, with its lightning-fast response times and problem-detecting tools, unlocks a new world of enhanced industrial safety and efficiency. Unlike traditional approaches that only react to problems, this proactive system identifies and addresses anomalies swiftly, leading to a more resilient and uninterrupted industrial environment. This seamless connection between detection and response ensures a robust industrial ecosystem where communication speed matches detection speed, marking a ground-breaking era in industrial innovation.

5.5.3 Case Studies Showcasing Predictive Maintenance Success Stories

Case Study 1: Aerospace Manufacturing

By embedding 6G-enabled sensors in aircraft manufacturing facilities, advanced monitoring capabilities can be achieved [19]. These sensors continuously gather detailed, real-time data about the machinery's performance. This data is then processed by advanced machine learning algorithms, which analyze and predict maintenance needs, based on the vast amount of data they receive.

Predictive analytics plays a crucial role in combining 6G connectivity with machine learning [14]. Machine learning algorithms analyze sensor data, detecting patterns and subtle changes, allowing for precise predictions of when maintenance is required. This foresight enables proactive scheduling [14], of maintenance during planned downtime, ensuring timely and efficient interventions, ultimately increasing accuracy and efficiency.

Predictive maintenance transforms operations by reducing unplanned maintenance, known for its high costs and disruptions. This efficiency allows aerospace production plants to optimize resource utilization and dramatically enhance operational performance, leading to substantial cost savings.

6G sensors enhance the reliability of crucial equipment in the aerospace industry. They work in tandem with machine learning algorithms, enabling predictive analytics to become an integral part of maintenance operations [20]. This proactive approach, where technology becomes a collaborative partner, ensures the longevity, efficiency, and cost-effectiveness of aerospace manufacturing processes [20].

Case Study 2: Power Generation

In power plants, 6G-linked sensors are deployed as technological pillars to monitor the well-being of generators and turbines. Equipped with 6G's speed and minimal delays, these sensors constantly collect real-time data. This data avalanche feeds machine-learning algorithms specifically designed for rapid processing and analysis [19]. These algorithms aim to forecast potential issues and detect anomalies that may signal inconsistencies in the machines' performance, enabling proactive action to prevent failures [19].

6G connectivity and machine learning work together to enable predictive maintenance, transforming power plant operations. Advanced analytics help predict potential issues, allowing for optimized scheduling of maintenance and repairs during planned outages, minimizing disruptions, and enhancing efficiency.

This strategy has numerous benefits. It has substantially reduced unplanned outages, which can be costly and problematic. This leads to significant savings in maintenance costs and enhances the overall reliability of the power plant. Beyond improving the reliability of turbines and generators, sensors connected to 6G networks and the analytical power of machine learning have revolutionized operations. This showcases the immense potential of proactive, technology-driven approaches within the power generation industry.

In these case studies, combining 6G connectivity with machine learning algorithms demonstrates its effectiveness for predictive maintenance and fault detection in various industries. Further exploring this combination, we will investigate the relationship between 6G and machine learning in autonomous systems and robotics. This integration not only improves the efficiency of industrial automation but also changes how autonomous systems and robots operate in 6G-connected environments.

Advanced 6G connectivity and machine learning have tangible benefits in industrial settings, enabling defect detection and predictive maintenance. As we explore the interplay between 6G and machine learning, we will examine the use of robots and autonomous systems. This integration not only enhances productivity but also transforms how these technologies interact with and adapt to dynamic 6G-connected environments.

5.6 Autonomous Systems and Robotics

5.6.1 Integration of Machine Learning into Autonomous Systems

The integration of machine learning (ML) in automated systems is revolutionizing industrial automation. 6G connectivity is crucial for this change, ensuring seamless communication and collaboration among autonomous entities. This section explores the synergy between ML algorithms and

6G technology, showcasing how they enhance the capabilities of autonomous systems in industrial applications. Uniting advanced technologies enhances the intelligence and adaptability of automated systems, enabling them to respond more effectively to ever-evolving 6G environments. This convergence marks a transformative era in industrial automation, where increased autonomy, responsiveness, and efficiency become fundamental characteristics of seamlessly interconnected systems.

Context-aware Decision Making: Incorporating machine learning algorithms into autonomous systems enables these systems to make informed decisions with contextual awareness [19]. They can learn from past experiences and adapt to changing conditions dynamically [19]. This is essential in industrial settings where circumstances can shift rapidly and unexpectedly.

Machine learning algorithms embedded in autonomous systems continuously gather past data to grasp patterns and variations. This learning process allows these systems to develop intelligence, enabling them to identify and understand complex situations. In dynamic industrial environments, autonomous systems enhanced with machine learning exhibit remarkable adaptability. They navigate scenarios with contextual understanding, making decisions based on both real-time inputs and accumulated knowledge from past encounters [19].

In industrial settings, where factors like production needs, surroundings, and equipment status are constantly shifting, the ability of self-driving systems enhanced by machine learning to make informed decisions is essential for efficiency. This synergy fosters a dynamic industrial ecosystem by allowing autonomous systems to navigate complex situations with adaptability, making the entire operation more responsive and adaptable.

Adaptive Navigation: 6G technology is crucial for the advancement of industrial automation, allowing real-time communication among self-operating machines. It serves as the communication backbone, facilitating the seamless adjustment of navigation paths based on the current environment. Machine learning algorithms play a vital role in enhancing this adaptability, synergistically working with 6G to create a dynamic duo. In the interconnected world of 6G networks, self-driving systems can communicate in real-time using their high speed and low delays. This allows them to constantly adjust and change their paths as the surroundings evolve. With 6G's rapid data exchange, autonomous systems stay agile and adaptable, enabling them to navigate obstacles, changing terrain, and unexpected events effectively.

Autonomous systems rely on machine learning for intelligent navigation [25]. These algorithms analyze sensor data to detect patterns and anomalies, informing navigation strategies. By processing real-time feedback, they optimize routes, adjusting courses based on prior knowledge. This adaptability enhances precision and efficiency, enabling autonomous systems to navigate industrial environments with greater agility and foresight [25].

In smart industrial settings, machine learning and 6G connectivity work together to create an ecosystem where automated systems can improve their navigation techniques and communicate instantly. This dynamic combination leads to seamless coordination between advanced AI decision-making and cutting-edge technology, allowing for efficient and adaptable operations.

5.6.2 Robotics Empowered by 6G Connectivity and Machine Learning

Machine learning algorithms working alongside ultra-fast 6G connections are revolutionizing industrial robotics. This ground-breaking fusion enables robots to operate more efficiently, precisely, and collaboratively than ever before.

6G connectivity and rapid, low-latency communication empower robots to interact and react instantaneously. Integrated machine learning algorithms simultaneously equip these systems with adaptive intelligence. By leveraging data-driven learning, robots can now optimize tasks, make intelligent choices, and navigate complex environments autonomously.

The integration of machine learning and 6G technology in industrial robotics is a breakthrough, enabling unprecedented efficiency and accuracy. Robots can now collaborate effectively, communicate continuously, and adapt to dynamic situations. This revolutionizes robotic systems, transforming them from mere tools into intelligent and supportive collaborators within industrial settings.

Collaborative Robotics (Cobots): Collaborative robotics (cobots) are evolving with the introduction of 6G connectivity [27]. This advanced connectivity enables seamless communication between robots and other devices, resulting in a more dynamic industrial ecosystem. 6G provides low latency and instantaneous communication, fostering real-time collaboration among robots and other industrial components [27]. Additionally, machine learning algorithms integrated into robotic systems enhance collaboration, transforming the interactions between robots, human workers, and other robots [27]. This synergistic relationship optimizes industrial processes and unlocks new possibilities for efficiency and innovation [27].

In today's interconnected world, robots leverage the high-speed connectivity of 6G to facilitate rapid communication [27]. This empowers them to synchronize and collaborate seamlessly in real time. Additionally, machine learning algorithms empower robots to learn from their experiences, adapt to dynamic environments, and optimize their coordination efforts. By harnessing the collective intelligence of machine learning, robots enhance their productivity and versatility. They can collaborate effectively with human counterparts on intricate tasks or work together in synchronized workflows, fostering greater efficiency and flexibility within the robotic workforce [27].

Working together, robots and humans streamline industrial processes and unlock innovative applications. This collaboration, powered by machine learning and 6G connectivity, transforms robots into more than just automated machines. They evolve into indispensable partners within the industrial ecosystem, orchestrating a seamless and efficient symphony of teamwork.

Learning from Human Interaction: By incorporating machine learning algorithms, robots gain the remarkable ability to learn from human interactions [28]. These algorithms enable robots to analyze data from human behaviors and adapt their actions accordingly [28]. This flexibility allows robots to operate effectively and responsively in industrial settings, enhancing the intuitiveness and efficiency of workflows [28].

Machine learning algorithms improve their ability to interpret complex cues and patterns when tasked with human-robot collaborations. By analyzing human feedback and observing interactions, algorithms can comprehend unspoken nuances in human behavior [28]. This enables robots and humans to form symbiotic partnerships, where robots adjust to human preferences, workstyles, and evolving requirements, fostering a mutually beneficial coexistence.

In fast-paced industrial settings where tasks and conditions fluctuate rapidly, the adaptability of robots enhanced with machine learning becomes crucial. These robots can adjust their actions swiftly and seamlessly, responding to evolving industrial requirements. This cutting-edge partnership leads to enhanced precision and productivity. Moreover, it paves the way for a future where human-robot collaboration is characterized by natural, flexible, and harmonious interactions within the dynamic industrial environment.

5.6.3 Diagrams Illustrating Communication Network in 6G-Enabled Autonomous Systems

Here's an explanation of each component:

Figure 5.4 shows the communication network between autonomous robots and drones,coordinated through edge computing nodes and a centralized control hub using 6G connectivity.

Centralized Control Hub:

- This serves as the network's main brain.
- It supervises and plans the actions of different independent organizations within the industrial setting.

Edge Computing Nodes:

- To process data locally, these nodes are positioned strategically across the environment.
- They speed up reaction times for jobs that require prompt attention and lessen the strain on the centralized control hub.

Robots:

- The two autonomous robots in the diagram are designated as "Robot 1" and "Robot 2."
- The edge computing nodes are connected to these robots.
- They can carry out a variety of duties in the industrial environment and interact with the centralized control hub.

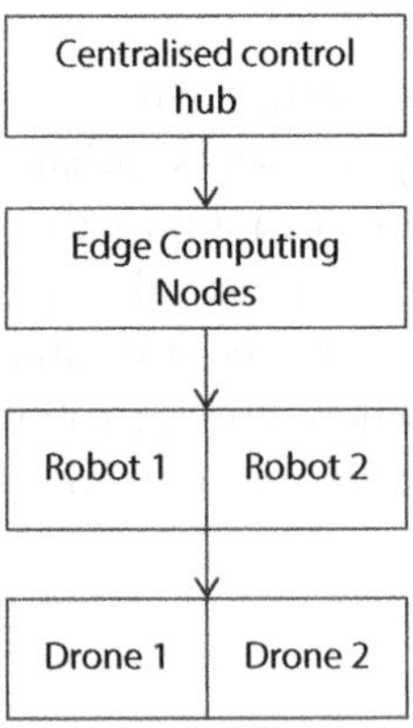

Figure 5.4 Communication network between autonomous systems.

Drones:

- The diagram includes two drones, labeled "Drone 1" and "Drone 2."
- Drones are essential for monitoring and surveillance within the industrial environment.
- They can communicate with the centralized control hub, edge computing nodes, and other autonomous entities.

Communication Lines:

- The diagram's lines show the channels of communication between the various parts.

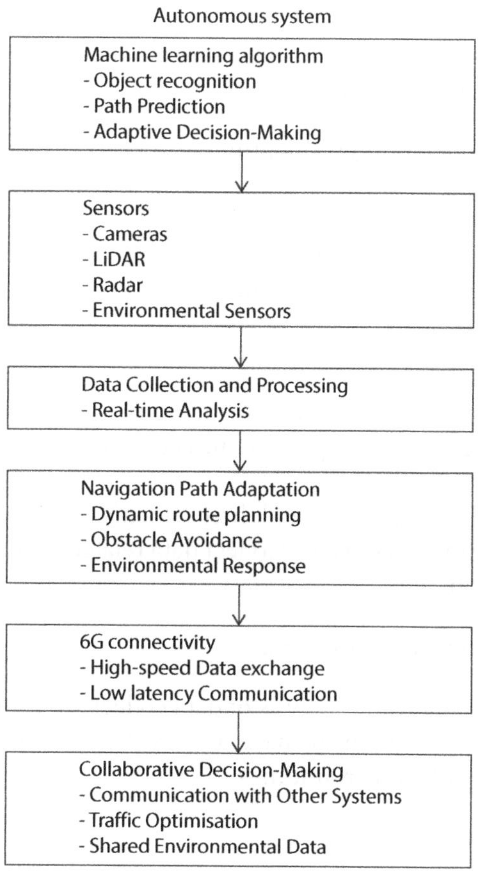

Figure 5.5 Adaptive navigation of autonomous systems.

- The robots and drones get communication from the centralized control hub through the edge computing modes.
- The bidirectional arrows indicate that feedback from independent entities is involved in addition to centralized communication.

This design illustrates the network architecture where data is handled at the periphery and in the center. 6G technology offers a high-speed, low-latency connection that helps the robots and drones work together effectively and react to data in real-time in the industrial setting.

Here's an explanation of each component:

Figure 5.5 demonstrates adaptive navigation of autonomous systems, where machine learning algorithms use sensor fusion and 6G connectivity to enable dynamic path planning and obstacle avoidance in real time.

Autonomous system: Represents the entire autonomous system
Machine learning algorithms:

- Object recognition: Identifying objects in the vehicle's environment.
- Path prediction: Predicting the likely path of objects.
- Adaptive Decision-Making: Making real-time decisions based on the analysis of data.

Sensors:

- Cameras: Capture visual information.
- Lidar: Uses laser light to measure distances and create detailed, accurate maps.
- Radar: Detects objects and their velocities using radio waves.
- Environmental sensors: Collect data related to weather, road conditions, etc.

Data Collection and Processing:

- Involves real-time analysis of data collected by sensors.
- Enables the system to have a correct and accurate understanding of its surroundings.

Navigation Path Adaption:

- Involves dynamic adjustments to the vehicle's route based on the analysis.

- Includes features like dynamic route planning, obstacle avoidance, and responses to changing environmental conditions.

6G Connectivity:

- Represents the connection to a 6G network.
- Provides high-speed data exchange and low-latency communication between the autonomous system and external sources.

Collaborative Decision-Making:

- Indicates the ability of the autonomous system to communicate with other systems.
- Allows for collaborative decision-making, traffic optimization, and sharing of environmental data for a collective understanding of the surroundings.

This figure shows how the autonomous system adjusts its navigation path and makes judgments in response to changing environmental conditions by integrating sensors, real-time data processing, machine learning algorithms, and 6G connectivity. To create a transportation system that is safer and more efficient overall, the collaborative aspect places a strong emphasis on communication between various autonomous systems.

As we progress through the chapter, we will delve into the critical aspects of security and privacy concerns in 6G-enabled industrial environments, examining strategies to ensure the integrity and confidentiality of data in this technologically advanced landscape.

5.7 Security and Privacy Concerns

5.7.1 Addressing Security Challenges in 6G-Enabled Industrial Environments

The convergence of machine learning and 6G in industries creates unprecedented advantages but also introduces security concerns [29]. Industries increasingly rely on connected devices and data-driven decision-making, necessitating robust security against potential threats. The increased interconnectivity and dependence on intelligent algorithms warrant a comprehensive security framework to protect sensitive data, prevent unauthorized access, and mitigate risks posed by cyberattacks [29]. Industries must navigate the transformative landscape of machine learning and 6G, balancing innovation with security measures to safeguard the integrity and reliability of industrial operations [29].

Network Security: The advanced connectivity of 6G networks expands the potential targets for cyberattacks, exposing individuals to heightened risks [30]. To mitigate these threats, robust security measures are crucial [30]. Encryption technologies, intrusion detection systems, and secure access controls are essential tools for bolstering defenses against unauthorized access and data breaches. Industries must adopt a proactive cybersecurity posture to maintain data integrity and privacy amid the evolving landscape of sophisticated cyberattacks made possible by 6G's capabilities [30].

Data Integrity: In the industrial realm enhanced by 6G, machine learning algorithms rely on data for decisions. Protecting data integrity is vital to prevent malicious tampering [31]. Blockchain technology presents a solution by offering secure, immutable records of data transactions. Blockchain establishes a distributed, tamper-proof ledger that ensures data history and provenance are transparent and trustworthy [31]. This enhances the reliability of data used by machine learning algorithms [31]. The convergence of blockchain, machine learning, and 6G creates a comprehensive approach to data security in the evolving landscape of interconnected industrial ecosystems [31].

5.7.2 Privacy Considerations in Machine Learning Applications

As 6G-connected industrial systems process and analyze immense amounts of personal data, privacy concerns arise due to the extensive use of machine learning [31, 32]. Complex interactions between machine learning algorithms and vast datasets, often containing sensitive information, necessitate stringent privacy regulations. Industries must strike a balance between innovation and protecting individuals' privacy within 6G-enabled industrial settings [31–33]. Robust privacy measures are crucial to ensure ethical and legal data handling, safeguarding the privacy rights of individuals in this dynamic environment.

Anonymization Techniques: In 6G-connected industrial environments, it's crucial to protect privacy by anonymizing data. During machine learning model training, organizations should remove personally identifiable information [34]. Additionally, techniques like differential privacy can be used to aggregate and anonymize data [34]. By implementing these measures, businesses can safeguard sensitive data and individuals' identities in the complex 6G era. This ensures that machine learning algorithms draw insights from anonymous and aggregated data, minimizing privacy risks [34].

Data Ownership and Consent: In 6G-connected manufacturing settings, preserving privacy involves defining data ownership rights and acquiring informed consent from users [35]. Open and transparent communication with all parties is essential to foster trust and awareness about data usage [35]. Industries must implement frameworks empowering users to manage and control their data. Additionally, they should promote an environment that prioritizes informed consent. By establishing clear guidelines and promoting open dialogue, businesses can strike a balance between technological advancements and privacy protection in the ever-evolving world of 6G-enabled industrial ecosystems [35].

5.7.3 Strategies for Ensuring Data Security and Privacy

Strategy 1: Multi-layered Security Protocols

In 6G-powered industries, effective security measures involve a layered approach [36]. This includes multiple layers of protection, such as intrusion detection, firewalls, and encryption [36]. By establishing these multiple barriers, businesses can improve their cyber security defenses. Even if one layer is compromised, the remaining layers provide additional protection against unauthorized access. This multi-layered strategy safeguards sensitive information, connected devices, and critical processes in the evolving world of 6G-connected industrial environments [36–38].

Strategy 2: Regular Security Audits and Updates

Regular security checks and software updates are crucial for promptly addressing vulnerabilities and bolstering security. Proactive measures allow for anticipation of threats and the preservation of a robust security posture. Continuous assessment and enhancement of security measures strengthen industries' defenses against evolving attack strategies within the dynamic 6G industrial landscape. Protecting data's integrity and privacy necessitates meticulous attention and swift response to vulnerabilities. These actions reinforce the overall security framework, enabling industries to effectively navigate the challenges of the constantly evolving cybersecurity environment.

Strategy 3: Privacy Impact Assessments

Before implementing new technologies or apps in industrial settings where 6G connectivity is prevalent, it's crucial to conduct privacy impact assessments [24]. These evaluations meticulously scrutinize potential privacy concerns to ensure that privacy protections are integrated into the design and implementation stages [24]. They serve as a proactive measure for industries to minimize the risk of unintended privacy violations [24]. By incorporating privacy considerations into the strategic planning process, businesses can reinforce their commitment to data protection while promoting the ethical adoption of technology in industrial contexts [24].

5.8 Conclusion

6G technology in industrial settings enables remarkable advancements by combining cutting-edge telecommunications and advanced algorithms. The convergence of 6G capabilities and machine learning applications across various industries drives a transformative journey towards Industry 4.0. This symbiotic relationship enhances operational efficiency and adaptability, laying the groundwork for a future where advanced connectivity and intelligent algorithms revolutionize industrial processes, leading to a surge of innovation and industrial advancements.

5.9 Future Prospects

The field of machine learning is expected to continue to grow and improve in the context of industrial settings in the upcoming 6G generation. Integrating these technologies is predicted to boost industrial processes' sustainability, resilience, and efficiency. Nonetheless, maintaining trust and fostering responsible implementation will hinge on the ongoing refinement of security safeguards and privacy concerns.

To fully harness the transformative potential of 6G and machine learning, collaboration between academia, industry, and regulation is crucial. Through sustained research, advancement, and adaptability, we can cultivate a cutting-edge industrial ecosystem that is interconnected and proactively addresses both current and future challenges and opportunities. This ecosystem will not only meet existing demands but will also reshape them, fostering an intelligent industrial landscape.

As machine learning and 6G technologies merge, they create a dynamic partnership that propels industries forward and reshapes the core of industrial systems. This convergence of cutting-edge technologies not only promises a technological transformation but also a profound shift in how industries operate, advance, and navigate the complexities of an evolving global landscape.

AI disclosure statement: The author acknowledges the use of AI-based tools for minor language editing or grammatical correction. However, all intellectual contributions, analyses, and conclusions presented in this chapter are entirely the author's own.

References

1. Elmeadawy, S. and M. Shubair, R., 6G wireless communications: Future technologies and research challenges. *2019 International Conference on Electrical and Computing Technologies and Applications (ICECTA)*, IEEE, 2019.
2. Shen, L.-H., Feng, K.-T., Hanzo, L., Five facets of 6G: Research challenges and opportunities. *ACM Comput. Surv.*, 55, 11, 1–39, 2023.
3. Akhtar, M.W., *et al.*, The shift to 6G communications: Vision and requirements. *Hum.-Centric Comput. Inf. Sci.*, 10, 1–275, 2020.
4. Ali, S., *et al.*, 6G white paper on machine learning in wireless communication networks. *arXiv preprint arXiv:2004.13875*, 2020.
5. Pan, C., *et al.*, Reconfigurable intelligent surfaces for 6G systems: Principles, applications, and research directions. *IEEE Commun. Mag.*, 59, 6, 14–20, 2021.
6. Kotsiantis, S.B., Zaharakis, I., Pintelas, P., Supervised machine learning: A review of classification techniques. *Emerg. Artif. Intell. Appl. Comput. Eng.*, 160, 1, 3–24, 2007.
7. Gourisaria, M.K., *et al.*, Application of machine learning in industry 4.0, in: *Machine learning: Theoretical foundations and practical applications*, pp. 57–87, 2021.
8. Chalapathy, R. and Chawla, S., Deep learning for anomaly detection: A survey. *arXiv preprint arXiv:1901.03407*, 2019.
9. Ghahramani, Z., Unsupervised learning, in: *Summer school on machine learning*, pp. 72–112, Springer Berlin Heidelberg, Berlin, Heidelberg, 2003.
10. Goodarzy, S., *et al.*, Resource management in cloud computing using machine learning: A survey. *2020 19th IEEE International Conference on Machine Learning and Applications (ICMLA)*, IEEE, 2020.
11. Wiering, M.A. and Van Otterlo, M., Reinforcement learning. *Adapt. Learn. Optim.*, 12, 3, 729, 2012.
12. Arulkumaran, K., *et al.*, A brief survey of deep reinforcement learning. *arXiv preprint arXiv:1708.05866*, 2017.
13. Zhao, Y., *et al.*, A comprehensive survey of 6G wireless communications. *arXiv preprint arXiv:2101.03889*, 2020.

14. Paolanti, M., *et al.*, Machine learning approach for predictive maintenance in industry 4.0. *2018 14th IEEE/ASME International Conference on Mechatronic and Embedded Systems and Applications (MESA)*, IEEE, 2018.
15. Giordani, M., *et al.*, Toward 6G networks: Use cases and technologies. *IEEE Commun. Mag.*, 58, 3, 55–61, 2020.
16. Chen, T., *et al.*, Machine Learning in Manufacturing towards Industry 4.0: From 'For Now' to 'Four-Know'. *Appl. Sci.*, 13, 3, 1903, 2023.
17. Aazam, M., Zeadally, S., Harras, K.A., Deploying fog computing in industrial internet of things and industry 4.0. *IEEE Trans. Ind. Inf.*, 14, 10, 4674–4682, 2018.
18. Li, X., *et al.*, Optimizing resources allocation for fog computing-based Internet of Things networks. *IEEE Access*, 7, 64907–649225, 2019.
19. Krupitzer, C., *et al.*, A survey on predictive maintenance for Industry 4.0. *arXiv preprint arXiv:2002.08224*, 2020.
20. Çınar, Z.M., *et al.*, Machine learning in predictive maintenance towards sustainable smart manufacturing in industry 4.0. *Sustainability*, 12, 19, 8211, 2020.
21. Kane, A.P., *et al.*, Predictive Maintenance using Machine Learning. *arXiv preprint arXiv:2205.09402*, 2022.
22. Mane, D., Detection of anomaly using machine learning: a comprehensive survey. *Int. J. Emerg. Technol. Adv. Eng.*, 12, 11, 134–152, 2022.
23. Gultekin, O., *et al.*, Real-time fault detection and condition monitoring for industrial autonomous transfer vehicles utilizing edge artificial intelligence, 2022.
24. Hakeem, A., Shimaa, A., Hussein, H.H., Kim, H.W., Security requirements and challenges of 6G technologies and applications. *Sensors*, 22, 5, 1969, 2022.
25. Han, D., *et al.*, A Survey on Deep Reinforcement Learning Algorithms for Robotic Manipulation. *Sensors*, 23, 7, 3762, 2023.
26. Kober, J., Bagnell, J.A., Peters, J., Reinforcement learning in robotics: A survey. *Int. J. Rob. Res.*, 32, 11, 1238–1274, 2013.
27. Bauer, A., Wollherr, D., Buss, M., Human–robot collaboration: a survey. *Int. J. Humanoid Rob.*, 5, 01, 47–66, 2008.
28. Semeraro, F., Griffiths, A., Cangelosi, A., Human–robot collaboration and machine learning: A systematic review of recent research. *Rob. Comput. Integr. Manuf.*, 79, 1024325, 2023.
29. Catak, FO., *et al.*, Security concerns on machine learning solutions for 6G networks in mmWave beam prediction. *Phys. Commun.*, 52, 1016265, 2022.
30. Sun, Y., *et al.*, When machine learning meets privacy in 6G: A survey. *IEEE Commun. Surv. Tutor.*, 22, 4, 2694–2724, 2020.
31. Velliangiri, S., *et al.*, Blockchain based privacy preserving framework for emerging 6G wireless communications. *IEEE Trans. Ind. Inf.*, 18, 7, 4868–4874, 2021.

32. Nguyen, V.-L., *et al.*, Security and privacy for 6G: A survey on prospective technologies and challenges. *IEEE Commun. Surv. Tutor.*, 23, 4, 2384–2428, 2021.
33. Ylianttila, M., *et al.*, 6G white paper: Research challenges for trust, security and privacy. *arXiv preprint arXiv:2004.11665*, 2020.
34. Xu, R., Baracaldo, N., Joshi, J., Privacy-preserving machine learning: Methods, challenges and directions. *arXiv preprint arXiv:2108.04417*, 2021.
35. Regulation, General Data Protection, *General data protection regulation (GDPR)*, Intersoft Consulting, 2018, Accessed in October 24.1.
36. Kazmi, S.H.A., *et al.*, Security Concepts in Emerging 6G Communication: Threats, Countermeasures, Authentication Techniques and Research Directions. *Symmetry*, 15, 6, 1147, 2023.
37. Sridhar, V., Rani, S., Pareek, P.K., Bhambri, P., Elngar, A.A. (Eds.), *Blockchain for IoT Systems: Concept, Framework and Applications*, 1st, Chapman and Hall/CRC, 2024, https://doi.org/10.1201/9781003460367.
38. Bhambri, P., Rani, S., Pareek, P.K., Paperless Paradigm: Intelligent Automation in Document and Record Management, in: *Generating Entrepreneurial Ideas with AI*, D. Darwish (Ed.), pp. 164–83, IGI Global, 2024, https://www.igi-global.com/book/hyperautomation-business-society/335477.

6

Wireless Infrastructure for Robust 6G IIoT Connectivity

Boudhayan Bhattacharya* **and Arpan Kisore Sarbadhikari**

Dept. of Computational Sciences, Brainware University, Kolkata, West Bengal, India

Abstract

This chapter addresses the pivotal role of wireless infrastructure in fostering resilient and efficient connectivity within the context of the Industrial Internet of Things (IIoT) and the upcoming 6th generation (6G) wireless technology. As industries increasingly embrace digital transformation through the implementation of Industry 4.0, the demand for a robust and reliable wireless communication framework becomes imperative for seamless integration and operation of industrial processes. The chapter begins by delineating the key features and expectations associated with 6G technology, its potential to revolutionize connectivity by providing ultra-reliable, low-latency communication with massive device connectivity. It explores the unique requirements of IIoT applications, discussing the challenges posed by the industrial environment, including harsh conditions, dynamic mobility, and stringent reliability demands. A detailed examination of wireless infrastructure components, such as edge computing, fog computing, and advanced communication protocols, is presented. The chapter highlights the critical role of components in ensuring resilient IIoT connectivity, optimizing data processing at the network edge, and minimizing latency for time-sensitive industrial applications. Practical use cases and industry examples illustrate the deployment of wireless infrastructure in diverse industrial sectors, showcasing the transformative impact on processes such as predictive maintenance, smart manufacturing, and supply chain optimization. Emphasis is placed on the integration of 6G capabilities to support emerging IIoT applications, enabling faster data transmission, improved network reliability, and enhanced security measures. The chapter also addresses considerations for the coexistence of multiple wireless technologies,

**Corresponding author*: mailforboudhayan@gmail.com; ORCID: 0009-0001-5094-6908
Arpan Kisore Sarbadhikari: ORCID: 0009-0002-2876-2034

Sita Rani, Pankaj Bhambri, Balamurugan Balusamy, Rishabha Malviya and Seifedine Kadry (eds.) Edge Intelligence for 6G-Enabled Industrial Internet of Things, (121–142) © 2026 Scrivener Publishing LLC

interoperability challenges, and the importance of standardization in ensuring seamless communication across heterogeneous IIoT devices and systems.

Keywords: 6G, edge computing, fog computing, time-sensitive networking, low power LAN

6.1 Introduction

The advent of the Sixth Generation (6G) of wireless technology promises to revolutionize the Industrial Internet of Things (IIoT) by providing unprecedented levels of connectivity, speed, and reliability. As industries increasingly rely on interconnected devices and systems to enhance efficiency, productivity, and automation, robust wireless infrastructure becomes critical. The 6G network, with its potential to deliver data rates up to 100 times faster than its predecessor, ultra-low latency, and enhanced security, offers a transformative leap forward for IIoT applications [1].

The foundation of a resilient 6G IIoT ecosystem lies in the development of advanced wireless infrastructure capable of supporting a massive number of connected devices. Unlike previous generations, 6G is expected to leverage a broad spectrum of frequencies, including millimeter waves and terahertz bands, to provide high bandwidth and support for high-density environments. This expanded spectrum capability is essential for accommodating the exponential growth in data traffic generated by industrial applications, such as real-time monitoring, predictive maintenance, and automated control systems.

Another critical aspect of 6G infrastructure is its ability to integrate with emerging technologies like edge computing and artificial intelligence (AI). By processing data closer to the source, edge computing reduces latency and bandwidth consumption, enabling real-time decision-making and efficient use of network resources. AI, on the other hand, enhances network management through predictive analytics, self-optimization, and automated troubleshooting, thereby ensuring consistent and reliable connectivity.

Security and privacy are also paramount in the 6G IIoT landscape, given the sensitive nature of industrial data and the increasing threat of cyberattacks. The wireless infrastructure must incorporate advanced encryption techniques, secure communication protocols, and robust authentication mechanisms to protect against unauthorized access and data breaches. Furthermore, the decentralized nature of 6G networks, characterized by the use of micro and nano-cells, necessitates a comprehensive approach to securing each network segment.

The deployment of 6G infrastructure will also require significant advancements in antenna technologies, including the development of massive MIMO (Multiple Input Multiple Output) systems and intelligent reflecting surfaces. These innovations aim to enhance signal quality, coverage, and energy efficiency, crucial for maintaining robust connectivity in challenging industrial environments, such as factories, warehouses, and remote locations.

In conclusion, the wireless infrastructure for robust 6G IIoT connectivity represents a significant leap forward in industrial automation and communication. By harnessing the capabilities of high-frequency bands, edge computing, AI, and advanced security measures, 6G promises to provide a scalable, secure, and efficient network solution that meets the demanding requirements of modern industrial applications. As we move towards a more connected and automated industrial future, the development and deployment of a resilient 6G wireless infrastructure will be pivotal in realizing the full potential of IIoT [2].

6.2 Key Features and Expectations of 6G Technology

- **(i)** 6G technology is poised to revolutionize wireless communication with several key features that are particularly beneficial for IIoT applications:
- **(ii)** Ultra-Reliable Low-Latency Communication (URLLC): 6G aims to provide extremely low latency (as low as 1 millisecond) and high reliability, which are critical for time-sensitive industrial processes such as robotic control, autonomous vehicles, and real-time monitoring systems.
- **(iii)** Massive Device Connectivity: With the capacity to connect a massive number of devices per square kilometer, 6G supports the dense sensor networks required for comprehensive monitoring and control in industrial settings.
- **(iv)** Enhanced Throughput and Capacity: 6G is expected to offer data rates up to 100 times faster than 5G, facilitating the rapid transmission of large volumes of data generated by IIoT devices.
- **(v)** Advanced AI Integration: 6G networks will leverage artificial intelligence for optimized resource allocation, predictive maintenance, and adaptive network management, enhancing the overall efficiency and reliability of IIoT systems.

(vi) Enhanced Security: 6G incorporates advanced security protocols and mechanisms to protect sensitive industrial data from cyber threats, ensuring secure communication channels.

6.3 Unique Requirements of IIoT Applications

(i) Industrial environments pose unique challenges for wireless communication systems, necessitating tailored solutions to meet specific requirements:
(ii) Harsh Conditions: Industrial settings often involve extreme temperatures, humidity, electromagnetic interference, and physical obstructions, requiring robust and resilient wireless infrastructure.
(iii) Dynamic Mobility: IIoT devices, such as autonomous guided vehicles and drones, are frequently in motion, demanding seamless handover and uninterrupted connectivity.
(iv) Stringent Reliability: Industrial processes are highly sensitive to delays and disruptions, necessitating ultra-reliable communication to maintain operational continuity and safety.
(v) Scalability: As industries expand their IIoT deployments, the wireless infrastructure must be scalable to accommodate the growing number of connected devices and increased data traffic.

6.4 Wireless Infrastructure Components for IIoT

The following components are integral to building a resilient wireless infrastructure for IIoT:

6.4.1 Edge Computing

Edge computing brings data processing closer to the data source, reducing latency and bandwidth usage. Edge computing is a transformative technology paradigm that brings computation and data storage closer to the sources of data generation, such as IoT devices, sensors, and local servers. Unlike traditional cloud computing, where data is sent to centralized data centers for processing, edge computing processes data at the "edge" of the network. This approach addresses several critical challenges associated with latency, bandwidth, security, and scalability, making it an essential component of modern digital infrastructure. This overview delves into the key aspects of edge computing, its advantages, applications, challenges, and future prospects [3].

6.4.1.1 *Key Concepts and Architecture*

At its core, edge computing decentralizes computing power by distributing it across various locations. The edge architecture typically involves multiple layers:

(i) **Edge Devices:** These are the data sources, such as IoT devices, sensors, smartphones, and industrial machines. They collect data and may perform preliminary processing.
(ii) **Edge Nodes:** These are intermediate devices or systems, such as local servers, gateways, or micro data centers, located near the data sources. They perform more complex data processing and analysis, often filtering, aggregating, and sending relevant data to the cloud.
(iii) **Cloud/Data Centres:** While edge computing reduces the reliance on centralized data centers, it doesn't eliminate them. Cloud infrastructure still plays a role in storing, managing, and analyzing large datasets and performing tasks that require extensive computational resources.

This layered architecture enables efficient data processing and management, allowing edge devices to interact with edge nodes and the cloud as needed.

6.4.1.2 *Key Benefits*

Key benefits for IIoT include:

(i). **Reduced Latency:** By processing data closer to where it is generated, edge computing significantly reduces the time it takes for data to travel to and from centralized data centers. This low latency is crucial for real-time applications, such as autonomous vehicles, augmented reality, and industrial automation, where delays of even a few milliseconds can be detrimental.

(ii). **Bandwidth Optimization:** Edge computing minimizes the amount of data that needs to be transmitted to the cloud. By performing data processing and filtering locally, only relevant data is sent to centralized servers. This optimization reduces bandwidth consumption and costs, especially important for applications generating large volumes of data, like video surveillance and smart city sensors [4].

(iii). **Enhanced Security and Privacy:** Keeping data close to its source can improve security and privacy by reducing the exposure of sensitive information during transmission. Edge computing allows for more granular control over data access and processing, making it easier to comply with regulations and protect against cyber threats.

(iv). **Scalability and Flexibility:** The decentralized nature of edge computing allows for scalable and flexible deployments. Organizations can easily expand their edge infrastructure by adding more edge nodes or devices as needed. This scalability is particularly beneficial in scenarios where infrastructure needs to grow quickly or dynamically, such as in disaster recovery or event-driven applications.

(v). **Reliability and Resilience:** Edge computing enhances the reliability of systems by enabling local data processing and decision-making, even in the event of network disruptions. This resilience is crucial for mission-critical applications, such as healthcare systems, industrial control systems, and emergency response operations.

(vi). **Fog Computing:** Fog computing extends cloud computing capabilities to the edge of the network, providing additional computational resources and storage closer to IIoT devices. Fog computing is an architectural paradigm that extends the cloud computing model to the edge of the network, aiming to provide a more efficient and effective means of processing and analyzing data. Coined by Cisco, the term "fog computing" refers to the layer of computing infrastructure that exists between the cloud and end devices, such as IoT sensors, smartphones, and other connected objects. This intermediate layer, often referred to as the "fog layer," brings processing, storage, and networking capabilities closer to where data is generated, thereby addressing some of the limitations associated with traditional cloud computing.

This overview explores the key concepts, advantages, applications, challenges, and future prospects of fog computing [5].

6.4.2 Architecture: Fog Layers and Nodes

6.4.2.1 Key Concepts and Architecture

Fog computing is designed to complement both cloud computing and edge computing by providing a continuum of resources from the core of the network to the edge. The fog layer consists of a distributed set of nodes, which can include routers, switches, gateways, servers, and even edge devices themselves. These nodes work together to perform data processing, storage, and communication tasks, thereby creating a more resilient and efficient computing environment.

(i) **Fog Nodes:** Fog nodes are the core components of fog computing. They are capable of handling various tasks, such as data filtering, aggregation, analytics, and decision-making. These nodes can be deployed at different points in the network, ranging from on-premises equipment to devices located at the edge. Fog nodes often work in conjunction with cloud resources, allowing for a hybrid computing model that leverages the strengths of both paradigms.

(ii) **Communication and Coordination:** Fog computing relies on robust communication and coordination mechanisms to manage the flow of data and tasks between fog nodes and the cloud. This involves efficient routing, load balancing, and resource allocation strategies to ensure optimal performance and reliability. The fog layer can also facilitate data sharing and collaboration between different nodes, enabling more comprehensive data analysis and insights.

(iii) **Data Management:** Data management in fog computing involves handling data across a distributed and heterogeneous environment. This includes data collection, storage, processing, and transmission. The fog layer can provide localized data storage and processing capabilities, reducing the need to send all data to the cloud. This not only conserves bandwidth but also enhances data security and privacy.

6.4.2.2 Key Benefits: Key Benefits for IIoT Include

(i) **Reduced Latency:** One of the primary advantages of fog computing is its ability to reduce latency by processing data closer to the source. This is particularly important for applications that require real-time or near-real-time responses, such as autonomous vehicles, industrial automation, and smart grid management. By minimizing the time it takes for data to travel to the cloud and back, fog computing enables faster decision-making and action.

(ii) **Bandwidth Efficiency:** Fog computing helps optimize bandwidth usage by performing data processing and filtering at the fog nodes. This reduces the amount of data that needs to be transmitted to the cloud, thereby lowering bandwidth costs and alleviating network congestion. This is especially valuable in scenarios where large volumes of data are generated, such as video surveillance or sensor networks.

(iii) **Enhanced Security and Privacy:** By keeping sensitive data closer to its source, fog computing can enhance security and privacy. Data can be processed and stored locally, reducing the exposure to potential threats during transmission. Additionally, fog nodes can implement security measures such as encryption, access control, and intrusion detection, further protecting data from unauthorized access and cyber-attacks [6].

(iv) **Scalability and Flexibility:** Fog computing provides a scalable and flexible infrastructure that can accommodate varying workloads and application requirements. Organizations can deploy and manage fog nodes according to their specific needs, whether it's for local processing, data analytics, or storage. This flexibility also allows for seamless integration with existing cloud and edge computing resources, creating a unified and adaptable computing environment.

(v) **Reliability and Resilience:** The distributed nature of fog computing enhances system reliability and resilience. Even if a fog node fails, other nodes can continue to operate and process data, ensuring continuous service. This is particularly important for mission-critical applications, such as healthcare monitoring, emergency response, and industrial control systems.

6.5 Advanced Communication Protocols

To support the high demands of IIoT applications, advanced communication protocols are essential:

6.5.1 Edge 5G NR (New Radio)

While 6G is on the horizon, 5G NR provides the foundation with features like URLLC and enhanced Mobile Broadband (eMBB), supporting a range of IIoT use cases. 5G NR (New Radio) is the global standard for the air interface of the Fifth Generation (5G) mobile networks. Developed by the 3rd Generation Partnership Project (3GPP), 5G NR is designed to provide faster data speeds, lower latency, increased capacity, and improved efficiency compared to previous generations of mobile networks, such as 4G LTE. The standard encompasses a wide range of technologies and innovations to support various applications, from enhanced mobile broadband (eMBB) to massive machine-type communications (mMTC) and ultra-reliable low-latency communications (URLLC) [7].

6.5.1.1 Key Features of 5G NR

(i) **Spectrum Flexibility:** 5G NR operates across a broad-spectrum range, including sub-1 GHz, mid-band (1-6 GHz), and high-band (millimeter-wave, mmWave, above 24 GHz) frequencies. This flexibility allows 5G networks to be deployed in different environments, from urban areas with high data traffic to rural regions requiring broader coverage. The use of mmWave bands, in particular, enables extremely high data rates and capacity, making 5G NR suitable for bandwidth-intensive applications.

(ii) **Massive MIMO (Multiple Input Multiple Output):** Massive MIMO technology, which employs a large number of antennas at the base station, is a cornerstone of 5G NR. It enhances spectral efficiency and network capacity by allowing multiple data streams to be transmitted and received simultaneously. This is especially beneficial in densely populated areas where many users need to be served simultaneously.

(iii) **Beamforming:** Beamforming is a technique used in 5G NR to direct radio signals more precisely toward users, improving signal quality and reducing interference. This targeted transmission enhances coverage, especially in challenging environments like urban canyons or indoor spaces.

(iv) **Network Slicing:** Network slicing enables the creation of multiple virtual networks within a single physical 5G infrastructure. Each slice can be tailored to specific use cases, providing customized services with different performance characteristics, such as high bandwidth for video streaming or low latency for real-time gaming. This flexibility allows service providers to meet diverse customer needs more efficiently.

(v) **Low Latency:** 5G NR aims to achieve ultra-low latency, potentially as low as 1 millisecond, depending on the application. This low latency is crucial for applications requiring real-time communication, such as autonomous vehicles, remote surgery, and industrial automation.

(vi) **Enhanced Mobile Broadband (eMBB):** eMBB is one of the primary use cases of 5G NR, focusing on providing faster data speeds and improved user experiences for mobile devices. This includes high-definition video streaming, virtual reality (VR), and augmented reality (AR) applications.

(vii) **Massive Machine-Type Communications (mMTC):** mMTC supports the connection of a massive number of IoT devices with minimal human intervention. This capability is essential for applications like smart cities, agriculture, and environmental monitoring, where many sensors and devices need to communicate simultaneously [8].

(viii) **Ultra-Reliable Low-Latency Communications (URLLC):** URLLC targets applications requiring highly reliable and low-latency communication, such as industrial automation, autonomous vehicles, and telemedicine. This use case demands stringent performance standards to ensure safe and efficient operation.

6.5.1.2 Deployment and Implementation

5G NR is being deployed globally in various phases, starting with non-standalone (NSA) deployments that use existing 4G LTE infrastructure and eventually transitioning to standalone (SA) deployments. In NSA mode, 5G NR operates alongside 4G LTE, providing enhanced data speeds and capacity. In contrast, SA mode relies solely on 5G infrastructure, offering lower latency, improved efficiency, and the full range of 5G features.

The deployment of 5G NR also involves significant infrastructure upgrades, including the installation of new base stations, small cells, and mmWave antennas. The rollout of 5G NR networks requires collaboration between telecom operators, equipment manufacturers, and regulatory bodies to address spectrum allocation, network planning, and standardization.

6.5.2 Time-Sensitive Networking (TSN)

TSN protocols ensure deterministic communication with guaranteed latency, synchronization, and reliability, crucial for industrial automation. Time-Sensitive Networking (TSN) is a set of IEEE standards that provide deterministic communication over Ethernet networks, ensuring the timely and reliable transmission of data. TSN is designed to support real-time applications that require precise timing and synchronization, such as industrial automation, automotive systems, and audio/video streaming. By offering features like low latency, low jitter, and high reliability, TSN enables Ethernet to be used in environments where timing and predictability are critical.

6.5.2.1 Key Features of TSN

(i). Time Synchronization (IEEE 802.1AS): TSN includes standards for precise time synchronization across the network. IEEE 802.1AS, also known as the Generalized Precision Time Protocol (gPTP), ensures that all devices on the network have a common sense of time, with synchronization accuracy typically in the range of microseconds. This feature is crucial for coordinating time-sensitive actions in distributed systems.

(ii). Traffic Scheduling and Shaping (IEEE 802.1Qbv, 802.1Qav): TSN introduces mechanisms for scheduling and shaping traffic, allowing for the prioritization of time-critical data over other types of traffic. IEEE 802.1Qbv, also known as the Time-Aware Shaper, enables the creation of time slots during which specific types of traffic can be transmitted, ensuring that high-priority data is delivered on time. IEEE 802.1Qav, the Forwarding and Queuing Enhancements for Time-Sensitive Streams, helps to manage network congestion and reduce latency by controlling the flow of traffic.

(iii). Frame Pre-emption (IEEE 802.1Qbu, IEEE 802.3br): Frame pre-emption allows certain high-priority frames to interrupt the transmission of lower-priority frames, reducing latency for critical data. This feature, defined in IEEE 802.1Qbu and IEEE 802.3br, ensures that urgent traffic can be delivered without being delayed by longer, non-critical frames [9].

(iv). Redundancy and Reliability (IEEE 802.1CB): TSN provides mechanisms for redundant data transmission to enhance network reliability. IEEE 802.1CB, also known as Frame Replication and Elimination for Reliability, enables the sending of multiple copies of a data frame over different network paths. If one path fails, the data can still be received *via* an alternate path, ensuring robust communication.

(v). Centralized Network Management (IEEE 802.1Qcc): TSN supports centralized network configuration and management, allowing for efficient setup and maintenance of time-sensitive networks. IEEE 802.1Qcc defines standards for centralized configuration, including the management of time synchronization, traffic scheduling, and network resources.

6.5.2.2 Deployment & Implementation

Deployment and Implementation of Time-Sensitive Networking (TSN) require careful planning, consideration of the specific requirements of the application, and an understanding of the underlying standards and technologies. TSN aims to provide deterministic, low-latency, and reliable communication over Ethernet, making it suitable for applications where timing and data integrity are critical. Here's a detailed guide to deploying and implementing TSN:

(i) Network Design and Planning:

a. Define Application Requirements: Determine the specific requirements for latency, jitter, bandwidth, reliability, and synchronization.

Identify the types of data flows (e.g., control data, multimedia, sensor data) and their priorities.

b. Topology Design: Design the network topology, considering the physical layout and logical structure.

Plan for redundancy to ensure high availability and reliability, using techniques like frame replication and elimination (IEEE 802.1CB).

c. **Selecting TSN Components:** Choose network devices (switches, routers, gateways) and end devices (controllers, sensors, actuators) that support TSN standards.

   Ensure compatibility and interoperability between devices from different vendors.

(ii) Implementation of TSN Standards:

a. **Time Synchronization (IEEE 802.1AS/gPTP):** Implement time synchronization across the network to ensure all devices have a common sense of time.

   Use Precision Time Protocol (PTP) for accurate clock synchronization, with grandmaster clocks providing the reference time.

b. **Traffic Scheduling and Shaping (IEEE 802.1Qbv, IEEE 802.1Qav):** Configure Time-Aware Shaper (TAS) to create time slots for scheduled traffic, ensuring timely delivery.

   Use credit-based shapers to manage traffic bursts and reduce congestion.

c. **Frame Pre-emption (IEEE 802.1Qbu, IEEE 802.3br):** Implement frame pre-emption to allow high-priority frames to interrupt ongoing transmissions, reducing latency for critical data.

d. **Redundancy and Reliability (IEEE 802.1CB):** Set up frame replication and elimination to provide fault tolerance.

   Use path control and reservation techniques to ensure alternate data paths in case of failures [10].

e. **Centralized Network Management (IEEE 802.1Qcc):** Implement centralized network configuration and management for efficient setup and control.

   Use network management software to monitor and configure TSN features across devices.

(iii) Configuration and Testing:

a. **Configuration:** Configure each device according to the network design, including time synchronization settings, traffic scheduling, and redundancy mechanisms.

   Set up VLANs and priority levels for different types of traffic.

b. **Testing and Validation:** Test the network to ensure it meets the required latency, jitter, and reliability standards.

Validate time synchronization accuracy across all devices.

Test failover mechanisms to ensure redundancy and high availability.

(iv) Deployment and Monitoring:

a. Gradual Deployment: Start with a pilot deployment in a controlled environment to identify and resolve issues.

Gradually scale up to full deployment, ensuring minimal disruption to existing operations.

b. Monitoring and Maintenance: Continuously monitor network performance, including latency, bandwidth usage, and synchronization accuracy.

Use network monitoring tools to detect and diagnose issues in real-time.

Regularly update firmware and software to maintain compatibility with new standards and security patches.

6.5.3 Low Power Wide Area Networks (LPWANs)

Technologies like NB-IoT and LoRaWAN enable long-range, low-power communication for remote IIoT devices, extending the reach of wireless infrastructure. Low Power Wide Area Network (LPWAN) is a category of wireless telecommunication technology specifically designed to support the needs of the Internet of Things (IoT). LPWAN technologies offer long-range communication with low data rates, minimal power consumption, and relatively low costs. This makes them ideal for applications where devices need to send small amounts of data infrequently over long distances, such as smart city infrastructure, agriculture, and industrial monitoring.

6.5.3.1 Key Features of LPWAN

(i) Long Range: LPWAN technologies are designed to provide connectivity over long distances, typically ranging from several kilometres in urban areas to tens of kilometres in rural settings. This is achieved by using low frequencies that can penetrate obstacles and propagate over long distances. The ability to cover large areas with minimal infrastructure is a significant advantage, particularly in rural or hard-to-reach locations.

(ii) **Low Power Consumption:** A defining feature of LPWAN is its low power consumption. Devices connected to an LPWAN can operate for years on small batteries, making them suitable for applications where frequent maintenance is impractical. This efficiency is achieved by optimizing protocols and limiting the data rate, which reduces the amount of energy required for transmission and reception [11].

(iii) **Low Data Rate:** LPWAN technologies typically support low data rates, ranging from a few kilobits per second (kbps) to a few hundred kbps. This is sufficient for many IoT applications, such as sending sensor readings, status updates, or control messages. The low data rate also contributes to energy efficiency, as devices spend less time in active transmission.

(iv) **Scalability:** LPWAN networks are highly scalable and can support a large number of devices. Depending on the specific technology and network design, LPWAN can accommodate thousands to millions of devices within a single network. This scalability is crucial for large-scale IoT deployments, such as smart cities, where numerous sensors and devices need to be connected.

(v) **Cost-Effectiveness:** LPWAN technologies are generally cost-effective to deploy and operate. They require minimal infrastructure, and the devices themselves are relatively inexpensive. Moreover, the long battery life of LPWAN devices reduces the cost associated with maintenance and battery replacement.

6.5.3.2 Deployment and Implementation

Deploying and implementing a Low Power Wide Area Network (LPWAN) involves several steps, from planning and design to deployment, operation, and maintenance. LPWAN technologies like LoRa, Sigfox, NB-IoT, and LTE-M each have unique requirements and characteristics, but they share common considerations in deployment. Here's an overview of the key aspects involved in deploying and implementing LPWAN networks.

6.5.3.2.1 Network Planning and Design

6.5.3.2.1.1 Use Case Definition

Before deployment, it's crucial to clearly define the use case for the LPWAN network. Different applications (e.g., smart metering, asset tracking, environmental monitoring) have varying requirements in terms of data rate, latency, coverage, and device density. Understanding these requirements helps in selecting the appropriate LPWAN technology and designing the network architecture.

6.5.3.2.1.2 Technology Selection

Selecting the right LPWAN technology depends on several factors:

- (i). **Data Rate and Latency:** LTE-M and NB-IoT offer higher data rates and lower latency compared to LoRa and Sigfox.
- (ii). **Coverage Area:** LoRa and Sigfox are suitable for large coverage areas, while NB-IoT and LTE-M leverage existing cellular networks.
- (iii). **Power Consumption:** All LPWAN technologies are designed for low power consumption, but the specific requirements may vary depending on the application.
- (iv). **Regulatory Compliance:** Considerations include spectrum availability and regulatory requirements, especially for technologies using unlicensed bands like LoRa and Sigfox.

6.5.3.2.1.3 Network Architecture

LPWAN networks typically use a star or star-of-stars topology. In a star topology, end devices communicate directly with a central gateway or base station. In a star-of-stars topology, multiple gateways connect to a central network server. The architecture chosen depends on factors such as coverage requirements, device density, and redundancy needs.

6.5.3.2.1.4 Deployment

- (i). **Site Survey and Planning:** Conducting a thorough site survey is essential for optimal network deployment. This involves assessing the geographical area, potential obstacles, and environmental conditions. The survey helps determine the number and placement of gateways or base stations needed to achieve the desired coverage and connectivity.
- (ii). **Gateway/Base Station Deployment:** For technologies like LoRa and Sigfox, gateways are strategically placed to maximize coverage and minimize interference. The height and location of gateways are critical factors, as they affect the

line-of-sight and signal strength. In NB-IoT and LTE-M, deployment is often simpler as these technologies use existing cellular infrastructure, although additional small cells may be deployed to improve coverage and capacity.

(iii). Device Deployment: Once the infrastructure is in place, end devices (e.g., sensors, meters, trackers) are deployed. These devices need to be configured to communicate with the network and may require calibration or tuning to optimize performance. Device placement is also important, particularly for applications like environmental monitoring, where sensor accuracy is crucial.

6.5.3.2.1.5 Network Integration and Testing

(i). Connectivity Testing: After deployment, the network undergoes rigorous testing to ensure connectivity and performance. This includes checking the signal strength, data transmission reliability, and latency. For cellular-based LPWAN technologies, this also involves verifying the device registration and data routing processes [12].

(ii). Data Management and Integration: LPWAN networks generate a large amount of data that needs to be collected, processed, and analyzed. Integrating the network with backend systems, such as data servers, cloud platforms, and analytics tools, is a critical step. This integration enables real-time monitoring, data analysis, and decision-making based on the collected data.

(iii). Security Implementation: Security is a major concern in LPWAN deployments, especially for critical infrastructure applications. Implementing encryption, secure authentication, and access control measures is essential to protect data integrity and prevent unauthorized access.

6.5.3.2.1.6 Operation and Maintenance

(i). Monitoring and Management: Ongoing monitoring is crucial for maintaining network performance and reliability. This involves tracking network metrics such as signal strength, device status, and data transmission rates. Network management platforms often provide dashboards and alerts to help operators monitor the network in real-time.

(ii). Firmware and Software Updates: Devices and gateways may require firmware or software updates to fix bugs, enhance features, or address security vulnerabilities. Over-the-air (OTA) updates are a common method for remotely updating devices without the need for physical intervention.

(iii). Maintenance and Support: Regular maintenance, such as replacing batteries in devices, is necessary to ensure continuous operation. Support teams need to be prepared to respond to issues like network outages, device malfunctions, or security incidents.

6.5.3.3 Common LPWAN Technologies

Several LPWAN technologies have emerged, each with its strengths and use cases. The most prominent ones include LoRa, Sigfox, NB-IoT, and LTE-M.

6.5.3.3.1 LoRa (Long Range)

LoRa is a proprietary LPWAN technology developed by Semtech Corporation. It uses the unlicensed ISM bands (typically around 868 MHz in Europe and 915 MHz in North America) and employs a modulation technique called Chirp Spread Spectrum (CSS). This technique is resistant to interference and multipath fading, making LoRa suitable for diverse environments. LoRa networks are typically deployed in a star topology, with devices communicating directly with gateways that relay data to a central network server. LoRa is widely used for applications like smart metering, agriculture, and asset tracking.

6.5.3.3.2 Sigfox

Sigfox is another LPWAN technology that operates in the unlicensed ISM bands. It focuses on ultra-narrowband communication, which allows for extremely low power consumption and long-range communication. Sigfox limits the payload size (up to 12 bytes per message) and the number of messages per device per day, making it suitable for applications where small amounts of data need to be transmitted sporadically. Sigfox provides a global network, making it an attractive option for international deployments.

6.5.3.3.3 NB-IoT (Narrowband IoT)

NB-IoT is a cellular LPWAN technology standardized by the 3rd Generation Partnership Project (3GPP). Unlike LoRa and Sigfox, NB-IoT operates in the licensed spectrum, typically within the bands allocated for LTE. NB-IoT offers excellent indoor coverage, low latency, and can support a high density of connected devices. It is ideal for applications like smart metering, environmental monitoring, and industrial automation. NB-IoT benefits from the security and reliability of cellular networks and can be integrated into existing LTE infrastructure, reducing deployment costs.

6.5.3.3.4 LTE-M (Long Term Evolution for Machines)

LTE-M is another cellular LPWAN technology standardized by 3GPP. It provides higher data rates compared to NB-IoT and supports features like mobility, voice communication (VoLTE), and real-time capabilities. LTE-M is suitable for applications that require more bandwidth or lower latency, such as wearables, fleet management, and real-time monitoring. Like NB-IoT, LTE-M operates in the licensed spectrum and can leverage existing cellular infrastructure.

6.6 Practical Use Cases and Industry Examples

6.6.1 Predictive Maintenance

Predictive maintenance leverages IIoT sensors and analytics to predict equipment failures before they occur, reducing downtime and maintenance costs. Wireless infrastructure plays a vital role by enabling real-time data collection and processing at the edge, facilitating timely maintenance interventions.

6.6.2 Smart Manufacturing

In smart manufacturing, interconnected machines and sensors work together to optimize production processes. Wireless infrastructure supports seamless communication between devices, enabling adaptive manufacturing processes, real-time quality control, and efficient resource management.

6.6.3 Supply Chain Optimization

Wireless connectivity in supply chain management enhances visibility and coordination across the supply chain. Real-time tracking of goods, automated inventory management, and data-driven decision-making are made possible through robust wireless networks

6.7 Integration of 6G Capabilities

6.7.1 Faster Data Transmission

6G technology enables faster data transmission rates, allowing IIoT systems to handle larger datasets and support more complex applications, such as high-definition video monitoring and advanced AI-driven analytics.

6.7.2 Improved Network Reliability

6G's ultra-reliable communication ensures continuous operation of critical industrial systems, reducing the risk of downtime and enhancing overall productivity.

6.7.3 Enhanced Security Measures

With advanced encryption and authentication mechanisms, 6G enhances the security of IIoT networks, protecting sensitive industrial data from cyber threats and ensuring secure communication channels.

6.8 Coexistence and Interoperability

6.8.1 Coexistence of Multiple Wireless Technologies

In industrial environments, multiple wireless technologies often coexist, each serving different applications and requirements. Ensuring harmonious coexistence involves careful frequency planning, interference management, and protocol coordination.

6.8.2 Interoperability Challenges

Interoperability between heterogeneous IIoT devices and systems is crucial for seamless communication. Standardization efforts, such as the development of common protocols and interfaces, are essential to achieve interoperability and enable the integration of diverse technologies.

6.8.3 Importance of Standardization

Standardization ensures that different IIoT devices and systems can communicate effectively, reducing complexity and enabling easier deployment and management of wireless infrastructure. Organizations like the IEEE and 3GPP play a key role in developing and promoting standards for IIoT and 6G technologies.

6.9 Conclusion

As industries continue to embrace digital transformation through IIoT, the development of robust wireless infrastructure is essential to support the demands of modern industrial applications. The advent of 6G technology promises to revolutionize IIoT connectivity, offering ultra-reliable, low-latency communication, massive device connectivity, and enhanced security. By leveraging components such as edge and fog computing, advanced communication protocols, and addressing the unique challenges of industrial environments, industries can achieve resilient and efficient IIoT connectivity. The integration of 6G capabilities will further enhance the potential of IIoT, enabling faster data transmission, improved network reliability, and secure communication, ultimately driving innovation and productivity in industrial sectors.

AI disclosure statement: The author acknowledges the use of AI-based tools for minor language editing or grammatical correction. However, all intellectual contributions, analyses, and conclusions presented in this chapter are entirely the author's own.

References

1. Zhang, Z., Xiao, Y., Ma, Z., Xiao, M., Ding, Z., Lei, X., Fan, P., 6G wireless networks: Vision, requirements, architecture, and key technologies. *IEEE Veh. Technol. Mag.*, 14, 3, 28–41, 2019.
2. Gupta, A. and Jha, R.K., A survey of 5G network: Architecture and emerging technologies. *IEEE Access*, 3, 1206–1232, 2015.
3. Park, S.Y. and Kwon, T., A comprehensive study on time-sensitive networking for industrial control systems: Applications, challenges, and research trends. *IEEE Commun. Surv. Tutor.*, 22, 4, 2933–2962, 2020.
4. Abbas, N., Zhang, Y., Taherkordi, A., Skeie, T., Mobile edge computing: A survey. *IEEE Internet Things J.*, 5, 1, 450–465, 2018.

5. Chiang, M. and Zhang, T., Fog and IoT: An overview of research opportunities. *IEEE Internet Things J.*, 3, 6, 854–864, 2016.
6. Delsing, J., *IoT automation: Arrowhead framework*, Boca Raton, FL: CRC Press, 2017.
7. Aazam, M., Khan, I., Alsaffar, A.A., Huh, E.N., Cloud of Things: Integrating Internet of Things and cloud computing and the issues involved, in: *Proceedings of the 2014 IEEE International Bhurban Conference on Applied Sciences and Technology (IBCAST)*, pp. 414–419, 2014.
8. Wollschlaeger, M., Sauter, T., Jasperneite, J., The future of industrial communication: Automation networks in the era of the Internet of Things and Industry 4.0. *IEEE Ind. Electron. Mag.*, 11, 1, 17–27, 2017.
9. Palattella, M.R., Dohler, M., Grieco, L.A., Rizzo, G., Torsner, J., Engel, T., Ladid, L., Internet of Things in the 5G era: Enablers, architecture, and business models. *IEEE J. Sel. Areas Commun.*, 34, 3, 510–527, 2016.
10. IEEE 802.1 Time-Sensitive Networking Task Group, Time-sensitive networking (TSN) standards, 2021, Retrieved from https://1.ieee802.org/tsn/rds, Retrieved from https://1.ieee802.org/tsn/.
11. Bhambri, P., Rani, S., Pareek, P.K., Financial Innovations: Intelligent Automation in Finance and Insurance Sectors, in: *Generating Entrepreneurial Ideas with AI*, D. Darwish (Ed.), pp. 226–43, IGI Global, 2024, https://doi.org/10.4018/979-8-3693-3354-9.ch012.
12. Bhambri, P. and Rani, S., Issues Related to Chatbots, in: *Design and Development of Emerging Chatbot Technology*, D. Darwish (Ed.), pp. 130–47, IGI Global, 2024, https://doi.org/10.4018/979-8-3693-1830-0.ch008.

7

Future Horizons: Emerging Trends in Edge Intelligence for IIoT

J. Vigneshwari*, K. Geetha, P. Senthamizh Pavai and L. Maria Suganthi

Faculty of Education, Dr. M.G.R. Educational and Research Institute, Chennai, Tamilnadu, India

Abstract

In the ever-evolving landscape of technology, the Industrial Internet of Things (IIoT) stands out as a transformative force, revolutionizing industries across the globe. At the heart of this revolution lies Edge Intelligence, a cutting-edge concept that promises to unlock new realms of efficiency, productivity, and innovation within the IIoT ecosystem. It represents the convergence of traditional industrial processes with advanced digital technologies, enabling seamless connectivity, data exchange, and real-time decision-making. However, processing, evaluating, and extracting meaningful insights quickly are severely hampered by the sheer volume and velocity of data created by IIoT devices.

Edge Intelligence becomes increasingly valuable in this context. By utilizing distributed computing resources located at the network edge, edge intelligence enables faster data processing, reduces latency, and enhances decision-making capabilities. This paradigm shift facilitates new levels of automation and control, significantly improving predictive maintenance and boosting operational efficiency. As a result, industrial organizations can fully harness the potential of their IIoT implementations. The ability to process data closer to where it is generated minimizes the delay associated with transmitting data to centralized cloud servers, leading to more timely and effective responses. This is particularly crucial for applications requiring real-time analysis and actions, such as in automated manufacturing systems and advanced robotics. With continuous advancements in this dynamic field, the IIoT is rapidly expanding. While the specific developments in

**Corresponding author*: vigneshwari.bed@drmgrdu.ac.in; ORCID: 0000-0003-2874-7360
K. Geetha: ORCID: 0000-0002-2121-3916
P. Senthamizh Pavai: ORCID: 0000-0003-0468-6188
L. Maria Suganthi: ORCID: 0000-0002-7323-8306

Sita Rani, Pankaj Bhambri, Balamurugan Balusamy, Rishabha Malviya and Seifedine Kadry (eds.) Edge Intelligence for 6G-Enabled Industrial Internet of Things, (143–162) © 2026 Scrivener Publishing LLC

2022 and beyond remain uncertain, several emerging trends are expected to shape the future of IIoT. This chapter aims to outline some anticipated developments that are likely to emerge, driving the next phase of innovation and growth in the IIoT landscape.

Keywords: Industrial Internet of Things, edge intelligence, technologies, connectivity, technological advancements, data processing

7.1 Introduction- An Outline on IIoT

IIoT technology gives businesses the ability to anticipate maintenance requirements, optimize resource usage, remotely monitor and manage equipment, and enhance overall operational performance.

Yifan Zhang gives a thorough introduction to the IIoT. The article describes the fundamental elements and technologies of the Internet of Things, such as communication networks, data analytics, and IoT devices. Zhang talks on the IIoT's present situation, its uses in a range of sectors, and its future advancements. Along with highlighting important issues including security, interoperability, and scalability, the study makes recommendations for future research areas in the area. This article is a useful tool for learning about the possibilities and reach of IIoT [17]. By applying advanced data analytics and machine learning algorithms, IIoT systems may provide valuable insights, facilitate predictive maintenance, and enable data-driven decision-making. Furthermore, IIoT solutions enable the fusion of modern information technology with traditional operational technologies, creating networked ecosystems that promote innovation and transformation across a range of industries, including manufacturing, transportation, energy, healthcare, and energy. Ultimately, the industrial internet of things (IIoT) represents a paradigm shift in industrial automation that has never been witnessed before, opening up previously unimaginable opportunities for long-term development, innovation, and optimization.

By utilizing the power of connected devices, sophisticated analytics, and real-time data to improve industrial processes and operations, the industrial internet of things (IIoT) is a revolutionary development in the industrial sector. As opposed to the more general internet of things (IoT), which includes personal and consumer applications, the IIoT is targeted at industrial and manufacturing settings. It entails the connection of industrial machinery with sensors, actuators, and other smart devices to facilitate data collecting and analysis for performance optimization, increased productivity, and decreased downtime [30].

Building a seamless, networked system of connected devices that can collaborate and communicate to improve industrial processes is the fundamental principle underlying IIoT. This link allows for the monitoring and administration of machinery and processes in real time and provides meaningful information that fosters innovation and decision-making. Manufacturing, energy, transportation, and healthcare are among the industries that are using IIoT solutions more often to satisfy sustainability goals, ensure safety, and boost productivity [34].

Edge computing, machine learning, cloud-based analytics, and cybersecurity are all part of the IIoT. Edge computing reduces latency and improves response times by processing data closer to the source. Cloud-based analytics can store and analyze large amounts of data, allowing for the identification of patterns and trends that may assist drive strategic decisions [4]. In the IIoT, cybersecurity is critical for protecting private information and ensuring the integrity of industrial systems. Machine learning and artificial intelligence boost IIoT by enabling automated decision-making, anomaly detection, and predictive maintenance [35].

In essence, IIoT is revolutionizing the industrial landscape by providing a robust framework for smart manufacturing and industrial automation. It empowers businesses to harness the full potential of data, drive efficiency, and remain competitive in an increasingly digital world [36].

7.2 Significance of IIoT

The Industrial Internet of Things (IIoT) offers numerous key benefits that drive its adoption and implementation across industrial sectors:

Enhanced Efficiency: IIoT enables real-time monitoring and analysis of equipment and processes, leading to improved operational efficiency and reduced downtime.

Predictive Maintenance: By collecting and analyzing data from sensors, IIoT systems can predict equipment failures before they occur, enabling proactive maintenance and minimizing costly unplanned downtime.

Cost reduction: IIoT solutions improve resource utilization, eliminate waste, and streamline operations, resulting in considerable cost savings for industrial enterprises.

Improved Safety: The IIoT allows for remote monitoring of hazardous surroundings and equipment, which helps to avoid accidents and assure worker safety.

Enhanced Quality Control: IIoT allows for continuous monitoring and analysis of industrial processes, assuring product quality and decreasing flaws.
Real-time Data Analysis: IIoT platforms offer real-time insights into operations, enabling data-driven decision-making and quick reactions to changing conditions.
Remote Monitoring and Control: IIoT allows for remote monitoring and control of equipment and processes, resulting in more flexibility and responsiveness in managing industrial operations.
Scalability and Flexibility: IIoT solutions can easily scale to accommodate changing business needs and can be customized to fit specific industrial requirements.
Integration with Existing Systems: IIoT platforms can seamlessly integrate with existing industrial systems and legacy equipment, allowing for incremental deployment and leveraging of existing investments.
Competitive Advantage: IIoT adoption can provide industrial organizations with a competitive advantage by enabling innovation, differentiation, and agility in responding to market demands [2].

To sum up, the extensive integration of IIoT technology provides a wide range of benefits that revolutionize industrial processes. IIoT gives enterprises the tools they need to prosper in a more connected and competitive world by allowing greater safety, predictive maintenance, cost savings, and increased efficiency, among other benefits. Adopting IIoT is a strategic requirement rather than merely a choice for businesses hoping to take the lead in the digital era.

7.2.1 IIoT vs IoT

IoT (Internet of Things)- The term "Internet of Things" (IoT) describes a network of commonplace items (things) that have been fitted with sensors, software, and other technologies to communicate and share data with other systems and devices online. These gadgets are frequently found in workplaces, wearable technology, and a range of consumer goods. Wearable fitness trackers, smart thermostats, and smart home assistants like Google Home or Amazon Echo are a few examples.
IIoT (Industrial Internet of Things)- IIoT, focuses the technology use and principles within industrial sectors such as manufacturing, energy, transportation, and healthcare. IIoT devices are deployed to monitor and optimize industrial processes, improve operational efficiency, reduce downtime, and enhance safety. Examples include remote monitoring

of machinery, predictive maintenance systems, and connected logistics platforms.

Hence, both IoT and IIoT involve the interconnectedness of devices and data exchange over the internet, IIoT specifically targets industrial applications and processes, whereas IoT encompasses a broader range of consumer and non-industrial applications.

IIoT brings more automation and self-monitoring to industrial machines. By connecting devices, enterprises can track activity, progress, and maintenance needs, ultimately improving operational efficiency. IIoT allows for unprecedented insights and business intelligence. It enables real-time data collection, analysis, and predictive maintenance, leading to better decision-making. With IIoT, you can monitor equipment health remotely, detect issues early, and prevent costly breakdowns. This proactive approach saves time and resources.

7.3 Future of IIoT

IIoT- is likely to expand and innovate rapidly in the future as industrial demands change and technology advances.

A paper by Debashis Bandyopadhyay and Arijit Bhattacharya explores the future trends and challenges associated with the Industrial Internet of Things (IIoT). The authors discuss how IIoT is expected to evolve with advancements in technology and its impact on various industrial sectors. They address key areas such as integration with emerging technologies, data management, cybersecurity concerns, and the development of smart manufacturing systems. The paper provides a comprehensive overview of how IIoT is likely to shape the future of industry, offering insights into both opportunities and potential obstacles [1].

Dominance of Edge Computing: By facilitating real-time data processing, analysis, and decision-making at the network edge, edge computing will be essential to the success of IIoT in the future. With its reduced latency, bandwidth consumption, and reliance on centralized cloud infrastructure, this method is perfect for industrial applications that require speed [23].
AI and Machine Learning Integration: Predictive maintenance, anomaly detection, and industrial process optimization will be made possible by the ongoing expansion of AI and ML algorithm integration into IIoT systems. IIoT solution adoption will increase as a result of new insights and efficiency made possible by AI-driven analytics [3].

5G Connectivity: The rollout of 5G networks will revolutionize IIoT connectivity, offering higher bandwidth, lower latency, and greater reliability. 5G technology will support mission-critical applications, enable real-time data transmission, and facilitate seamless integration of IIoT devices across industries.
Cyber security Enhancement: As IIoT deployments grow in scale and complexity, cyber security will remain a top priority. Industrial enterprises will invest in advanced security measures such as block chain technology, zero-trust architecture, and AI-powered threat detection to safeguard IIoT networks and data from cyber threats [31].
Interoperability Standards: Interoperability will become increasingly important as IIoT ecosystems expand. Standardization efforts will drive interoperability, enabling seamless communication and data exchange between disparate IIoT systems and devices, fostering collaboration and innovation across industries.
Sustainability Focus: Sustainability will emerge as a key consideration in IIoT deployments, driven by environmental responsibility and energy efficiency goals. IIoT solutions will increasingly incorporate green technologies.
Digital twin technology: It generates dynamic virtual clones of real assets, is expected to become widely used in Industrial Internet of Things (IIoT) applications. Digital twins provide complete insights into the status and operation of industrial assets by combining real-time data from sensors and IoT devices. This capacity enables real-time monitoring, modeling, and optimization, allowing for more effective decision-making processes.

The use of digital twins is revolutionizing the industrial environment by allowing predictive maintenance, which identifies and addresses possible faults before they cause costly downtime. This proactive strategy not only extends the life of equipment, but it also lowers maintenance costs and increases overall asset reliability. Furthermore, digital twins allow the modeling of many situations, enabling businesses to optimize operations and execute changes in minimum cost and risk. As a consequence, firms may increase their operational efficiency and production. Businesses may improve supply chain management, maximize resource use, and promote innovation by developing new goods and services with digital twin technology. The combination of artificial intelligence and machine learning with digital twins expands their capabilities, enabling more accurate forecasts and automated decision-making.

7.4 Edge Intelligence

In 2024, a significant trend propelling Industrial IoT (IIoT) forward is the ongoing advancement of edge computing. As data volumes from IoT devices continue to grow exponentially, companies are increasingly adopting edge computing solutions to handle data processing and analysis closer to the source. This transition not only minimizes latency but also addresses bandwidth limitations, facilitating instantaneous decision-making and enabling industries to fully leverage their data assets.

Edge intelligence in the IIoT represents a shift in data processing and decision-making. This localized approach optimizes bandwidth usage, improves data privacy and security, and reduces operational costs by decreasing the need for extensive data transmission to centralized servers. Moreover, edge intelligence enhances the scalability and adaptability of IIoT systems. It allows for dynamic adjustments to changing conditions without constant reliance on centralized infrastructure.

Additionally, edge intelligence supports advanced applications such as predictive maintenance, augmented reality (AR) for remote assistance, and real-time quality control in manufacturing. These applications not only improve efficiency but also lead to significant cost savings by preventing downtime and reducing waste. In the healthcare sector, edge intelligence facilitates real-time patient monitoring and diagnostics, enhancing patient care and operational efficiency. In transportation and logistics, edge intelligence enables smarter traffic management, real-time tracking of goods, and enhanced fleet management, leading to more efficient and cost-effective operations. In agriculture, it supports precision farming practices, optimizing resource use and increasing crop yields while minimizing environmental impact.

Overall, edge intelligence enables enterprises to fully realize the potential of IIoT by providing quicker, more efficient, and cost-effective results. By embracing this technology, industries may significantly increase their performance, productivity, and profitability, propelling the next wave of industrial innovation and growth.

7.4.1 Edge AI for Autonomous Decision-Making

Edge AI is experiencing a surge in adoption, driving autonomous decision-making at the network's edge. By deploying AI algorithms directly on edge devices, industries can process data locally, reducing dependence on continuous communication with centralized servers. This not only reduces latency, but also improves privacy and security measures. Edge AI enables IoT devices to make fast important choices, increasing the efficiency and responsiveness of industrial operations. Organizations may optimize operations, reduce downtime, and increase overall productivity by leveraging real-time data analysis and decision-making capabilities at the edge. This decentralized approach to AI enables enterprises to maximize the value of their data while assuring quick and effective decision-making in changing contexts [29].

A Paper by Zhang, Li, and Zhang provides an in-depth exploration of Edge AI and its role in autonomous decision-making. The paper highlights the advantages of Edge AI, such as reduced latency, improved privacy, and enhanced efficiency. It also examines various use cases and applications where Edge AI can significantly impact autonomous systems, including smart cities, autonomous vehicles, and industrial automation. The authors address key challenges and propose solutions for effectively implementing Edge AI in these scenarios [16].

As Edge AI continues to evolve, it promises to revolutionize industrial processes, driving innovation and competitiveness in the ever-evolving landscape of IoT technologies. In essence, the edge computing shows the ways and reshapes the globe in various aspects. Mainly,

- Using AI-powered edge computing solutions to process and analyze data in real-time at the network's edge.
- Integration of edge computing with 5G networks to enable high-speed, low-latency communication between edge devices and centralized systems.
- Evolution of edge intelligence to support more complex analytics and decision-making capabilities, facilitating predictive maintenance and process optimization.
- Decentralization of edge intelligence, with edge devices collaborating autonomously and reducing dependence on centralized infrastructure.
- Advancements in edge intelligence enabling applications such as autonomous robotics and remote monitoring in industrial environments.
- Emerging trends driving innovation, efficiency, scalability, and agility in IIoT deployments.

7.4.2 Artificial Intelligence (AI) and Machine Learning (ML)

Artificial Intelligence: A Modern Approach. Stuart Russell and Peter Norvig's fundamental textbook on artificial intelligence is extensively used in education. It addresses a wide range of AI subjects, including problem solving, knowledge representation, learning techniques, and robotics. The book gives a thorough review of machine learning techniques, artificial intelligence ideas, and practical applications, making it an essential resource for understanding AI and ML [21, 23].

Artificial Intelligence (AI) and Machine Learning (ML) play integral roles in IIoT systems, transforming industrial processes and operations by the following-

- **Predictive Maintenance**: This approach helps prevent unexpected downtime, reduce maintenance costs, and extend the lifespan of machinery.
- **Quality Control**: Utilizing advanced sensors and image recognition technology to swiftly identify defects and deviations in production lines. This ensures high-quality products, reduces waste, and minimizes the need for manual inspections.
- **Process Optimization**: Streamlining manufacturing processes through continuous monitoring and data analysis. IIoT technologies enable real-time adjustments to optimize workflows, improve production efficiency, and reduce operational costs.
- **Energy Management**: Implementing IIoT solutions to monitor and manage energy consumption across facilities. This helps identify inefficiencies, optimize energy usage, and lower energy costs by adjusting settings and schedules based on real-time data.
- **Supply Chain Management**: Leveraging IIoT for accurate demand forecasting and inventory optimization. Real-time data and analytics enhance visibility into the supply chain, allowing for better planning, reduced stockouts, and minimized excess inventory.
- **Safety and Security**: Employing IIoT systems to detect hazards and security threats proactively. Sensors and surveillance systems monitor for environmental conditions, unauthorized access, and equipment malfunctions, improving workplace safety and security [25].

- **Autonomous Systems**: Deploying autonomous vehicles and robots to perform repetitive and complex tasks within industrial settings. These systems enhance productivity, reduce human error, and allow for 24/7 operations with minimal supervision.

7.5 The 4.0 Technology

Industry 4.0 is rapidly evolving and radically changing production processes and business models. These technologies facilitate the development of smart factories, where machines are networked and capable of self-optimizing their performance, and they also increase operational efficiency and decision-making [19]. Businesses are using data-driven insights to boost efficiency and encourage innovation as the industrial industry embraces digital transformation. This change not only promotes economic expansion but also tackles important issues like sustainability and resource optimization [20]. As a result, implementing Industry 4.0 technology is thought to be a crucial first step for businesses looking to stay competitive in a global market that is becoming more digital [18].

7.5.1 The 4.0 Solution

The report by Kagermann, Wahlster, and Helbig is a cornerstone text for comprehending Industry 4.0. It offers strategic advice for implementing Industry 4.0 technology and processes. The paper describes the vision for Industry 4.0, which includes the integration of cyber-physical systems, IoT, and advanced manufacturing technologies. It also discusses problems, potential consequences, and the procedures required to shift to a more digital and automated industrial environment [6, 37, 38]. 4.0 solutions refer to the integration of advanced technologies, often referred to as Industry 4.0, to revolutionize industrial processes and operations. This solution encompasses the following key elements:

Connectivity: Utilizing IoT devices and sensors to collect real-time data from equipment, machinery, and production lines. These devices are interconnected through wireless networks, enabling seamless communication and data exchange [32].
Data Analytics: Employing advanced analytics techniques, including AI and ML, to analyze the vast amounts of data generated by IIoT devices.

This analysis provides valuable insights into process efficiency, predictive maintenance, quality control, and other aspects of industrial operations.
Automation: Implementing automation technologies to streamline processes and reduce manual intervention. This includes robotic process automation (RPA), autonomous systems, and smart control systems that can adjust operations based on real-time data and analytics insights.
Integration: Integrating disparate systems and technologies within the industrial environment to create a cohesive and interconnected ecosystem. This involves connecting IIoT devices with existing enterprise systems, such as ERP (Enterprise Resource Planning) and MES (Manufacturing Execution Systems), to enable seamless data flow and decision-making across the organization.
Optimization: Continuously optimizing industrial processes and operations based on data-driven insights and feedback. This includes identifying opportunities for efficiency improvements, cost reductions, and quality enhancements, and implementing corresponding changes to drive continuous improvement.

Thus, the 4.0 Solution in IIoT is a comprehensive approach to digital transformation in the industrial sector, employing cutting-edge technologies to boost innovation, efficiency, and competitiveness. In the Industry 4.0 age, enterprises may unleash new prospects for development and success by leveraging the power of connection, data analytics, automation, integration, and optimization.

7.6 Challenges and Considerations for Adopting IIoT Trends

Adopting Industrial Internet of Things (IIoT) trends presents various challenges and considerations for organizations. Some of the key challenges and considerations include:

Security: Ensuring the security of IIoT devices, networks, and data is paramount. With increased connectivity comes a higher risk of cyber threats, including data breaches, malware attacks, and unauthorized access. Organizations must implement robust cyber security measures to protect their IIoT infrastructure and mitigate potential risks.
Interoperability: Integrating IIoT devices and systems from different vendors can be challenging due to interoperability issues. Standardization

efforts are underway to address this challenge, but organizations may still face compatibility issues when deploying IIoT solutions across their operations.

Data management: Effective data management techniques are necessary to handle the enormous volumes of data produced by IIoT devices. This include gathering, storing, processing, analyzing, and visualizing data to derive useful insights and promote thoughtful decision-making [9].

Scalability: Scaling IIoT solutions to accommodate growing data volumes and expanding operations can be complex. Organizations need scalable architectures and platforms that can support their evolving needs while maintaining performance, reliability, and security [11, 13].

Skills Gap: It might be difficult to find and keep qualified workers with experience in IIoT technologies, such as cloud computing, data analytics, cyber security, and IoT development. To increase internal skills, organizations could have to spend money on training and development initiatives or turn to outside partners and service providers.

Regulatory Compliance: Compliance with industry regulations and data privacy laws, such as GDPR (General Data Protection Regulation) and HIPAA (Health Insurance Portability and Accountability Act), is essential when deploying IIoT solutions, especially in regulated industries like healthcare and manufacturing [11].

Return on Investment (ROI): Calculating the ROI of IIoT investments can be challenging due to the complex nature of these initiatives and the long-term nature of their impact. Organizations must carefully evaluate the costs, benefits, and risks associated with adopting IIoT trends to ensure they deliver tangible business value [10].

Change Management: Implementing IIoT technologies often requires significant organizational change, including new processes, workflows, roles, and responsibilities. Effective change management strategies are essential to ensure smooth adoption and acceptance of IIoT initiatives by employees and stakeholders [14].

While IIoT developments generally present enormous promise for innovation and efficiency in industrial processes, enterprises must successfully manage a number of obstacles and concerns in order to fully grasp these prospects. Through proactive and creative approaches to these obstacles, firms may optimize the advantages of IIoT adoption and foster long-term, sustainable corporate success [12].

7.7 6G and Future Horizons

6G, the upcoming sixth generation of wireless technology, is set to revolutionize communication by building on the advancements of 5G and introducing several cutting-edge features and applications. At its core, 6G will deliver higher data rates, potentially reaching 1 terabit per second, alongside ultra-low latency, facilitating real-time applications like autonomous vehicles, remote surgery, and interactive gaming. Terahertz communication and quantum technologies will be integral, offering high bandwidth and unbreakable encryption for secure communications. The integration of artificial intelligence and machine learning will allow for self-optimizing networks that adapt to user needs, while semantic communication will enable a deeper understanding of data, improving services like language translation and AI interactions [26].

6G will also support innovative applications such as immersive extended reality experiences, real-time holographic communication, and wireless brain-computer interfaces, transforming industries like healthcare, entertainment, and education. The technology will underpin smart cities and infrastructure by enabling intelligent traffic management, energy-efficient buildings, and responsive urban environments [5]. Cyber-physical systems and digital twins will benefit from enhanced real-time data interactions, optimizing manufacturing, healthcare, and urban planning [7, 28].

6G is not just another iteration of mobile communications; it's a transformative leap beyond mere connectivity. Imagine a distributed neural network that seamlessly fuses the physical, cyber, and biological worlds. Some insights about it are below-

- eMBB+ (Enhanced Mobile Broadband+): This evolution of enhanced mobile broadband will revolutionize human-centric communication. It'll power immersive experiences in extended reality (XR), telepresence, and more. Think augmented reality (AR), virtual reality (VR), and mixed reality (MR) applications that redefine how we live, learn, work, and travel.
- URLLC+ (Ultra-Reliable Low-Latency Communications+): URLLC+ builds on ultra-reliable low-latency communication. It's critical for Industry 4.0, autonomous driving, and household management. Picture robots, UAVs, and advanced human-machine interfaces working seamlessly, with strict latency and reliability requirements [8].

- Sensing and AI: These are new usage scenarios in the 6G era. Sensing technologies will enable us to perceive our environment at an unprecedented level, while native AI will enhance decision-making and automation.

Cyber security enhancements are crucial as IIoT networks expand, protecting against increasingly sophisticated threats. Implementing robust security protocols and leveraging blockchain technology can provide decentralized and tamper-proof data management solutions. Interoperability standards will ensure seamless integration and communication between diverse IIoT devices and systems, enhancing overall system efficiency [15]. The focus on sustainability within IIoT initiatives will drive the development of eco-friendly solutions, optimizing energy consumption, and minimizing environmental impact. Digital twin technology, which creates virtual replicas of physical assets, will enable real-time monitoring, simulation, and optimization of industrial processes, further enhancing efficiency and reducing costs.

Additionally, 6G will focus on sustainability and energy efficiency, aiming to reduce the environmental impact of digital infrastructure. Network slicing and virtualization will allow for tailored services, improving resource allocation and network efficiency. The integration of space-air-ground networks will provide seamless global connectivity, addressing connectivity challenges in underserved areas. As 6G evolves, it will face challenges such as technological complexity, regulatory issues, and privacy concerns, but its potential to transform society and drive innovation is immense, making it a key enabler of future technological advancements [27].

7.8 Benefits of Investing in IIoT

Investing in the IIoT offers numerous benefits for businesses. Firstly, it improves efficiency and productivity by enabling real-time monitoring and control of industrial processes, leading to optimized operations and reduced downtime. Enhanced predictive maintenance minimizes equipment failures and reduces maintenance costs. IIoT also increases operational visibility through data analytics, aiding informed decision-making and better supply chain management. Cost savings arise from optimized processes, reduced downtime, and efficient resource utilization. Additionally, IIoT enhances safety by monitoring environmental conditions and ensuring compliance with regulatory standards [22].

Quality control improves as IIoT detects defects early, leading to higher-quality products and reduced waste. Supply chain management benefits from real-time data on inventory and shipment tracking, optimizing operations and reducing lead times. The scalability and flexibility of IIoT systems allow businesses to adapt to growth and technological advancements. Data-driven decision-making is facilitated by vast amounts of data generated by IIoT, providing valuable insights. This technological edge offers a competitive advantage, improving customer satisfaction through better product quality, timely delivery, and efficient service. Overall, IIoT transforms operations, driving efficiency and growth in a competitive market [24].

7.8.1 Planning and Implementation of IIoT

It requires a strategic and methodical approach to ensure success. Start by defining clear objectives, such as improving operational efficiency or reducing downtime, and establish key performance indicators (KPIs) to measure success. Assess your current infrastructure to identify gaps and determine the necessary upgrades or additions. Choose an IIoT platform that is scalable, compatible with existing systems, and equipped with robust security features. It's advisable to begin with a pilot project to test the technology in a specific area, which helps manage risks and refine the implementation strategy before a full-scale rollout [33].

Focus on effective data management by ensuring high-quality data collection and utilizing advanced analytics tools for actionable insights. Prioritize security by implementing encryption, secure communication protocols, and access controls to protect against cyber threats. Ensure interoperability by using standardized protocols and collaborating with vendors to integrate seamlessly with existing systems. Invest in training and change management to support employees in adapting to new technologies and processes. Regularly monitor the performance of IIoT systems, optimize them based on data insights, and plan for scalability to accommodate future growth. Engage stakeholders throughout the process, maintain clear communication, and track the financial and operational benefits to measure and report on ROI. By adopting these practices, organizations can effectively navigate the complexities of IIoT implementation and realize significant improvements in efficiency, productivity, and overall business performance [34].

7.9 Conclusion

With trends like edge computing dominance, AI integration, 5G connectivity, cybersecurity enhancement, interoperability standards, sustainability focus, and adoption of digital twins predicted to drive innovation and transformation in industrial connectivity and automation, the future of IIoT is incredibly promising. Organizations must adopt these tendencies as IIoT develops to fully realize the promise of this revolutionary technology [36].

At the forefront of technological advancement is edge intelligence, poised to revolutionize the future world in profound ways. By decentralizing data processing and analysis, edge intelligence empowers devices to make real-time decisions, reducing latency and enhancing responsiveness across diverse applications. This paradigm shift optimizes bandwidth usage, improves privacy and security, and fosters scalability and flexibility in distributed computing environments [35].

Edge intelligence enables advanced tasks to be performed locally on edge devices, catalyzing industry transformation across healthcare, transportation, manufacturing, agriculture, and smart cities. In healthcare, it leads to improved patient care through real-time monitoring and diagnostics. In transportation, it streamlines logistics and enhances safety with intelligent traffic management systems. In manufacturing, it boosts productivity through predictive maintenance and automation. In agriculture, it supports precision farming practices that increase yields and reduce resource usage. In smart cities, it promotes sustainable urban development with efficient resource management and intelligent infrastructure.

Furthermore, the integration of AI in IIoT systems allows for deeper data insights, driving smarter automation and decision-making processes. AI-powered analytics enable predictive and prescriptive maintenance, reducing downtime and operational costs. 5G connectivity enhances IIoT applications by providing ultra-reliable, low-latency communication, essential for mission-critical operations.

As edge intelligence continues to evolve, it promises to unlock new opportunities for innovation, efficiency, and resilience, shaping a future where the boundaries between physical and digital realms blur, and intelligent systems seamlessly integrate into everyday life. This integration will lead to a more connected, efficient, and sustainable world, where industries are transformed, and new possibilities are continually realized. By embracing these trends and investing in IIoT technologies, organizations can position themselves at the cutting edge of industry innovation, driving growth, and maintaining competitive advantage in an increasingly digital and interconnected world [8].

AI disclosure statement: The author acknowledges the use of AI-based tools for minor language editing or grammatical correction. However, all intellectual contributions, analyses, and conclusions presented in this chapter are entirely the author's own.

References

1. Bandyopadhyay, D. and Bhattacharya, A., The future of Industrial Internet of Things (IIoT): Trends and challenges. *IEEE Access*, 9, 65222–65235, 2021, https://doi.org/10.1109/ACCESS.2021.3075174.
2. Bertolini, M. and Gregori, A., The impact of industrial internet of things on manufacturing and maintenance strategies. *Procedia CIRP*, 72, 234–239, 2018, https://doi.org/10.1016/j.procir.2018.03.013.
3. Feng, C., Han, P., Zhang, X., Yang, B., Liu, Y., Guo, L., Computation offloading in mobile edge computing networks: a survey. *J. Netw. Comput. Appl.*, 202, 5, 103366, 2022.
4. Satria, D., Park, D., Jo, M., Recovery for overloaded mobile edge computing. *Future Gener. Comput. Syst.*, 70, 8, 138–147, 2017.
5. Gubbi, J., Buyya, R., Marusic, S., Internet of things (IoT): A vision, architectural elements, and future directions. *Future Gener. Comput. Syst.*, 29, 7, 1645–1660, 2013, https://doi.org/10.1016/j.future.2013.01.010.
6. Gilchrist, A., *Industry 4.0: The Industrial Internet of Things*. 1st ed. Berkeley, CA: Apress. ISBN 978-1-4842-2046-7 (print); 978-1-4842-2047-4 (eBook). doi:10.1007/978-1-4842-2047-4, 2016.
7. Lee, J., Bagheri, B., Kao, H.A., A cyber-physical systems architecture for industry 4.0-based manufacturing systems. *Manuf. Lett.*, 3, 18–23, 2015, https://doi.org/10.1016/j.mfglet.2014.12.001.
8. Xing, L., Cascading failures in internet of things: review and perspectives on reliability and resilience. *IEEE Internet Things J.*, 8, 1, 44–64, 2021.
9. Miller, B. and Xu, L., Addressing the challenges of big data in IIoT: A review of data management strategies. *J. Ind. Inf. Integr.*, 18, 100155, 2020, https://doi.org/10.1016/j.jii.2020.100155.
10. Sundararajan, V. and Deshmukh, A., The economic impact of industrial internet of things (IIoT) and its implications for business strategy. *J. Bus. Res.*, 102, 280–292, 2019, https://doi.org/10.1016/j.jbusres.2019.04.015.
11. Zhang, Y. and Wang, N., A survey on security and privacy issues in industrial IoT. *IEEE Access*, 9, 140122–140137, 2021, https://doi.org/10.1109/ACCESS.2021.3119740.

12. Wang, J., Li, X., Liu, Y., Integration of IIoT with legacy systems: Challenges and solutions. *J. Manuf. Syst.*, 54, 221–229, 2020, https://doi.org/10.1016/j.jmsy.2020.01.001.
13. Nicolai, J. and Peltonen, K., Scalability issues in IIoT: A framework for addressing infrastructure constraints. *Comput. Ind.*, 89, 95–107, 2017, https://doi.org/10.1016/j.compind.2017.04.003.
14. Schroeder, R. and Smith, S., Change management strategies for IIoT adoption: Best practices and case studies. *Int. J. Prod. Econ.*, 210, 56–67, 2019, https://doi.org/10.1016/j.ijpe.2019.01.012.
15. Vogel, W. and Martin, A., Interoperability challenges in IIoT: Standards and solutions. *J. Syst. Softw.*, 136, 118–131, 2018, https://doi.org/10.1016/j.jss.2017.11.012.
16. Zhang, X., Li, X., Zhang, L., Edge AI: A new frontier for autonomous decision-making. *IEEE Internet Things J.*, 7, 5, 3786–3797, 2020. https://doi.org/10.1109/JIOT.2019.2969555.
17. Zhang, Y., Industrial Internet of Things: A comprehensive review and future research directions. *IEEE Access*, 6, 38060–38072, 2018, https://doi.org/10.1109/ACCESS.2018.2859238.
18. Hermann, M., Pentek, T., Otto, B., Design principles for Industrie 4.0 scenarios, in: *2016 49th Hawaii International Conference on System Sciences (HICSS)*, IEEE, pp. 3928–3937, 2016.
19. Kagermann, H., Wahlster, W., Helbig, J., Recommendations for implementing the strategic initiative INDUSTRIE 4.0. Final report of the Industrie 4.0 Working Group, 2013.
20. Lasi, H., Fettke, P., Kemper, H.G., Feld, T., Hoffmann, M., Industry 4.0. *Bus. Inf. Syst. Eng.*, 6, 4, 239–242, 2014.
21. https://dl.acm.org/doi/10.1145/3486674.
22. https://www.iot83.com/top-5-iiot-trends-you-cant-miss-in-2024/.
23. http://www.jatit.org/volumes/Vol100No13/31Vol100No13.pdf.
24. https://ubisense.com/industrial-iot-what-to-expect-in-2024/.
25. Russell, S. and Norvig, P., *Artificial Intelligence: A Modern Approach*, 3rd ed., Pearson Education, 2010.
26. https://www.huawei.com/en/huaweitech/future-technologies/6g-the-next-horizon.
27. https://www.hcltech.com/blogs/accelerating-to-future-ready-networks-navigating-the-6g-horizon-beyond-2024.
28. https://www.mckinsey.com/industries/technology-media-and-telecommunications/our-insights/shaping-the-future-of-6g.
29. https://link.springer.com/chapter/10.1007/978-3-031-55718-7_5.
30. Sisinni, E., Saifullah, A., Han, S., Jennehag, U., Gidlund, M., Industrial internet of things: Challenges, opportunities, and directions. *IEEE Trans. Ind. Inf.*, 15, 6, 4122–4137, 2019, https://doi.org/10.1109/TII.2019.29056781.

31. Wu, M., Song, J., Hu, J., Zhang, Z., Research on the architecture of Internet of Things, in: *Proceedings of the 3rd International Conference on Advanced Computer Theory and Engineering (ICACTE)*, IEEE, pp. 484–487, 2014, https://doi.org/10.1109/ICACTE.2010.5579493.
32. Zhu, Q., Wang, R., Chen, Q., Liu, Y., Qin, W., IOT Gateway: Bridging wireless sensor networks into Internet of Things, in: *Proceedings of the IEEE/IFIP International Conference on Embedded and Ubiquitous Computing*, IEEE, pp. 347–352, 2010, https://doi.org/10.1109/EUC.2010.58.
33. Boyes, H., Hallaq, B., Cunningham, J., Watson, T., The industrial internet of things (IIoT): An analysis framework. *Comput. Ind.*, 101, 1–12, 2018, https://doi.org/10.1016/j.compind.2018.04.015.
34. Gilchrist, A., *Industry 4.0: The Industrial Internet of Things*, Apress, 2016, https://doi.org/10.1007/978-1-4842-2047-4.
35. Lee, I. and Lee, K., The Internet of Things (IoT): Applications, investments, and challenges for enterprises. *Bus. Horiz.*, 58, 4, 431–440, 2015, https://doi.org/10.1016/j.bushor.2015.03.008.
36. Sisinni, E., Saifullah, A., Han, S., Jennehag, U., Gidlund, M., Industrial internet of things: Challenges, opportunities, and directions. *IEEE Trans. Ind. Inf.*, 14, 11, 4724–4734, 2018, https://doi.org/10.1109/TII.2018.2852491.
37. Bhambri, P. and Rani, S., Issues Related to Chatbots, in: *Design and Development of Emerging Chatbot Technology*, D. Darwish (Ed.), pp. 130–47, IGI Global, 2024, https://doi.org/10.4018/979-8-3693-1830-0.ch008.
38. Rani, S. and Bhambri, P., Industry 4.0 Framework and Applications, in: *AI-Driven Digital Twin and Industry 4.0: A Conceptual Framework with Applications*, 1st, S. Rani, P. Bhambri, S. Kumar, P.K. Pareek, A.A. Elngar (Eds.), pp. 1–14, CRC Press, 2024, https://doi.org/10.1201/9781003395416.

Part 2

ADVANCES AND APPLICATIONS OF EDGE INTELLIGENCE FOR 6G ENABLED INDUSTRIAL INTERNET OF THINGS

8

Connecting the 6G Autonomous Worlds with Real Time Edge Intelligence (Autonomous Vehicle)

Hemant Kumar Saini

School of Computer Science Engineering & Technology, Bennett University (The Times Group), Greater Noida, India

Abstract

The story, which views 6G as a disruptive factor in the development of wireless technology, predicts a move away from simple connectivity and towards a world of "connected intelligence." The relevance of intelligent solutions, powered by data-centric machine learning and artificial intelligence, becomes significant for sensible function as one moves beyond the capabilities of 5G and looks ahead to the future of 6G networks. Such applications cover a wide range of industries, such as improved user experiences, improved manufacturing processes, autonomous urbanization, smart machines. This chapter centers on providing a forward-thinking overview of 6G edge intelligence, highlighting its function in creating all-encompassing worldwide connection. This explores the various concerns like end-user viewpoints, pricing concerns, security, and privacy in the various edge computing paradigms. Moreover, some important investigations with enablers and obstacles that arise during the creation of Intelligent Edge services have been addressed. Significantly, this focus aims to enable the Industrial Internet of Things (IIoT) by satisfying the latency requirements with dependent modules, applications in intelligent transportation systems, as examples to stand out.

In addition, there is an introduction of the notion of edge computing, that places the computational assets to the network periphery breaking with conventional cloud-centric models and emphasizing efficiency and closeness when interacting with data sources.

Email: hemantrhce@rediffmail.com; ORCID: 0000-0002-2759-2654

Sita Rani, Pankaj Bhambri, Balamurugan Balusamy, Rishabha Malviya and Seifedine Kadry (eds.) Edge Intelligence for 6G-Enabled Industrial Internet of Things, (165–180) © 2026 Scrivener Publishing LLC

***Keywords*:** 6G, industrial internet of things, autonomous vehicle, edge intelligence, decision making, IoT, AI

8.1 Introduction

The advent of Sixth Generation (6G) and its integration with edge intelligence heralds a new era in the Internet of Everything, facilitating seamless connectivity among people, vehicles, devices, and the cloud anytime and anywhere. The increasing prevalence of next-generation smart services in wireless networks is transforming lifestyles and enhancing overall eminence. With the 6G numerous users over the world connect the virtuality into reality with the internet application.

However, the realization of 6G's complete vision, encompassing immersion, materialization, and interoperability, remains hindered by constraints such as limited resources, computing power, and sensory devices. Consequently, now is the opportune moment to actualize this vision by integrating 6G with edge-enabled artificial intelligence (AI). This integration not only addresses the existing limitations but also try to extend connectivity to the realm of vehicular networks.

To support the performance, new features, and services of future 6G networks, edge intelligence (EI) [1] motorized by artificial intelligence (AI) practice , essential component that lacks in 5G networks is fully functional. It is also expected to play a major enabling role in these networks. As a result, the goal of this chapter is to give a new direction of the researchers to sustain the various high speed communications at the edges only which cut off the overheads. From the past few years demand of AI in ICT covers the world variety of applications, including driverless cars, smart city operations, video/audio surveillance, and intelligent personal assistants. Industry 4.0 revolutions transform the industries by making them digital and automize every sector. There is an increasing requirement to manage new tradeoffs in design considerations as computer and software use grows. These factors include giving priority to privacy and security issues and resolving energy and timing limits in calculations and data transmissions. The availability of high-performance, reasonably priced computing and the exponential growth in data created by a wide range of ubiquitous devices [2], from industrial robots to personal cellphones, are responsible for the recent advances that have led to the surge in interest in artificial intelligence.

Moreover, with the high utilization of the IoT based surroundings which generated the large data volume demands the attention with the solid foundation for the significant trend towards. The use of TinyML model emphasizes the importance of operations at the edge. Incorporating this consideration into computational models necessitates an extension of the centralized cloud computing model to the edge locations. By using these methods, the process and storage are placed closer to the end users and data sources. In [3], the context of 6G, edge intelligence is poised to play a significant role in furthering these benefits. Additionally, the capabilities of edge intelligence are expected to pave the way in improving the edge services.

The integration of intelligence in edge computing give rise to rapid emergence of novel business opportunities and innovations across various interdisciplinary domains. Mostly, the Fog computing is used to drive the processes at the edges altering the scenario from the central to cloud.

An especially pertinent definition for 5G and future systems comes from the endless access initiative within the European Telecommunications Standards Institute (ETSI). This architecture allows applications and services to be executed at the edge by running a movable periphery platform on the movable host. Through standardized APIs (application interfaces), such as support for network slicing and access to base station data, the ETSI endless edge connects various application at edges with their services. Installation of smart applicative services with or without the user domains are vicinity to them, or even over the boundaries of network domains, is the fundamental definition of edge intelligence from a network perspective. Edge intelligence is essentially the ability to process data at an ever-higher degree and to filter information at the edge. With the growing edges intelligence, it is a remarkable milestone of forging AI into nodes also [4]. This permits incremental learning and the possible exchange of learned information with other edge nodes that are comparable to one another, hence providing optimized or new value-added services. Anticipatedly, telecom sector with the fastest growth of 6G communication shifts the complete market from centralized resources to edge arrangements in an intelligent way. Furthermore, edge intelligence becomes critical in the ecosystem where humans tend to merge with machines, like in workplaces, and where safety concerns are paramount. As devices like Coral and Jetson that can compute artificial intelligence (AI) they become more prevalent but are still in infancy. The current AI solutions, however, need a lot of time, energy, and resources. Boolean algebra transistors are still commonly employed in several machine learning and deep neural network techniques for large-scale digital calculations over large datasets. Future predictions call for a rise in the quantity and size of datasets that are available, along with more demanding AI performance standards for near real-time, ultra-low latency applications. Long-term sustainability of this trend may be questionable, though, as chipset technologies are not developing as quickly as AI solutions to fulfill the demands and expectations of the market. A viable remedy is provided by nanophotonic technology, which can efficiently execute DNN tasks like matrix multiplication at nearly the speed of light. There is a bottleneck in transferring the data between processor and memory whose one solution is to execute calculations inside memory structures. Systems-on-a-Chip (SoC) combines general processor with the intelligent application specific engines such as Adaptive Computing Acceleration Engine (ACAE), are considered to benefit greatly from in-memory computing [4].

Moreover, one area of current 5G development that receives little attention is the software that underpins AI development. Performance, memory limitations, and productivity are some of the reasons behind the differences in tools, techniques, and procedures used in the development of various end user edge resources apps. Divergence results in established roles for various devices in the design and implementation process, impeding the flow of software between devices—a phenomenon referred to as "liquid software." Future 6G networks will not be able to locate intelligence within the network architecture without liquid software; therefore, decisions on where to put intelligence must be made during the design phase because computations cannot be easily moved without advance planning.

8.2 Evolutions

Over time, wireless communication technology has advanced with the goal of offering secure, dependable, and fast communication. With the numerous deployments that have occurred throughout the years, wireless network development has progressed from 1G to 6G. We describe each evolution in the following discussions, along with its uses and drawbacks.

8.2.1 1G Communication

The United States launched the 1G system in 1980s with the Advanced Mobile Phone System (AMPS) [5]. This system had a 50MHz bandwidth and operated in the 824–894 MHz frequency range. This system uses frequency division multiple access (FDMA) to divide the bandwidth into 30

KHz sub-channels, allowing numerous users to send data at the same time. In addition, the Nordic nations—Norway, Denmark, Switzerland, Finland, and Sweden—developed the Nordic Mobile Telephone (NMT) standard for 1G in 1981. It could handle voice calls at up to 2.4 Kbps by the 1980s. However, the original technology had issues with handoffs, signal quality, and handling international phone and conference calls, mail service across the telecom network. The introduction of the 2G network generation came later to rectify these issues.

8.2.2 2G Communication

Finland developed and deployed the second-generation (2G) network in the 1990s using the Global System for Mobile (GSM) standards [6]. This signaled the change from the 1G analogue system to a digital one and the addition of voice call encryption for increased security. Time Division Multiple Access (TDMA), used by GSM, divides the channel bandwidth according to time periods. Later, additional digital standards including Japan's Personal Digital Cellular (PDC) and the United States' Digital AMPS (D-AMPS) adopted TDMA. In the United States, Code Division several Access (also known as CDMA) evolved as an alternative to Time Division Multiplexing (TDMA), allowing several network users to transmit data simultaneously based on uniquely given code sequences. 2G introduced capabilities like conference calls, call holding, short message services (SMS), and multimedia message services (MMS) in addition to enabling international roaming voice calls. General Packet Radio Service (GPRS), also known as 2.5G, was made possible by the further development of GSM technology. It brought with it specialized services like Wireless Application Protocol (WAP) for internet communication, including email and access to the World Wide Web (WWW) [7]. Higher data rates were made available by Enhanced Data Rates for GSM Evolution (EDGE), a further advancement of GPRS. Notwithstanding these developments, 2G networks were unable to support high-bandwidth applications like video conferencing and navigation services. The third-generation (3G) network was developed in response to this constraint.

8.2.3 3G Communication

NTT DoCoMo first unveiled third-generation (3G) technology in Japan in 2001. It works on the International Mobile Telephone (IMT)-2000 standard. Improving Quality of Service (QoS), expanding coverage, and offering services to users anywhere were its main goals [8]. With this development, audio compression over conversations could be used at a reduced cost for high data rate video conferencing and video downloads. In particular, packet-based 3.5G, or High-Speed Downlink Packet Access (HSDPA), was introduced, providing downlink data rates of 8–10 Mbps. Another version, known as 3.75G or High-Speed Uplink Packet Access (HSUPA), was intended for interactive gaming. Nevertheless, 3G was still unable to provide support for high definition (HD) mobile TV, 3D movies, and IP telephony. Fourth-generation (4G) networks were developed as a result of these constraints.

8.2.4 4G Communication

The Fourth Generation (4G) network system was unveiled in the latter part of the 2000s. It is an all-IP network system made to transport voice, data, multimedia, and internet services more quickly, more securely, and for less money. In 2009, 4G technology began to be utilized commercially. It provides 1GPS speed and 100 Mbps speed at low and high mobility respectively. The Long-Term Evolution (LTE) based -Advanced Pro, commonly referred to as 4.5G, is the result of additional improvements made to the LTE standard to boost mobile broadband and connectivity. Notwithstanding these developments, 4G had difficulties supporting image-processing-intensive applications like augmented reality, smart linked automobiles, and machine vision. The creation of the fifth-generation (5G) network followed as a result.

8.2.5 5G Generation

5G communication was developed with the aim of best Quality of Service (QoS), low latency and broad spectrum. It is basically designed for applications of the augmented reality (AR) with the industrial revolutions. Enhanced Mobile Broadband (eMBB) is built to accommodate apps like augmented reality (AR) and Ultra-High Definition (UHD) films [9]. In the meanwhile, mMTC specifies that each square kilometer must contain one million inexpensive, low-power devices with a 10-year battery life. Applications combining several sensors, controllers, and actuators, such as industrial automation and smart homes, require this capability to provide high dependability (99.99%) at very low latencies. Year wise progression of 1G to 6G evaluation in mentioned in Figure 8.1.

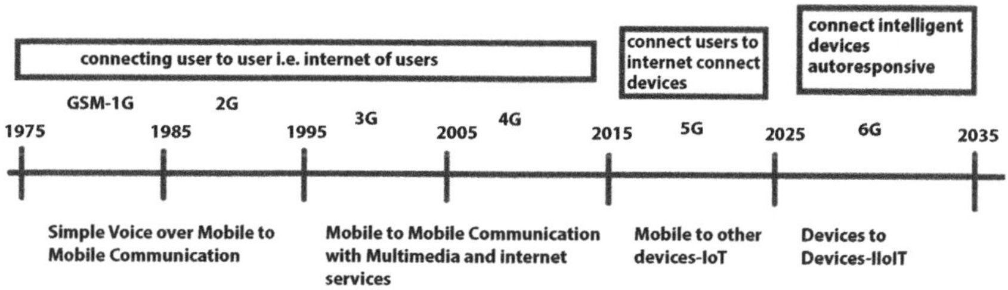

Figure 8.1 Technology progression over 1 G to 6G evolution.

8.2.6 6G Communication

By addressing more stringent requirements, the current research on Sixth Generation (6G) technology seeks to advance the "Internet of Everything" into an "Intelligent Internet of Everything." High data speeds, improved energy efficiency, massively distributed low-latency control, increased dependability, and the incorporation of linked intelligence *via* ML and DL are a few of these. It is also expected that 6G would function over a very wide range of frequency bands [10]. With the help of this technology, services would be able to adjust to many aspects like traffic volume, network topology, user mobility, and social networking context. Furthermore, it is anticipated that 6G will perform well in emergency or extreme scenarios, adapting to changes in traffic patterns, infrastructure availability, and spatial-temporal device density.

8.3 Issues in 6G Edges

Recently, there has been a major shift in the focus of Internet-of-Vehicle (IoV) networks from only linked cars to connected intelligence. It is anticipated that cellular vehicular-to-everything (C-V2X) and dedicated short-range communications (DSRC) would combine to form the future of vehicular communications. Currently, "802.11p/DSRC" and "C-V2X" are at the center of the battle between vehicular communication protocols. The benefit of "802.11p" is that the European Commission and the Department of Transportation have approved it for use at 5.9 GHz, allowing it to be implemented in basic short-range communications. But in the case of "Driver-less V2X," things are not the same. Given the large amount of data anticipated in mobile edge communication (MEC), maintaining 802.11p would necessitate considerable changes to the existing standard. In this

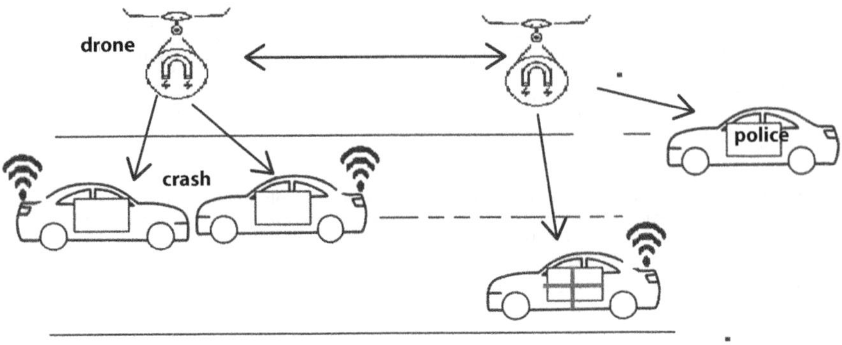

Figure 8.2 Edge based communication between vehicles.

regard, it is believed that the novel features of C-V2X in B5G/6G would be extremely important. The development of MEC and AI has been fueled by autonomous driving, a promising application that has improved daily life and led to the flowering of edge intelligence (EI) [10]. Under this structure, Edge based drones with the artificial intelligence collects the data and process to the base stations (BS), as shown in Figure 8.2.

Higher accuracy and lower latency inference computing for AVs can be accomplished by implementing an edge based intelligent server. However, there are a number of intrinsic problems with computing and communication with constrained bandwidth and computational resources, data security, and privacy, which are roadblocks to the intended drive in 6G.

AI technology greatly influenced the human life in the modern world, where data is an essential resource for a variety of organizations. As a result, edge artificial intelligence (edge AI) is a revolutionary learning model that has gained acceptance in both academia and industry [11]. With the help of this paradigm, AI models may be installed directly on devices, enabling real-time data processing and model inference. In addition to expanding AI's potential applications, edge AI signals the start of a new age defined by the "Internet of Everything." But even with all of its promise, there are still several problems with the edge AI paradigm and its applications that need to be fixed.

1. Elevated Latency: The proliferation of massive data in edge AI, involving numerous remote devices transmitting and processing extensive data sets, presents a persistent challenge of high latency within the current network environment. This bottleneck has consistently impeded the widespread adoption of edge AI [11].

2. Fragile Stability: Since the existing network is only capable to train the small scale model, hence the large-scale model training is in demand with edge AI.
3. Limited safety: The contemporary design falls short in meeting the security requirements of the multitude of remote devices linking to cloud servers today [9]. Moreover, the network's openness presents greater difficulties for the security of the existing network design.

The concept of AI embedded 6G edge has arisen to address these issues. This paradigm denotes how well AI technology and 6G mobile communication technology are working together. 6G mobile communication technology advances edge AI by delivering fastly and robustly. Additionally, users data get more secure in intelligent way through the 6G advance slicing technique [12]. Consequently, 6G seems to be the best for deployment of the next decade wireless communication.

8.4 6G with Edge

Leveraging and elevating the foundations laid by 4G/5G mobile communication technology, 6G mobile communication embodies a sophisticated communication framework that seamlessly incorporates sagacity, network, power capabilities. In comparison to 4/5G, 6G boasts of numerous advantages like throughput, energy, packet transmission, coverage, processing performance [13]. With improvements in broadcast rate, passage solidity, location precision, and of over 100 times, 6G outperforms 5G. 6G broadcast with the rate of 1 Tbit/s and a network latency of less than 1 ms, greatly improving consumers' quality of experience (QoE). In terms of positioning accuracy, 6G can precisely cover circumference of 1 m range in outside and 10 cm inside. Notably, 6G networks coalesce the autonomous vehicles with ground communication, offer global coverage across land and sea. In terms of security, 6G adopts endogenous security technology, strengthening its resistance to unknown security threats compared to conventional plug-in and patch-type system defense machine. By combining edge computing and artificial intelligence, edge AI realize the end user data with machine learning paradigms. The incessant advances in the edge energy assures the endeavor of new forthcoming 6G [14]. In the new world of the internet of everything, EI offers the impending proficient and precise intellectual steering vehicles, using computation potential of edge servers (e.g., roadside stations) [14]. The real-world use of 6G technology is made easier by the development of edge intelligence. Benefits from 6G edge intelligence include high performance, computing offload, and low latency. Thus, there are three main advantages to applying 6G-oriented edge intelligence:

1) Equitable Data Storage: In conventional cloud computing, data generated at end nodes transmits for further processing towards the cloud causing heightened demand on cloud servers. Edge intelligence minimizes the redundancy in data storage through parity distribution of the data at numerous edge nodes.
2) Effective Data Transmission: In comparison to cloud networks, the layered architecture of 6G edge AI guarantees faster transmission speeds, which lowers the need for internet capacity. This facilitates faster information transfer and communication and offers a platform for virtual services to respond quickly.
3) High Reliability: Spatial multiplexing technology will be employed by 6G-oriented edge intelligence in the future, guaranteeing a chance of less than one in a million for communication interruptions. This significant upgrade significantly raises the standard of the user experience. One of three architectures is usually adopted by edge AI when it comes to model training.
4) Centralized architecture: In this architecture, the cloud server manages the data generated by AI models and their inferences. The data required for AI model training is generated and collected by remote terminal devices, which are placed at the edge layer and include smart watches, cellphones, automobiles, and security cameras. The cloud server then uses the data that these edge devices have uploaded to train AI models, which are then made available for model inference.
5) Decentralized architecture: Every edge computing node in this architecture is given the task of training an AI model. This architecture uses the local data to train independently the AI model and processed updated data eventually shared over the networks.
6) A cross design combines elements of decentralized and centralized design patterns. The edge terminal is used for sharing and training, while the edge server serves as the central

entity. To be more precise, the edge server updates the AI model globally and uses network connections to send it to edge nodes. Using the cloud server's advantages in computational power and resources, training data from edge nodes may be uploaded in real time for centralized training.

8.5 Edge Intelligence with Autonomous Vehicle

In the realm of the latest research, a new paradigm has emerged, integrating AI technology into edge computing, referred to as edge intelligence (EI). This integration holds the potential to facilitate efficient computing and intelligent decision-making, particularly in enhancing road safety. Several applications of EI in autonomous driving have garnered attention, including:

1) Object Detection: In autonomous vehicles like drones, real-time data is continuously captured using sensors during driving. AI techniques process this data, providing instructions for safe and efficient driving by timely and accurately identifying objects in the surroundings [15]. However, the computational cost is substantial, and EI plays a pivotal role in effectively reducing this overhead.
2) Traffic Flow Prediction: As autonomous vehicles become more commonplace and the need for intelligent transportation systems to meet growing demands is made clear, timely and reliable traffic flow data is essential for safe navigation. EI, in conjunction with the driverless revolution, extends computation resources to handle real-time, time-consuming tasks, serving as a significant advantage.
3) Intelligent Decision-Making: Recent years have witnessed a focus on various autonomous applications, such as online path planning, aimed at enhancing road safety by avoiding collisions. With feasible path planning, autonomous vehicles (AVs) took decisions decisive drills based on their surroundings. This becomes especially crucial in the context of the 5G/6G paradigm. EI offers a deep learning approach deployed at the edge [16]. Applications like Google Maps suffers from the delays due to which the novel AVs try to collect data at the edges with minimum delays in limited

timeframe. Therefore, smart, opportune, and consistent decisions become achievable for Avs [17], particularly in scenarios with dynamically changing surroundings.

8.6 Forthcoming Edge Driven AI Based 6G in Autonomous Vehicular Applications

In today's world, almost every industry incorporates the modern art of AI in their manufacturing processes, leading to extensive data collection facilitated by the internet of things (IoT). This proliferation of connected devices and rapid computer processing has significantly impacted various aspects of present-day life. Evolution of IIot is mentioned in Figure 8.3. Despite the current influence of AI and IoT [18], there is a continued need for advanced services in the future across various applications, including:

(i) Three dimension mobility,
(ii) Industrial and production preservation,
(iii) Medicare,
(iv) Learning and instructional programs
(v) Communication and leisure.,
(vi) e-shopee,
(vii) Preservation of the ecosystem

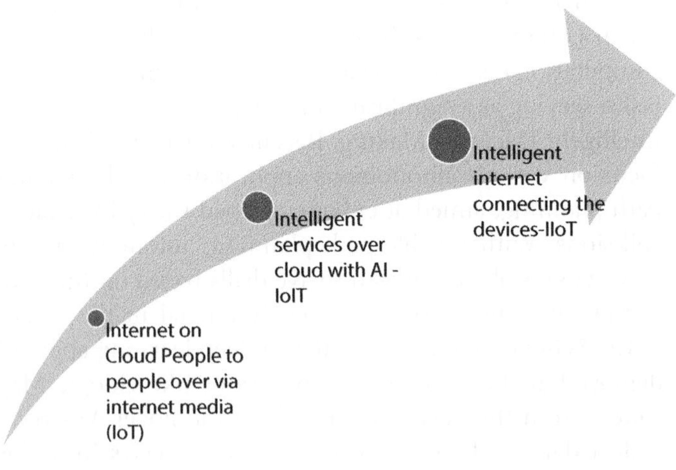

Figure 8.3 Evolution of IIoT.

As the functionality increases, there is a greater need to ensure competent, protected, healthy, and flexible services. This evolution marks the transition from the "Internet of Things" to the "Internet of Intelligent Things." With a plethora of the aforementioned services, the IIoT connect over the internet efficiently and securely.

The new generation 6G communication-driven artificial intelligence has the potential to be extremely important in this situation. In contrast to edge computing initiatives by cloud service providers such as Google, Amazon, and Microsoft, 6G allows telecom operators to more tightly integrate processing and communication. For instance, edge intelligence can be automatically deployed by 6G base stations, although doing so requires both computation and communication resources. This aids for the telecom operators which would regain the market.

In 6G era linked objects are more intelligent that they can carry large data with minimum complexity in a sophisticated and intelligent approach where many applications are relying on such data. Introducing intelligence at the edge is a key feature that will guarantee the effectiveness of next 6G wireless networks. Simultaneously, it serves as an enabling technology for various applications of wireless communications. AI concentrated on the specific application of the local environments, network architectures, cooperative frameworks, and the need to balance performance and costs. one such method demonstrated optimizing 6G with AI in [19].

It is essential to ensure secure and reliable 6G nonstop services, the reliance on AI for edge must be diminished. Combination of the platform orchestration and infrastructure gives the best optimization to render the services. To achieve maximum flexibility, developing" design all conceivable combinations of "micro services" on the edge nodes, 6G ontology seems to be required.

8.7 Future Perspective of Edge Intelligence in Vehicles

Research on autonomous driving spans a broad spectrum, from completely automated driving without human interaction to basic driver aid systems like lane-keeping assistance and traffic sign recognition. An intriguing application with driverless cars, usually trucks, moves in coordination. This convoy, led by a platoon leader, relies on wireless communication technologies for data exchange. As the number of vehicles increases, potential congestion in communication mediums may arise. In such cases, edge intelligence (EI) efficiently processes data within platoons and from all street users, providing fast and reliable data processing. Enthusiastic superior dispensation units situated with base stations or roadside units offer edge intelligence functionality [20].

Various applications of intelligent healthcare arena leverage AI-driven in-network devices for daily activities. These latency-sensitive devices exchange privacy-susceptible data and surveillance cameras, generate substantial data volumes. The requirement for edge-resident elucidation becomes evident in environments like smart hospitals, where extensive data services are essential. Environmental sensing, specifically air quality monitoring, collects and processes AI data, which is offloaded on edges.

With the continuous growth of technology and the demand for mobile-centric applications, the future tactile internet with 6G demonstrates great potential for edge intelligence. However, since mobile devices are battery-based, the ongoing development of Collaborative Robots (COBOTS) is in progress, aiming to establish alliance with individual and reduces battery usage [21, 22].

The evolution towards deploying the Intelligent era at the edges providing services standing with the high performance computing support in the next forthcoming decades could fulfill the demands of huge data in 6G networks. Initial deployments may use pre-trained, enabling real-time action based on collected information. Data processing and training will need to be distributed even with the increased power of edge devices. AI accelerator application-specific integrated circuits are one example of a new hardware component being developed with the goal of increasing performance while lowering expenses and energy usage. Long-term solutions may involve technologies like nanophotonics for complex operations or information storage. The combination of communication and learning, guided by learning-driven design principles, will lead to secure users copyrights in distributed fashion at the edge networks.

AI disclosure statement: The author acknowledges the use of AI-based tools for minor language editing or grammatical correction. However, all intellectual contributions, analyses, and conclusions presented in this chapter are entirely the author's own.

References

1. Wang, J., Jiang, C., Zhang, H., Ren, Y., Chen, K.C., Hanzo, L., Thirty Years of Machine Learning: The Road to Pareto-Optimal Wireless Networks. *IEEE Commun. Surv. Tutor.*, 22, 3, 1472–1514, thirdquarter 2020.

2. Zhang, K., Zhu, Y., Leng, S., He, Y., Maharjan, S., Zhang, Y., Deep learning empowered task offloading for mobile edge computing in urban informatics. *IEEE Internet Things J.*, 6, 5, 7635–47, Mar. 2019.
3. Li, K., *et al.*, Computation Offloading in Resource-Constrained Multi-Access Edge Computing, in: *IEEE Transactions on Mobile Computing*, vol. 23, no. 11, pp. 10665–10677, Nov. 2024, doi: 10.1109/TMC.2024.3383041.
4. Zhang, J., Li, F., Ye, F., Wu, H., Autonomous Unknown-Application Filtering and Labeling for DL-based Traffic Classifier Update, *arXiv preprint arXiv:2002.06359*, Feb. 2020.
5. Xiong, K., Leng, S., Chen, X., Huang, C., Yuen, C., Guan, Y.L., Communication and Computing Resource Optimization for Connected Autonomous Driving, in: *IEEE Transactions on Vehicular Technology,* vol. 69, no. 11, pp. 12652–12663, Nov. 2020, doi: 10.1109/TVT.2020.3029109.
6. Deng, B., Jiang, C., Wang, J., *et al.*, Beam scheduling with various mission demands in data relay satellite systems. *J. Commun. Inf. Netw.*, 6, 4, 396–410, 2021.
7. Chowdhary, K.R., Natural Language Processing, in: *Fundamentals of Artificial Intelligence.* Springer, New Delhi, 2020. https://doi.org/10.1007/978-81-322-3972-7_19.
8. Zhang, B., Davoodi, A., Hu, Y.H., Exploring energy and accuracy tradeoff in structure simplification of trained deep neural networks. *IEEE J. Emerg. Sel. Top. Circuits Syst.*, 8, 4, 836–848, Dec. 2018.
9. Singh, G., Chelini, L., Corda, S., Javed Awan, A., Stuijk, S., Jordans, R., Corporaal, H., Boonstra, A.-J., Near-memory computing: Past, Present, and Future. *Microprocess. Microsyst.*, 71, 102868, 2019, ISSN 0141-9331, https://doi.org/10.1016/j.micpro.2019.102868.
10. Zhou, Z., Chen, X., Li, E., Zeng, L., Luo, K., Zhang, J., Edge intelligence: Paving the last mile of artificial intelligence with edge computing. *Proceedings of the IEEE*, 2019.
11. Zhang, X., Wang, Y., Lu, S., Liu, L., Lanyu xu, W.S., OpenEI: An Open Framework for Edge Intelligence. *Distributed Computing Systems (ICDCS) 2019 IEEE 39th International Conference on*, pp. 1840–1851, 2019.
12. Deng, S., Zhao, H., Fang, W., Yin, J., Dustdar, S., Zomaya, A.Y., Edge Intelligence: The Confluence of Edge Computing and Artificial Intelligence, in: *IEEE Internet of Things Journal,* vol. 7, no. 8, pp. 7457–7469, Aug. 2020, doi: 10.1109/JIOT.2020.2984887.
13. Letaief, K.B., Chen, W., Shi, Y., Zhang, J., Zhang, Y.J.A., The roadmap to 6G: AI empowered wireless networks. *IEEE Commun. Mag.*, 57, 8, 84–90, Aug. 2019.
14. Ivkovic, Z., Stavness, I., Gutwin, C., *et al.*, Quantifying and mitigating the negative effects of local latencies on aiming in 3d shooter games, in: *Proceedings of the 33rd Annual ACM Conference on Human Factors in Computing Systems*, ACM, New York, pp. 135–144, 2015.

15. Rasheed, A., San, O., Kvamsdal, T., Digital twin: values, challenges and enablers from a modeling perspective. *IEEE Access*, 8, 21980–22012, 2020.
16. Liu, Y., Peng, J., Kang, J., *et al.*, A secure federated learning framework for 5G networks. *IEEE Wirel. Commun.*, 27, 4, 24–31, 2020.
17. Saini, H.K. and Jain, K., A Novel Deep Energy Efficient Hello Packet Scheduling for Ad Hoc Networks in Unmanned Aerial Vehicles. *Eng. Sci.*, 22, 843, 2023. http://dx.doi.org/10.30919/es8d843.
18. Huang, X., Zhang, K., Wu, F., *et al.*, Collaborative machine learning for energy-efficient edge networks in 6G. *IEEE Netw.*, 35, 6, 12–19, 2021.
19. Mozumder, M.A.I.I, Sheeraz, M.M., Athar, A., Aich, S., Kim, H.-C., Overview: Technology Roadmap of the Future Trend of Metaverse based on IoT, Blockchain, AI Technique, and Medical Domain Metaverse Activity, in: *2022 24th International Conference on Advanced Communication Technology (ICACT)*, PyeongChang Kwangwoon_Do, Korea, Republic of, pp. 256–261, 2022, doi: 10.23919/ICACT53585.2022.9728808.
20. Park, J., Samarakoon, S., Shiri, H., K. Abdel-Aziz, M., Nishio, T., Elgabli, A., Bennis, M., Extreme URLLC: Vision, Challenges, and Key Enablers, arXiv:2001.09683, Jan. 2020.
21. Bhambri, P., Rani, S., Pareek, P.K., Paperless Paradigm: Intelligent Automation in Document and Record Management, in: *Generating Entrepreneurial Ideas with AI*, D. Darwish (Ed.), pp. 164–83, IGI Global, Hershey, PA 17033, USA, 2024, https://www.igi-global.com/book/hyperautomation-business-society/335477.
22. Sridhar, V., Rani, S., Pareek, P.K., Bhambri, P., Elngar, A.A. (Eds.), *Blockchain for IoT Systems: Concept, Framework and Applications*, 1st, Chapman and Hall/CRC, New York, 2024, https://doi.org/10.1201/9781003460367.

9

Performance Improvement of 6G Internet of Things Using Converged Super Hybrid [CPU+GPU] HPC Infrastructure and Edge AI

B.N. Chandrashekhar[1]* **and V. Geetha**[2]

[1]*Department of Computer Science and Engineering, Amity University, Bengaluru, Karnataka, India*
[2]*School of Management, Reva University, Bengaluru, Karnataka, India*

Abstract
In recent years, many data centers have transitioned from a centralized model to an edge computing approach. This brings computing closer to the point of use, reducing latency and improving performance. Enterprises, cloud service providers, and telecom companies invest heavily in digital edge data centers to optimize IOT-based HPC benchmark applications like streaming video, telemedicine, and factory automation. What is lacking is a solid software environment to effectively realize HPC from powerful edge AI systems. The main objective of this chapter is to improve the performance of 6G IOT-based benchmark HPC applications on hybrid HPC infrastructure on edge devices equipped with parallel accelerators focusing on software environments including programming models and benchmark methods to overcome the performance issues and optimal resource utilization. The proposed approach to achieve this goal is through optimal workload distribution and AI- based Intra-node and Internode communication on CPUs and GPUs-based HPC infrastructure. To achieve this goal, we propose optimized analytical workload partitioning strategies based on parameters such as the computing capability of CPU and GPU, available cores on the CPU and GPU, Clock rate of CPU and GPU, and memory bandwidth. To improve the performance of intra-node and internode communication we use an AI-based CNN algorithm with a zero-copy technique based on applications on hybrid HPC infrastructure.

**Corresponding author*: cnaikodi@gmail.com

Sita Rani, Pankaj Bhambri, Balamurugan Balusamy, Rishabha Malviya and Seifedine Kadry (eds.) Edge Intelligence for 6G-Enabled Industrial Internet of Things, (181–198) © 2026 Scrivener Publishing LLC

***Keywords*:** Artificial intelligence (AI), central processing units (CPUs), graphics processing unit (GPU), and high-performance computing (HPC), Internet of Things (IoT)

9.1 Introduction

The potential of Edge AI [Artificial Intelligence] has been unlocked by recent advancements in edge computing, IoT device adoption, and AI efficacy. This has created previously unthinkable new potential for edge AI, such as assisting radiologists in hospital pathology identification, operating cars on freeways, and assisting with plant pollination. Edge computing, which has its roots in the 1990s when content delivery networks were established to offer web and video content from edge servers placed close to users, is a topic of discussion and implementation for many experts and corporations.

Nowadays, practically all businesses have work functions where edge AI deployment can be advantageous. The next wave of AI computing is being driven by edge applications, which enhance our quality of life at home, at work, in school, and on public transportation. Neural networks have been used in a variety of data management and data engineering scenarios due to artificial intelligence of things rapid development and many advantages [1–6].

9.1.1 Edge Computing with AI

What is Edge AI?

The use of AI applications in devices located throughout the real world is known as Edge AI. The reason it's dubbed "edge AI" is that, as opposed to being done centrally in a cloud computing facility or private data center, the AI calculation is done close to the user at the network's edge, near the location of the data [7]. Due to the internet's worldwide reach, any location can be considered the network's edge. It might be a retail outlet, factory, hospital, or any of the gadgets we see all around us, including phones, autonomous vehicles, and traffic lights.

How Does Edge AI Technology Work?

Machines must be able to reproduce human intellect to emulate human abilities such as seeing, detecting objects, driving, speaking, walking, and so on. As shown in Figure 9.1 AI mimics human cognition by using a data

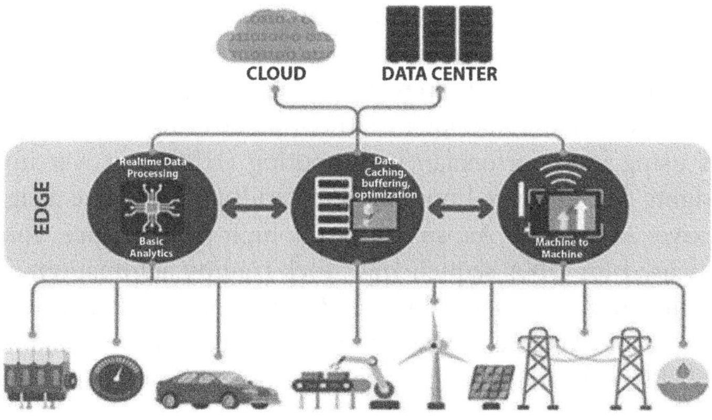

Figure 9.1 Lifecycle of an edge AI application.

structure known as a deep neural network. By being presented with several samples of a certain question type together with the appropriate responses, these DNNs are trained to respond to question kinds.

Due to the enormous volume of data needed to train an accurate model and the requirement for data scientists to work together on model configuration, this training process, known as "deep learning," frequently takes place in a data center or the cloud. The model progresses from training to becoming an "inference engine" that can respond to inquiries from the actual world. The inference engine in edge AI deployments operates on a computer or other device in remote areas like homes, factories, hospitals, automobiles, and satellites. When the AI detects an issue, the problematic data is typically transferred to the cloud for additional training of the initial AI model, which eventually takes the position of the edge inference engine.

9.1.2 HPC Infrastructure

HPC technology utilizes clusters of powerful processors that work in parallel to process large multi-dimensional datasets, also known as big data, and solve intricate problems at incredibly high speeds. HPC systems typically outperform commodity desktops, laptops, or server systems by more than a million times in terms of speed.

Supercomputers have historically served as the main HPC system paradigm. Millions of processors or processor cores are included in these specially designed-computers. Supercomputers still exist today; the fastest one is the US-based Frontier, which can process information at a quintillion floating-point operations per second (flops), or 1.102 exaflops. Organizations are, however, increasingly choosing to operate HPC solutions on clusters of fast computers, either on-site or in the cloud [9].

Tasks using high-performance computing (HPC) uncover important new insights that advance human understanding and create a significant competitive advantage. As an example, high-performance computing (HPC) is used for DNA sequencing, stock trading automation, and artificial intelligence (AI) algorithms and simulations. AI algorithms and simulations, for example, power autonomous cars, which instantly process terabytes of data coming from IoT sensors, radar, and GPS systems to make quick decisions.

9.1.2.1 Multicore Architecture

Multicore processors are integrated circuits that contain two or more processor cores to improve performance and reduce power consumption. These processors allow for more efficient simultaneous processing of multiple tasks through parallel processing and multithreading. A dual-core setup is akin to having multiple individual processors in a computer but with a faster connection between them due to being plugged into the same socket. By making use of multicore processors, one can increase CPU performance while maintaining safe operation in terms of heat generation, all while staying within the practical bounds of semiconductor design and fabrication [8].

The execution engine, often known as a core, is the primary component of every processor. This core is designed primarily to process data and execute commands from software applications that are kept in the computer's memory. It has been noted over time that every new CPU design has a unique set of drawbacks. These days, multicore computers might include [12, 24], or even more processor cores, as Figure 9.2 illustrates. The idea behind multiprocessor motherboards, which have two or four different processor sockets, is similar to that of multicore processors. The final product stays the same. The use of processor components that feature fast clocking is how current processors achieve their great performance.

Multicore processors come with several considerations. Performance on computers is not always improved by simply adding more processing cores. Applications and the operating system must be able to distribute software instructions to make use of and recognize the numerous cores. Concurrently allocating distinct threads to different processor package

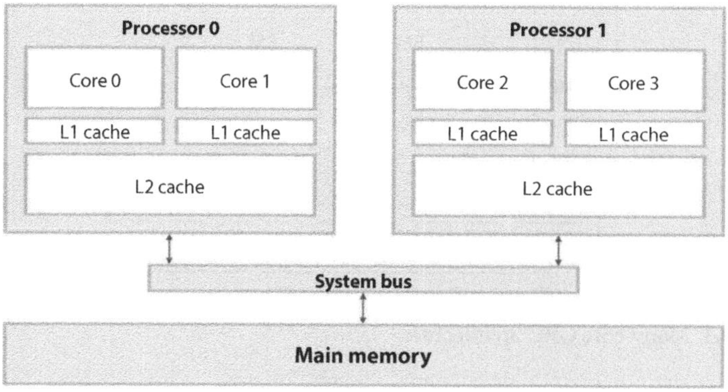

Figure 9.2 Architecture of multi-core processors.

cores is required for this allocation. It could be necessary to restructure some applications to make the most of multicore processor platforms. If not, all CPU cores will be idle and only the first default core will be used.

Additionally, the additional cores do not directly multiply the performance advantage. For example, the performance of a CPU does not double with the addition of a second core, nor does it quadruple with the addition of a quad-core processor. This is because the CPU shares parts of its architecture, like system memory, external buses, and internal or cache memory.

There are practical restrictions on the benefits of having several cores, notwithstanding their potential significance. However, because the cores in the same package are closer to one another and have fewer components and shorter distances between them, the acceleration is usually better than in a traditional multiprocessor system.

9.1.2.2 Many-Core Architecture

The rapidly expanding video and gaming industries developed lightweight many-core GPUs to overcome the architectural problems with CPUs and increase GFLOPS per video frame in high-end gaming applications. In Figure 9.3 the GPU architecture is displayed. A variety of highly threaded streaming multiprocessors (SMs) make up the architecture. Streaming processors (SPs) or several cores that share an instruction cache and control circuitry are a feature of each SM. The instructions are carried out in SIMD (single instruction multiple data) mode by individual SMs. Dynamic random-access memory (DRAM) is a type of global memory that is unique to each GPU and speeds up sophisticated computation and graphics

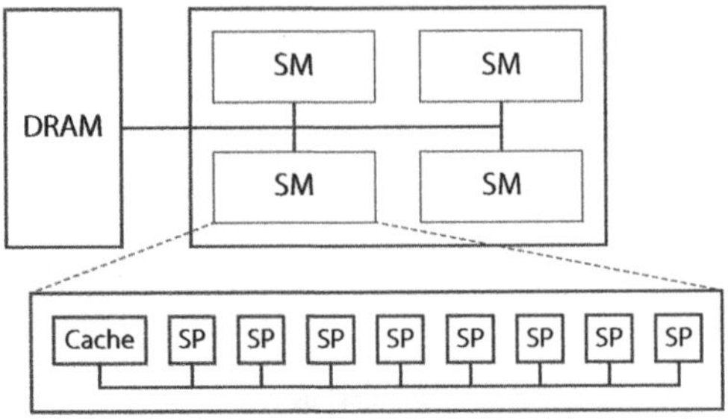

Figure 9.3 Many-core GPU architecture.

rendering [9]. Applications that are not graphical are supported by GPUs of the latest generation. GPUs can offer thread-level parallelism according to their computing power. GPU uses a tiny amount of memory.

The GPU's highly parallel architecture has made it useful in a variety of applications, including large-scale simulation, medical imaging, deep learning, machine learning, and artificial intelligence. Nevertheless, there are drawbacks to GPU. To fully utilize the many-core GPU computing power, the algorithms must be written with GPU architecture in mind. If not, high-performance computing programs will not be able to fully exploit all of a system's resources. The performance of the application is harmed by this underutilization. Without the assistance of the CPU, the multicore GPU unit is unable to operate on its own.

9.1.2.3 Hybrid [CPU+GPU] Architecture

In massively parallel HPC applications, performance can be further enhanced by combining CPU-GPU architecture (hybrid). Although CPU and GPU are designed from different perspectives, combining their features leads to better performance in many HPC applications. A CPU-GPU heterogeneous architecture with two CPUs and two GPUs is shown in Figure 9.4. I/O chipsets facilitate CPU-GPU connection, and they are linked to the I/O Hub *via* PCIE and Quick Path Interconnect Link (QPI). Separate memory exists for CPUs and GPUs (DRAM) [9].

In addition to doing certain computational tasks, the CPU is in charge of managing programs, assigning work to the GPUs, starting GPU computations, and reading the results from the GPUs. The massively parallel computation is carried out by the GPUs.

A lot of scientific and industrial advances are built on HPC. Research labs, the entertainment sector, financial services, artificial intelligence, and

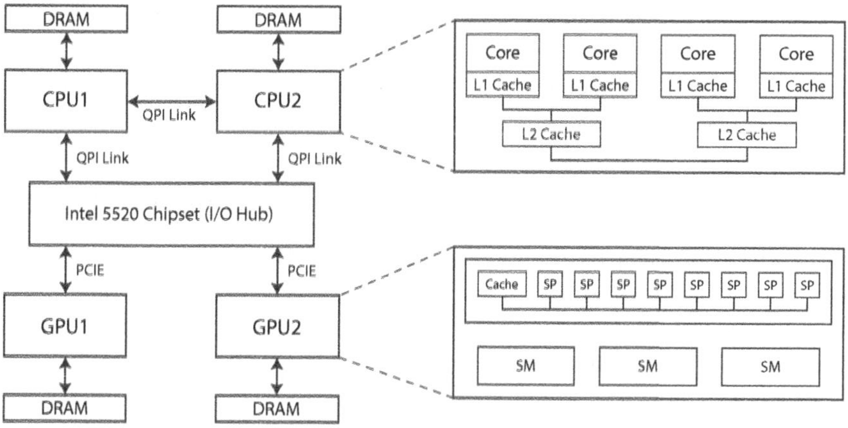

Figure 9.4 Multi- cores CPU-GPU hybrid architecture.

the oil and gas business are among the main industries that benefit from HPC. As the name suggests, HPC applications process massive amounts of data quickly, thus they require a lot of processing power. One of the main forces behind the advancements in computer hardware is the need for such high-performance computing capability. One such system is the hybrid one, which combines CPUs and GPUs.

9.2 Proposed Converged Super Hybrid [CPU+GPU] HPC Infrastructure and Edge AI

Over the next ten years, scientific instruments will be improved to give ten to one hundred times more sensitivity and resolution. This will necessitate a matching scale-up in processing and storage. The data generated by these improved instruments will surpass the limitations of Moore's law and pose a threat to conventional data center operating models that are exclusively reliant on HPC.

We are entering an era where edge computing needs AI and high-performance computing (HPC) to stay up with these new capabilities. Multimodality is becoming more and more common in contemporary edge AI real-time applications. High-speed input/output, graphics, streaming technologies, vision and imaging AI, and more are all included. It is quite hard to create and maintain these applications [28–30]. Climbing them is more difficult. Artificial intelligence and high-performance computing are not necessarily related; in this chapter, we will explain what the combined use of HPC and AI offers to both the enterprise and scientific computing landscape. Jump in to see whether mixing these technologies would make a worthwhile investment for your use case.

9.2.1 Overview of Converged HPC Infrastructure and Edge AI

Versatility is another basic thought. Edge computing in information centers empowers an increment in associated gadgets by decreasing the strain on centralized foundations [22, 23]. This move toward localized handling opens entryways to a superior gadget network shown in Figure 9.5.

Nowadays, retailers are utilizing edge AI to make strides in client involvement and stock administration and to analyze client behavior for ideal item arrangement in walkways. With edge computing's quick information preparation, retailers can present voice requests or product-search functionalities to improve shopping involvement.

So also, edge-based AI is also being utilized in mechanical settings to guarantee useful security, counting collision location and shirking for AMRs, robot-human interaction, and recognizing breaches in obstructions or erroneous utilization of individual defensive gear. High-performance edge computing permits AI applications to be tried and tested [with] inside controlled situations without influencing the rest of an organization's operations. Once victory is accomplished, it can be scaled in advance,

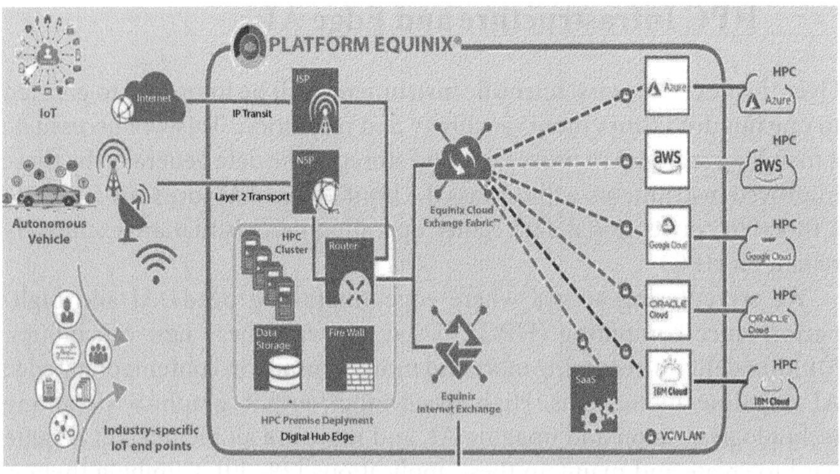

Figure 9.5 HPC+ Edge AI.

and conveyed by combining the control of information center models. This could lead to iterative changes, which can include up to major changes in productivity and adequacy [9].

Once the models have been tuned in and are prepared for generation, the AI-powered shrewd application can be conveyed (and naturally upgraded as required). The shrewdly AI-powered application running at the edge can presently help make real-time choices based on the information it is handling. The edge gadget keeps up a neighborhood demonstration, empowering information examination and decision-making at the point of the information era. Furthermore, it can occasionally share recently collected information from sensors, cameras, and other sources with the worldwide demonstration at the center information center. This guarantees that the AI/ML show remains precise by consolidating the most recent information overhauls as essential dispersed AI permits for the quick emphasis of AI models, giving conclusion to clients with the foremost up-to-date forms. Moreover, this approach empowers low-power gadgets to get to AI capabilities by interfacing with an adjacent "supercloud" information center for induction.

With expansive dispersed systems and code, information can be brought near to the 6G organized, near to the conclusion client, guaranteeing there's no punishment no matter where the conclusion client is. Dispersed computing system-based information centers around the world are connected through the edge that works as an enormous framework capable of moving information and code around for the most elevated execution. AI specialists reliably hook with adjusting precision and achievability. Conducting additional model training directly at the edge, rather than only in centralized servers. In case the conclusion user's gadget needs the computational capabilities to perform deduction, it must communicate with the centralized framework to overcome its computational restrictions. Such strategies unavoidably present information exchange costs and open up the hazard of operational disappointment. Be that as it may, if edge gadgets are taught inside information center foundations to handle AI forms requesting tall computational control amid the induction stage, it altogether supports the general application's unwavering quality.

It's challenging to resolve the issue because advancements in AI, such as generative AI and large language models (LLMs), only increase the demand for computing resources. Whereas there's developing mindfulness of the carbon impression issue related with the IT industry, and numerous organizations are taking noteworthy steps to address the issue. Semiconductor companies are contributing intensely to chip plans that improve vitality productivity for processors and memory models. In expansion, hyperscale's such as Amazon Web Administrations, Purplish blue, Google Cloud and other cloud suppliers are continually finding better energizing approaches to maximize vitality proficiency through operational optimization. Be that as it may, as request for computing assets proceeds to develop and gets to be more conveyed among numerous cloud situations, it's apparent that organizations require a more bound together and comprehensive approach to observing, measuring and optimizing the carbon effect of their computing utilization. And, out of the blue, the key to really minimizing computer-related carbon outflows might lie in a program organization's capacity to organize and oversee their cloud situations.

9.2.2 Proposed Converged Super Hybrid [CPU+GPU] HPC Infrastructure and Edge AI

Figure 9.6 shows that the design required for HPC executions has numerous likenesses with AI usage. Both utilize tall levels of computing and capacity, expansive memory capacity, transfer speed, and high-bandwidth textures to realize what comes about, regularly by preparing enormous information sets of increasing size. Profound learning could be an extraordinary coordinate for issues tended to by HPC that include exceptionally expansive, multidimensional information sets. For example, Quantify used

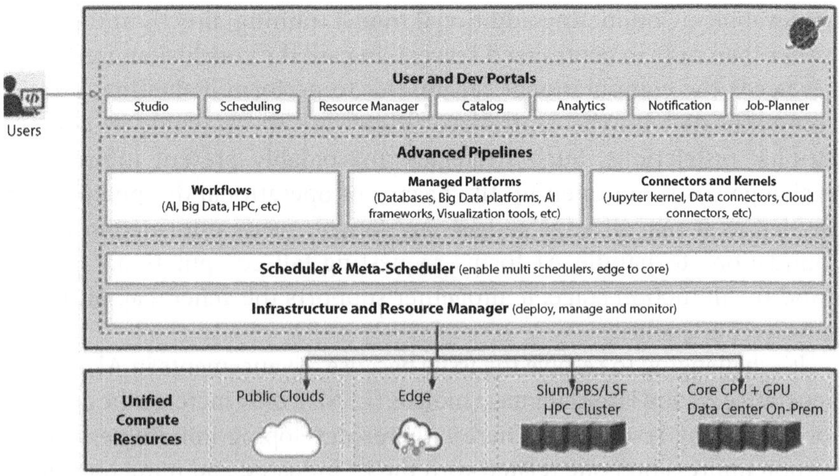

Figure 9.6 Proposed HPC and edge AI infrastructure.

Intel-powered AI to make derivative valuation in financial markets 700 times faster than traditional methods, giving almost real-time results for common valuation tasks.

AI and HPC are being combined seriously across the HPC field. Later achievements of this program have been detailed in plasma material science [10], cosmology [11], gravitational wave astronomy [12], tall vitality material science [13], multi courier astronomy [14], materials science [15], information administration of unstructured datasets [16, 17], and hereditary information [18], among others.

These accomplishments share a common string, specifically, the calculations created to quicken the preparing of AI models in HPC stages have a solid exploratory component. To date, there's no thorough system to compel the perfect set of hyper-parameters that guarantees fast merging and ideal execution of AI models as the number of GPU hubs is expanded to quicken the preparing organize. Moreover, it is standard that conveyed preparing calculations in HPC stages are benchmarked utilizing idealized neural arrange models [19].

9.2.3 Innovation in 6G IOT

To address the longer-term needs, 6G networks will incorporate the advantages of 5G models while also using contemporary innovations. This indicates that various innovations will impact 6G communication frameworks.

Due to the IoT devices' rapid expansion in providing keen cities with remote networks, there is an unforeseen need for improvement in order to provide thick systems with a reliable network [24]. The demonstration of flying automobiles [25], enhanced reality [26], and healthcare [27] necessitate high data transfer rates, cellular energy, and moo idleness conceivable with the imagine 6G systems as shown in Figure 9.7.

As a significant advancement in connecting disparate electronic devices with distant systems, IoT aims to link everything to the Web and create a connected world where information detection, preparation, and communications are carried out organically and without human intervention [20]. In conclusion, users can benefit from IoT data gathered from ubiquitous mobile devices, such as sensors, actuators, smart phones, PCs, and radio frequency identification devices [21].

Compared to the 5G versatile organize, the following era 6G versatile organize is anticipated to donate enormous scope and improved versatility to back IoT network and benefit conveyance. The Lead research program

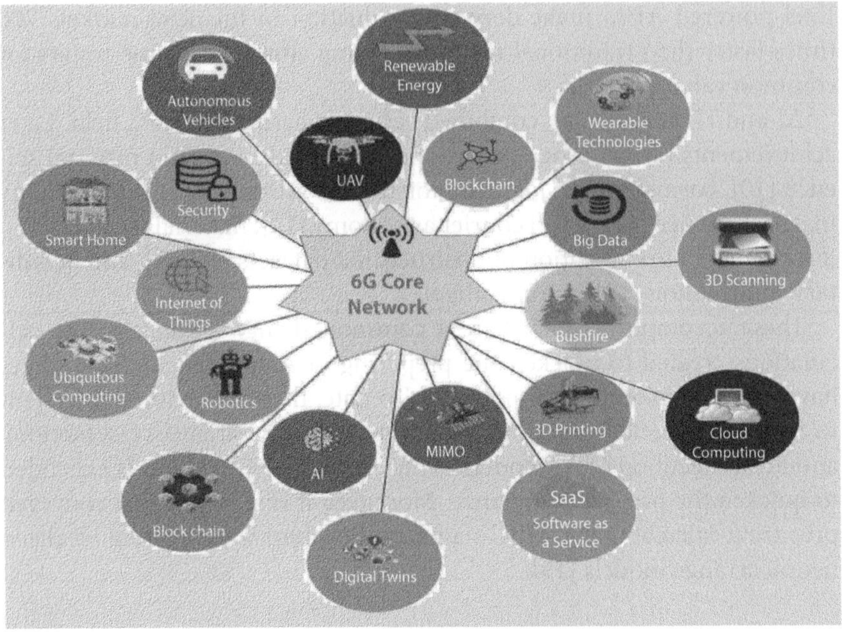

Figure 9.7 Visualize 6G based applications.

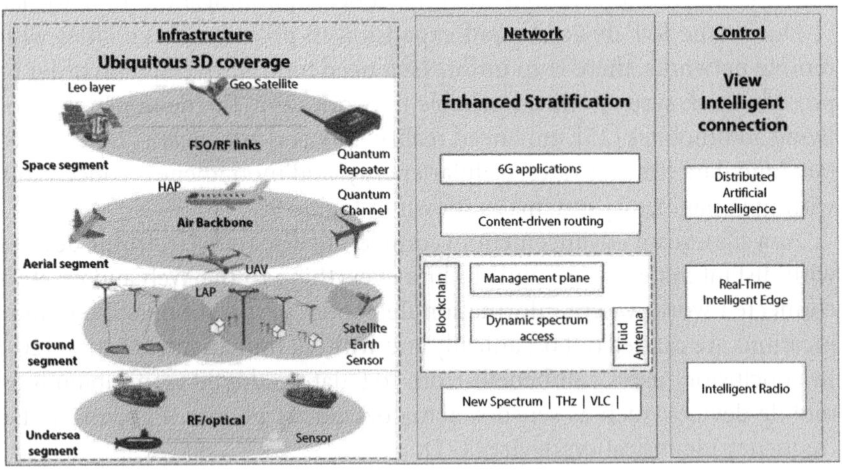

Figure 9.8 6G IoT based architecture.

for 6G was initially carried out to co-create an environment for developing next-generation communication technologies and fostering collaboration between industry, academia, and government.

The core of the 6G remote systems will be revealed by the explanation of underutilized worldview alterations. The global reach of the space, ground, discuss, and ocean coordinate systems will be provided by the 6G systems. In Figure 9.8 [31–33], the 6G engineering outline is shown. By using lackey communication, unmanned aerial vehicles, and maritime communication, the reach and functionality of distant communication systems may be greatly increased.

9.3 Performance Optimization

9.3.1 AI-Based Intra-Node and Internode Communication on CPUs and GPUs-Based HPC Infrastructure

The explanation of unused worldview shifts will give the pith of the 6G remote systems. 6G systems will connect networks across space, land, air, and sea worldwide. The outline of the 6G engineering is displayed in Figure 9.9 [31]. The scope and run of the remote communication systems can be amplified broadly through the utilization of lackey communication, UAVs, and sea communication.

Software engineers can create flexible parallel programs using MPI, which describes send/receive, one-sided, and group communication operations. MPI is compatible with nearly all parallel computing designs. The most well-known MPI executions also provide highly optimized

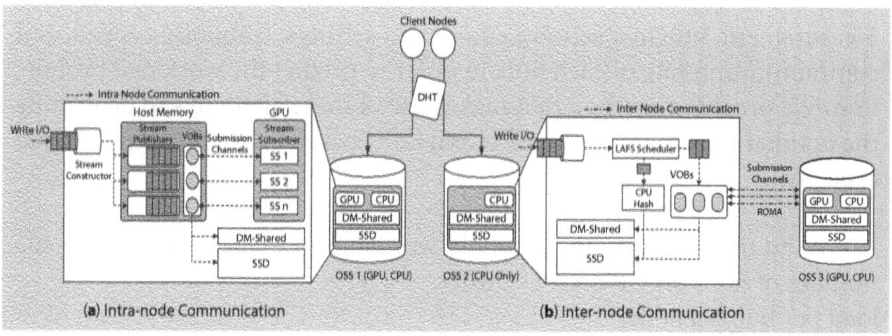

Figure 9.9 Intra-node and Inter-node Communication.

intranode communication between centers and processors on the same hub, even though MPI is mostly renowned for its high-performance internode communication.

MPICH2 is an open-source usage of MPI standard. Planned for high-performance communication, MPICH2 is built on the Enemy communication subsystem [32], and bolsters intranode message-passing through shared memory and internode communication by utilizing arrange modules outlined for systems. The adversary organize module API productively underpins high-performance RDMA-style systems as well as TCP. MPICH2 abstracts associations between two forms with a virtual channel information structure that stores state data related to the association. In this work, we center on intranode GPU local communication and thus will adjust fundamentally to foe.

These days, programming clusters with GPU speeding agents are commonly used for the combined CUDA+MPI parallel programming show. In this paradigm, internode parallelism is managed using MPI, while intranode parallelism is conveyed within the CUDA display.

9.3.2 Optimal Workload Distribution

In this section, an ideal workload conveyance approach is shown, where each hub of a homogenous CPU/GPU cluster receives the task. If we assign the CPU too much work, it won't be enough to keep it busy between memory exchange and GPU part delivery, and the inactivity won't be effectively concealed. However, in the unlikely event that we give the CPU too much work at that point, the GPU component must wait for the CPU to finish the assignments and produce the result.

We are addressing the CPU and GPU's equipment details and computing speed in this effort. We are considering several factors, including issue measurement, hub inspections, equipment settings, computing speed, and communication rate of each hub, in order to predict the workload proportion. We present a method that makes use of these attributes to determine the optimal workload for the CPU and GPU based on their computational capacity.

Let W be the measure of the whole workload per cluster, $Nnode$ be the number of hubs on CPU-GPU cluster.
load per hub is $Lnode$,
NC speaks to a number of cores.

when we relegate the complete HPC application workload *W* to hubs-based cluster, we got to compute the stack for person hubs *Lnodei* utilizing condition 9.1 by considering factors like the number of nodes with the same capability *Nnode* and the workload size W. Achieving a viable workload split requires taking the CPU and GPU's compute speeds into account. If this isn't done, there will usually be severe load awkwardness because the fast GPU will keep waiting for the moderate CPU to finish its workload, which results in deficient execution.

$$Lnode = \frac{W}{Nnode} \tag{9.1}$$

target HPC applications on individual nodes in a cluster are computed using Equation 9.1. Hence, the load on the CPU [*LCP*] is computed using equation

$$Lcp = Lnode \times \frac{CP_{flops}}{(nodeFlops)} \tag{9.2}$$

nodeFlops are nothing but the sum of CPU flops and GPU flops present in that node then the Equation 9.1 can be re written as shown in 9.2

$$Lcp = Lnode \times \frac{CP_{flops}}{(CP_{flops} + GP_{flops})} \tag{9.3}$$

$$LCP_{core} = \frac{LCP}{Nc} \tag{9.4}$$

where,

$LCP - load\ on\ cpu$

To find out the load on GPU Equation (9.3) can be modified as follows

$$L_{GPi} = (L_{nodei} - L_{CPi}) \tag{9.5}$$

Equation 9.5 is now used to obtain the load on GPUs, or *LGPi*.

Assign the remaining workload to the available number of GPUs in the corresponding nodes in a cluster after calculating the proportion of the workload ratio to the CPU.

9.3.3 Evaluation of Performance

Performance improvement through efficient use of computational resources is the main objective of hybrid implementation. The performance of the application is evaluated in this work using GFLOPs and execution time. The formula is used to calculate the GFLOPs.

$$Gflops = \left[\frac{Nop}{ET}\right] * 10^{-9}$$

where,

Nop= Number of operations

ET= Execution time in seconds

AI disclosure statement: The author acknowledges the use of AI-based tools for minor language editing or grammatical correction. However, all intellectual contributions, analyses, and conclusions presented in this chapter are entirely the author's own.

References

1. Bibri, S.E., Alahi, A., Sharifi, A., Krogstie, J., Environmentally sustainable smart cities and their converging AI, IoT, and big data technologies and solutions an integrated approach to an extensive literature review. *Energy Inf.*, 9, 1, 1–43, 2023, https://doi.org/10.1186/s42162-023-00259-2.
2. Gourisaria, M.K., Jee, G., Harshvardhan, G.M., Konar, D., Singh, P.K., Artificially intelligent and sustainable smart cities, in: *Sustainable Smart Cities. Studies in Computational Intelligence*, vol. 942, P.K. Singh, M. Paprzycki, M. Essaaidi, S. Rahimi (Eds.), Springer, Cham, 2023.
3. Iris-Panagiota, E. and Egleton, T.E., Artificial intelligence for sustainable smart cities, in: *Handbook of Research on Applications of AI, Digital Twin, and Internet of Things for Sustainable Development*, B.K. Mishra (Ed.), pp. 1–11, IGI Global, 2023, 10.4018/978-1-6684-6821-0.ch001.
4. Yigitcanlar, T., Mehmood, R., Corchado, J.M., Green artificial intelligence: toward an efficient Sustain. *Equit. Technol. Smart Cities Futures*, 13, 16, 8952, 2021, https://www.mdpi.com/2071-1050/13/16/895.
5. Ab-Rahman, A., Hamid, U.Z., Chin, T.A., Emerging technologies with disruptive effects: a review. *Perintis e-J.*, 7, 111–128, 2017.
6. *Greenfield Radical Technologies: the Design of Everyday Life*, Verso Books, 2018.
7. Edge AI, https://blogs.nvidia.com/blog/what-is-edge-ai.

8. Multicore processor, 2023, https://www.techtarget.com/searchdatacenter/definition/multi-core-processor.
9. high-performance computing (HPC)THINK, 2024, https://www.ibm.com/topics/hpc, https://venturebeat.com/ai/how-high-performance-computing-at-the-edge-is-reshaping-data- center-intelligence/.
10. Svyatkovskiy, A., Kates-Harbeck, J., Tang, W., Training distributed deep recurrent neural networks with mixed precision on gpu clusters, in: *Proceedings of the Machine Learning on HPC Environments, MLHPC'17*, New York, NY, USA, Association for Computing Machinery, 2017.
11. Khan, A., Huerta, E.A., Wang, S., Gruendl, R., Jennings, E., Zheng, H., Deep learning at scale for the construction of galaxy catalogs in the Dark Energy Survey. *Phy. Lett. B.*, 795, 248–58, 2019.
12. Hongyu, S., Huerta, E.A., Zhao, Z., Deep Learning at Scale for Gravitational Wave 13. Parameter Estimation of Binary Black Hole Mergers, arXiv e-prints, page arXiv:1903.01998, Mar 2019.
14. Guest, D., Cranmer, K., Whiteson, D., Deep learning and its application to lhc physics. *Annu. Rev. Nucl. Part. Sci.*, 68, 1, 161–81, 2018.
15. Huerta, E.A., *et al.*, Enabling real-time multi-messenger astrophysics discoveries with deep learning. *Nat. Rev. Phys.*, 1, 600–8, 2019.
16. Ward, L., Blaiszik, B., Foster, I., Assary, R.S., Narayanan, B., Curtiss, L., Machine learning prediction of accurate atomization energies of organic molecules from low-fdelity quantum chemical calculations. *MRS Commun.*, 9, 3, 891–9, 2019.
17. Marini, L., Gutierrez-Polo, I., Kooper, R., Satheesan, S.P., Burnette, M., Lee, J., Nicholson, T., Zhao, Y., McHenry, K., Clowder: Open source data management for long tail data, in: *Proceedings of the Practice and Experience on Advanced Research Computing, PEARC'18*, New York, NY, USA, Association for Computing Machinery, 2018.
18. Padhy, S., Jansen, G., Alameda, J., Black, E., Diesendruck, L., Dietze, M., Kumar, P., Kooper, R., Lee, J., Liu, R., Marciano, R., Marini, L., Mattson, D., Minsker, B., Navarro, C., Slavenas, M., Sullivan, W., Votava, J., Zharnitsky, I., McHenry, K., Brown dog: Leveraging everything towards autocuration, in: *2015 IEEE International Conference on Big Data (Big Data)*, pp. 493–500, Oct 2015.
19. Blatti, C., Emad, A., Berry, M.J., Gatzke, L., Epstein, M., Lanier, D., Rizal, P., Ge, J., Liao, X., Sobh, O., Lambert, M., Post, C.S., Xiao, J., Groves, P., Epstein, A.T., Chen, X., Srinivasan, S., Lehnert, E., Kalari, K.R., Wang, L., Weinshilboum, R.M., Song, J.S., Jongeneel, C.V., Han, J., Ravaioli, U., Sobh, N., Bushell, C.B., Sinha, S., Knowledge-guided analysis of 'omics' data using the KnowEnG cloud platform. *PLoS Biol.*, 18, 1, e3000583, 2020. https://doi.org/10.1371/journal.pbio.3000583.
20. He, K., Zhang, X., Ren, S., Sun, J., Deep residual learning for image recognition, 2015.

21. Saeed, N., Al-Naffouri, T.Y., Alouini, M.-S., Around the World of IoT/ Climate Monitoring Using Internet of X-Things. *IEEE Internet Things Mag.*, 3, 2, 82–83, June 2020, doi: 10.1109/MIOT.2020.9125423.
22. Al-Jarrah, M.A., Yaseen, M.A., Al-Dweik, A., Dobre, O.A., Alsusa, E., Decision Fusion for IoT-Based Wireless Sensor Networks. *IEEE Internet Things J.*, 7, 2, 1313–1326, Feb. 2020, doi: 10.1109/JIOT.2019.2954720.
23. Internet Available: of Things 2016, 2016, Cisco, [Online]. https://www.cisco.com/c/dam/en/us/products/collateral/se/internetof-things/at-a-glance-c45-731471.pdf.
24. Number to 125 of Connected billion IoT by Devices 2030, will 2021. Surge [Online].
25. Available: https://news.ihsmarkit.com/prviewer /releaseonly/slug/number-connected-iot-devices-will-surge-125-billion -2030.
26. Liang, J., Li, L., Zhao, C., A transfer learning approach for compressed sensing in 6G-IoT. *IEEE Internet Things J.*, 8, 20, 15276–15283, 2021.
27. Saeed, N., Al-Naffouri, T.Y., Alouini, M.-S., Wireless communication for flying cars. *Front. Commun. Networks*, 2, 689881, 2021.
28. Petrov, V., Gapeyenko, M., Paris, S., Marcano, A., Pedersen, K.I., Extended reality (XR) over 5G and 5G-advanced new radio: Standardization, applications, and trends, *arXiv preprint arXiv:2203.02242*, 2022.
29. Lu, Y. and Zheng, X., 6G: A survey on technologies, scenarios, challenges, and the related issues. *J. Ind. Inf. Integr.*, 19, 100158, 2020.
30. Huang, T., Yang, W., Wu, J., Ma, J., Zhang, X., Zhang, D., A survey on green 6G network: architecture and technologies. *IEEE Access*, 7, 175758–175768, 2019.
31. Buntinas, Mercier, G., Gropp, W., Implementation and shared-memory evaluation of MPICH2 over the Nemesis communication subsystem, in: *Recent Advances in Parallel Virtual Machine and Message Passing Interface, ser. Lecture Notes in Computer Science*, vol. 4192, B. Mohr, J. Trff, J. Worringen, J. Dongarra (Eds.), pp. 86–95, Springer Berlin, Heidelberg, 2006, doi 10.1007/118.
32. Bhambri, P. and Rani, S., Issues Related to Chatbots, in: *Design and Development of Emerging Chatbot Technology*, D. Darwish (Ed.), pp. 130–47, IGI Global, 2024, https://doi.org/10.4018/979-8-3693-1830-0.ch008.
33. Sridhar, V., Rani, S., Pareek, P.K., Bhambri, P., Elngar, A.A. (Eds.), *Blockchain for IoT Systems: Concept, Framework and Applications*, 1st, Chapman and Hall/CRC, 2024, https://doi.org/10.1201/9781003460367.

10

Embedding Privacy into Industrial IoT System

N. Ambika

Department of Computer Science, Jain College Vasavi Campus, Bangalore, India

Abstract

The previous recommendation covers a wide range of categories, including the collection of data from manufacturing execution systems, inspection of equipment in chemical factories, remote expert-supported machine maintenance, and e-commerce warehouse operations. It incorporates industrial wearable technology such as gloves, rings, smart glasses, smart watches, and wearable printers. It is built on three main elements: equipping front-end operators with industrial wearable gadgets, enhancing their capabilities through wearable data-gathering systems and sensors, and improving communication with wireless networks, enabling real-time connections with backend administrators and onsite operators. The project spans e-commerce warehouse operations, remote expert-supported machine maintenance, equipment inspection in chemical plants, and data collection in manufacturing systems. It consists of three primary components, including a cloud-based cyber system with two sections: a cloud-based corporate information system designed for business processes execution, and cloud-based computing resources for carrying out recognition operations that demand substantial computer power, such as voice and gesture recognition. The suggestion enhances security of the network by encrypting the data uniquely. The work enhances security by 11.98%.

***Keywords*:** Sensors, IIoT, business process, cloud-based systems, privacy, hash key generation

Email: ambika.nagaraj76@gmail.com; ORCID: 0000-0003-4452-5514

Sita Rani, Pankaj Bhambri, Balamurugan Balusamy, Rishabha Malviya and Seifedine Kadry (eds.) Edge Intelligence for 6G-Enabled Industrial Internet of Things, (199–216) © 2026 Scrivener Publishing LLC

10.1 Introduction

The Industrial Internet of Things (IIoT) [25, 26] is the game-changing network of interconnected sensors, instruments, and devices transforming industrial operations. By seamlessly collecting, exchanging, and analyzing data, IIoT enhances operational efficiency, boosts productivity, and empowers better decision-making.

Key Components of IIoT

- Sensors and Actuators: The physical layer [13] in IoT is critical for seamless operation. It is comprised of sensors that gather system information and actuators that execute instructions. Actuators are essential for tasks such as door locking, lighting control, user alerting, and temperature regulation. Meanwhile, sensors provide valuable feedback to the system's controller. This controller processes sensor data, computes it, and sends instructions to the actuators. These instructions, based on the variance between sensor readings and desired values, ensure that the system maintains the desired physical quantities. Cutting-edge devices that accurately capture data from the physical environment (e.g., temperature, pressure, vibration) and swiftly execute actions based on that data.
- The term "Internet of Things" describes "connectivity" which refers to the process of uniting intelligent devices and management systems through network connections for creating an automated world without major human participation. The linked network includes various applications such as health monitoring and smart utilities together with integrated logistics which results in a hyper-automated environment. The data collection process from sensors and devices enables operational performance enhancement and increases business process speed while enabling this transformation. The various disciplines encompassed by industrial IIoT applications include motion control as well as machine-to-machine interactions combined with predictive maintenance for smart-grid energy management through big data analytics and smart cities alongside networked medical systems. Mumtaz, *et al.*, [15] are designed to meet a

set of demanding yet interconnected requirements. Robust communication networks (wired or wireless) seamlessly facilitate the exchange of data between devices and centralized systems.

- Data Storage and Analytics [20]: The industrial internet of things system relies heavily on big data since multiple contemporary technologies generate this information. Cyber-Physical Systems (CPS) unite physical production devices with built-in computation capabilities as well as internet-based networking elements. The combination of IoT devices and integration enables IIoT systems to produce extensive raw data streams which result in big data formation. The system functions independently within industrial environments but it also provides integration capability with existing CPS for executing predetermined tasks. The sensing functions of IoT devices enable the production of beneficial big data which proves essential for enterprise value development. The combination of CPS with IoT devices creates vast back-end cloud usage to enable Big Data Analytics (BDA) implementations [3] processes. IIoT systems [9, 15] are responsible for processing big data from both inbound enterprise operations and outbound customer activities. The raw data necessitates further processing in its initial stages to enhance quality and align with IIoT applications. Data wrangling and cleaning methodologies help in selecting relevant datasets from historical data or processing data streams from real-time data. Advanced platforms and software efficiently store, process, and dissect data to derive actionable insights, enabling informed decision-making.
- User Interfaces: As the IIoT continues to grow, machinery in industrial processes is increasingly equipped with advanced capabilities such as sensing, identification, processing, communication, analytics, and networking. These innovations enable the remote monitoring and control of industrial objects across existing network infrastructure. In the realm of process industries, the presence of efficient alarm systems shows a pivotal role in ensuring economic, safe, along with efficient operation. Overloading of alarm systems can significantly disrupt their crucial function. Additionally, in line with modern economic principles, companies are

expected to optimize the utilization of machinery, including the expanding array of IoT devices, with minimal human intervention. This undertaking [7] involves the development and implementation of analytic models using Hadoop/Java and data mining approaches. Data mining encompasses a suite of algorithms for uncovering unknown patterns or relationships within historical datasets. These patterns can be leveraged to classify or forecast situations based on relevant facts or factors. Once these insights are unearthed, they are validated through the application of the identified patterns to new subsets of data. Furthermore, machine learning algorithms can automate the discovery of these patterns and facilitate their application to dynamic decision-making. Intuitive tools and dynamic dashboards empower operators to effortlessly monitor and command industrial processes with precision and control.

Benefits of IIoT

- Enhanced Efficiency: The IIoT devices have become essential for monitoring industrial systems, permitting for the gathering, combined transmission, and analysis of data to drive business intelligence and enhance decision-making processes. However, the reliance on communication networks for transmitting critical industrial information heightens the vulnerability of industrial systems to potential information leakage and security attacks. These devices are widely deployed to monitor manufacturing processes and the environment, with data being sent to a cloud or centralized storage service. Real-time monitoring and automation drive operational efficiency to new heights. The proposal [2] advocates for transferring certificate validation operations from resource-constrained IIoT devices to the IIoT border router, which serves as a more resource-rich networking device through the application of In-Network Computing (INC) and data plane programming (DPP). This strategic approach offers enhanced security and efficiency by effectively leveraging the capabilities of the IIoT border router.
- Economical Operations: Substantial cost savings are obtained *via* predictive maintenance and resource efficiency.

The objective of the initiative [10] is to create an innovative fog federation for industrial networks termed cost-efficient computation offloading (CeCO). CeCO efficiently allocates IIoT data among fog devices under the oversight of a master fog controller, ensuring cost optimization by considering the weighted energy-delay cost of IIoT devices while adhering to various constraints. To effectively process emergency-based service requests and route them to fog devices *via* the shortest path, this research also proposes a frequency control mechanism for IIoT devices, a controller-based device adaptation approach, and a policy-based reinforcement learning strategy. It is obvious from testing data that the CeCO approach performs better than baseline methods, maximizing performance and cost utilization for industrial applications by up to 13% to 18%.

- Superior Safety: Monitoring systems boost workplace safety by swiftly identifying and addressing potential risks. The proposed RSA algorithm [1] boasts of a robust 512-bit four-prime number configuration. Seamless device authentication is achieved through the use of a hash signature. Our innovative resource scheduling as well as security system for IIoT data features quatern comprehensive layers. The IIoT sensing device layer is equipped with cutting-edge devices and sensors, strategically positioned to gather and transmit data to the cloud layer through the gateway. To safeguard against unauthorized access to the IIoT data, a rigorous registration and login process for IIoT devices is implemented. The gateway layer plays a pivotal role in aggregating connectivity, enabling seamless communication between diverse devices and sensors and fostering interoperability across standards, protocol. The fog layer efficiently handles the reception and allocation of tasks in the form of requests from cluster heads, leveraging advanced machine learning algorithms such as the SoftMax deep neural network to allocate tasks to a cloud server. Our cloud layer serves as the ultimate end-user interface, ensuring device authentication, efficient data storage, and seamless decision-making capabilities, empowering users and decision-makers to interact seamlessly.

- Informed Decision Making: Harness data-driven insights for strategic planning and informed decision-making. The first case study [8] involves the optimization of logistic systems using a quantum approximate optimization algorithm. This can be pragmatic to smart factories involved in logistics as well as product shipping. The second case study emphasizes on the execution of a quantum neural network (QNN) in the finance sector. This approach may be used to price-related data analysis, future opportunity discovery, and forecasting in smart factories in a quicker, scalable, and more efficient way. There are four major layers to the system. The first layer, known as the device layer, is made up of many IoT devices and data sources that smart factories utilize to acquire information depending on their individual demands. Names, gender, IP addresses, and identification numbers are examples of customer and personal information that may be included in this data. Quantum terminals, which are small quantum computers with a minimum size of one qubit, are inserted into the second layer, also referred to as the edge layer. These terminals have the capacity to turn classical bits that represent data from the device layer into qubits that the cloud layer quantum cloud server can grasp. This arrangement allows efficient and effective decision-making in smart factories by automatically conducting the required quantum computations at the cloud layer, doing away with the need for quantum programmers or specialists. Additionally, a hybrid quantum-classical model that can conduct hybrid computations is located in the edge layer. The cloud layer, which contains the quantum server, is the final tier of the system. This quantum server, which is run by quantum machines, is in charge of executing the various computations that the smart factory clients have requested.
- Limitless Scalability: IIoT systems seamlessly adapt to evolving industrial needs, ensuring readiness for new challenges and opportunities. In the IoT/IIoT Devices layer [21], a cutting-edge drone diligently monitors weather conditions. It utilizes advanced technology to pre-process weather data before securely transmitting it to the weather station. All transactions are meticulously recorded on a blockchain, with the drone and the base station serving as

integral miners. Furthermore, the AI Services layer enhances decision-making processes using sophisticated AI models. The fusion of edge computing and blockchain technology stands poised to revolutionize the scalability of IIoT.

Project categories [12] include data collecting of manufacturing execution systems, equipment inspection in chemical factories, machine maintenance with remote expert support, and operations of e-commerce warehouses. It incorporates gloves, rings, smart glasses, smart watches, and wearable printers, among other areas of industrial wearable technology. It has three main elements. The front-end operators are furnished with industrial wearable gadgets. Wearable data-gathering systems and sensors improve their capacity. Wireless networks improve their capacity for communication. It can build a real-time link with backend administrators and other onsite operators. Project areas include e-commerce warehouse operations, machine maintenance with remote expert help, equipment inspection in chemical plants, and data collection in manufacturing systems. These projects include wearable printers, gloves, rings, smart glasses, and smartwatches. It consists of three primary components. Cloud-based Cyber System is divided into two sections. The first is a corporate information system that is cloud-based. The primary function of this system is to execute business processes. The equivalent of actual objects and people are also digitally registered. Cloud-based computing [5, 17] resources make up the second. The recognition operations are not completed on the front-end side because the recognition of human intentions (such as voice and gesture recognition) requires a large amount of computer power.

The suggestion enhances security of the network by encrypting the data uniquely. They derive the parameters from the device number and the location of the respective nodes using Merkle tree algorithm. This is inserted into the encryption algorithm to derive the encryption key. This key is used to encrypt the data and system creates a hash key using the device number, which is embedded at the end of the device. The work enhances security by 11.98%.

Drawbacks

- The system may require some amount of human intervention which will lead to manipulation of data (compromised users).

10.2 Background

Homomorphic encryption [18] is a groundbreaking method that enables secure data processing while maintaining encryption. Through this innovative technique, computations can be performed on encrypted data, ensuring data privacy and security.

- Key Generation: A public as well as private key pair is produced for encryption and decryption, respectively.
- Encryption: The plaintext data is encrypted using the public key, resulting in ciphertext.
- Computation: Specific algebraic operations (addition, multiplication, etc.) can be performed directly on the ciphertext, corresponding to equivalent operations on the plaintext.
- Decryption: The result of homomorphic operations is decrypted using the private key to obtain the final plaintext result. This powerful encryption technique allows for secure data processing, offering peace of mind and confidence in data privacy and security.

A Merkle tree [4, 6, 11], called as hash tree, is a powerful data structure in the fields of cryptography and computer science. Its purpose is to efficiently and securely verify the integrity and consistency of data. The tree's structure is based on a binary format, with each leaf node representing a hash of a data block and each non-leaf node representing a hash of its child nodes.

Working of a Merkle tree
Structure of a Merkle Tree:
The tree's leaves are where the hashes of the real data bits are saved. The numbers of each non-leaf node's child nodes are combined to form the node itself. The Merkle root, the largest node, is a picture of the consistency of the whole collection.

Construction of a Merkle Tree:

- Hashing Data Blocks: Each data block (e.g., transaction data) is hashed to produce the leaf nodes.

- Pairing and Hashing: Hashes are paired and hashed again to form the parent nodes. For example, for data blocks D1, D2, D3, D4, the corresponding hashes are H(D1), H(D2), H(D3), H(D4). These hashes are paired and hashed to form the parent nodes.

Verification with a Merkle Tree:

- Merkle Proof: To verify a specific data block without revealing the entire dataset, a Merkle proof is used. This proof includes the sibling hashes along the path from the leaf node to the root.

Verification Process: The verifier can reconstruct the path up to the root by hashing the data block with the provided proof hashes and then comparing the result to the Merkle root. A match between the reconstructed root and the stored Merkle root verifies the data block's inclusion in the dataset.

10.3 Literature Survey

The work of Zolanvari, Yang, Khan, Jain, & Meskin, [22] is a cutting-edge, high-performing XAI model that sets the standard for transparency and accuracy without compromising the selection as well as performance of the primary AI. This model offers lightning-fast reasoning on numerical data, making it ideal for real-time numerical applications. With a focus on realistic along with up-to-date datasets for network-based IDSs, TRUST XAI is a versatile as well as powerful tool which can be applied to any complex AI model, including artificial neural networks with specific configurations.

The designed privacy-preserving architecture [19] encompasses three fundamental layers: the device, network, and application levels, respectively. Important parameters, including the threshold value, transaction value, and trust score, are rigorously initialized in the unique reputation-based trust estimate technique. The amount of deals is used to calculate the reputation score once the trust score value and the total number of collected traits have been determined. Transaction sensor data is widely obtained as output during the off-chain data storage process, and the accessible hash value is made. The content-addressed hash value is estimated and safely saved in the server's InterPlanetary File System (IPFS) if it is found to be genuine. The information is then safely saved by sensor devices in the distributed hash table, and the targeted hash value is sent to the BlockCloud and BlockFog platforms for smooth data access activities in the future.

Project categories [12] include data collecting of manufacturing execution systems, equipment inspection in chemical factories, machine maintenance with remote expert support, and operations of e-commerce warehouses. It incorporates gloves, rings, smart glasses, smart watches, and wearable printers, among other areas of industrial wearable technology. It has three main elements. The front-end operators are furnished with industrial wearable gadgets. Wearable data-gathering systems and sensors improve their capacity. Wireless networks improve their capacity for communication. It can build a real-time link with backend administrators and other onsite operators. Project areas include e-commerce warehouse operations, machine maintenance with remote expert help, equipment inspection in chemical plants, and data collection in manufacturing systems. These projects include wearable printers, gloves, rings, smart glasses, and smartwatches. It consists of three primary components. Cloud-based Cyber System is divided into two sections. The first is a corporate information system that is cloud-based. The primary function of this system is to execute business processes. The equivalent of actual objects and people are also digitally registered. Cloud-based computing resources make up the second. The recognition operations are not completed on the front-end side because the recognition of human intentions (such as voice and gesture recognition) requires a large amount of computer power.

The lifecycle [14] consists of two key stages development, operation, and maintenance phases. Creating suitable security guides and suggestions during these phases is vital. Either the asset owner and service providers may integrate normal commercial things into their system design or they may have specifically made goods produced for their system. The maintenance stage, which includes resolving security concerns and software upgrades, may include informing the asset owner, service providers, and product suppliers of security-related events that impact the functioning IIoT systems and components. Each organization must establish and apply the essential security problem management methodologies and processes in its cybersecurity maintenance plans.

10.4 Previous System

The recommendation [12] encompasses several critical aspects of IIoT, targeting diverse industrial applications such as:

1. Manufacturing Execution Systems (MES) Data Collection: Harnessing IIoT for real-time data collection from MES to elevate production monitoring and control.
2. Equipment Inspection in Chemical Factories: Employing IIoT sensors and devices for thorough equipment inspections to ensure safety and optimize efficiency.
3. Remote Expert-Supported Machine Maintenance: Facilitating remote experts to assist in machine maintenance through connected devices and real-time data sharing.
4. E-commerce Warehouse Operations: Enhancing warehouse operations with IIoT-enabled tracking, monitoring, and automation technologies.

The integration of industrial wearable technology plays a pivotal role in IIoT implementation. This includes:

- Wearable Gadgets: Gloves, rings, smart glasses, smart watches, and wearable printers specifically designed for industrial use.
- Wearable Data-Gathering Systems: Sensors embedded in wearables to collect and transmit data in real-time.
- Enhanced Communication: Wireless networks enabling seamless, real-time communication between front-end operators and backend administrators.

The IIoT project focuses on three primary areas:

- Empowering Front-End Operators:
  - Cutting-Edge Wearable Gadgets: Equipping operators with state-of-the-art wearable devices to enhance efficiency and streamline data collection.
  - Enhanced Capabilities: Elevating operator functionality through real-time data and sensory inputs.
- Wearable Data-Gathering Systems and Sensors:

    - Comprehensive Data Collection: Integration of sensors in wearables to gather crucial operational data.
    - Real-Time Monitoring: Enabling real-time monitoring and feedback mechanisms.
- Improved Communication Networks:
    - Robust Wireless Networks: Establishment of reliable wireless communication channels for seamless real-time data exchange and coordination.
    - Integrated Backend Systems: Ensuring seamless connectivity between on-site operators and backend systems for smooth operations.

Cloud-Based Cyber System: The cornerstone of our IIoT framework is a cutting-edge cloud-based cyber system, which includes:

- Corporate Information System:
    - Efficient Business Processes Execution: A cloud-based system designed to manage and execute various business processes seamlessly.
- Cloud-Based Computing Resources:
    - Advanced Recognition Operations: Utilizing cloud computing power for demanding recognition tasks such as voice and gesture recognition.
    - Streamlined Data Processing: Ensuring scalable and efficient processing of the enormous quantity of data produced by IIoT devices and sensors.

10.5 Proposed System

The work follows the previous work [12]. Table 10.1 covers the assumptions of the work. Table 10.2 contains the notations of the work.

- *Encryption stage-* All the sensors are responsible to send the readings to the server. They derive the parameters from the device number and the location of the respective nodes using Merkle tree algorithm. This is inserted into the encryption algorithm to originate the encryption key. This key is used to encrypt the data and system creates a hash key using the device number, which is embedded at the end of the device. Table 10.3. represents of algorithm used to generate Encryption key. Table 10.4 represents algorithm to generate hash key.

Table 10.1 Assumptions of the work.

• All the sensing devices sending readings are capable of encrypting data using homomorphic encryption. They obtain the parameters from the device number (unique).
• They embed the hash key of the device number at the end of the message.

Table 10.2 Notations used in the system.

Notations	Description
N_1	Node
L_1	Location of the device
D_1	Device number
E_1	Encryption key
H_1	Hash key
M_A	Merkle tree algorithm
P_1	Parameter

Table 10.3 Algorithm used to generate encryption key.

- *Step 1* – Input the parameters to the algorithm (location details -24 bits; Device number- 30 bits)
- *Step 2* – Add 6 '0' bits to the end of location details to make it 30 bits
- *Step 3* – Insert location details in even position of resultant bits and device number in odd position of resultant bits
- *Step 4* – Apply mathematical function {in this work we have applied the following function - $\sin^{-1} \sum_0^{60} \int_0^2 \textit{Resultant bits}$

Table 10.4 Algorithm to generate hash key.

- *Step 1* – Input the parameters to the algorithm (location details -24 bits; Device number- 30 bits, data bits -262 bits)
- *Step 2* – Truncate all the bits (316 bits -resultant bits)
- *Step 3* – Divide the resultant bits into 4 halves
- *Step 4* – Xor first and second halve bits (resultant 1 -79 bits)
- *Step 5* – Xor third and fourth halve bits (Resultant 2-79 bits)
- *Step 6* – Apply right circular shift on resultant 1 bits (4 bits right circular shift)
- *Step 7* – Apply left circular shift on resultant 2 bits (4 bits left circular shift)
- *Step 8* – Apply Xor on resultant 1 and resultant 2 bits to obtain hash key

10.6 Analysis of the Work

The previous recommendation [12] covers a wide range of categories, including the collection of data from manufacturing execution systems, inspection of equipment in chemical factories, remote expert-supported machine maintenance, and e-commerce warehouse operations. It incorporates industrial wearable technology such as gloves, rings, smart glasses, smart watches, and wearable printers. It is built on three main elements: equipping front-end operators with industrial wearable gadgets, enhancing their capabilities through wearable data-gathering systems and sensors, and improving communication with wireless networks, enabling real-time connections with backend administrators and onsite operators. The project spans e-commerce warehouse operations, remote expert-supported machine maintenance, equipment inspection in chemical plants, and data collection in manufacturing systems [16, 23, 24]. It consists of three primary components, including a cloud-based cyber system with two sections: a cloud-based corporate information system designed for business processes execution, and cloud-based computing resources for carrying out recognition operations that demand substantial computer power, such as voice and gesture recognition. The suggestion enhances security of the network by encrypting the data uniquely. They derive the parameters from the device number and the location of the respective nodes using Merkle tree algorithm. This is inserted into the encryption algorithm to derive the encryption key. This key is used to encrypt the data and system creates a hash key using the device number, which is embedded at the end of the device. The work enhances security by 11.98%. Figure 10.1 portrays the same.

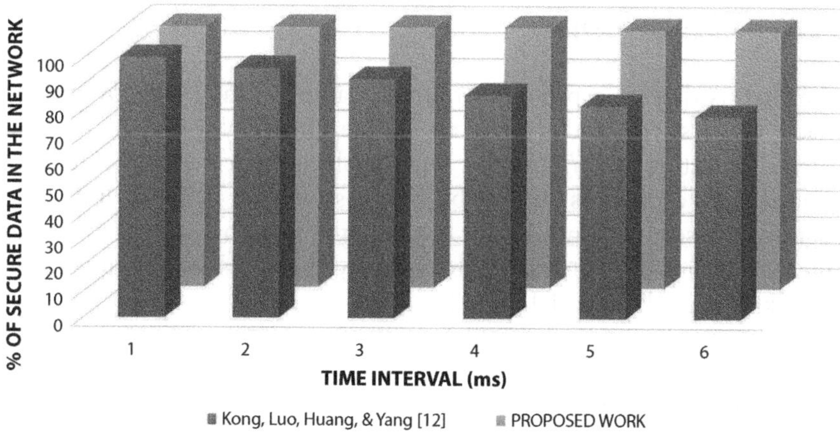

Figure 10.1 Comparison of secure data in the network. *[alt-text – Different colour of bars]*

10.7 Simulation

The work is simulated in NS2. Table 10.5 contains the parameters used in the work.

Table 10.5 Parameters used in the work.

Description	Parameters
Dimension of the network	200m*200m
Number of nodes in the network	5
Number of compromised nodes	2
Length of location	24 bits
Length of device number	30 bits
Length of encryption key	300 bits
Length of hash key	79 bits
Length of data bits	262 bits
Time of simulation	60 m

10.8 Future Scope

The IIoT is driving a profound transformation in industries by linking machines, systems, and devices to elevate efficiency, productivity, and safety. The future of IIoT herald's remarkable advancements in efficiency, productivity, as well as sustainability across a wide range of industrial sectors. The seamless integration of cutting-edge technologies, enhanced interoperability, and fortified cybersecurity measures will be pivotal in unlocking the full potential of IIoT.

10.9 Conclusion

The previous recommendation covers a wide range of categories, including collecting data from manufacturing execution systems, inspecting equipment in chemical factories, providing remote expert-supported machine maintenance, and managing e-commerce warehouse operations. It involves the use of industrial wearable technology such as gloves, rings, smart glasses, smart watches, and wearable printers. The recommendation is based on three main elements: equipping front-end operators with industrial wearable gadgets, enhancing their capabilities through wearable data-gathering systems and sensors, and improving communication with wireless networks to enable real-time connections with backend administrators and onsite operators. The project spans e-commerce warehouse operations, remote expert-supported machine maintenance, equipment inspection in chemical plants, and data collection in manufacturing systems. It consists of three primary components, including a cloud-based cyber system with two sections: a cloud-based corporate information system designed for business process execution, and cloud-based computing resources for carrying out recognition operations that require substantial computer power, such as voice and gesture recognition. The suggestion enhances network security by encrypting the data uniquely. It derives the parameters from the device number and the location of the respective nodes using the Merkle tree algorithm. This information is then inserted into the encryption algorithm to derive the encryption key, which is used to encrypt the data. The system also creates a hash key using the device number, which is embedded at the end of the device. This approach enhances security by 11.98%.

AI disclosure statement: The author confirms that no artificial intelligence (AI)-generated content or AI-assisted writing tools were used in the preparation of this chapter (including summaries and the abstract). All text, analysis, and conclusions are the result of the author's original work.

References

1. Abuhasel, K.A. and Khan, M.A., A secure industrial internet of things (IIoT) framework for resource management in smart manufacturing. *IEEE Access*, 8, 117354–64, 2020.
2. Atutxa, A., Astorga, J., Barcelo, M., Urbieta, A., Jacob, E., Improving efficiency and security of IIoT communications using in-network validation of server certificate. *Comput. Ind.*, 144, 103802, 2023.
3. Babar, M., Alshehri, M.D., Tariq, M.U., Ullah, F., Khan, A., Uddin, M.I., *et al.*, IoT-Enabled Big Data Analytics Architecture for Multimedia Data Communications. *Wirel. Commun. Mob. Comput.*, 2021, 1–9, 2021.
4. Chelladurai, U. and Pandian, S., Hare: A new hash-based authenticated reliable and efficient modified merkle tree data structure to ensure integrity of data in the healthcare systems. *J. Ambient Intell. Hum. Comput.*, 1–15, 2021.
5. Devare, M.H., Cloud Computing and Innovations, in: *Applying Integration Techniques and Methods in Distributed Systems and Technologies*, G. Kecskemeti (Ed.), pp. 1–33, IGI Global, US, 2019.
6. Dhumwad, S., Sukhadeve, M., Naik, C., Manjunath, K.N., Prabhu, S., A peer to peer money transfer using SHA256 and Merkle tree, in: *23rd Annual International Conference in Advanced Computing and Communications (ADCOM)*, Bangalore, India, IEEE, pp. 40–3, 2017.
7. Domova, V. and Dagnino, A., Towards intelligent alarm management in the age of IIoT, in: *Global Internet of Things Summit (GIoTS)*, pp. 1–5, IEEE, Geneva, Switzerland, 2017.
8. El Azzaoui, A., Salim, M., Park, J., Secure and Reliable Big-Data-Based Decision Making Using Quantum Approach in IIoT Systems. *Sensors*, 23, 10, 4852, 2023.
9. Fernández-Caramés, T. and Fraga-Lamas, P., Use Case Based Blended Teaching of IIoT Cybersecurity in the Industry 4.0 Era. *Appl. Sci.*, 10, 16, 5607, 2020.
10. Hazra, A. and Amgoth, T., CeCO: Cost-efficient computation offloading of IoT applications in green industrial fog networks. *IEEE Trans. Ind. Inform.*, 18, 9, 6255–63, 2021.
11. Hu, B. and Gharavi, H., Smart grid mesh network security using dynamic key distribution with merkle tree 4-way handshaking. *IEEE Trans. Smart Grid*, 5, 2, 550–8, 2013.
12. Kong, X.T., Luo, H., Huang, G.Q., Yang, X., Industrial wearable system: the human-centric empowering technology in Industry 4.0. *J. Intell. Manuf.*, 30, 2853–69, 2019.

13. Mohamed, K.S., IoT physical layer: Sensors, actuators, controllers and programming, in: *The Era of Internet of Things: Towards a Smart World*, pp. 21–47, Springer, Cham, 2019.
14. Mugarza, I., Flores, J., Montero, J., Security Issues and Software Updates Management in the Industrial Internet of Things (IIoT) Era. *Sensors*, 20, 24, 7160, 2020.
15. Mumtaz, S., Alsohaily, A., Pang, Z., Rayes, A., Tsang, K.F., Rodriguez, J., Massive Internet of Things for industrial applications: Addressing wireless IIoT connectivity challenges and ecosystem fragmentation. *IEEE Ind. Electron. Mag.*, 11, 1, 28–33, 2017.
16. Munirathinam, S., Industry 4.0: Industrial internet of things (IIoT), in: *Advances in Computers*, vol. 117, no. 1, pp. 129–64, Elsevier, 2020. doi - 10.1016/bs.adcom.2019.10.010.
17. Nagaraj, A., *Introduction to Sensors in IoT and Cloud Computing Applications*, Bentham Science Publishers, UAE, 2021.
18. Ogburn, M., Turner, C., Dahal, P., Homomorphic encryption. *Procedia Comput. Sci.*, 20, 502–9, 2013.
19. Selvarajan, S., Srivastava, G., Khadidos, A.O., Baza, M., Alshehri, A., Lin, J.C., An artificial intelligence lightweight blockchain security model for security and privacy in IIoT systems. *J. Cloud Comput.*, 12, 1, 38, 2023.
20. ur Rehman, M.H., Yaqoob, I., Salah, K., Imran, M., Jayaraman, P.P., Perera, C., The role of big data analytics in industrial Internet of Things. *Future Gener. Comput. Syst.*, 99, 247–59, 2019.
21. Wu, Y., Dai, H.N., Wang, H., Convergence of blockchain and edge computing for secure and scalable IIoT critical infrastructures in industry 4.0. *IEEE Internet Things J.*, 8, 4, 2300–17, 2020.
22. Zolanvari, M., Yang, Z., Khan, K., Jain, R., Meskin, N., Trust xai: Model-agnostic explanations for ai with a case study on iiot security. *IEEE Internet Things J.*, 10, 4, 2967–78, 2021.
23. Bhambri, P., Rani, S., Pareek, P.K., Financial Innovations: Intelligent Automation in Finance and Insurance Sectors, in: *Generating Entrepreneurial Ideas with AI*, D. Darwish (Ed.), pp. 226–43, IGI Global, 2024, https://doi.org/10.4018/979-8-3693-3354-9.ch012.
24. Rani, S. and Bhambri, P., Industry 4.0 Framework and Applications, in: *AI-Driven Digital Twin and Industry 4.0: A Conceptual Framework with Applications*, 1st, S. Rani, P. Bhambri, S. Kumar, P.K. Pareek, A.A. Elngar (Eds.), pp. 1–14, CRC Press, 2024, https://doi.org/10.1201/9781003395416.
25. Ambika, N., Secure integration of IIoT Environment in Industry 4.0, in: *Human-Centric Integration of Next-Generation Data Science and Blockchain Technology*, pp. 287–298, Academic Press, 2025.
26. Ambika, N., Authenticated integration of data science and IoT with Blockchain in IIoT environment, in: *Human-Centric Integration of 6G-Enabled Technologies for Modern Society*, pp. 119–127, Academic Press, 2025.

11

Exploring Novel Directions in Edge Intelligence for Industrial Internet of Things (IIoT)

T. Thangarasan[1*], R. Keerthana[2], J. Nagaraj[3], S. Vani[4] and R.M. Dilip Charaan[5]

[1]*Madanapalle Institute of Technology & Science, Madanapalle, Andhra Pradesh, India*
[2]*K.S.R. College of Engineering, Tiruchengode, Tamil Nadu, India*
[3]*Panimalar Engineering College, Chennai, Tamil Nadu, India*
[4]*SRM Institute of Science and Technology, Kattankulathur, Chennai, Tamil Nadu, India*
[5]*Vel Tech Rangarajan Dr. Sagunthala R&D Institute of Science and Technology, Avadi, Chennai, Tamil Nadu, India*

Abstract

The Industrial Internet of Things (IIoT) is transforming industries, with Edge Intelligence playing a crucial role in optimizing systems for enhanced efficiency and performance. This abstract explores emerging concepts in IIoT Edge Intelligence. Decentralized Edge Intelligence Ecosystems address scalability and bandwidth challenges by utilizing distributed network intelligence for data processing and resource optimization. Real-time Anomaly Detection and Predictive Maintenance focus on improving edge device machine learning models for faster, more accurate identification of device failures and maintenance needs. Federated Learning for Edge Devices enhances data privacy by training models on raw devices instead of aggregating data. Energy-Efficient Edge Computing introduces strategies like hardware optimization and renewable energy integration to improve energy efficiency. Integration of AR and VR in IIoT offers immersive interfaces for operators, enhancing operations and training. Edge-based Data Fusion aims to combine data

**Corresponding author*: thangarasan89@gmail.com; ORCID: 0000-0002-3511-3166
R. Keerthana: ORCID: 0009-0001-4898-4075
J. Nagaraj: ORCID: 0000-0002-2888-0762
S. Vani: ORCID: 0000-0001-7328-0638
R.M. Dilip Charaan: ORCID: 0009-0002-1332-4592

Sita Rani, Pankaj Bhambri, Balamurugan Balusamy, Rishabha Malviya and Seifedine Kadry (eds.) Edge Intelligence for 6G-Enabled Industrial Internet of Things, (217–248) © 2026 Scrivener Publishing LLC

from various sources for better situational awareness. Distributed Edge Intelligence Marketplaces encourage collaboration by allowing edge devices to share processing power and access expert knowledge. Edge-to-Cloud Orchestration seeks to balance data flow and resource allocation between edge devices and cloud servers, enhancing IIoT system functionality. These advancements in AI for IIoT are crucial for real-time data analysis and intelligent decision-making, promising to revolutionize industrial applications.

***Keywords*:** Industrial internet of things (IIoT), edge intelligence, decentralized edge intelligence ecosystems, predictive maintenance, federated learning, energy-efficient edge computing, augmented reality (AR), virtual reality (VR)

11.1 Introduction to the Internet of Things

The Internet of things (IoT) refers to the network where objects (home appliances, vehicles, appliances, etc.) are integrated with sensors, computers and other technologies to connect and transfer data to other devices and systems on [1], the internet. These objects, called "smart" devices, can communicate and interact with others on the internet, and can be monitored and controlled remotely [1]. Let's take a closer look at the main features of IoT:

11.1.1 Key Components of IoT

1. **Devices/Sensors:** Collect data from your surroundings. This can range from temperature sensors in your home to sensors in industrial machinery.
2. **Connectivity:** Devices need to connect to an IoT platform to exchange data. This can be done *via* various wireless protocols such as Wi-Fi, Bluetooth, cellular networks, and more.
3. **Data Processing:** Once data has been collected and transferred to the cloud or processed locally, it must be analyzed and converted into useful information.
4. **User Interface:** Provide useful insights or data to end-users *via* app notifications, email, or other channels.

11.1.2 Applications of IoT

- **Smart Homes:** IoT devices such as smart thermostats, smart lights, and security cameras can help improve home comfort and security [2].

- **Healthcare:** Wearable devices can track a patient's vital signs in real time, providing critical information to healthcare providers to help manage illnesses or prevent them from worsening.
- **Agriculture:** IoT sensors can monitor soil moisture and nutrients, control water use, and improve resource management in farming operations [2].
- **Industrial Automation:** The internet of things enables more efficient and dependable industrial operations through predictive maintenance of equipment and manufacturing process optimization.
- **Smart Cities:** IoT applications can manage traffic, save energy, and enhance public safety by connecting public services and infrastructure.

11.1.3 Challenges of IoT

- **Security:** IoT devices are connected and frequently collect sensitive data; they make ideal targets for cyberattacks. Ensuring the security of IoT devices is critical.
- **Privacy:** With devices collecting personal data, ensuring that it is handled correctly is a major concern.
- **Interoperability:** With numerous manufacturers and protocols, ensuring devices can communicate effectively is frequently a challenge.
- **Data Overload:** Massive amounts of data are generated by IoT devices, making it difficult to manage, process, and store.

11.2 Industrial Internet of Things (IIoT)

Industrial internet of things (IIoT) is the application of IoT technologies to industrial settings, with a focus on automating and exchanging data to improve operational efficiency, machinery performance, and industrial processes [3]. Here's a closer look at the components, applications, and benefits of IIoT, as well as the challenges it faces.

11.2.1 Key Components of IIoT

1. **Sensors and Actuators:** These are essential for data collection and action in industrial settings. They monitor variables

such as temperature, pressure, and vibration and can control machinery using data inputs.

2. **Industrial Communication Networks:** Unlike consumer IoT, IIoT necessitates robust, dependable communication systems capable of handling large amounts of data transfer under industrial conditions. Industrial Ethernet, Fieldbus, and wireless technologies are widely used.
3. **Edge Computing Devices:** Edge computing devices are used to process data on-site while reducing latency. These devices can analyze sensor data in real time and make critical decisions without sending it to the cloud.
4. **Data Analytics and Machine Learning:** Advanced analytics are used on the data to extract insights, predict maintenance requirements, and optimize processes [3, 4].
5. **Industrial Cloud Platforms:** These platforms combine data from various sources to provide a comprehensive view of operations and enable deep analytics, often with the help of AI.

11.2.2 Applications of IIoT

- **Predictive Maintenance:** Sensors monitor equipment and predict failures before they happen, lowering downtime and maintenance costs.
- **Asset Tracking and Management:** Real-time monitoring of asset conditions and locations to improve logistics and reduce theft or loss.
- **Smart Manufacturing:** Automation and data exchange make production lines more efficient, improve product quality, and reduce waste.
- **Energy Management:** Monitoring and managing energy consumption to improve efficiency and lower costs in industrial operations [4].
- **Supply Chain Optimization:** Real-time data from IIoT devices can help improve inventory management, delivery times, and supply chain visibility.

11.2.3 Benefits of IIoT

- **Increased Efficiency:** Automation and more precise control over manufacturing processes result in increased throughput and lower operating costs.
- **Enhanced Safety:** Monitoring systems can predict dangerous equipment malfunctions and, if necessary, shut down machinery, thereby increasing workplace safety.
- **Improved Quality:** Continuous monitoring ensures that products are manufactured within the specified parameters, which improves product quality [5].
- **Economic Benefits:** Reduced operational costs, increased productivity, and reduced downtime all contribute to improved economic outcomes for industrial businesses.

11.2.4 Challenges of IIoT

- **Cybersecurity Risks:** The more connected an industrial system is, the more vulnerable it is to cyber threats. Industrial systems often control critical infrastructure, making security paramount.
- **Integration Complexity:** Integrating new IIoT technologies into existing industrial systems can be difficult and expensive.
- **Data Privacy and Sovereignty:** Data generated in industrial settings can be sensitive, so controlling who has access to it is critical [5].
- **Skill Gaps:** When it comes to deploying, managing, and maintaining IIoT systems, the workforce frequently lacks the necessary skills.

11.3 Decentralized Edge Intelligence Ecosystems

Decentralized Edge Intelligence Ecosystems are network architectures in which decision-making processes and intelligence are distributed at the network's edge rather than being centralized in a cloud or a single data center [6]. This approach takes advantage of edge devices' proximity to data sources—such as IoT devices, sensors, and mobile phones—to perform data processing locally, reducing latency, bandwidth consumption, and reliance on central servers [6]. Here are some important components and advantages of decentralized edge intelligence ecosystems:

11.3.1 Components

1. **Edge Devices:** These are network peripheral devices that can process and store data. Smartphones, routers, internet-of-things devices, and embedded systems are some examples.
2. **Edge Nodes:** These can be gateways or local servers that add computational power and storage close to the edge devices.
3. **Distributed Data Analytics:** Algorithms and models that can be executed locally on edge devices or nodes, enabling real-time data processing and decision-making.
4. **Communication Infrastructure:** Efficient and secure communication protocols allow devices and nodes to share insights and coordinate actions without constantly connecting to a central server [7].
5. **Decentralized Management:** Tools and protocols for managing devices, security, and operations without centralized control, frequently utilize technologies such as block chain for security and data integrity.

11.3.2 Benefits

- **Reduced Latency:** Local data processing allows for faster decision-making, which is critical for applications that require real-time or near-real-time responses.
- **Bandwidth Savings:** Local data processing reduces the amount of data sent to the cloud, lowering bandwidth requirements and associated costs.
- **Improved Privacy:** Data can be processed locally, reducing the need to transmit sensitive information over a network.
- **Scalability:** By distributing processing tasks across multiple edge devices, the system can scale more effectively than traditional centralized systems [7].
- **Resilience:** Decentralization is more resistant to failures and cyber-attacks because there is no single point of failure.

11.3.3 Real-Time Anomaly Detection and Predictive Maintenance

Real-time anomaly detection and predictive maintenance are critical components of modern industrial operations, particularly as the Industrial Internet of Things (IIoT) gains traction [7]. These technologies use data analytics, machine learning, and IIoT devices to detect unusual conditions that could indicate a failure and predict when maintenance should be performed to avoid such failures [8]. Here's a detailed breakdown of each aspect.

11.3.3.1 Real-Time Anomaly Detection

Real-time anomaly detection entails continuously monitoring and analyzing data from various sensors and systems to identify patterns or behaviors that are out of the ordinary. Here's how it works.

1. **Data Collection:** Machine sensors collect operational data in real time, including temperature, pressure, vibration levels, and more.
2. **Data Processing:** The data is either processed locally using edge computing or transferred to a centralized data center or cloud for analysis.
3. **Anomaly Detection Models:** These models, which are frequently developed using machine learning techniques, compare real-time data to historical data and learned patterns to detect any deviations.
4. **Alerts and Actions:** If an anomaly is detected, the system can notify operators or automatically adjust the operation to address the problem.

11.3.3.2 Technologies Used

- **Machine Learning Algorithms:** Clustering, neural networks, and isolation forests are among the techniques used to learn from historical data and detect anomalies in real time [8].
- **Edge Computing:** Allows data processing near the source, reducing latency, which is critical for timely anomaly detection [9].

11.3.3.3 Predictive Maintenance

Predictive maintenance uses the data and insights gained from real-time monitoring to predict when and which components will require maintenance before failing [9]. The steps involved are:

1. **Condition Monitoring:** Continuous monitoring of equipment condition *via* sensors.
2. **Health Assessment:** Analyzing collected data to determine the health and performance of equipment.
3. **Predictive Analytics:** Using statistical models and machine learning to forecast potential failures based on current and past data.
4. **Maintenance Scheduling:** Preparing maintenance tasks in advance to avoid unexpected equipment failures and downtime.

11.3.4 Benefits

- **Reduced Downtime:** Maintenance can be scheduled during non-critical times to prevent unexpected failures.
- **Cost Efficiency:** Increases the lifespan of machinery by maintaining it before it sustains severe damage.
- **Enhanced Safety:** Reduces the risk of equipment failure, which could endanger operators.

11.3.5 Challenges

- **Data Quality and Quantity:** Effective anomaly detection and predictive maintenance necessitate high-quality and abundant data, which can be difficult to obtain in complex industrial settings.
- **Integration with Existing Systems:** Integrating new technologies into existing machinery and software systems can be technically difficult and costly [9].
- **Skilled Personnel:** Advanced predictive maintenance systems must be designed, implemented, and maintained by highly skilled personnel.

- **False Positives/Negatives:** Machine learning models may generate false alerts, resulting in unnecessary maintenance actions or missed failures.

11.3.6 Applications

- These technologies are applicable in a variety of industries, including manufacturing, energy, transportation, and utilities, where equipment failures can cause significant operational disruptions and safety risks [10].
- Combining real-time anomaly detection with predictive maintenance allows industries to not only detect and respond to immediate anomalies, but also anticipate and prevent future issues, resulting in more stable, efficient, and cost-effective operations.

11.4 Federated Learning for Edge Devices

Federated Learning (FL) is a technique that enables machine learning models to be trained across multiple decentralized devices or servers that store local data samples without exchanging them. This technique is especially useful for edge devices, where data privacy, security, and bandwidth efficiency are critical considerations [10]. Here's a detailed look at Federated Learning for edge devices:

11.4.1 Key Concepts

1. **Local Training:** Each edge device trains a local model using its own data. This means that data never leaves the device, thereby protecting privacy and lowering the risk of data breaches.
2. **Model Aggregation:** The locally trained models are periodically sent to a central server, where they are combined to create a global model. This aggregation usually involves averaging the weights of the local models.
3. **Iteration:** The global model is then transmitted back to the edge devices, where the process is repeated. The global model improves over time as a result of multiple rounds of local training and aggregated data.

11.4.2 Benefits

1. **Data Privacy:** Federated Learning addresses the privacy concerns associated with centralized data collection by keeping data on edge devices.
2. **Reduced Bandwidth:** Only model updates (which are typically smaller than raw data) are sent to the central server, minimizing bandwidth consumption.
3. **Scalability:** Federated Learning can scale across millions of edge devices, leveraging their collective computational power and data.

11.4.3 Challenges

1. **Communication Overhead:** While Federated Learning reduces the need to send large amounts of data, frequent communication is still required for model updates.
2. **Device Heterogeneity:** Edge devices can differ significantly in terms of computational power, battery life, and connectivity, affecting the consistency and efficiency of model training [11].
3. **Non-IID Data:** Data on edge devices is frequently not distributed in an independent and identical manner (non-IID), complicating the training process and model convergence [11].

11.4.4 Applications

- **Healthcare:** Federated Learning can be used to train models on medical data from various hospitals while protecting patient privacy.
- **Smart Homes:** Devices in smart homes can collaborate to improve automation and security features.
- **Finance:** Banks can use Federated Learning to detect fraud across multiple branches while protecting sensitive customer information.
- **Autonomous Vehicles:** Vehicles can collaborate to improve their navigation and safety systems by sharing model updates rather than raw data [19, 20].

11.4.5 How it Works

1. **Initialization:** A global model is initialized and sent to all participating edge devices.
2. **Local Training:** Each edge device trains the global model on its local dataset for a specified number of epochs.
3. **Model Upload:** The locally trained models are uploaded to a central server.
4. **Aggregation:** The central server aggregates the local models to update the global model.
5. **Distribution:** The updated global model is sent back to the edge devices, and the process repeats.

11.4.6 Example Workflow

1. **Start Global Model Training:**
   - Initialize a global model.
   - Distribute the model to edge devices.
2. **Local Model Training:**
   - Each device trains the model locally using its own data.
   - Local training results (model updates) are sent back to the central server.
3. **Model Aggregation:**
   - The central server aggregates the received local models.
   - The aggregated model (global model) is updated and redistributed to the edge devices.
4. **Iterative Process:**
   - Repeat the local training and model aggregation steps until the global model converges or meets performance criteria.

11.4.7 Key Algorithms

- **Federated Averaging (FedAvg):** A common FL algorithm in which the central server averages the weights of the local models before updating the global model [12].

11.4.8 Technical Considerations

- **Secure Aggregation:** Ensure that the model aggregation process respects the privacy of individual updates.

- **Fault Tolerance:** Handling device failures and intermittent connectivity gracefully.
- **Resource Management:** Efficiently using edge devices' computational resources without depleting their batteries or interfering with their primary functions.

Federated Learning for edge devices offers a promising solution to leverage distributed data while addressing privacy and bandwidth concerns [12]. It enables the creation of robust and scalable machine learning models capable of operating effectively in a variety of decentralized environments.

11.5 Energy-Efficient Edge Computing

Energy-efficient edge computing is concerned with optimizing the use of energy in edge devices and infrastructure to extend battery life, lower operational costs, and reduce environmental impact [13]. This is especially important because edge devices frequently operate in resource-constrained environments, requiring them to strike a balance between performance and power consumption [13]. Here are the key strategies, technologies, and advantages associated with energy-efficient edge computing:

11.5.1 Key Strategies

1. **Dynamic Voltage and Frequency Scaling (DVFS):** Adjusts voltage and frequency based on workload to reduce power consumption during low-demand periods.
2. **Task Offloading:** Compute-intensive tasks are offloaded to nearby edge servers or the cloud, reducing the load on energy-constrained edge devices.
3. **Efficient Data Transmission:** Utilizes data compression, local aggregation, and selective transmission to reduce energy consumption for data communication.
4. **Adaptive Resource Management:** Dynamically allocates resources based on current needs, avoiding over-provisioning and unnecessary energy use.
5. **Sleep Modes and Power Gating:** Implements deep sleep modes and powers off unused components when the device is idle to save energy.

6. **Energy-Aware Scheduling:** Tasks are scheduled based on their energy consumption profiles and deadlines, with low-energy operations being prioritized whenever possible.

11.5.2 Technologies and Techniques

1. **Low-Power Hardware:**
    - Utilizes energy-efficient processors, like ARM Cortex, with low power consumption.
2. **Edge AI and Inference Optimization:**
    - Optimizes machine learning models for edge devices through quantization and pruning to reduce computational requirements.
3. **Energy Harvesting:**
    - Uses renewable energy sources like solar panels and kinetic energy to power edge devices.
4. **Fog Computing:**
    - Uses intermediate nodes (fog nodes) between the cloud and edge devices to process data closer to the source, reducing the energy costs associated with long-distance data transmission.
5. **Data Caching and Prefetching:**
    - Caches frequently accessed data locally and prefetches data based on predictive algorithms to reduce the need for energy-intensive data retrievals.

11.5.3 Benefits

- **Prolonged Battery Life:**
    - Essential for mobile and remote edge devices, ensuring longer operational periods without frequent recharging or battery replacement.
- **Cost Savings:**
    - Reduces operational costs by lowering energy consumption and improving the efficiency of edge computing operations.
- **Environmental Impact:**
    - Minimizes the carbon footprint of edge computing by reducing overall energy use.

- **Enhanced Performance:**
  - Balances performance and energy efficiency, ensuring that devices can operate optimally without excessive power drain.

11.5.4 Challenges

- **Complexity of Implementation:**
  - Developing and implementing energy-efficient algorithms and hardware can be challenging and require specialized expertise.
- **Trade-offs with Performance:**
  - Balancing performance and energy efficiency is crucial for meeting application needs.
- **Heterogeneous Environments:**
  - Implementing uniform energy-efficient strategies in edge environments can be challenging due to their high heterogeneity in hardware capabilities and energy requirements.

11.5.5 Applications

- **IoT Networks:**
  - Energy-efficient edge computing is essential for IoT networks that require devices to operate for extended periods on limited power sources.
- **Smart Cities:**
  - Optimizes energy use of edge devices to support smart city applications such as traffic management, environmental monitoring, and public safety.
- **Healthcare:**
  - Energy-efficient edge computing extends battery life and improves reliability for wearable health monitors and remote patient monitoring.
- **Industrial Automation:**
  - Ensures continuous operation of industrial IoT devices and sensors in demanding environments, without frequent maintenance or power disruptions.

11.5.6 Example Approaches

- **Edge Computing Frameworks:**
  - Utilizing frameworks like Apache, Edgent or EdgeX Foundry that provide tools and libraries to develop energy-efficient edge applications.
- **Machine Learning Models Optimization:**
  - Applying techniques like TensorFlow Lite or ONNX for running machine learning models efficiently on edge devices.
- **Energy-Aware Software Development:**
  - Developing software with energy-efficient coding practices, such as minimizing background processes and optimizing code for low-power operation.

Implementing energy-efficient edge computing strategies allows for the development of more sustainable and cost-effective systems capable of operating reliably in a wide range of applications, from consumer electronics to critical industrial systems [13].

11.6 Integration of Augmented Reality (AR) and Virtual Reality (VR)

The incorporation of Augmented Reality (AR) and Virtual Reality (VR) into a variety of fields has fundamentally altered our interactions with digital content and the physical world [14]. These technologies provide immersive experiences that can benefit productivity, entertainment, education, and a variety of other industries. Here's a detailed look at AR and VR, including their integration, applications, benefits, and challenges:

11.6.1 Key Concepts

- **Augmented Reality (AR):** Enhances the real world by superimposing digital content, such as images, videos, or 3D models, onto the physical environment *via* smartphones, tablets, or AR glasses.
- **Virtual Reality (VR):** Creates a fully immersive digital environment that replaces the physical world, typically accessed *via* VR headsets.

11.6.2 Integration of AR and VR

The combination of AR and VR technologies, known as Extended Reality (XR), enables a wide range of immersive experiences, from partial augmentation to full immersion [14]. This integration can provide a smooth transition between the real and virtual worlds, enhancing a variety of applications.

1. **Mixed Reality (MR):** It combines elements of AR and VR, allowing digital and physical objects to coexist and interact in real time. Microsoft HoloLens and Magic Leap are notable examples.
2. **Immersive Analytics:** Uses both AR and VR to visualize complex data in intuitive and interactive ways, thereby improving decision-making and comprehension.

11.6.3 Applications

1. **Education and Training:**
   - **AR:** Improves learning materials with interactive 3D models and real-time information overlays.
   - **VR:** Offers immersive training simulations for scenarios such as medical procedures, flight training, and industrial equipment operation.
2. **Healthcare:**
   - **AR:** Assists in surgeries by overlaying critical information, such as patient vitals and surgical guides, onto the surgeon's view.
   - **VR:** Facilitates therapy for mental health conditions, pain management, and rehabilitation through controlled virtual environments.
3. **Retail:**
   - **AR:** Enables virtual try-ons for clothing and accessories or visualizing furniture in a customer's home.
   - **VR:** Creates virtual stores where customers can explore and purchase products in a fully immersive environment.
4. **Entertainment and Gaming:**
   - **AR:** Adds interactive elements to real-world environments in mobile games and live events.
   - **VR:** Provides fully immersive gaming experiences, virtual concerts, and interactive storytelling.

5. **Real Estate:**
   - **AR:** Visualizes modifications to existing structures or overlays property information during tours.
   - **VR:** Offers virtual tours of properties, allowing potential buyers to explore homes remotely.
6. **Manufacturing and Maintenance:**
   - **AR:** Guides workers through complex assembly processes or maintenance tasks with step-by-step instructions.
   - **VR:** Simulates production environments for training and process optimization.

11.6.4 Benefits

- **Enhanced User Experience:** AR and VR provide more engaging and interactive experiences compared to traditional interfaces.
- **Improved Training and Education:** Immersive simulations and interactive content can significantly enhance learning outcomes.
- **Increased Efficiency:** AR can streamline workflows by providing real-time information and guidance, while VR can simulate complex scenarios for planning and training.
- **Remote Capabilities:** Both technologies enable remote collaboration, visualization, and training, reducing the need for physical presence.

11.6.5 Challenges

- **Technical Limitations:** High computational requirements, latency issues, and the need for advanced hardware can limit the widespread adoption of AR and VR.
- **Cost:** Developing and implementing AR/VR solutions can be expensive, particularly for high-quality experiences [14].
- **User Comfort:** VR can cause motion sickness and eye strain for some users, while AR devices need to be comfortable for prolonged use.
- **Content Development:** Creating high-quality, interactive AR and VR content requires specialized skills and tools.
- **Privacy and Security:** As AR and VR devices collect and process large amounts of data, ensuring user privacy and data security is crucial.

11.6.6 Future Trends

1. **Advancements in Hardware:** Improved AR glasses and VR headsets with higher resolution, better field of view, and more ergonomic designs.
2. **5G Integration:** Faster and more reliable connectivity enabling real-time AR/VR experiences without latency issues.
3. **AI Integration:** Enhancing AR/VR experiences with artificial intelligence for more intelligent interactions and personalized experiences [14].
4. **Cross-Platform Experiences:** Development of platforms that seamlessly integrate AR and VR, providing a cohesive user experience across devices.
5. **Enterprise Adoption:** Increased use of AR/VR in industries like healthcare, manufacturing, and retail for training, maintenance, and customer engagement.

The integration of AR and VR technologies promises to revolutionize various fields by providing more immersive, interactive, and efficient ways to visualize and interact with information [14]. As technology continues to evolve, the potential applications and benefits of AR and VR will continue to expand, shaping the future of digital interaction.

11.7 Edge-Based Data Fusion

Edge-based data fusion refers to the process of integrating data from multiple sources at the edge of the network, close to where the data is generated, to enhance decision-making, reduce latency, and optimize the use of network and computational resources [15]. This approach leverages the computational capabilities of edge devices to process and combine data locally, thereby reducing the need to transmit large volumes of raw data to central servers or cloud platforms. Here's a comprehensive look at edge-based data fusion, its components, applications, benefits, and challenges:

11.7.1 Key Components

1. **Data Sources:**
   - **Sensors and IoT Devices:** Collect raw data such as temperature, humidity, video footage, audio signals, etc.

- **Edge Devices:** Process data locally and serve as the primary units for data fusion.

2. **Data Fusion Algorithms:**
   - **Low-Level Fusion:** Combines raw data from multiple sensors to produce refined sensor data.
   - **Intermediate-Level Fusion:** Integrates features extracted from sensor data, such as patterns or signals.
   - **High-Level Fusion:** Merges interpreted data or decisions to provide a holistic understanding or decision-making.
3. **Edge Computing Infrastructure:**
   - **Edge Nodes:** Devices or servers located near data sources that perform data fusion and processing tasks.
   - **Network Connectivity:** Reliable and efficient communication protocols to facilitate data exchange between devices.
4. **Software Frameworks:**
   - Platforms and libraries that support data fusion processes, such as Apache Edgent, EdgeX Foundry, or custom-developed solutions.

11.7.2 Applications

1. **Smart Cities:**
   - **Traffic Management:** Fusion of data from traffic cameras, sensors, and GPS devices to optimize traffic flow and reduce congestion.
   - **Public Safety:** Combining data from surveillance cameras, environmental sensors, and social media feeds to enhance situational awareness and emergency response.
2. **Industrial Automation:**
   - **Predictive Maintenance:** Merging data from various sensors on machinery to predict equipment failures and schedule maintenance.
   - **Quality Control:** Integrating data from different stages of the production line to monitor and ensure product quality.
3. **Healthcare:**
   - **Patient Monitoring:** Fusion of data from wearable devices, medical records, and environmental sensors to monitor patient health in real-time.

- **Diagnostics:** Combining imaging data, lab results, and patient history for more accurate diagnoses.

4. **Agriculture:**
   - **Precision Farming:** Integrating data from soil sensors, weather stations, and satellite imagery to optimize irrigation, fertilization, and pest control.
   - **Crop Monitoring:** Merging data from drones, sensors, and ground-based observations to assess crop health and yield.
5. **Autonomous Vehicles:**
   - **Navigation:** Fusion of data from LIDAR, radar, cameras, and GPS to enable safe and efficient navigation.
   - **Obstacle Detection:** Combining sensor data to detect and respond to obstacles in real-time.

11.7.3 Benefits

- **Reduced Latency:** By processing data at the edge, decisions can be made more quickly, which is critical for time-sensitive applications.
- **Bandwidth Efficiency:** Local data fusion reduces the need to transmit large amounts of raw data to central servers, conserving bandwidth.
- **Enhanced Privacy and Security:** Sensitive data can be processed locally, minimizing the risk of exposure during transmission.
- **Improved Reliability:** Edge-based processing can continue to operate even if connectivity to central servers is lost.

11.7.4 Challenges

- **Heterogeneous Data Sources:** Integrating data from diverse sources with varying formats, resolutions, and update rates can be complex.
- **Computational Constraints:** Edge devices often have limited computational power and storage compared to central servers, posing challenges for complex data fusion tasks.
- **Synchronization:** Ensuring that data from different sources is synchronized correctly for accurate fusion.

- **Security and Privacy:** Protecting data at the edge from unauthorized access and ensuring secure communication between devices.

11.7.5 Implementation Strategies

1. **Distributed Processing:** Distribute data fusion tasks across multiple edge devices to balance the load and enhance efficiency.
2. **Hierarchical Fusion:** Implement multi-layered data fusion, where initial fusion occurs on individual edge devices, and further fusion is performed at higher-level edge nodes or gateways.
3. **Machine Learning:** Employ machine learning models for complex data fusion tasks, such as pattern recognition and anomaly detection, tailored for edge deployment.
4. **Adaptive Algorithms:** Use adaptive data fusion algorithms that can dynamically adjust based on the available resources and current data conditions.

11.7.6 Future Trends

- **5G Integration:** Enhanced connectivity provided by 5G networks will support faster and more reliable data exchange between edge devices.
- **AI and Edge Computing:** Increasing use of artificial intelligence for more sophisticated data fusion tasks at the edge.
- **Edge-to-Cloud Continuum:** Developing seamless integration between edge computing and cloud resources for balanced processing and storage.
- **Standardization:** Efforts to standardize protocols and frameworks for edge-based data fusion to ensure interoperability and ease of deployment.

Edge-based data fusion holds significant promise for various industries by enabling faster, more efficient, and more secure data processing and decision-making directly at the point of data generation [15]. As technology advances, the capabilities and applications of edge-based data fusion will continue to expand, offering new opportunities for innovation and optimization.

11.8 Distributed Edge Intelligence Marketplaces

Distributed Edge Intelligence Marketplaces represent an emerging paradigm where computational resources, data, and AI models are traded in decentralized networks to enable real-time, intelligent processing at the edge of the network [16]. These marketplaces facilitate the sharing and monetization of edge resources, promoting collaboration and innovation while optimizing the use of distributed computational assets. Here's a detailed look at the concept, components, benefits, challenges, and potential applications of Distributed Edge Intelligence Marketplaces.

11.8.1 Key Concepts

1. **Edge Intelligence:**
   - Combining edge computing with AI to perform data processing and inference tasks locally on edge devices.
2. **Marketplaces:**
   - Platforms that facilitate the buying, selling, and sharing of computational resources, data, and AI models.
3. **Distributed Networks:**
   - Utilizing decentralized architectures, often supported by blockchain technology, to ensure trust, security, and transparency in transactions.

11.8.2 Components

1. **Edge Devices:**
   - Devices like smartphones, IoT sensors, gateways, and local servers that provide computational resources and generate data.
2. **Market Platform:**
   - A decentralized platform that connects resource providers with consumers. This platform manages transactions, resource allocation, and ensures compliance with agreed terms.
3. **Blockchain Technology:**
   - Used to create a secure and transparent ledger of transactions, ensuring trust among participants without the need for a central authority.

4. **Smart Contracts:**
   - Self-executing contracts with the terms of the agreement directly written into code, facilitating automated transactions and enforcement.
5. **AI Models and Algorithms:**
   - Pre-trained models and algorithms available for purchase or sharing to enable edge intelligence.

11.8.3 Benefits

1. **Resource Optimization:**
   - Efficient utilization of underused computational resources at the edge, reducing the need for central cloud resources and associated costs.
2. **Reduced Latency:**
   - Performing computations closer to the data source decreases latency, which is critical for real-time applications.
3. **Scalability:**
   - Leveraging a distributed network of edge devices allows for scalable solutions without heavy reliance on centralized infrastructure.
4. **Enhanced Privacy and Security:**
   - Local processing minimizes the need to transmit sensitive data over the network, enhancing privacy and security.
5. **Monetization Opportunities:**
   - Resource owners can monetize their underutilized assets, and developers can sell or license their AI models.

11.8.4 Challenges

1. **Interoperability:**
   - Ensuring compatibility among diverse devices, platforms, and protocols is a significant challenge.
2. **Quality Assurance:**
   - Maintaining the quality and reliability of resources and services provided through the marketplace.
3. **Security Concerns:**
   - Protecting against cyber threats and ensuring the integrity and confidentiality of transactions and data.

4. **Regulatory Compliance:**
   - Adhering to varying regulatory requirements across different regions and industries.
5. **Network Management:**
   - Efficiently managing and orchestrating a decentralized network of edge devices to avoid bottlenecks and ensure smooth operation.

11.8.5 Potential Applications

1. **Smart Cities:**
   - Facilitating the exchange of computational resources and data for applications such as traffic management, energy optimization, and public safety [16].
2. **Healthcare:**
   - Enabling secure, real-time processing of patient data from wearable devices and medical sensors for diagnostics and monitoring.
3. **Industrial IoT:**
   - Supporting predictive maintenance, quality control, and process optimization through localized data processing and AI.
4. **Retail:**
   - Enhancing customer experiences with personalized services, real-time inventory management, and smart store operations.
5. **Agriculture:**
   - Optimizing farming practices through real-time data analysis from various sensors and devices deployed in the field.

11.8.6 Implementation Strategies

1. **Decentralized Infrastructure:**
   - Building a robust, decentralized infrastructure leveraging blockchain and edge computing technologies.
2. **Incentive Mechanisms:**
   - Designing effective incentive mechanisms to encourage participation from resource providers and consumers.

3. **Standardization:**
   - Developing standards and protocols to ensure interoperability and seamless integration of diverse resources.
4. **AI and Machine Learning:**
   - Utilizing AI to optimize resource allocation, predict demand, and enhance the overall efficiency of the marketplace [16].
5. **User-Friendly Platforms:**
   - Creating intuitive platforms that simplify the process of buying, selling, and managing resources and services.

11.8.7 Future Trends

1. **AI-Driven Marketplaces:**
   - Increasing use of AI to automate marketplace operations, enhance user experiences, and improve decision-making processes.
2. **Edge-to-Edge Collaboration:**
   - Enabling direct collaboration and resource sharing between edge devices without the need for central coordination.
3. **Hybrid Cloud-Edge Solutions:**
   - Integrating edge intelligence marketplaces with traditional cloud services to provide flexible and scalable solutions.
4. **Regulatory Frameworks:**
   - Development of regulatory frameworks to ensure fair practices, security, and compliance in decentralized marketplaces.
5. **Emerging Technologies:**
   - Leveraging emerging technologies such as 5G, advanced cryptography, and quantum computing to enhance the capabilities and efficiency of edge intelligence marketplaces [17].

Distributed Edge Intelligence Marketplaces represent a promising frontier in the evolution of edge computing and AI. By enabling the decentralized exchange of resources, data, and intelligence, these marketplaces can drive innovation, enhance efficiency, and unlock new economic opportunities across various industries [18].

11.9 Edge-to-Cloud Orchestration

Edge-to-cloud orchestration involves the coordinated management of computational workloads and data across both edge and cloud environments [18]. This approach leverages the strengths of edge computing—such as low latency, real-time processing, and reduced bandwidth usage—alongside the vast computational power and storage capabilities of cloud computing. Effective orchestration ensures that tasks are dynamically allocated to the most appropriate resources based on factors like latency requirements, data sensitivity, and computational intensity [12]. Here's an in-depth look at edge-to-cloud orchestration, its components, benefits, challenges, and use cases:

11.9.1 Key Components

1. **Edge Devices:**
   - **Sensors and Actuators:** Collect real-time data from the physical world.
   - **Edge Gateways:** Aggregate data from sensors and perform preliminary processing.
2. **Cloud Infrastructure:**
   - **Cloud Servers:** Provide large-scale data processing and storage capabilities.
   - **Data Lakes and Warehouses:** Centralized repositories for storing and analyzing large datasets.
3. **Orchestration Platform:**
   - **Management Layer:** Interfaces for monitoring and controlling resources across edge and cloud.
   - **Scheduling Algorithms:** Decide where to execute tasks based on current conditions and policies [8].
   - **Data Management:** Ensures data is efficiently transferred, stored, and processed between edge and cloud.
4. **Network Connectivity:**
   - **High-Speed Networks:** Reliable and fast connections to facilitate data transfer.
   - **5G and IoT Protocols:** Enable low-latency and high-bandwidth communication.

11.9.2 Benefits

1. **Optimized Performance:**
    - Ensures that time-sensitive tasks are processed at the edge to minimize latency, while resource-intensive tasks leverage the cloud's computational power.
2. **Cost Efficiency:**
    - Reduces bandwidth costs by processing data locally and only sending necessary data to the cloud.
3. **Scalability:**
    - Combines the scalability of cloud resources with the localized processing of edge devices, enabling seamless scaling of applications.
4. **Improved Security and Compliance:**
    - Sensitive data can be processed locally to comply with privacy regulations, while less sensitive data can be offloaded to the cloud [14].
5. **Enhanced Reliability:**
    - Provides redundancy and failover capabilities by distributing workloads across multiple environments.

11.9.3 Challenges

1. **Complexity of Management:**
    - Managing resources and workloads across distributed environments can be complex and require sophisticated orchestration tools.
2. **Interoperability Issues:**
    - Ensuring seamless integration and communication between diverse edge devices and cloud services.
3. **Latency and Bandwidth Constraints:**
    - Balancing the need for real-time processing with the limitations of network latency and bandwidth.
4. **Security Risks:**
    - Ensuring secure data transfer and processing across multiple environments and addressing potential attack vectors [13].
5. **Resource Allocation:**
    - Dynamically allocating resources based on changing workloads and network conditions.

11.9.4 Use Cases

1. **Smart Cities:**
   - **Traffic Management:** Real-time processing of traffic data at the edge for immediate insights, with historical data analysis performed in the cloud.
   - **Public Safety:** Edge devices can process video feeds for real-time surveillance, while the cloud can be used for long-term storage and analysis [16].
2. **Healthcare:**
   - **Remote Monitoring:** Wearable devices process health data locally to provide instant feedback, with aggregated data sent to the cloud for in-depth analysis.
   - **Telemedicine:** Combines edge processing for real-time diagnostics with cloud resources for comprehensive patient records management.
3. **Manufacturing:**
   - **Predictive Maintenance:** Edge devices monitor machinery and detect anomalies in real-time, while the cloud performs predictive analytics on collected data.
   - **Quality Control:** Real-time inspection data is processed at the edge, and cloud resources analyze trends and patterns over time.
4. **Retail:**
   - **Customer Experience:** Edge computing powers in-store personalized experiences, while cloud computing supports broader analytics and inventory management.
   - **Supply Chain Optimization:** Edge devices track goods in transit, with the cloud coordinating overall logistics and supply chain strategies.
5. **Agriculture:**
   - **Precision Farming:** Sensors process environmental data locally for immediate actions, while cloud analytics help in long-term planning and forecasting.
   - **Crop Monitoring:** Edge devices provide real-time monitoring and control, while the cloud integrates data for comprehensive farm management.

11.9.5 Implementation Strategies

1. **Hybrid Architectures:**
   - Implementing a hybrid architecture that leverages both edge and cloud resources to optimize performance and cost.
2. **Federated Learning:**
   - Utilizing federated learning to train machine learning models across edge devices without centralized data collection, enhancing privacy and efficiency [15].
3. **Containerization and Microservices:**
   - Deploying applications as containerized microservices that can run seamlessly on both edge and cloud environments.
4. **AI and ML Integration:**
   - Using AI and ML to dynamically optimize workload distribution and resource allocation based on real-time conditions and historical data [14].
5. **Standardization:**
   - Adopting standards and protocols to ensure interoperability and ease of integration between different devices and platforms.

11.9.6 Future Trends

1. **5G and Beyond:**
   - The adoption of 5G will enhance connectivity, reduce latency, and support a larger number of connected devices, making edge-to-cloud orchestration more efficient.
2. **Edge AI:**
   - Increasing deployment of AI capabilities at the edge to enable more intelligent and autonomous decision-making.
3. **Blockchain:**
   - Using blockchain technology to secure transactions and data exchange in decentralized edge-to-cloud environments.
4. **Autonomous Systems:**
   - Development of autonomous systems that can self-manage and optimize their operations across edge and cloud resources.

Edge-to-cloud orchestration is a pivotal strategy for modern computing, enabling more efficient, secure, and scalable solutions across various industries [11]. By leveraging the strengths of both edge and cloud computing, businesses can achieve better performance, cost savings, and flexibility in their operations.

11.10 Conclusion

The exploration of novel directions in Edge Intelligence for the Industrial Internet of Things (IIoT) highlights the transformative potential of decentralized ecosystems, real-time anomaly detection, predictive maintenance, federated learning, energy-efficient computing, and the integration of AR/VR technologies [12]. These advancements offer significant improvements in efficiency, latency reduction, and privacy, which are crucial for the optimization of IIoT systems [15].

Decentralized edge intelligence ecosystems enable distributed data processing, reducing the reliance on centralized cloud infrastructures and enhancing system responsiveness [11]. Real-time anomaly detection and predictive maintenance leverage advanced machine learning models to foresee and mitigate potential equipment failures, thus minimizing downtime and operational costs. Federated learning addresses privacy concerns by enabling localized model training on edge devices, ensuring data security while maintaining the benefits of global model improvements [13].

Energy-efficient edge computing is increasingly vital, incorporating hardware optimizations and renewable energy sources to sustain edge infrastructure. The integration of AR and VR technologies into IIoT applications enhances operational efficiency, providing immersive, context-aware interfaces for operators and maintenance staff. Edge-based data fusion and distributed edge intelligence marketplaces further exemplify the shift towards more collaborative and resource-optimized IIoT environments [14].

Edge-to-cloud orchestration ensures a balanced approach, optimizing data flow and task distribution between edge devices and cloud servers [12]. This dynamic interplay supports scalable, efficient, and reliable IIoT systems, ready to meet the evolving demands of industrial applications.

In conclusion, the ongoing innovations in Edge Intelligence for IIoT represent a significant leap towards smarter, more autonomous industrial operations [13]. As these technologies continue to evolve, they will play an instrumental role in shaping the future of industrial automation, enhancing productivity, and fostering sustainable growth across various sectors.

AI disclosure statement: The author acknowledges the use of AI-based tools for minor language editing or grammatical correction. However, all intellectual contributions, analyses, and conclusions presented in this chapter are entirely the author's own.

References

1. Xu, L.D., Xu, E.L., Li, L., Industry 4.0: state of the art and future trends. *Int. J. Prod. Res.*, 56, 8, 2941–2962, 2018, doi:10.1080/00207543.2018.1444806.
2. Zhou, K., Liu, T., Zhou, L., Industry 4.0: Towards future industrial opportunities and challenges, in: *2015 12th International Conference on Fuzzy Systems and Knowledge Discovery (FSKD)*, IEEE, pp. 2147–2152, 2015, doi:10.1109/FSKD.2015.7382284.
3. Satyanarayanan, M., The emergence of edge computing. *Computer*, 50, 1, 30–39, 2017, doi:10.1109/MC.2017.9.
4. Shi, W., Cao, J., Zhang, Q., Li, Y., Xu, L., Edge computing: Vision and challenges. *IEEE Internet Things J.*, 3, 5, 637–646, 2016, doi:10.1109/JIOT.2016.2579198.
5. Wang, L. and Gu, T., Predictive maintenance of industrial systems using machine learning approaches. *Procedia CIRP*, 88, 303–308, 2020, doi:10.1016/j.procir.2020.05.052.
6. Khan, M.A., Afzal, M., Umair, M., Lee, J., Lee, M.Y., Smart anomaly detection using machine learning techniques for a sustainable smart city. *Sustainability*, 12, 3, 802, 2020, doi:10.3390/su12030802.
7. McMahan, H.B., Moore, E., Ramage, D., Hampson, S., y Arcas, B.A., Communication-efficient learning of deep networks from decentralized data, in: *Artificial Intelligence and Statistics*, pp. 1273–1282, PMLR, 2017, doi:10.48550/arXiv.1602.05629.
8. Konečný, J., McMahan, H.B., Yu, F.X., Richtárik, P., Suresh, A.T., Bacon, D., Federated learning: Strategies for improving communication efficiency, *arXiv preprint arXiv:1610.05492*, 2016, doi:10.48550/arXiv.1610.05492.
9. Liu, Y. and Han, G., A survey on edge computing systems and tools. *Proc. IEEE*, 107, 8, 1537–1562, 2018, doi:10.1109/JPROC.2019.2921977.
10. Murshed, M., Murphy, C., Hou, D., Khan, A., Ananthanarayanan, G., Smyl, S., Machine learning at the network edge: A survey, in: *2019 6th IEEE International Conference on Cyber Security and Cloud Computing (CSCloud)*, IEEE, pp. 35–40, 2019, doi:10.1109/CSCloud.2019.00014.
11. Azuma, R.T., A survey of augmented reality. *Presence Teleoperators Virtual Environ.*, 6, 4, 355–385, 1997, doi:10.1162/pres.1997.6.4.355.
12. Anthes, C., García-Hernández, R.J., Wiedemann, M., Kranzlmüller, D., State of the art of virtual reality technology, in: *2016 IEEE Aerospace Conference*, IEEE, pp. 1–19, 2016, doi:10.1109/AERO.2016.7500674.

13. Luo, S., Bai, Y., Zhou, W., Jiang, H., Edge computing for mobile augmented reality: Offloading framework and challenges. *IEEE Netw.*, 32, 2, 48–55, 2018, doi:10.1109/MNET.2018.1700203.
14. Zhang, C. and Vasilakos, A.V., Data fusion in sensor networks: A survey, in: *Handbook of Sensor Networks*, pp. 379–417, Springer, 2018, doi: 10.1007/978-0-387-78059-3_14.
15. Shi, W. and Dustdar, S., The promise of edge computing. *Computer*, 49, 5, 78–81, 2016, doi:10.1109/MC.2016.145.
16. Zhu, Q., Loke, S.W., Trujillo-Rasua, R., Jiang, Y., Xiang, Y., Applications and security in edge computing systems: A survey. *IEEE Internet Things J.*, 8, 4, 3489–3510, 2020, doi:10.1109/JIOT.2020.3003281.
17. Satyanarayanan, M., The role of edge computing in cloud computing. *IEEE Cloud Comput.*, 4, 6, 84–89, 2019, doi:10.1109/MCC.2017.3791011.
18. Luan, T.H., Gao, L., Li, Z., Xiang, Y., Weerasuriya, P., Sun, L., Fog computing: Focusing on mobile users at the edge, *arXiv preprint arXiv:1901.07722*, 2019, doi:10.48550/arXiv.1901.07722.
19. Bhambri, P., Rani, S., Pareek, P.K., Financial Innovations: Intelligent Automation in Finance and Insurance Sectors, in: *Generating Entrepreneurial Ideas with AI*, D. Darwish (Ed.), pp. 226–43, IGI Global, 2024, https://doi.org/10.4018/979-8-3693-3354-9.ch012.
20. Rani, S. and Bhambri, P., Industry 4.0 Framework and Applications, in: *AI-Driven Digital Twin and Industry 4.0: A Conceptual Framework with Applications*, 1st, S. Rani, P. Bhambri, S. Kumar, P.K. Pareek, A.A. Elngar (Eds.), pp. 1–14, CRC Press, 2024, https://doi.org/10.1201/9781003395416.

12

6G Network: Integrating Wireless Networks and Machine Learning for Connected Edge Intelligence

B. Prabha[1]*, V. Praveen[2] and M.R. Santhoosh[2]

[1]Department of Artificial Intelligence and Machine Learning, Panimalar Engineering College (Autonomous), Chennai, Tamil Nadu, India
[2]SRM Institute of Science and Technology, Vadapalani Campus, Chennai, Tamil Nadu, India

Abstract

The rapid growth of artificial intelligence (AI) applications is propelling the ongoing evolution of wireless networks. The advent of 6G is anticipated to be transformative, ushering in a shift from merely connecting devices to fostering "connected intelligence." However, contemporary state-of-the-art AI systems, relying on deep learning and big data analytics, demand substantial computation and communication resources, leading to notable issues such as latency, energy consumption, network congestion, and privacy concerns during both training and inference phases. Addressing these challenges, the integration of model training and inference capabilities into the network edge emerges as a disruptive technology, poised to seamlessly amalgamate sensing, communication, computation, and intelligence. This paper envisions scalable and trustworthy edge AI systems, presenting an integrated approach that combines wireless communication strategies with decentralized machine learning models. It introduces innovative design principles for wireless networks, service-driven resource allocation optimization methods, and a comprehensive end-to-end system architecture supporting edge AI. The discussion extends to application scenarios, providing insights to propel the industrialization and commercialization of edge AI systems in the context of 6G networks.

**Corresponding author*: jemi.prabha@gmail.com; ORCID: 0000-0003-4392-9058
V. Praveen: ORCID: 0009–0001–0750–7248
M.R. Santhoosh: ORCID: 0009–0001–0473–3549

Sita Rani, Pankaj Bhambri, Balamurugan Balusamy, Rishabha Malviya and Seifedine Kadry (eds.) Edge Intelligence for 6G-Enabled Industrial Internet of Things, (249–270) © 2026 Scrivener Publishing LLC

Keywords: 6G networks, edge AI, connected intelligence, wireless communication, decentralized machine learning, resource allocation

12.1 Introduction

6G networks are about to change how we connect with each other, thanks to their ambitious goals and cutting-edge abilities. These networks are aiming for data speeds that go beyond 1 terabit per second, making communication lightning-fast for things like augmented reality and high-definition video streaming. They're also working on reducing delays to less than one millisecond, which is super important for things like self-driving cars and remote surgery. Another big goal is connecting tons of devices, up to a million in each square kilometer. This will make it easy to bring IoT devices into smart cities and industries seamlessly. And to top it off, they're focusing on being more energy-efficient with cool ideas like energy harvesting and smart network management to help save the environment and cut down on costs. Plus, they're making sure our data stays safe with strong encryption and smart security protocols [9].

But wait, there's more! 6G networks are going to introduce some really cool new features. They're bringing in advanced AI algorithms to make the networks smarter, more efficient, and better at managing traffic and resources. This means less waiting and more smooth experiences for us. And get this – they're going to support all kinds of new tech like virtual reality, augmented reality, holographic communication, and immersive telepresence. It's going to feel like we're right there in the action! They're even using satellite communication to reach far-off places and make sure everyone gets connected, no matter where they are. And they're doing all of this while keeping an eye on the planet, working to reduce carbon emissions, cut down on electronic waste, and promote eco-friendly practices every step of the way. So yeah, 6G networks are not just faster and smarter – they're also more sustainable and ready to meet the ever-growing needs of our digital world [20].

12.1.1 Definition and Importance of Edge Intelligence in the 6G Context

Edge intelligence is all about being smart right where the action is – at or near where data is created, usually at the edge of the network [27]. When it comes to 6G networks, this kind of intelligence is super important because it helps make communication systems work better, faster, and more smoothly by spreading out the computing and decision-making tasks. Here's why edge intelligence matters so much in the world of 6G [7].

1. **Reduced Latency:** Handling data close to where it's generated means fewer delays. This is crucial for applications like self-driving cars, factory automation, and virtual reality that need instant responses.
2. **Bandwidth Optimization:** Edge intelligence is like a filter for data before it gets sent out, which means less data has to travel across the network. This saves bandwidth and reduces traffic jams, especially in places where the network is already pretty busy.
3. **Enhanced Privacy and Security:** By keeping sensitive data close by, edge intelligence lowers the risk of data breaches during transmission. This keeps your private information safer and more secure.
4. **Scalability and Flexibility:** Edge intelligence can adapt and allocate resources on the fly based on what's needed.

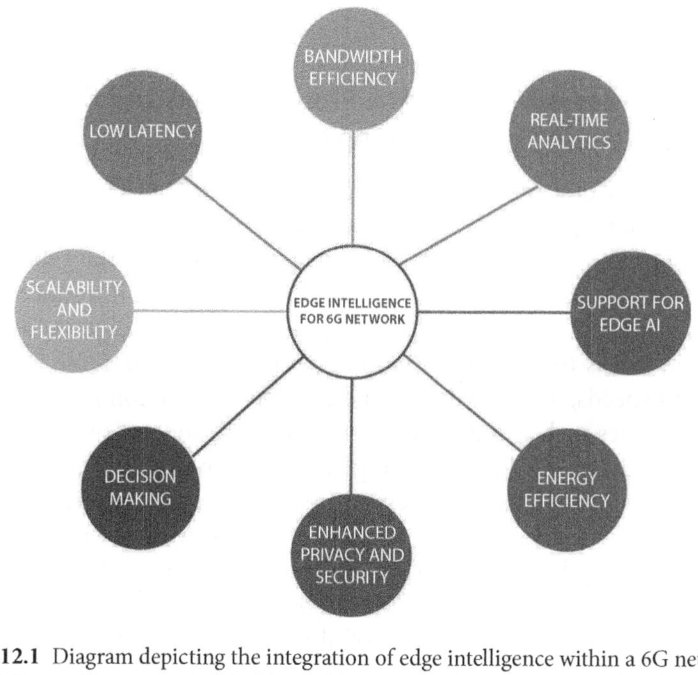

Figure 12.1 Diagram depicting the integration of edge intelligence within a 6G network, highlighting various connected devices and data processing nodes situated at the network edge.

This makes it great for handling lots of IoT devices and handling different workloads in different situations.

5. **Support for Edge-AI Applications:** Bringing AI smarts to the edge of the network lets us do cool things like real-time analytics, predicting when machines need maintenance, and providing services that understand their surroundings. This makes edge devices smarter and more capable.

So, integrating edge intelligence into 6G networks isn't just a small change – it's a big deal that makes wireless communication smarter, faster, and more adaptable to all the new digital stuff. Integration of Edge Intelligence in a 6G Network— This diagram illustrates the architecture of a 6G network with edge intelligence, showcasing the various connected devices (e.g., IoT devices, sensors) and data processing nodes distributed at the network edge. It highlights how data is processed locally near the source, reducing latency and enhancing real-time decision-making capabilities within the network as shown in Figure 12.1.

12.2 Evolution of Wireless Networks for Edge Intelligence

12.2.1 Historical Perspective: From 1G to 6G and the Evolution of Edge Computing

The evolution of wireless communication from 1G to 6G networks has brought about a profound transformation, accompanied by the rise of edge computing [6]. It all began with basic analog voice calls in the 1980s during the era of 1G. Subsequent generations like 2G, 3G, and 4G introduced digital transmission and data services, shaping the mobile landscape we see today. However, it was the arrival of 5G that truly changed the game, delivering super-fast speeds, minimal delays, and extensive device connectivity, thanks to technologies such as millimeter-wave spectrum and massive MIMO.

At the same time, edge computing evolved from simply reducing latency by processing data closer to users to becoming a widespread distributed computing approach. Initially focused on improving user experiences, edge computing has now become indispensable for supporting applications sensitive to delays and managing the vast amounts of data generated by IoT devices. With the promises of ultra-low latency and enhanced connectivity in 6G networks, the importance of edge computing has grown

Table 12.1 Historical Perspective: From 1G to 6G and the Evolution of Edge Computing - This table outlines the progression of wireless communication technologies from 1G to the projected 6G, highlighting advancements in data rate, latency, connection density, coverage, and energy efficiency for each generation.

Generation	Year	Data rate	Latency	Connection density	Coverage	Energy efficiency
1G	1980s	Up to 2.4 kbps	High	Low	Limited	Low
2G	1990s	Up to 50 kbps	Moderate	Moderate	Improved	Moderate
3G	2000s	Up to 2 Mbps	Moderate	High	Widespread	Moderate
4G	2010s	Up to 1 Gbps	Low	High	Extensive	High
5G	2020s	Up to 10 Gbps	Ultra-Low	Very High	Ubiquitous	Very High
6G	2030s	Projected > 10 Gbps	Projected Ultra-Low	Projected Very High	Projected Ubiquitous	Projected Very High

even further [2]. Table 12.1 provides a historical perspective, tracing the evolution from 1G to 6G alongside the development of edge computing.

6G networks are preparing to seamlessly integrate edge computing, leveraging its capabilities to make quick decisions, optimize network resources, and support a wide range of applications. The combination of 6G and edge computing is poised to unlock groundbreaking innovation, especially with the integration of AI at the network edge to enable intelligent services and applications. This collaboration between 6G networks and edge computing holds tremendous promise across various sectors such as autonomous vehicles, smart cities, healthcare, and industrial automation. As we enter this new phase of connectivity evolution, the merger of 6G networks with edge computing represents a fundamental shift, offering improved performance, reliability, and transformative opportunities in the digital era. The progression of wireless networks from 1G to 6G, highlighting key technological advancements such as digital voice, mobile internet, high-speed broadband, and intelligent connectivity is shown in Figure 12.2.

12.2.2 Key Technological Advancements Enabling Edge Intelligence in 6G Networks

Several important technological advances are set to make edge intelligence a reality in 6G networks, transforming how data is handled and used at

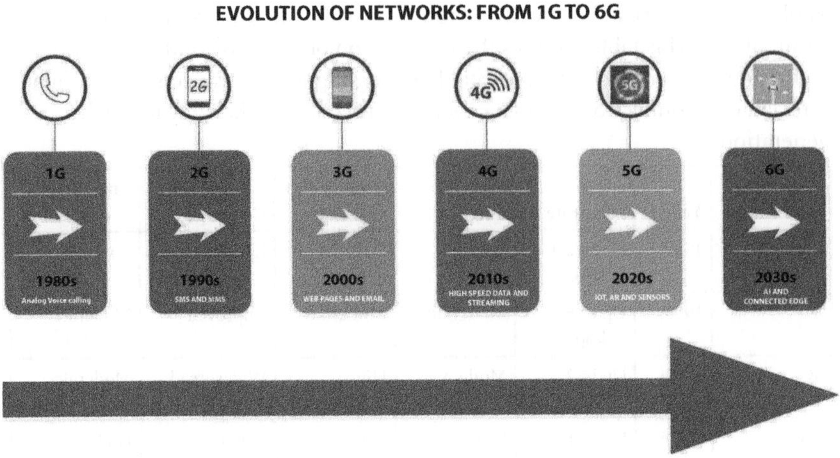

Figure 12.2 Timeline graph showing the progression of wireless networks from 1G to 6G, emphasizing key technological advancements.

the network edge. One key development is the integration of advanced AI algorithms directly into edge devices. This allows for real-time analysis of data without needing central cloud servers. Additionally, the widespread adoption of edge computing infrastructure, like edge servers and nodes, provides the computational power needed for complex AI tasks at the network edge.

Furthermore, improvements in communication technologies, such as faster wireless connectivity and lower latency, enable seamless communication among edge devices and ensure quick data transmission for analysis [24]. The rise of federated learning techniques allows edge devices to work together on training AI models using local data while keeping sensitive information secure on the device.

Moreover, the creation of specialized hardware accelerators like GPUs and TPUs designed for edge computing enhances the efficiency and performance of AI tasks at the network edge. Security and privacy measures, like homomorphic encryption and differential privacy, ensure that sensitive data remains protected during processing and analysis at the edge.

Additionally, integrating blockchain technology creates a secure and transparent framework for data exchange and transactions, enhancing trust and accountability in edge intelligence systems. Advancements in edge orchestration and management tools also make it easier to deploy and manage edge intelligence applications, ensuring scalability, reliability, and efficient use of resources in 6G networks [28]. These technological advancements together make edge intelligence in 6G networks possible, leading to a new era of decentralized, smart, and responsive communication systems.

12.3 Challenges in Integrating AI with Wireless Networks

Integrating AI into wireless networks faces several challenges. These include limited resources for wireless devices, delays that affect AI's real-time decision-making, and the need for energy-efficient AI algorithms to save device battery life [4]. Concerns about data privacy and security also come up when sensitive information is transmitted, and scalability becomes an issue as more devices join the network. In wireless setups, interference and signal changes can disrupt AI's performance, so we need strong adaptation methods. Additionally, complying with AI and wireless communication rules makes integration more complex. Overcoming these challenges will require teamwork and innovative solutions to ensure smooth AI integration with wireless networks.

12.3.1 Latency and Real-Time Processing Requirements

Reducing delays and achieving real-time responses are big challenges when combining AI with wireless networks, especially for tasks that need quick decision-making like autonomous vehicles and industrial automation. Delays caused by sending and processing data can really affect how well these systems work, which is super important for keeping interactions smooth and users happy. Wireless networks naturally have some delays because of things like how long it takes signals to travel and how data is processed. [5], talked about how important it is to minimize these delays, saying we need to make every step of handling data—from collecting it at the edge to making decisions—as efficient as possible. That's where edge computing comes in—it helps by doing most of the work closer to where the data is, so it doesn't have to travel far. This means we can respond much faster, which is crucial for real-time tasks on wireless networks.

Also, [1] talked about new ways to speed up AI using special processors and other technologies. This makes AI work faster, which helps reduce delays and lets us do real-time tasks at the edge. Plus, we can improve how networks work by using smarter ways to send data, like making sure important data gets through quickly and using better coding methods.

These tricks can really speed up how data moves, cutting down delays. And using edge caching and content delivery networks (CDNs) helps too—they store often-used data closer to users so we don't have to fetch it from far away, which saves time.

12.3.2 Energy Efficiency and Resource Optimization

When integrating AI with wireless networks, one of the most important considerations is how efficiently energy is used and resources are optimized. This is especially crucial because many wireless devices have limited resources, and there's a growing need for communication systems that are environmentally friendly. Using energy efficiently not only helps devices last longer on a single charge but also reduces costs and lessens the impact on the environment. To improve energy efficiency, one approach is to develop AI algorithms and models specifically tailored for devices with limited resources. These algorithms aim to strike a balance between being computationally complex enough to deliver accurate results and using less energy to perform tasks, thus maintaining performance while reducing energy consumption [8].

Another key aspect is edge computing, which plays a vital role in energy efficiency by reducing the amount of data that needs to travel to centralized servers. This reduction in data transmission lowers energy consumption associated with wireless communication. Edge computing allows for local data processing at the edge of the network, making use of nearby computational resources and cutting down on energy-intensive communication.

12.3.3 Privacy and Security Concerns in Edge AI Systems

Privacy and security are critical concerns in edge AI systems due to the sensitive nature of data processed at the network edge, as discussed by [22]. Edge devices handle personal and confidential information, raising worries about unauthorized access, data breaches, and privacy violations. The decentralized nature of edge computing introduces more vulnerabilities and attack points, increasing the risk of cyber threats and malicious activities. Furthermore, edge AI systems may lack robust encryption and authentication measures, making them susceptible to data interception and tampering during transmission. To tackle these challenges, techniques like differential privacy and homomorphic encryption are crucial for protecting sensitive data and preserving user privacy. Implementing strong access controls and authentication protocols is vital to prevent unauthorized access to edge devices and data. Compliance with data protection regulations such as GDPR and CCPA is essential to ensure legal and regulatory adherence regarding data privacy and security. Continuous monitoring, threat detection, and incident response are key for identifying and mitigating security breaches in edge AI systems. Collaborative efforts among stakeholders are necessary to effectively address privacy and security concerns and build trust among users of edge AI systems through transparent disclosure and user awareness initiatives.

12.4 Machine Learning Models for Edge Computing

Machine learning models used in edge computing are specially crafted to work efficiently on edge devices with limited resources. Their goal is to reduce latency and energy usage, as highlighted by [26]. These models are typically lightweight and optimized for making quick decisions at the network edge. Techniques like model quantization, pruning, and compression are commonly used to shrink the model size and complexity. These edge machine learning models are designed to use local data for making inferences, which lessens the need to send data to centralized servers and boosts privacy. Additionally, federated learning allows collaborative model training across distributed edge devices while maintaining data privacy. Transfer learning methods enable edge devices to leverage pre-trained models and adapt them to local situations, reducing the reliance on extensive training data. Continuous learning strategies are also employed, enabling edge models to adapt and improve their performance as they operate, ensuring adaptability in changing environments and evolving needs. Overall, machine learning models tailored for edge computing enable smart decision-making and real-time analytics at the network edge, enhancing the efficiency and responsiveness of edge computing systems.

12.4.1 Overview of Decentralized Machine Learning Algorithms

Decentralized machine learning algorithms, as explained by [14], are designed to facilitate collaborative model training across numerous distributed nodes without relying on a central server. These algorithms simplify the aggregation of local model updates from each node to collaboratively train a global model while maintaining data privacy. One common approach is federated learning, where local models use data from individual nodes, and only the model updates are shared with a central server for aggregation. Another method is peer-to-peer (P2P) learning, where nodes

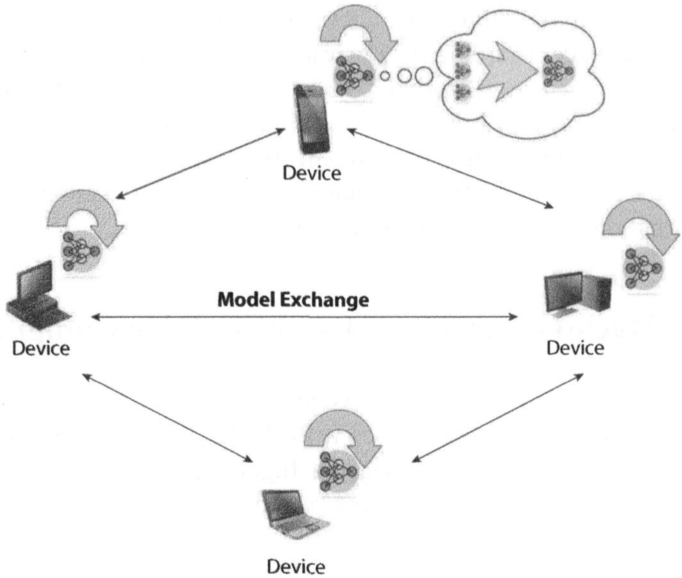

Figure 12.3 Illustration demonstrating peer-to-peer learning among edge devices, where devices share model updates directly with each other without a central server.

exchange model parameters directly with each other in a decentralized manner. These algorithms are particularly useful in scenarios where data is sensitive or spread across multiple locations, such as IoT networks or edge computing environments. Figure 12.3 provides an illustration of the decentralized nature of P2P learning.

12.4.2 Model Compression and Optimization Techniques for Edge Devices

Compression and optimization techniques are vital for deploying machine learning models on edge devices with limited resources, as highlighted by Han *et al.* [8]. These methods ensure efficient inference while minimizing the computational and memory demands. Figure 12.4 shows the illustration of the aggregation of local models from multiple devices into a global model within a federated learning framework. Quantization, for example, reduces parameter precision by compressing them into smaller bit widths, which conserves memory and decreases computational complexity. Pruning removes redundant connections and parameters, reducing the model's size without affecting its performance. Weight sharing techniques like weight tying and matrix factorization further reduce the parameter

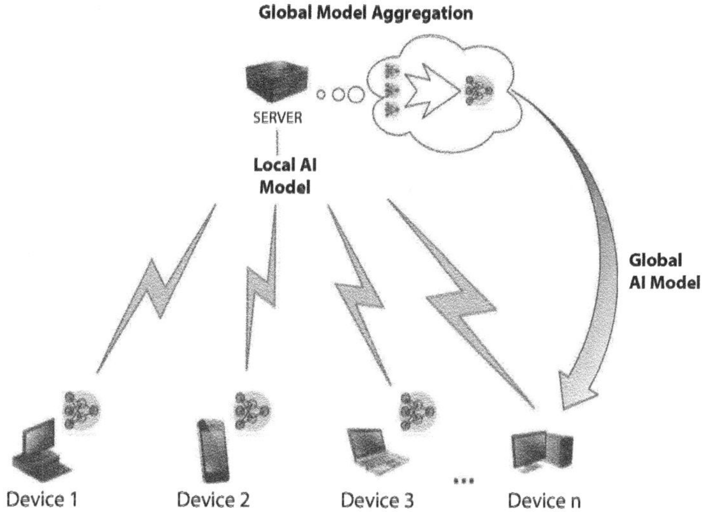

Figure 12.4 Diagram illustrating the aggregation of local models from multiple devices into a global model within a federated learning framework.

count, optimizing memory usage. Knowledge distillation transfers insights from a complex model to a simpler one, maintaining performance in a more compact form. Sparsity promotes sparse representations by setting many parameters to zero, making computation and storage more efficient. Dynamic quantization adjusts parameter precision based on runtime constraints, optimizing performance as required [11]. Hybrid architectures combine deep neural networks with lightweight algorithms to strike a balance between accuracy and efficiency. Methods such as Neural Architecture Search (NAS) and model pruning explore various designs to find compact and efficient model architectures tailored to edge devices. Together, these techniques enable the deployment of powerful machine-learning models on edge devices, unlocking a wide array of intelligent applications while conserving computational resources.

12.4.3 Federated Learning and Collaborative Intelligence at the Edge

Federated learning and collaborative intelligence, as described by [13], are revolutionary concepts in distributed machine learning that offer powerful capabilities while prioritizing data privacy and security. In federated learning, model training happens locally on edge devices using decentralized data, with only model updates shared with a central server for aggregation.

This method enables collaborative model training across an edge device network without centrally storing sensitive data, ensuring privacy and compliance with data regulations. Collaborative intelligence utilizes the collective intelligence of edge devices to jointly learn and make inferences from decentralized data sources [12], facilitating real-time decision-making and insights at the network edge. By utilizing the computational resources of edge devices and integrating local insights, federated learning and collaborative intelligence empower edge networks to handle complex machine learning tasks while minimizing latency and communication overhead. Moreover, these approaches enable adaptive and context-aware learning [13], allowing edge devices to continuously improve their models based on local feedback and environmental cues.

12.5 Design Principles for Edge AI Systems in 6G

Xu *et al.*, [25] underlines the importance of design principles for edge AI systems in 6G networks, emphasizing their critical role in ensuring scalability, efficiency, and reliability. The primary focus for these systems is to minimize latency by processing data locally at the network edge, reducing the reliance on transmitting data to centralized servers. This requires utilizing distributed computing resources and optimizing communication protocols for real-time decision-making. Energy efficiency is a significant concern, leading edge AI systems to adopt power-efficient hardware and algorithms to prolong device battery life and minimize environmental impact [14]. Privacy and security [15] are also key priorities, necessitating robust encryption, authentication [16, 17], and access control mechanisms to effectively safeguard sensitive data.

12.5.1 Scalable Architecture for Edge AI Deployment

A scalable architecture for edge AI deployment [19], leverages distributed edge servers, optimized machine learning models, and service-driven resource allocation. This architecture prioritizes low-latency processing, efficient data management, and robust security measures. By dynamically allocating resources based on service requirements and employing interoperable standards, it ensures flexibility, reliability, and scalability in edge computing environments. Additionally, continuous monitoring and management capabilities enable real-time optimization and resilience. Overall, this architecture facilitates efficient edge AI deployment, empowering

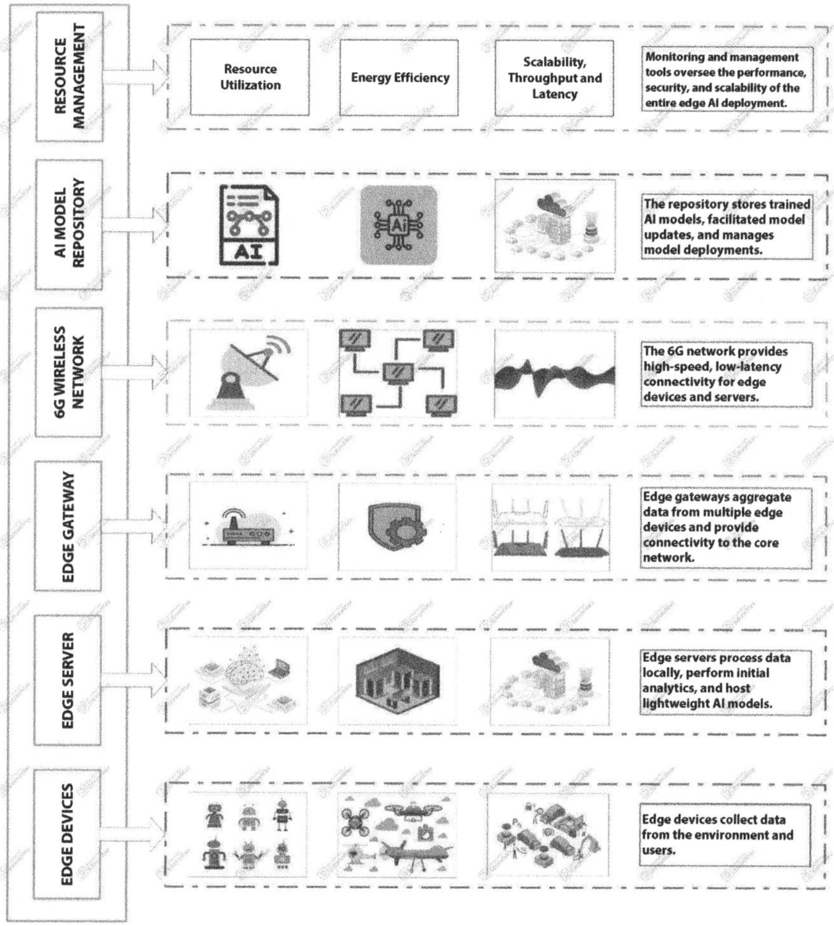

Figure 12.5 Architecture diagram showing the scalable design for deploying artificial intelligence at the network edge, including various layers and components.

organizations to deliver intelligent services at the network edge. The scalable design for deploying artificial intelligence at the network edge, including various layers and components is shown in Figure 12.5.

12.5.2 Service-Driven Resource Allocation and Management

Service-driven resource allocation and management is a critical aspect of optimizing the performance and efficiency of edge AI systems. This approach involves dynamically allocating computing resources based on the requirements of specific services or applications, ensuring optimal utilization while meeting quality of service (QoS) objectives. At the heart of service-driven resource allocation is the ability to prioritize and allocate resources based on the demands of different services. This involves continuously monitoring service-level metrics such as latency, throughput, and resource utilization and dynamically adjusting resource allocations accordingly. For example, resources can be allocated based on the urgency of a particular service request or the criticality of the application. Moreover, service-driven resource allocation requires intelligent workload scheduling mechanisms to efficiently distribute computing tasks across available resources. This may involve prioritizing critical tasks, optimizing task placement to minimize communication overhead, and dynamically scaling resources to handle fluctuating workloads.

Furthermore, service-driven resource management incorporates mechanisms for resource optimization and consolidation. This includes techniques such as virtualization, containerization, and server consolidation

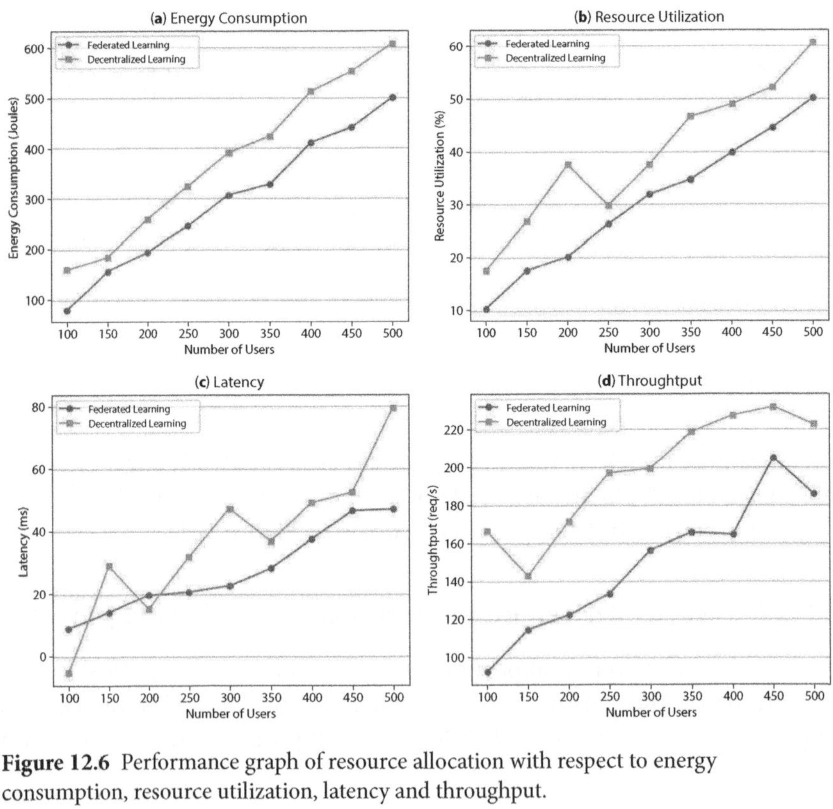

Figure 12.6 Performance graph of resource allocation with respect to energy consumption, resource utilization, latency and throughput.

to maximize resource utilization and minimize energy consumption while ensuring service performance is shown in Figure 12.6. Additionally, service-driven resource allocation and management should be adaptive and responsive to changes in the environment, such as fluctuations in demand, network conditions, and hardware failures. This requires continuous monitoring and analysis of system metrics and the ability to dynamically reconfigure resources in real-time.

12.5.3 Edge-to-Cloud Continuum: Balancing Computation between Edge and Central Servers

The concept of the edge-to-cloud continuum, as outlined by, encompasses a spectrum of computing resources ranging from edge devices to centralized cloud servers. Finding the right balance in distributing computational tasks across this spectrum involves optimizing where tasks are performed based on factors such as latency requirements, data sensitivity, and resource availability [21]. Edge computing plays a crucial role in enabling low-latency processing and real-time decision-making near data sources, thereby reducing the reliance on centralized servers and minimizing communication overhead. However, there are instances where centralized cloud processing remains advantageous, particularly for handling complex or resource-intensive tasks, as well as for long-term data analysis and storage. To achieve an optimal balance, it is necessary to dynamically allocate tasks between the edge and cloud based on workload demands. This dynamic allocation ensures efficient utilization of resources while meeting performance and scalability requirements across the continuum. Such an approach enhances system responsiveness, reliability, and scalability, enabling organizations to effectively leverage the strengths of both edge and cloud computing in a cohesive manner [22].

12.6 Applications and Use Cases of Edge Intelligence in 6G Networks

Edge intelligence in 6G networks [18], refers to the integration of AI and computational capabilities at the network edge, enabling real-time data processing, analysis, and decision-making closer to the data source. Some notable examples include autonomous vehicles, where edge intelligence ensures rapid decision-making for safe navigation; smart cities, where it optimizes traffic management and enhances environmental monitoring;

healthcare, with remote patient monitoring and personalized treatment recommendations; industrial IoT, for predictive maintenance and real-time equipment monitoring; and augmented reality/virtual reality, providing low-latency content delivery and immersive user experiences. Overall, edge intelligence in 6G networks enables efficient, responsive, and intelligent systems, transforming industries and enhancing user experiences.

12.6.1 Smart Cities and IoT Applications Leveraging Edge AI

Smart cities leverage various IoT devices [15] and sensors to collect massive amounts of data from urban environments. Edge AI, by processing this data locally at the edge of the network, offers several benefits in terms of speed, efficiency, and scalability. Here are some specific applications of edge AI in smart cities and IoT:

- **Traffic Management**: Edge AI can analyze real-time data from traffic cameras, sensors embedded in roads, and GPS-enabled vehicles to optimize traffic flow, predict congestion, and manage traffic signals dynamically.
- **Public Safety and Security**: Edge AI enables intelligent video analytics for real-time monitoring of public spaces, identifying suspicious behavior, and detecting anomalies such as accidents or criminal activities.
- **Waste Management**: Smart waste management systems equipped with sensors can monitor garbage levels in bins and optimize waste collection routes. Edge AI can analyze this data to predict fill levels, schedule pickups efficiently, and reduce operational costs while keeping cities cleaner and more sustainable.
- **Environmental Monitoring**: Edge AI can process data from environmental sensors measuring air quality, temperature, humidity, and pollution levels.

12.6.2 Autonomous Vehicles and Intelligent Transportation Systems

Autonomous vehicles (AVs) and intelligent transportation systems (ITS) [23] are revolutionizing the way people and goods are transported, offering numerous benefits in terms of safety, efficiency, and sustainability.

Edge AI plays a critical role in enabling the development and deployment of AVs and ITS by processing data in real-time and facilitating intelligent decision-making.

- **Enhanced Situational Awareness**: Edge AI enables AVs to maintain a comprehensive understanding of their environment by continuously analyzing sensor data and identifying potential hazards or risks in real-time. This enhances situational awareness and allows AVs to anticipate and react to unpredictable events on the road effectively.
- **Dynamic Route Optimization**: Edge AI enables AVs to optimize their routes dynamically based on real-time traffic conditions, road closures, and weather updates. By processing data locally, AVs can adapt their navigation strategies in response to changing circumstances, minimizing travel time and improving overall efficiency.
- **Collision Avoidance Systems**: Edge AI powers advanced collision avoidance systems in AVs, which can detect and respond to potential collisions with other vehicles, pedestrians, or obstacles on the road. By analyzing sensor data in real-time, AVs can apply brakes, steer, or take evasive action to prevent accidents and ensure passenger safety.
- **Traffic Management and Optimization**: Edge AI extends beyond individual AVs to facilitate intelligent traffic management and optimization in ITS.

12.6.3 Healthcare, Industry 4.0, and Other Verticals Benefiting from Edge Intelligence

Edge intelligence offers significant benefits across various verticals, including healthcare, Industry 4.0, and several others [3]. Here's how edge intelligence is transforming these sectors:

12.6.3.1 Healthcare

- Remote Patient Monitoring: Employing edge intelligence enables the continuous monitoring of patients' vital signs and health parameters through wearable devices and sensors. Real-time analysis of this data at the edge facilitates early detection of health issues and timely intervention.

- Telemedicine: Edge intelligence supports high-quality video consultations and remote diagnostics in telemedicine. By processing medical imaging data and patient records locally, edge devices ensure low latency and secure data transmission.
- Personalized Medicine: Edge AI analyzes genomic data, patient history, and real-time physiological data to tailor treatment plans and medications for individual patients. This personalized healthcare approach enhances treatment outcomes and patient satisfaction.

12.6.3.2 Industry 4.0

- Predictive Maintenance: Edge intelligence enables predictive maintenance of industrial machinery by analyzing sensor data to detect signs of equipment failure beforehand. This minimizes downtime, reduces maintenance costs, and prolongs the lifespan of assets.
- Smart Manufacturing: Edge AI optimizes production processes by analyzing real-time data from sensors, machines, and production lines. This enhances efficiency, quality control, and resource utilization in manufacturing settings.
- Supply Chain Optimization: Edge intelligence facilitates real-time tracking and monitoring of goods across the supply chain. By analyzing data from RFID tags, GPS trackers, and other IoT devices at the edge, companies can optimize inventory management, logistics, and delivery processes.

12.7 Future Directions and Emerging Trends

12.7.1 Predictions for the Evolution of Edge Intelligence beyond 6G

The advancement of edge intelligence beyond 6G networks, as discussed by [10], is poised for a significant transformation towards ultra-low latency, high-bandwidth communication, and distributed intelligence. This progress is expected to lead to the use of more autonomous edge devices, employing advanced AI algorithms [25] for making decisions locally. This will improve response times and ensure privacy.

12.7.2 Integration of Quantum Computing, Blockchain, and Other Emerging Technologies with Edge AI

Combining quantum computing, blockchain, and other new technologies with edge AI brings big opportunities to change many industries and improve how decentralized computing works. Quantum computing is super powerful and can do really complex tasks that were impossible before. When we mix quantum computing with edge AI, like what talked about, it makes machine learning algorithms work better. This means quicker decision-making and more accurate insights right at the edge of the network. Blockchain is famous for being secure and transparent, which is crucial for edge AI systems dealing with sensitive data. By using blockchain, edge AI systems can make sure data is safe, transactions are secure, and everyone in the network can trust each other. This is super important in areas like healthcare, finance, and supply chain management where privacy and trust are huge concerns. Overall, bringing quantum computing, blockchain, and new tech together with edge AI is changing how computers work in a big way. It makes things more efficient, secure, and scalable. As these technologies get better and work together more [29–31], they'll keep changing industries, sparking new ideas, and shaping how decentralized computing grows in the future.

12.8 Conclusion

The fast development of AI in wireless networks is changing how devices connect, moving towards a concept called "connected intelligence." But this shift brings challenges like delays, energy use, network congestion, and privacy worries with today's AI systems. With 6G networks, there's a chance to solve these issues by focusing on putting AI at the network's edge. This lets us blend sensing, communication, computing, and smarts smoothly, creating scalable and dependable edge AI systems. This article suggests a mixed approach that combines wireless strategies with decentralized machine learning. It suggests smart design ideas for network setups, efficient ways to allocate resources, and complete system setups that support edge AI. It also looks beyond just tech problems to consider different ways these systems can be used. By sharing insights into how to make edge AI systems work in 6G networks, this article aims to push forward in making efficient, secure, and scalable AI-powered wireless networks for the future.

AI disclosure statement: The author confirms that no artificial intelligence (AI)-generated content or AI-assisted writing tools were used in the preparation of this chapter (including summaries and the abstract). All text, analysis, and conclusions are the result of the author's original work.

References

1. Bui, N., Zorzi, M., Poor, H.V., A Review of Predictive Maintenance Management Solutions: State of the Art and Prospects for the Future. *IEEE Access*, 8, 180934, 2020, https://doi.org/10.1109/ACCESS.2020.3022765.
2. Buzzi, S., Santamaria, I., Zappone, A., AI at the Edge for 6G Wireless Networks: Benefits and Challenges. *IEEE Trans. Wirel. Commun.*, 21, 2, 1357, 2022.
3. Chen, M., Mao, S., Zhang, Y., Leung, V.C., Letaief, K.B., Deep Learning for Remote Health Monitoring Systems: A Survey. *IEEE Access*, 6, 47965, 2018.
4. Chen, Y., Jiang, H., Yu, F.R., Huang, T., Zhang, H., Artificial Intelligence in Wireless Networks: Opportunities, Challenges, and Research Directions. *IEEE Wirel. Commun.*, 27, 4, 47, 2020.
5. Chen, M., Zhang, Y., Zhao, S., Mao, Y., Wireless Network Meets Artificial Intelligence: A Survey. *IEEE Commun. Surv. Tutor.*, 21, 3, 2574, 2019, https://doi.org/10.1109/COMST.2019.2907070.
6. Feng, T., Zhang, L., Chen, Y., Hu, F., Kato, N., Edge intelligence in 6G networks: Challenges, solutions, and future trends. *IEEE Wirel. Commun.*, 28, 2, 48, 2021.
7. Guo, J., Sheng, M., Kang, J., Zhou, T., Wu, D., Edge intelligence in 6G networks: Challenges, solutions, and future trends. *Future Gener. Comput. Syst.*, 116, 566, 2021.
8. Han, S., Mao, H., Dally, W.J., Deep Compression: Compressing Deep Neural Networks with Pruning, Trained Quantization and Huffman Coding, *arXiv preprint arXiv:1510.00149,* 2015. [Online]. Available: https://arxiv.org/abs/1510.00149.
9. Hossain, M.S., Muhammad, G., Vu, H.L., Abdel-Maguid, M., 6G Networks: Vision, Requirements, Architecture, and Key Technologies. *IEEE Access*, 9, 50535, 2021.
10. Huang, W., Zhang, Q., Cheng, H., Yang, J., Chen, H.H., Edge Intelligence Beyond 5G and 6G: A Review and Outlook. *IEEE Internet Things J.*, 8, 18, 14901, 2021.
11. Jiang, H., Zhu, G., Zong, Z., Lu, Y., Mao, S., Edge Intelligence in 6G: Vision, Requirements, and Key Technologies. *IEEE Wirel. Commun.*, 28, 5, 17, 2021.
12. Khan, R.U., Khan, S.U., Zaheer, R., Khan, A., A Comprehensive Review of Emerging Technologies: Integration of Quantum Computing, Blockchain,

and Other Emerging Technologies with Edge AI. *IEEE Access*, 8, 81716, 2020, https://doi.org/10.1109/ACCESS.2020.2980737.

13. Kairouz, P., McMahan, H.B., Avent, B., Bellet, A., Bennis, M., Bhagoji, A.N., *et al.*, Advances and open problems in federated learning, *arXiv preprint arXiv:1912.04977,* 2019. [Online]. Available: https://arxiv.org/abs/1912.04977.
14. Konečný, J., McMahan, H.B., Yu, F.X., Richtárik, P., Suresh, A.T., Bacon, D., Federated Learning: Strategies for Improving Communication Efficiency, *arXiv preprint arXiv:1610.05492*, 2016. [Online]. Available: https://arxiv.org/abs/1610.05492.
15. Li, Q., Xu, L.D., Zhao, S., Liu, L., A survey on the edge computing for the Internet of Things. *IEEE Access*, 6, 6900, 2018.
16. Liu, Y., Zhang, J., Guan, X., Zhang, Y., Chen, H.H., Artificial Intelligence in Wireless Networks: A Comprehensive Survey. *IEEE Internet Things J.*, 7, 1, 38, 2020, https://doi.org/10.1109/JIOT.2019.2944056.
17. Lu, W. and Liu, Y., Edge Intelligence Empowered 6G Wireless Networks: A Comprehensive Survey. *IEEE Commun. Surv. Tutor.*, 24, 1, 31, 2022.
18. Mahdavinejad, M.S., Rezvan, M., Javadi, H.H.S., Abolhasani, M.M., Adibi, P., Internet of Things for Smart Cities: Technologies and Applications. *Information*, 8, 3, 1, 2017, https://doi.org/10.3390/info8030098.
19. Satyanarayanan, M., Bahl, P., Caceres, R., Davies, N., The Case for VM-based Cloudlets in Mobile Computing. *IEEE Pervasive Comput.*, 8, 4, 14, 2009, https://doi.org/10.1109/MPRV.2009.82.
20. Sharma, P., Zhang, Y., Yu, F.R., Nallanathan, A., Zomaya, A.Y., An Overview of 6G Networks: Vision, Applications, and Research Challenges. *IEEE Netw.*, 35, 6, 59, 2021.
21. Shi, W., Cao, J., Zhang, Q., Li, Y., Xu, L., Edge Computing: Vision and Challenges. *IEEE Internet Things J.*, 3, 5, 637, 2016, https://doi.org/10.1109/JIOT.2016.2579198.
22. Tang, J. and Nambi, S., Privacy and Security in Edge Computing: A Review. *IEEE Access*, 9, 94706, 2021, https://doi.org/10.1109/ACCESS.2021.3097024.
23. Tian, Y., Xu, F., Wang, D., Zhang, Y., Tian, H., The Study on Traffic Management System Based on Edge Computing and IoT, in: *Proceedings of the 2020 International Conference on Big Data and Computing*, ACM, pp. 70–74, 2020, https://doi.org/10.1145/3429216.3429233.
24. Wang, J., Lin, W., Zhang, Z., Integration of AI into Edge Computing for 6G Networks: Challenges and Opportunities. *IEEE Trans. Ind. Inf.*, 18, 2, 1073, 2022.
25. Xu, J., Wang, X., Chen, J., Liu, C., Wang, F., Jin, D., Design and Implementation of AI-Based Edge Computing Systems: A Comprehensive Survey. *IEEE Access*, 9, 61228, 2021, https://doi.org/10.1109/ACCESS.2021.3070729.
26. Yang, Y., Liu, Y., Chen, M., Zhang, Q., Edge Intelligence: Paving the Last Mile of Artificial Intelligence with Edge Computing. *Proc. IEEE*, 108, 9, 1655, 2020, https://doi.org/10.1109/JPROC.2020.3008401.

27. Zhang, H., Luo, X., Lu, X., Wang, C., Zhang, Y., Edge Intelligence-Enabled 6G Networks: Challenges and Opportunities. *IEEE Trans. Cogn. Commun. Netw.*, 8, 1, 4, 2022.
28. Zhang, J., Huang, T., Dong, M., Zhang, Z., Edge Intelligence in 6G Networks: Opportunities and Challenges. *IEEE Internet Things J.*, 8, 23, 18752, 2021.
29. Zhang, Y., Zhang, Y., Sun, X., Liu, C., Edge computing for smart cities: A survey. *IEEE Access*, 7, 148231, 2019.
30. Bhambri, P., Rani, S., Kumar, S., Sinha, V.K., Big Data Analytics with Digital Twin for Industrial Applications, in: *AI-Driven Digital Twin and Industry 4.0: A Conceptual Framework with Applications*, 1st ed., S. Rani, P. Bhambri, S. Kumar, P.K. Pareek, A.A. Elngar (Eds.), pp. 105–126, CRC Press, Boca Raton, FL, USA, 2024, https://doi.org/10.1201/9781003395416.
31. Bhambri, P., Rani, S., Pareek, P.K., Paperless Paradigm: Intelligent Automation in Document and Record Management, in: *Generating Entrepreneurial Ideas with AI*, D. Darwish (Ed.), pp. 164–83, IGI Global, Hershey, PA, USA, 2024, https://www.igi-global.com/book/hyperautomation-business-society/335477.

13

Securing the Hyper-Connected World: Security, Privacy and Research Challenges in IoT

Gagneet Kaur[1,2]*, Komal Singh[3], Pankaj Bhambri[2] and Sandeep Kumar Singla[2]

[1]*Department of Computer Science and Engineering, I.K. Gujral Punjab Technical University, Jalandhar, Punjab, India*
[2]*Guru Nanak Dev Engineering College, Ludhiana, Punjab, India*
[3]*Department of Electrical Engineering, Indian Institute of Technology, Ropar, Punjab, India*

Abstract

The Internet of things (IoT) becomes popular and supported by many applications after it was introduced for the first time in 2006. It interconnects objects with each other such as machine-to-machine, to communicate wirelessly without intervention of humans. Time to time updating is done in wireless sensor networks (WSNs), Radio Frequency Identification (RFID) for communication between different objects without consideration of place, surroundings and time.

This chapter aims at systematic study of research challenges of IoT security and data security in a hyper-connected world. The chapter begins with the discussion of why there is a need of "security and privacy in IoT" and how security will maximize while designing IoT systems for providing end-to-end security. Firstly, we explain the security architecture of IoT; because security issues in IoT is not only similar to security issues in the internet, mobile communications, and WSNs. Different network configuration, access control, authentication, and privacy issues are there in IoT.

**Corresponding author*: jaggigagneet@gmail.com; ORCID: 0000-0002-1049-6623
Komal Singh: ORCID: 0000-0002-1337-0014
Pankaj Bhambri: ORCID: 0000-0003-4437-4103
Sandeep Kumar Singla: ORCID: 0009-0002-6313-3460

Sita Rani, Pankaj Bhambri, Balamurugan Balusamy, Rishabha Malviya and Seifedine Kadry (eds.) Edge Intelligence for 6G-Enabled Industrial Internet of Things, (271–284) © 2026 Scrivener Publishing LLC

Secondly, we discuss various security issues and open challenges in different applications of IoT. Several attacks and data theft issues arise in many applications of IoT. These issues can be resolved by applying security techniques.

Keywords: Security architect, security principles, Internet of Things, security patches, RFIDs

13.1 Introduction

The internet of things (IoT) becomes popular and supported by many applications after it was introduced for the first time in 2006. It interconnects objects with each other such as machine-to-machine, to communicate wirelessly without intervention of humans. Time to time updating is done in wireless sensor networks (WSNs), Radio Frequency Identification (RFID) for communication between different objects without consideration of place, surrounding and time [7, 17]. IoT attracts various industries and markets by enabling automation and opportunities. The greatest advancement in IoT comes through introducing smart city concept. That gives various business opportunities to citizens of smart cities with smart automation, smart objects, smart living, smart home, etc. [17].

With the increase of use of IoT in various applications, main research concern in IoT till now is efficiently connecting a greater number of devices together. Mobile phones are no longer just for communication with people. IoT upgrades the use of mobile phone by communicating it with dumb devices containing sensors [11].

Devices made up of sensors and controllers progressively become intelligent for providing support in smart applications in security, healthcare, industry and vehicle transportations. By looking on popularity of IoT, it already presumes that in the future billions of devices will be interlinked together *via* the internet; which will lead us to hyper-connected world. So, security issues are common in the world of hyper-connections. Many new security threats will arise that will affect the life of the citizens and their privacy. Designing cross-layer security mechanism for IoT is not easy [12].

This chapter aims at systematic study of research challenges of IoT security and data security in a hyper-connected world. The chapter begins with the discussion of why there is need of "security and privacy in IoT" and how security will maximize while designing IoT systems for providing end-to-end security. Firstly, we'll explain the security architecture of IoT. Because security issues in IoT is not only similar to security issues in the internet, mobile communications, and WSNs. Different network configuration, access control, authentication, and privacy issues are there in IoT.

Secondly, we'll discuss various security issues and open challenges in different applications of IoT. Several attacks and data theft issues arise in many applications of IoT. These issues can be resolved by applying security techniques.

13.1.1 Security Framework for Privacy & Security in a Hyper-Connected World

The term IoT refers to the ability of day-to-day objects around us to be connected to the internet for transmission and reception of data—such as smart home automations systems which allows you to turn on or off lights when you leave or enter; smart meters help electricity providers to analyze the consumption of power of consumers; smart bands share your activities with your friend when you go run or biked, and internet enabled security cameras which allow you to watch over home even from far. In the medical area, medical devices connected over the internet which help doctors to monitor serious diseases of their patients to control their illness. According to some researchers, six years ago, the total number of objects or things connected over internet exceeds the total number of people in the world. It presumes that, as of the 2020, over 20 million devices will be connected over the internet [12]. Data sharing between millions of devices also has various risks of breeching data.

As of risks, researchers identified that IoT has many security risks. Such as it,

a) enables breech in data security due to unauthorized access;
b) misuses user's information;
c) suffers security attacks on other connected devices; and other
d) personal safety risk.

Researchers also mention that privacy risks may emanate from collection of data containing personal information, locations, physical movements and habits. Some third-party companies might use such data for other technologies and companies, to meet their potential results.

As for designing a security framework, three parts of security are important. These are:

a) **Confidentiality**
   It basically is the set of rules that enables the accessibility of personal information to a smaller number of users. It helps to secure the important data from unauthorized access.
b) **Availability**
   It enables the accessibility of data only to main user, not to third party users. It is achieved by maintaining hardware and, updating of the system timely.

c) **Integrity**
Integrity is achieved by maintaining correctness of data. It depends upon trustworthiness of data. While transmitting data from one end to another, it needs to be assured that data should not breached and accessed by unauthorized users. IoT devices shares large amount of data like, medical information and, banking transactions. This data is transmitted over same shared platform. That leads to security risk.

13.2 Security Attacks & Open Challenges

In this, we will cover the different security attacks and open challenges in IoT applications.

13.2.1 Smart Buildings

1. Smart buildings equipped with connected devices such as IoT networks, sensors, and their processing with building automation systems, parking systems, security systems, and fire detection. The smart building system enables single control system to control all other systems of building and sharing their data for analysis [3]. Smart buildings generates huge amount of data (historical and real time data). That data further used for processing to generate predictive analysis based results for optimization of assets and consumption of resources, using artificial intelligence and machine learning algorithms. Apart from benefits offered by smart building in management of resources and ease of living, there are many security threats that come from different sources [15].

Some researchers identifies that poorly installed equipment by electricians who have no knowledge about security enables the open access of building management system controllers *via* open internet [15]. That becomes the reason of security attacks. One research shows that the data of search engines can unveil the information of many insecure building management systems throughout the world.

Another research reveals the major security issue in temperature controller systems used in smart buildings, hospitals and super-markets [14]. Research shows that anyone could access temperature controllers using browsers because these systems used insecure default passwords and protocols. In 2016, an attack on Dyn company hijacked the computing resources of the company which leads to congestion of network and interruption of services in America [2, 10]. Mirai malware was used for attack on CCTV cameras and recorders. This malware wipes the data of IoT devices that were protected with default username and passwords.

Vulnerabilities:

Whole systems of smart buildings are complex that leads to a range of weak security. These are,

a) Computer Security Flaws in the software of devices and gateways of firms.
b) Using insecure protocols and, default passwords for surveillance devices causes vulnerability issues.
c) No physical security to wired networks and internal devices.
d) Limited access or visibility to state of security of interconnected devices and systems.
e) Improper management of procedure and policies in cryptographic keys.
f) Lack of security upgradation of systems.

The insecure security system of smart building invites many attackers by exposing them to weaknesses. These issues can be resolved by implementing confidentiality, availability and, integrity. That is possible only after understanding the weak points of interconnections of the whole smart building. The process of threat modeling helps to point out security issues and controls, such as

a) Authentication, encryption and integration security over communications
b) Audit security events
c) Using security patches
d) Configuration of network management
e) Network segmentation
f) Authorized access controls
g) Tamper alarms
h) By deploying secure gateways

13.2.2 Healthcare Industry

IoT offers various services in healthcare industry such as, reduction in operational cost, remote monitoring, improvement in treatment and, diagnosis. Several healthcare products were used to control connectivity of device and physical accessibility, in healthcare organizations and hospitals like controlled environment. IoT enhances the mobility and remotely accessibility of healthcare devices [13]. IoT expands the area of healthcare industry by introducing digital health. Digital health is the combination of health and care. It includes telehealth, wearable devices, health information technology, and mobile health. Mobile health offers health services *via* wearable devices, monitoring devices, and smart mobile phones [8]. The data of digital health devices further shared with external healthcare professionals for monitoring details of patients. Sharing and handling data of patient comes under security concerns. Security of digital healthcare devices includes the factors such as management and portability of devices, the platform on which the devices are connected, and the architecture of network [16]. A poor security causes the serious issues in the ability of device to deliver effective service to patient. Security services are different for different types of devices.

Vulnerabilities

From research, it shows that several vulnerabilities are reported in health devices from then till now. List of reported vulnerabilities are growing day by day likely due to the increase in number of devices in use. In 2008, hackers remotely accessed the "Implantable Defibrillator" which directly harms the safety of the user. Researchers found out that anyone can remotely access and shut down the device [8].

In 2013, researchers show that multiple numbers of medical devices are secured with hard coded passwords. But this became the major vulnerability of devices because if some devices have same passwords, then anyone can access other devices having similar passwords. User had no ability to change the password manually [13].

In 2015, vulnerability is reported in "Patient Controlled Infusion System (Hospira LifeCare)" because of its connectivity with other devices and systems. The connectivity issue caused a potential impact on security of device. This vulnerability allows anonymous remote access and control of devices which impacts the flow of medication through veins of patient [13].

In 2018, a major vulnerability of personal data collection is reported in wearable gadgets like "Fitness Tracker Data API (Polar)" which directly impact on security of user's privacy. Anyone can access personal information, location data, and identify identity of user like military personnel [13]. These vulnerabilities can also cause physical harm to users, including death, if used indiscreetly. But fortunately, these issues have not yet used in such ways. This shows that there is a need to recognize issues in security and fix them. Improvement in security of healthcare devices is a main concern. Complexities that arise with the IoT for health industry are [5].

a) Healthcare service providers,
b) Network platform,
c) Environment in which devices are operating,
d) Device ownership/providers,
e) User authentication,
f) Device authentication,
g) Confidentiality, availability and integrity of data

13.3 Solutions & Security Architecture for Healthcare Industry

Different security solutions developed for different types of healthcare devices. There is no single solution to solve the issues of security. A wide variety of devices are here in use as healthcare [18]. Those who are deploying IoT in healthcare need to be aware about the wide range of vulnerabilities while designing a device [4]. A security of device focuses on key principles of IoT security framework.

a) Confidentiality,
b) Availability, and
c) Integrity

Several risks also arise while designing security framework for device using these traditional principles.

13.3.1 Confidentiality Risks

It includes risk of unauthorized access while sharing and collecting patient's data between systems and devices. Different regional and national regulations defined these risks like- health sector regulation in America and regulation of protection of data in Europe [6]. Because some organizations use patient data for medicinal research, so protecting identity of patient and personal information is also a main concern.

13.3.2 Availability Risks

These risks can result from malware attacks. In 2017 UK, Wanna cry ransomware attack caused the disruption in the service of devices [13]. This attack made the devices unable to record data, manage history, and monitor readings.

13.3.3 Integrity Risks

It arises when changes in data affects the patient's healthcare record. With the help of healthcare devices, it allows doctors to monitor the health and information while overseeing the treatment of patients. More data increases the risk of miss-analysis and miss-calculation of data.

13.4 Automotive IoT

Using IoT in vehicles broadens the capabilities of vehicles. Now, vehicles are no longer only for moving from one place to another. IoT connects vehicles to devices which enhances the accessibility of vehicle from anywhere. IoT connects the cars over the network called CV2X that helps to connect vehicles together [19]. Connected vehicles enable fast data transmission and enhance the response time of drivers. Predictive analysis is the crucial feature of IoT automotive. The sensors are used to collect information of different components of car and transmit it to platform [20–22]. Then, that data is further used for processing by an algorithm for analyzing the future outcomes. Several features provided by IoT in automotive are:

a) Time and driver management
b) Real-time location monitoring
c) Route management
d) Automotive maintenance system
e) In-vehicle information and telematics
f) Autonomous vehicle

13.4.1 Vulnerabilities

Apart from advancement in automotive industry, IoT increases the ease and comfort of living. But it also opens many safety and privacy issues. Some vulnerabilities of automotive IoT are here:

a) Flaws in software applications
b) Lack and low integrity of segmentation between critical and non-critical applications
c) Loop holes in end point integrity
d) Cryptographic tampering
e) Weak peer authentication

In 2015, an experiment was done to prove the vulnerabilities of connected cars. The experimental research shows the massive impact on security of vehicle. In this experiment, a team of two guys was able to hack the vehicle that was just ten miles away from them [9]. They were able to change the music, project images on dashboard screen, pull on seatbelts, engage the horn, and disable breaks. This experiment found the major vulnerability in the connecting platform which connects the phones with navigation and entertainment system of the vehicle. In 2016, research team of the University of Michigan's cyber security show that they were able hack commercial vehicles *via* standards used for communication and networking in commercial vehicles [1].

13.4.2 Safety Measures

Important safety measures are necessary for protection of data and human life. These are:

a) Segmentation and isolation
   If any area of system is damaged or breached, then that system should operate to quarantine.
b) Security Updates
   Timely security updates are important for the system. If there are any breaches that are disclosed, then security updates implement crucial patches to that problem.
c) Evidence Capture
   In this safety measure, investigation is done to recognize defects in designs and malfunctions of a system.
d) Third-party Collaboration
   Collaboration between researchers and industry is needed to look for issues in security while designing new technologies.
e) Safety by design
   Designing safety measures while developing, designing and testing of system.

13.5 Issues of Risks Arise in Key Security Principles of Security Architecture

Table 13.1 identifies the causes of vulnerabilities in major IoT application areas and the risks they pose to confidentiality, integrity, and availability.

Table 13.1 Causes of vulnerabilities in the major IoT application areas and their associated risks to confidentiality, integrity, and availability.

Major application areas	Smart buildings	Healthcare industry	Automotive industry
Confidentiality risks	1. Open networks, 2. Poor security systems, 3. Lack of timely up-dating	1. Single network frame (where all devices are inter-connected), 2. Poor security architecture, 3. Unauthorized access	1. Poor network security, 2. Using open gateways, 3. Third party software
Integrity risks	1. Open ports, 2. Low or lack of encryption key management	1. Hard coded passwords, 2. Same key management for encryption	1. Open ports, 2. Using low security network standards
Availability risks	1. Single control system, 2. Lack of web security	1. Single network hub for all devices, 2. Third party access	1. Network failure, 2. Complex supply chain

13.6 Solutions for Issues of Risks Arise in Key Security Principles of Security Architecture

Table 13.2 below are the solutions designed for resolving issues that pose risks in security and privacy.

Table 13.2 Solutions to mitigate security and privacy risks.

Major application areas	Smart building	Healthcare industry	Automotive industry
Confidentiality risks	1. By using security protocols for connectivity of devices. 2. Time-to-time updating of softwares.	1. By managing authenticity of data and devices. 2. By using secure network connections. 3. Time-to-time updating of systems to patch loopholes of systems, if any occurs.	1. By using secure connections. 2. Managing authenticity of third party softwares.
Integrity risks	1. By using standard encryption keys to encrypt data for transmission. 2. Use reliable platforms for sharing information of devices over the network.	1. Use reliable platforms for sharing information of devices over the network. 2. By managing authenticity of users. 3. Timely updating security passwords. 4. By using secure encryption standards.	1. By not using third party systems that can interrupt the transmission of data.

(*Continued*)

Table 13.2 Solutions to mitigate security and privacy risks. (*Continued*)

Major application areas	Smart building	Healthcare industry	Automotive industry
Availability risks	1. Keep building access control system up to date and running. 2. Detect potential problems proactively. 3. Ensure central IoT system is continuously available.	1. Ensure devices are up-to-date. 2. Check data-backups. 3. Use network interrupt detection systems.	1. By optimizing visibility of automotive parts and routing through supply chain. 2. By using risk management systems. 3. Insist on accurate cost control and deep visibility to the supply chain. 4. By applying stringent quality reporting and visibility.

AI disclosure statement: The author acknowledges the use of AI-based tools for minor language editing or grammatical correction. However, all intellectual contributions, analyses, and conclusions presented in this chapter are entirely the author's own.

References

1. Achiiles, D. and Maria., S., Internet of Things (IoT) and Agricultural Unmanned Aerial Vehicles (UAVs) in smart farming: A comprehensive review. *Internet Things*, 2020.

2. Kreb, B. and Krebs on Security, Hacked cameras, DVRs Powered Todays Massive Internet Outage, October 2016, https://krebsonsecurity.com/2016/10/hacked-cameras-dvrs-powered-todays-massive-internet-outage/.
3. Can You Trust Your Smart Building? Whitepaper, in: *IoT Security Foundation*, 2019, https://www.iotsecurityfoundation.org/wp-content/uploads/2019/07/IoTSF-Smart-Buildings-White-Paper-PDFv2.pdf.
4. IETF, Key words for use in RFCs to Indicate Requirement Levels.
5. *IoT Security reference architecture for the healthcare industry, Whitepaper*, IoT Security Foundation, 2019, https://www.iotsecurityfoundation.org/wp-content/uploads/2018/12/IoTSF-IoT-Security-Compliance-Framework-Release-2.0-December-2018.pdf.
6. IoT Security Foundation, IoT Security Compliance Framework release 2.0, 2018.
7. ISO/IEC 80001 Application of Risk Management for IT Networks Incorporating Medical Devices, 2010.
8. Carter, J. and OWASP, Defense in depth, 2020, https://owasp.org/www-project-reverse-engineering-and-code-modification-prevention/.
9. Keertikumar, M., Shubham, M., Banakar, R.M., Evolution of IoT in smart vehicles: An overview, in: *2015 International Conference on Green Computing and Internet of Things (ICGCIoT)*, 2015.
10. Mathews, L. and Forbes, Criminals Hacked A Fish Tank To Steal Data From A Casino, July, 2017, https://www.forbes.com/sites/leemathews/2017/07/27/criminals-hacked-a-fish-tank-to-steal-data-from-a-casino/.
11. Dachyar, M., Zagloel, T.Y.M., Saragih, L.R., Knowledge growth and development: internet of things (IoT) research, 2006–2018. *Heliyon*, 5, 8, e02264, 2019. https://doi.org/10.1016/j.heliyon.2019.e02264.
12. Ammar, M., Russello, G., Crispoa, B., Internet of Things: A survey on the security of IoT frameworks. *J. Inf. Secur. Appl.*, 38, 8–27, 2018. https://doi.org/10.1016/j.jisa.2017.11.002.
13. National Institute of Standards and Technology, Framework for Improving Critical Infrastructure Cybersecurity, https://nvlpubs.nist.gov/nistpubs/CSWP/NIST.CSWP.04162018.pdf.
14. Kane, P. and Safety Detective, Major Security Breach Found in Hospital and Supermarket Refrigeration Systems, 2019, https://www.safetydetectives.com/blog/rdm-report/.
15. SC Media and Barth, B., Researchers develop proof-of-concept malware for attacking Building Automation Systems, Jan. 2019, https://insight.scmagazineuk.com/.
16. US Department of Homeland Security, Recommended Practice: Improving Industrial Control System Cybersecurity with Defense-in-Depth Strategies, https://ics-cert.us-cert.gov/sites/default/files/recommended_practices/NCCIC_ICS-CERT_.
17. Vermesan, O. and Friess, P., *The University of Michigan's cybersecurity*, pp. 189–192, River Publishers, 2015.

18. World Health Organisation Constitution, 1946.
19. Kim, Y., Oh, H., Kung, S., Proof of Concept of Home IoT Connected Vehicles. *Sensors*, 17, 6, 1289, 2017. https://doi.org/10.3390/s17061289.
20. Devi, Y.U. and Rukmini, M.S.S., IoT in connected vehicles: Challenges and issues — A review, in: *2016 International Conference on Signal Processing, Communication, Power and Embedded System (SCOPES)*, 2017.
21. Bhambri, P., Rani, S., Kumar, S., Sinha, V.K., Big Data Analytics with Digital Twin for Industrial Applications, in: *AI-Driven Digital Twin and Industry 4.0: A Conceptual Framework with Applications*, 1st, S. Rani, P. Bhambri, S. Kumar, P.K. Pareek, A.A. Elngar (Eds.), pp. 105–26, CRC Press, 2024, https://doi.org/10.1201/9781003395416.
22. Kaur, J., Bhambri, P., Rani, S., Digital Twin Enabling Technologies, Applications, and Challenges, in: *AI-Driven Digital Twin and Industry 4.0: A Conceptual Framework with Applications*, 1st, S. Rani, P. Bhambri, S. Kumar, P.K. Pareek, A.A. Elngar (Eds.), pp. 90–104, CRC Press, 2024, https://doi.org/10.1201/9781003395416.

14

Edge-to-Cloud Synergy: Enhancing IIoT Capabilities

Cynthia Jayapal[1]*, K. Ulagapriya[2], K.V.M. Shree[3] and A. Poonguzhali[4]

[1]Department of Computer Science and Engineering, RV University, Bengaluru, India
[2]Department of Computer Science and Engineering, Vels Institue of Science Technology and Advanced Studies, Chennai, Tamil Nadu, India
[3]Department of Artificial Intelligence and Data Science, Dhanalakshmi Srinivasan Engineering College, Perambalur, Tamil Nadu, India
[4]Department of Electronics and Communication Engineering, Sri Sairam College of Engineering, Bangalore, Karnataka, India

Abstract

Integration of edge computing and cloud services creates an ecosystem that harnesses the Industrial IoT(IIoT) potential to enhance real-time monitoring and analytics capability. IIoT enables the integration of devices, machines, sensors, and actuators in an industry with an IoT framework. This enhances the performance of the industry by aiding in effective decision-making and preventive maintenance. Edge computing aids in data filtering, monitoring, and triggering for action at the industrial site; and cloud computing aids in storing data and performing data analytics for effective production and preventive maintenance. The synergy between cloud and edge aids in optimal performance. Digital Twins are used to simulate, remotely monitor, and analyze the IIoT entities in real-time. The steps involved are Data collection from sensors at the edge side, Edge Intelligence using ML Algorithms, Data filtering and aggregation, Digital Twin Integration, Edge Cloud connectivity, Real-time monitoring, Data Analytics, Preventive Maintenance, and Real-time decision-making. 6G Terahertz communication aids in connecting a massive number of devices and sensors with ultra-low latency, high reliability, and responsiveness. It also provides enhanced security and privacy features with

**Corresponding author*: cynthia.j.it@kct.ac.in; ORCID: 0000-0002-9318-7948
K. Ulagapriya: ORCID: 0000-0001-9276-9308
K.V.M. Shreel: ORCID: 0009-0008-0817-8125
A. Poonguzhali: ORCID: 0000-0001-5393-9861

Sita Rani, Pankaj Bhambri, Balamurugan Balusamy, Rishabha Malviya and Seifedine Kadry (eds.) Edge Intelligence for 6G-Enabled Industrial Internet of Things, (285–320) © 2026 Scrivener Publishing LLC

highly accurate spatial detection and satellite integration. Digital Twin is used to virtually represent the physical asset of an IIoT system and is used for remote monitoring, predictive analytics and preventive maintenance. Blockchain technology can be used to store critical data from IIoT devices in a distributed digital ledger and is used to provide enhanced security in an untrusted environment with time stamping and integrity.

Keywords: IIoT, edge computing, cloud computing, digital twin, 6G, blockchain

14.1 Introduction

The convergence of edge computing and cloud services has emerged as an essential paradigm in the Industrial Internet of Things (IIoT), enabling unprecedented possibilities for revolutionizing industrial operations. In this era of interconnected devices, machines, sensors, and actuators, IIoT is at the forefront, enabling seamless integration within industrial frameworks in addition to real-time monitoring and analytics. However, to entirely realize the potential of IIoT and address the evolving requirements of modern business enterprises, a symbiotic relationship between edge computing and cloud services is necessary.

This chapter explores how the combination of edge computing, cloud services, 6G communication, digital twin and blockchain technologies can considerably improve the competences of IIoT. By integrating these technologies seamlessly, industries can leverage every aspect of IIoT to improve performance, make more accurate decisions and implement proactive maintenance strategies. Edge computing is essential for processing data at the network's edge, enabling real-time data filtering, monitoring, and action triggering on the industrial site. Cloud services, on the other hand, provide a robust infrastructure for storing enormous amounts of data and performing complex analytics, enabling industries to acquire actionable insights to optimize production processes and maintenance tasks.

Digital twins are simulated copies of physical resources that enable real-time simulation, remote monitoring, predictive analytics, and proactive maintenance of IIoT entities. This promotes a paradigm shift in industrial operations, which improves efficiency and dependability. The capacity to monitor physical assets in real time allows organizations to optimize operations, reduce downtime, and improve dependability and safety. As more firms adopt IIoT, the use of digital twins is expected to become more widespread, creating new possibilities for innovation.

This chapter discusses the essential steps involved in utilizing the potential of edge-to-cloud synergy. These steps include gathering data from various sensors, using machine learning algorithms to power edge intelligence, filtering and aggregating the data, integrating digital twin, connecting edge and cloud, monitoring the system in real time, performing data analytics, executing preventive maintenance, and making real-time decisions. Furthermore, the introduction of 6G terahertz communication is set to change the game by enabling uninterrupted communication between an enormous number of devices and sensors, with ultra-low latency, high reliability, and enhanced security features.

In addition, this chapter highlights the importance of utilizing blockchain technology to maintain the security and integrity of data within industrial internet of things (IIoT) ecosystems. By utilizing blockchain's distributed ledger capabilities, critical data from IIoT devices can be securely stored, timestamped, and verified, which helps to reduce risks in untrusted environments and ensure the continuity of industrial processes. This chapter also provides a comprehensive understanding of how combining edge and cloud technologies can enhance IIoT capabilities and drive innovation in industrial landscapes. Our main objective is to pave the way for a future where industries can thrive in a data-driven ecosystem that is interconnected. The chapter aims to offer insights into the practical benefits that this paradigm shift can offer, which can lead to sustainable growth and development.

14.1.1 Foundations of Industrial IoT

The IIoT is built on a combination of key elements that together transform business processes. Sensors and actuators are installed in machines to seamlessly collect instantaneous information about various objects that are not at the core of the industrial internet of things (IIoT). This information is then transmitted to a trusted network to enable remote monitoring and communication with the device. IIoT platforms use advanced data collection technologies and processing capabilities to transform raw data into valuable information. This facilitates quality control, process optimization, and preventive maintenance. Integrity and reliability are ensured through security measures that protect against cyber threats and ensure proper integration of various businesses and devices. A scalable and flexible infrastructure designed to keep pace with changing business requirements and technological developments allows the industry to adapt and evolve in dynamic situations. IIoT improves human-machine interaction by enabling operators to monitor, measure, and optimize business processes with unprecedented efficiency and accuracy. This is achieved through an intuitive interface and intelligent analytics.

14.1.1.1 Evolution of Industry IoT

The network of networked machines, sensors, and devices in industrial settings that exchange data and communicate with one another to enhance productivity, stimulate innovation, and optimize operations is known as the IIoT. The IIoT [1], is designed for manufacturing industries, energy, transportation, and healthcare, in contrast to the consumer-oriented IoT, which is focused on improving daily living [2]. The convergence of multiple technical developments can be linked to the evolution of the IIoT. Industries first used manual methods and stand-alone machinery. However, the groundwork for IIoT was established with the introduction of digital technologies like sensors, actuators, and automation systems. Real-time data collecting from industrial assets was made possible by these technologies, opening the door for proactive maintenance plans and better decision-making.

With the increasing prevalence and affordability of connectivity technologies such as Ethernet, Wi-Fi, and cellular networks, industries started integrating their fragmented systems and devices into unified IIoT networks. This evolution was made possible by cloud computing, which offered scalable processing and storage capacities for the enormous volumes of data produced by IIoT devices. Additionally, developments in edge computing made it possible for data processing to take place nearer to the source, which decreased latency and made it possible for important applications to respond more quickly. Furthermore, the development of AI and machine learning has enabled IIoT systems to autonomously evaluate data patterns, forecast equipment failures, and optimize production processes. As new technologies appear and industries embrace digital transformation projects, the evolution of IIoT keeps accelerating. A wide range of industries are now implementing IIoT solutions, which give businesses all around the world cost savings, efficiency benefits, and competitive advantages. It is anticipated that IIoT will continue to merge the digital and physical domains, bringing in an era of linked supply chains, smart factories, and predictive maintenance.

14.1.1.2 Components of IIoT Ecosystem

The IIoT ecosystem consists of several interconnected parts that work together to promote innovation, streamline operations, and allow data-driven decision-making in industrial settings.

Figure 14.1, illustrates the components of IIoT system. The components of an IIoT system are—

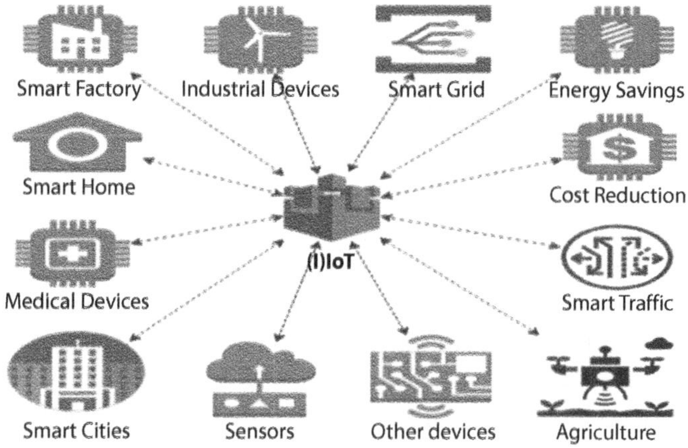

Figure 14.1 Components of IIoT systems.

Sensors and Actuators: These are the foundational elements of IIoT, which gather information from physical assets and start operations in response to commands or circumstances. Actuators allow for the automation and remote control of machinery and equipment, while sensors keep an eye on a variety of characteristics like humidity, vibration, temperature, and pressure. Connectivity Infrastructure: To transfer data between systems and devices, IIoT depends on reliable communication networks. Wireless technologies such as Bluetooth, Zigbee, Wi-Fi, and cellular networks enable mobility and flexibility in data transfer, wired technologies like Ethernet and fieldbus protocols offer dependable connectivity within industrial contexts. Edge Devices and Gateways: At the edge of the network, edge devices, and gateways carry out data preprocessing, aggregation, and filtering functions in their capacity as middlemen between sensors and the cloud. Through the reduction of latency, bandwidth usage, and dependency on cloud infrastructure, these devices provide instantaneous data analysis and make decisions at the network edge.

Cloud Platforms: Cloud computing platforms deliver scalable processing and storage, of enormous volumes of data collected by IIoT devices. By making data storage, processing, and visualization easier, these systems help businesses get practical insights, put predictive maintenance plans into place, and streamline industrial procedures [3]. The author's emphasis on creating a cloud-based digital twin production system is indicative of their conviction that cutting-edge technologies, including cloud computing and digital twins, can completely alter conventional manufacturing processes. Analytics and Artificial Intelligence (AI): AI algorithms and advanced analytics are essential for deriving valuable insights from IIoT data. While machine learning algorithms allow for autonomous decision-making and process optimization, predictive analytics techniques help firms anticipate equipment failures, detect maintenance needs, and optimize production schedules.

Cybersecurity Solutions: Cybersecurity is essential to protect sensitive industrial data and defend against cyber threats as linked devices and data exchange within IIoT networks proliferate. To reduce risks and guarantee data integrity and confidentiality, IIoT cybersecurity solutions include intrusion detection, access control, encryption, authentication, and security monitoring techniques. Integration and Interoperability Standards: Within IIoT ecosystems, compatibility and interoperability across heterogeneous systems and devices are guaranteed by integration platforms and standards [4]. The smooth connection and data exchange between sensors, actuators, control systems, and business IT systems is made possible by common protocols like MQTT, OPC UA, and RESTful APIs. Human-Machine Interface (HMI): Operators and decision-makers may monitor, evaluate, and control industrial processes with the use of user interfaces and visualization tools, which offer intuitive dashboards and analytics dashboards. With the help of HMIs [5], users can collaborate in real-time, monitor remotely, and visualize data, which helps them respond to changing conditions and make wise decisions.

The IIoT ecosystem is built on the elements mentioned above, which enable companies to leverage automation, connectivity, and data-driven insights to improve productivity, streamline processes, and foster innovation.

14.1.1.3 Role of IIoT in Industrial Transformation

The IIoT is playing a critical and diverse role in driving major changes across all elements of industrial processes, leading to an industrial transformation. [6], advances how various technologies work together to improve productivity, efficiency, and adaptability in contemporary industrial environments, opening the door to more intelligent and well-optimized manufacturing procedures.

The following are some crucial functions of IIoT in the industrial transformation:

Data-Driven Decision Making: The IIoT enables real-time data collection from industrial environments, processes, and assets. Cloud computing platforms provide scalable processing and storage for the large amounts of data produced by IoT devices. With the help of this data, firms may make well-informed decisions by analyzing performance measures, spotting inefficiencies, and streamlining procedures to cut costs and boost output.

Predictive Maintenance: Predictive maintenance solutions can be implemented by enterprises by utilizing IIoT sensors and analytics. These tactics include increasing asset lifespan, decreasing downtime, cutting maintenance expenses, and forecasting possible breakdowns using equipment data analysis. Process Optimization: IIoT makes process optimization easier by offering insights into resource usage, energy consumption, and operational effectiveness [7]. By identifying bottlenecks, streamlining processes, and optimizing production schedules, organizations may use IIoT data to improve throughput, cut waste, and boost overall performance. Supply Chain Management: The movement and state of items in transit are monitored by IIoT, which improves visibility and traceability throughout the supply chain. Organizations may reduce risks like theft, damage, or spoiling, enhance inventory management, and streamline logistics with real-time tracking and monitoring capabilities.

Quality Control: IIoT makes it possible to continuously monitor and analyze metrics related to product quality throughout the production process. Through real-time deviation detection and swift corrective action implementation, companies may guarantee consistent product quality, minimize defects, and improve customer satisfaction.

Safety and Compliance: By tracking ambient conditions, identifying hazards, and warning staff members of possible dangers, IIoT improves workplace safety. IIoT data can also make it easier to comply with industry norms and regulations, guaranteeing adherence to safety procedures and lowering operational and legal risks [8].

Innovation and Product Development: IIoT encourages innovation by giving users access to copious amounts of data that can support R&D activities. Businesses can use IIoT information to spot market trends, foresee client wants, and create new goods and services that cater to changing consumer tastes and desires. Business Model Transformation: With the use of IIoT, businesses can transition from conventional product-centric business models to service-oriented ones with consumption, subscription [9], or performance-based pricing. Value-added services, such as asset tracking, predictive maintenance, and remote monitoring, help businesses build stronger client connections and generate new revenue streams. IIoT has a revolutionary role in the industrial transformation process, enabling businesses to stay competitive in an increasingly digital and connected world by streamlining processes, boosting productivity, and stimulating innovation. The IIoT, is a global industry-reshaping force that boosts productivity, creativity, and competitiveness through data-driven insights, predictive maintenance, and creative business models. It plays a critical part in the industrial transformation process by enabling firms to increase efficiency, streamline processes, and seize new growth prospects. IIoT will have a profound effect on industrial sectors as it develops, influencing supply chain management, manufacturing, and other areas in the future.

14.1.2 Understanding Edge Computing

14.1.2.1 Overview of Edge Computing

Cloud computing services can be extended to the edge of a network through an edge computing model. In this case, the main objective of this model is to make decisions that are as near as possible to the source of data by serving as a bridge between cloud data centers and edge devices/sensors. The problem with moving all the data from the net's edge to a cloud data center for processing is latency issues and exceeding network bandwidth capacity. It seems like the best way out would be to do data processing close to device/sensor [10]. This may not be new; placing compute resources adjacent to data sources. Edge computing solves many problems associated with cloud computing when it brings flexible resources closer to end-users at the net's edge, unlike distributed and hosted resources in other clouds.

14.1.2.2 Need of Edge Computing for IIoT Applications

IIoT can be revolutionized by edge computing. This, instead of transmitting it to a central server, lets IIoT devices store, process and analyze data on their own. There is usually a feedback loop in place in most IoT systems that involves constant transmission of data; reception of feedback and analyzing the input information. Real-time or historical analytics may be performed on large amounts of data using artificial intelligence (AI/ML) algorithms.

Edge computing comprises networking, storage and computation services at or near the physical location of users or data sources. Deploying technology closer to these locations offers faster, more dependable services for users with improved user experiences while enabling businesses to launch new types of latency-sensitive applications as well. Edge computing when combined with IoT enables enterprises to allocate jobs across IoT devices in a more flexible manner, enhance performance while introducing new use cases like low-latency, high-throughput messages which cannot be supported by conventional IoT.

14.1.2.3 Operational Benefits of Edge Computing

IoT applications are often used as monitoring systems that collect and analyze data and ask for educated responses. IoT application may process data on a daily basis, hourly basis or it can be event driven. IoT devices usually send back few packets to an evaluation center at the central control platform. Edge computing minimizes bandwidth by transferring long-term storage information only to a central base instead of entire data. Managing security is another headache for organizations with numerous internet of things gadgets [11]. Massive number of connected devices could be employed by attackers in launching DDoS attacks. One however; edge computing does not inherently offer better security than private clouds but the in-house solution simplifies handling security challenges. For instance, it is helpful in adhering to rules regarding data sovereignty and local data protection [12].

14.1.2.4 Edge Computing Architectures

Three main selections for architecture of edge computing are as follows.

Clean edge: Every compute resource should be located on premises. This is best for companies having regulatory or safety concerns over cloud migrations, hence requiring the making of high initial capital investments. A thick-edge connected to the cloud: Deploy data centers, edge computing devices and resources on the cloud. This allows for an enterprise to make use of pre-existing investments in on-premise data centers, as well as the cloud for gathering, analyzing and storing some data. A thin edge connected to the Cloud: This approach directly connects resources at the edge to the cloud without necessarily going through on-premises data center. It is also lightest and most flexible method with minimal expenses incurred. However, it lacks control of business conditions and possible security issues may arise.

The combination of edge computing and cloud services creates an ecosystem that leverages IIoT's potential in enhancing real-time monitoring and analytics capabilities. The integration of IIoT enables devices, machines, sensors & actuators to be incorporated into various industries through common framework of IoT. This enhances industrial productivity by aiding in making good decisions and preventive services. Edge computing tools for data filtering, monitoring and action in industrial spaces; and cloud computing tools to store data and perform data analytics for efficient production and preventive maintenance. Digital twins are used for virtual simulation, remote monitoring as well as analyzing IIoT components in real time. Data collection from edge sensors is done. Edge Intelligence with ML algorithms is in use. Data filtering and aggregation is conducted. Digital twin integration and edge cloud connectivity aids in real-time monitoring, data analytics and preventive maintenance and real-time decision making. The role of 6G terahertz is to have ultra-low latency, high reliability and sensitivity enabling communication devices and sensors. It also provides enhanced security and privacy features and space detection and satellite integration.

14.1.3 Cloud Computing

14.1.3.1 Overview of Cloud Computing

Cloud computing refers to the utilization of internet-based resources for various purposes, including storage, software, and other services. Users can access these resources on-demand, based on their needs without having to invest in physical infrastructure like servers or software licenses. Cloud services can be accessed from anywhere with an internet connection, allowing users to run applications and access data remotely. It provides scalability, allowing users to scale their resources up or down based on demand. This flexibility enables businesses to adapt to changing requirements without incurring significant costs or downtime. Cloud services can be deployed globally, making applications and data accessible to users worldwide. This global reach enables businesses to reach a wider audience and operate across geographical boundaries.

Edge computing and cloud services collaborate to create an ecosystem that leverages the potential of industrial IoT enabling real-time monitoring and analytics. Industrial IoT integrates devices, machines, sensors, and actuators into industries employing the internet of things framework. It improves industrial productivity by promoting effective decision-making and preventive services. Edge computing provides solutions for data filtering, monitoring, and taking action in industrial settings; and cloud computing tools for storing and analyzing information for enhancing production efficiency and preventive maintenance. Digital twins are employed to simulate IIoT entities in real-time, monitor them remotely, and then evaluate them.

The phases are outlined below: Data gathering from edge sensors, edge intelligence employing machine learning algorithms, data filtering and aggregation, Digital Twin integration, edge cloud connectivity, real-time monitoring, data analytics, preventive maintenance, and real-time decision-making. 6G Terahertz is useful for connecting communication devices and sensors with ultra-low latency, great reliability, and sensitivity. It also has enhanced security and privacy features that include space detection and satellite integration.

14.1.3.2 Cloud Services for Industrial Applications and Their Impact on IIoT

Cloud services are instrumental in driving industrial applications and revolutionizing the landscape of the IIoT. Infrastructure as a Service (IaaS) provisions virtualized resources, allowing industries to scale infrastructure dynamically, while Platform as a Service (PaaS) accelerates IIoT application development and deployment. Software as a Service (SaaS) solutions streamline the adoption of IIoT technologies. Big data and analytics services empower industries to analyze vast data streams, enhancing operational efficiency and enabling predictive maintenance. Machine learning and AI services enable intelligent IIoT applications for real-time decision-making and anomaly detection. Security and compliance services ensure data integrity and regulatory adherence. Together, these cloud offerings catalyze IIoT adoption, fostering innovation, scalability, and agility in industrial processes, ultimately driving enhanced productivity and competitiveness in Industry 4.0.

14.1.3.3 Benefits and Challenges of Cloud Integration

Cloud integration offers numerous benefits for IIoT deployments. Firstly, it facilitates seamless connectivity and data sharing across disparate devices and systems, enhancing interoperability and collaboration within industrial environments. Secondly, cloud integration enables scalable storage and processing of massive volumes of IIoT data, allowing organizations to leverage advanced analytics and machine learning algorithms for predictive maintenance, process optimization, and decision-making. Additionally, cloud integration reduces upfront infrastructure costs and complexity, as organizations can leverage cloud-based services and platforms on a pay-as-you-go basis, eliminating the need for large capital investments in hardware and software. Moreover, cloud integration provides enhanced flexibility and agility, enabling rapid deployment and scaling of IIoT solutions to meet evolving business requirements and market demands.

Despite its benefits, cloud integration in IIoT also presents several challenges. Firstly, data silos can arise due to segregated data repositories controlled by different departments or systems, hindering data accessibility and integration efforts. Secondly, ensuring security and compliance becomes paramount when migrating sensitive IIoT data to the cloud, requiring robust security measures and adherence to regulatory requirements. Thirdly, vendor lock-in poses a risk as organizations may become overly dependent on a single cloud provider, limiting flexibility and potentially increasing costs. Additionally, managing the complexity of integrating diverse IIoT devices, protocols, and platforms can be challenging, requiring careful planning and execution. Finally, ongoing maintenance and monitoring are essential to ensure the smooth operation and performance of cloud-integrated IIoT systems, necessitating proactive management of updates, performance, and potential issues to minimize downtime and disruptions. Overall, addressing these challenges effectively is critical to realizing the full potential of cloud integration in IIoT and achieving desired business outcomes.

14.1.4 Synergizing Edge and Cloud Technologies

Edge computing is an emerging technology that is revolutionizing the way businesses access and process data [13]. It offers several advantages over traditional cloud computing, such as reduced latency, cost savings, better data security, and privacy, improved scalability, and higher performance.

14.1.4.1 Conceptual Framework of Edge-to-Cloud Synergy

Edge computing and cloud computing are interdependent technologies that form a symbiotic relationship. While edge computing handles local data processing, cloud technology provides centralized resources and services for more extensive and resource-intensive tasks [14]. They create a holistic computing ecosystem that enhances application performance across various domains. Figure 14.2 illustrates the synergy between edge and cloud.

Performance of Edge Computing
The network performance of edge computing is characterized by its ability to,

Handle Data at the Source: Efficiently processes data center generated by network edge, ensuring low latency and real-time interactions.

Reduce Network Congestion: By processing data locally, edge computing minimizes internet congestion, ensuring smooth data transmission and optimal network constraints.

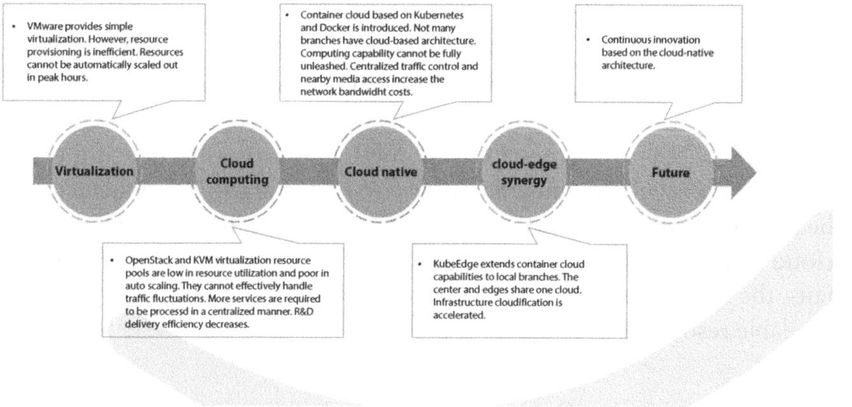

Figure 14.2 Cloud-to-edge synergy.

Enable Real-Time Interactions: Edge computing enables applications such as virtual reality, augmented reality, and IoT devices to interact with minimal delays, providing a seamless user experience.

14.1.4.2 Integrating Edge and Cloud for Enhanced Performance

Combining edge computing and cloud computing can significantly improve overall system performance through strategic allocation of computing resources [15]. This combination is often referred to as edge-cloud or fog computing. Reduce latency: Edge computing moves computing resources closer to data sources, reducing travel time for data to and from the cloud. This is especially important for applications that require real-time or low-latency processing, such as IoT devices, autonomous vehicles, and augmented reality.

Bandwidth Optimization: Edge devices can process and filter data before sending only relevant data to the cloud. This reduces the amount of data sent over the network, optimizes bandwidth usage, and reduces congestion. Enhanced security: Edge computing allows data to be processed locally, reducing the need to transmit sensitive data over the network. Important data can be processed at the edge and only aggregated or anonymous data is sent to the cloud, improving overall security. Work offline: Devices at the edge can continue to work even when disconnected from the cloud. It can handle critical tasks by processing local data and ensuring continuous operation in remote or offline scenarios. Machine learning at the edge: Applying machine learning models at the edge enables real-time insights into locally collected data. The learned model can be updated periodically from the cloud, ensuring that edge devices take advantage of the latest improvements, rather than relying solely on local processing. Edge Intelligence: Edge devices can analyze local data and provide instant insights without relying on cloud computing. This is especially important in applications where quick decisions are important in manufacturing or healthcare. Fault tolerance: By distributing computing tasks to edge and cloud resources, systems become more resilient to failure. If a component fails, the system can adapt by reducing downtime and redirecting tasks to available resources.

14.1.4.3 Achieving Optimal Balance in IoT Operations

The process of "load balancing" involves distributing heavy processing loads among a small number of processing nodes to improve system performance. A distributed system environment is the practice of distributing the load among many distributed system nodes to increase resource utilization and task response time [16].

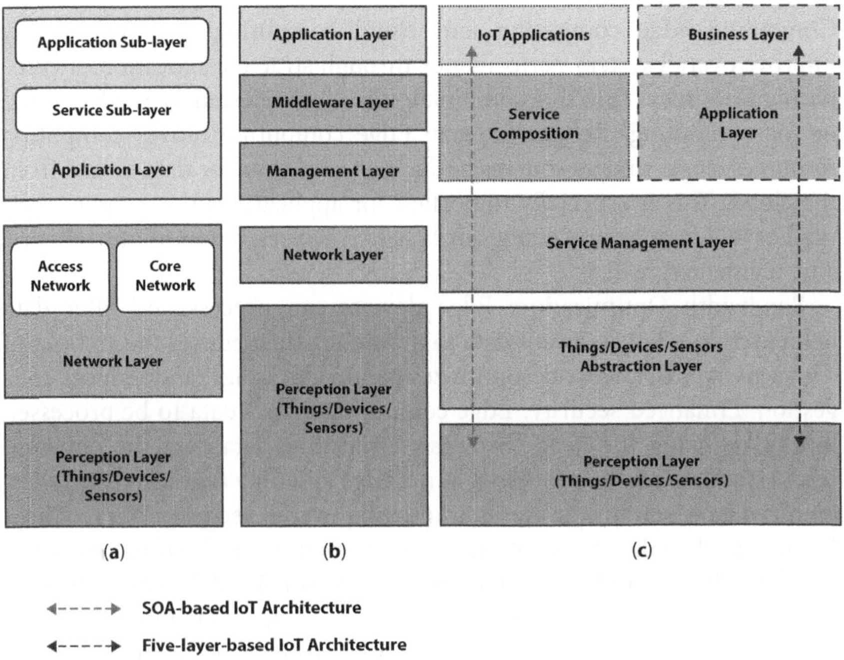

Figure 14.3 SoA-based IoT architecture.

Figure 14.3, illustrates Service Oriented Architecture (SoA) for IoT. IoT network optimization offers many benefits for traffic management, operational efficiency, energy savings, latency reduction, higher throughput, and faster utilization when scaling or deploying IoT services and devices in the network. The synergistic integration of edge and cloud technologies offers a powerful framework for enhanced performance in various applications. As edge and cloud technologies continue to evolve, their collaborative integration provides a versatile solution for achieving optimal performance, efficiency, and adaptability across diverse computing landscapes.

14.1.5 Steps in Edge-to-Cloud Integration

14.1.5.1 Data Collection from Edge Devices

In the dynamic landscape of industrial internet of things (IIoT) environments, effective data management at the edge is paramount for seamless operations and insightful decision-making. Edge IoT ecosystems rely on robust processes encompassing device discovery, connectivity, data acquisition, processing, storage, and analysis to harness the full potential of connected devices and sensors. This comprehensive approach ensures that data is efficiently collected, transformed, and utilized to drive actionable insights while adhering to stringent security and compliance standards. Integrating diverse methods of data acquisition such as polling, real-time data streams, and event-driven collection, Edge IoT environments orchestrate a symphony of interconnected devices and systems, laying the foundation for optimized performance and unparalleled operational intelligence.

In the initial phases of establishing an industrial internet of things (IIoT) ecosystem, the process begins with device discovery and connectivity. This entails the identification of compatible devices within the industrial environment and establishing secure communication links utilizing appropriate protocols and interfaces. Once devices are discovered and connected, the focus shifts to device configuration and integration. This involves setting up communication parameters tailored to the specific requirements of the connected devices, ensuring seamless data exchange. Moreover, devices are seamlessly integrated into the gateway and broader IoT infrastructure to foster interoperability and facilitate efficient data flow across the ecosystem.

Data Acquisition approaches:
Polling Method: Periodically polling devices at regular intervals for data updates must happen. They're suitable when real-time data updates are not

critical, and network capacity allows frequent communication between devices.
Real-Time Data Streams: Receiving continuous data streams in real time from sensors or connected devices is essential for applications that require immediate insights or rapid decision-making.
Event-Driven Collection: Triggering data collection based on specific events or conditions optimizes resource usage by collecting data only when necessary.

14.1.5.2 Data Filtering, Aggregation, and Compression

Edge computing, with its data reduction [17], and strategies, revolutionizes how we handle IoT data. By implementing techniques such as compression, aggregation, and filtering at the edge, unnecessary or redundant data is eliminated before transmission or storage. This results in faster response times and reduced network traffic – critical for edge devices with limited processing power and storage capacity.

Data Sampling: Data sampling involves selecting a subset of data points from a larger dataset for analysis. In EC, data sampling is often used to reduce the volume of data transmitted from edge devices to central servers or cloud platforms. By capturing representative samples, edge devices can conserve network bandwidth and computational resources while still providing valuable insights for analysis and decision-making.
Data Compression: Data compression techniques are used to reduce the size of data payloads transmitted between edge devices and centralized servers. Compression algorithms such as gzip, zlib, or lightweight compression techniques tailored for IoT devices help minimize network bandwidth usage and storage requirements while preserving essential information. Data compression is especially beneficial in EC scenarios where network bandwidth is limited or costly.
Data Filtering: Data filtering involves the selective processing or exclusion of data based on predefined criteria or conditions. In EC, data filtering mechanisms are implemented at the edge to discard irrelevant or redundant data before transmission to higher-level processing nodes. Filtering criteria may include data relevance, quality thresholds, or event triggers, allowing edge devices to focus computational resources on processing meaningful data while discarding noise or irrelevant information.
Data Aggregation: Data aggregation techniques consolidate and summarize multiple data streams into a more compact representation, reducing

the volume of data transmitted across the network. In EC environments, edge devices often collect data from multiple sources or sensors distributed across a network. Aggregating this data at the edge before transmission to central servers or cloud platforms helps minimize network congestion, latency, and processing overhead. Aggregation methods may include simple averaging, summing, or more complex statistical techniques tailored to specific application requirements.

14.1.5.3 Edge Intelligence with Machine Learning Algorithms

At the forefront of edge computing (EC) lies a sophisticated integration of artificial intelligence (AI) algorithms [18], with machine learning (ML) methodologies playing a central role in optimizing resource utilization, enabling informed decision-making, and seamlessly adapting to dynamic environments. Spanning from traditional ML algorithms to the intricate architectures of deep learning (DL) models, the adaptive strategies of reinforcement learning (RL) techniques, the collaborative nature of federated learning (FL), and the evolutionary principles of evolutionary algorithms (EAs), each AI paradigm injects distinctive strengths and applications into the ever-evolving EC landscape. By delving into the intricacies of these algorithms, stakeholders can effectively tap into the transformative potential of intelligent edge systems, igniting innovation, bolstering scalability, and enhancing efficiency across a diverse spectrum of industries and domains.

Traditional ML algorithms encompass supervised, semi-supervised, and unsupervised learning paradigms. Supervised methods like SVM, boosting, and random forests rely on labeled data for model training. Semi-supervised techniques such as label propagation and graphical models leverage both labeled and unlabeled data. Unsupervised algorithms like K-means clustering and PCA autonomously discover patterns within data. Despite their effectiveness, traditional ML algorithms exhibit sensitivity to datasets, diminishing returns with large datasets, and demand intricate feature engineering. Nonetheless, they offer advantages like lower energy consumption, reduced computing power requirements, and straightforward deployment compared to DL and RL. In the context of edge computing (EC), the appropriate ML algorithm can be selected based on resource constraints and task specifics, allowing traditional ML to find its niche within EC.

Deep Learning: Deep learning (DL) mimics the brain's functionality, autonomously extracting high-level features from raw data for classification and prediction tasks. DL models, structured in multiple layers, include

DNNs, CNNs, and RNNs. DNNs, with multiple hidden layers, enhance learning capacity through layered representations. CNNs, with convolution layers, excel in feature extraction and image recognition tasks. RNNs are proficient in modeling sequential data, with variants like LSTM mitigating the issue of information decay over time. DL surpasses traditional ML in natural language processing, computer vision, and EC-specific applications such as anomaly detection and task scheduling. The distributed nature of EC aligns with DL's capacity to process data locally, promoting its integration into EC frameworks.

Reinforcement Learning and Deep Reinforcement Learning: Reinforcement learning (RL) trains models *via* dynamic interactions with the environment, aiming to maximize cumulative rewards. RL algorithms like Q-learning and DQN tackle decision-making problems in EC resource management and scheduling. However, complex environments pose challenges such as slow convergence and high memory consumption. DRL, particularly DQN, addresses these issues by approximating Q-values using deep neural networks. Despite its advantages, DRL encounters instability, especially when using nonlinear functions for Q-function approximation. Solutions like experience replay mitigate this challenge, enhancing the stability and effectiveness of DRL in EC applications.

Federated learning (FL) facilitates collaborative model training while preserving user privacy and data security across distributed environments. Local models are trained on privacy-sensitive data and aggregated into a global model on a central server. In EC, FL addresses concerns regarding data privacy and scalability, enabling model training across multiple edge nodes without centralizing raw data. Collaborative model training under privacy constraints emerges as a research hotspot, reflecting FL's relevance and potential in EC frameworks.

Evolutionary Algorithms: Evolutionary algorithms (EAs) draw inspiration from biological evolution mechanisms, offering optimization solutions for EC tasks. Algorithms like PSO, GA, and DE iteratively optimize variables through fitness evaluation, selection, reproduction, and variation steps. EAs find applications in resource scheduling, load balancing, and task scheduling in EC environments. Although briefly introduced, EAs demonstrate promise in addressing optimization challenges within EC, complementing the capabilities of ML and DL algorithms.

14.1.5.4 Establishing Edge-Cloud Connectivity

Establishing seamless connectivity between edge devices and cloud infrastructure is essential for enabling real-time data processing, analysis, and decision-making in distributed environments. Key considerations for establishing edge-cloud connectivity include:

Edge Device Configuration: Configure edge devices with appropriate networking protocols, security mechanisms, and data processing capabilities to ensure seamless communication with cloud services. Edge devices should be equipped to securely transmit data, authenticate with cloud platforms, and handle intermittent network connectivity and bandwidth constraints.
Edge Data Processing: Implement edge computing capabilities to preprocess, filter, and aggregate data locally before transmission to the cloud. Edge data processing minimizes latency, conserves bandwidth, and reduces dependence on centralized cloud resources for real-time analytics and decision-making.
Cloud Integration: Integrate edge devices with cloud services, platforms, or APIs to enable seamless data exchange, synchronization, and orchestration between edge and cloud environments. Cloud integration facilitates data storage, analysis, visualization, and collaboration across distributed computing resources while ensuring data consistency, security, and compliance.
Hybrid Architectures: Adopt hybrid cloud-edge architectures that leverage the strengths of both edge and cloud computing paradigms to optimize performance, scalability, and cost-effectiveness. Hybrid architectures enable workload orchestration, data replication, and resource allocation across edge and cloud environments based on workload characteristics, latency requirements, and cost considerations.

By integrating digital twins for simulation [19], and establishing robust edge-cloud connectivity, organizations can unlock new opportunities for predictive maintenance, performance optimization, and innovation across diverse industries and applications. These initiatives enable organizations to harness the power of real-time data analytics, simulation, and collaboration to drive operational excellence, enhance customer experiences, and accelerate digital transformation initiatives.

14.1.5.5 Real-Time Monitoring and Control

In edge computing environments, real-time monitoring and control systems are essential for overseeing the status and performance of edge devices and processes. For instance, in a smart manufacturing facility, sensors embedded in production equipment continuously collect data on parameters like temperature, pressure, and machine health. This data is then processed in real-time by monitoring software, which provides insights into equipment performance and environmental conditions. If anomalies or deviations from normal operating parameters are detected, the system can trigger immediate alerts or corrective actions, such as adjusting machine settings or notifying maintenance personnel. By promptly addressing issues and optimizing processes in real-time, organizations can ensure uninterrupted production, minimize downtime, and maximize operational efficiency in dynamic edge environments.

14.1.5.6 Enabling Real-Time Decision-Making

Edge computing environments facilitate real-time decision-making by providing access to timely and relevant data insights at the point of action. By processing and analyzing data locally on edge devices, organizations can reduce latency, conserve network bandwidth, and respond rapidly to changing conditions or events. Real-time decision-making frameworks leverage machine learning algorithms, rules engines, and event processing systems to automate decision-making processes and execute predefined actions based on predefined rules or conditions. This capability enables organizations to optimize operational efficiency, enhance customer experiences, and capitalize on emerging opportunities in dynamic and fast-paced environments, ensuring agility and responsiveness in decision-making processes.

14.1.6 6G Terahertz Communication Revolution

14.1.6.1 Introduction to 6G Terahertz Communication

The introduction of 6G terahertz (THz) connectivity is a major advancement in wireless technology. With ultra-low latency measured in microseconds and speeds of tens of terabits per second, 6G THz communications promises to revolutionize the entire communications landscape. Experiences, real-time applications, and the integration of millions of devices into the online ecosystem are made possible by new technologies. Additionally, by providing high-speed connectivity to poor and remote areas, 6G terahertz communications have the potential to bridge the digital divide, foster inclusion, and connect people around the world. As 6G networks continue to evolve, they have the potential to support business expansion, drive innovation, and influence future global communications models.

14.1.6.2 Framework for Using Edge Intelligence in the 6G Industrial Internet of Things (IIoT)

To use edge intelligence in the 6G Industrial Internet of Things (IIoT), a framework combined with the latest technology is needed, and 6G to play a strong role using networking and edge computing [20]. Figure 14.4 illustrates the synergy between edge computing and 6G networks.

An example description of the main activities is given below:

Network infrastructure optimization: To support smart applications, there must first be a 6G network infrastructure. This requires placing antennas, base stations, and small cells to ensure there is no interference and poor connectivity in the area [21]. Use the high bandwidth and low latency of 6G to realize fast data transfer between end devices and the cloud.

Deployment of edge devices: In business environments, edge devices, including servers, routers, and gateways, are deployed at the edge of production facilities. Network– These edge devices form the basis of edge intelligence, making it easier to process, analyze and share data.

Edge Analytics and Machine Learning: Use edge analytics and machine learning algorithms to instantly measure streaming data and provide better insights [22]. Use techniques such as defect detection, predictive

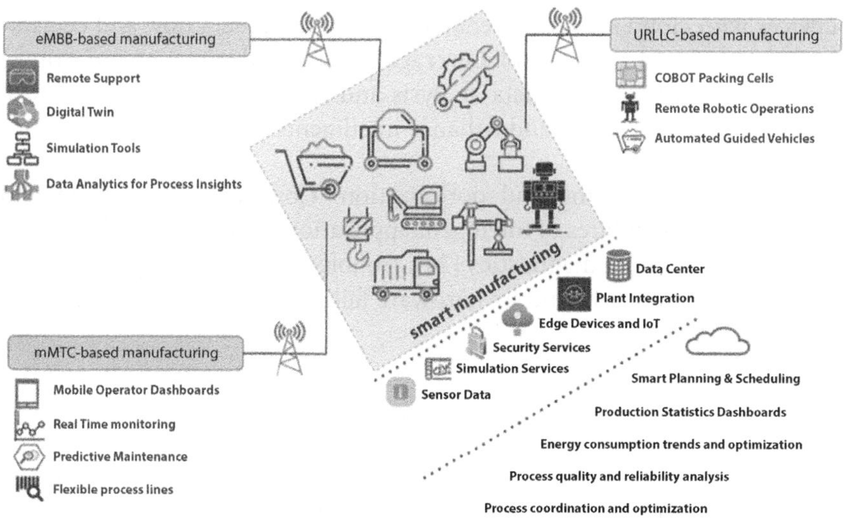

Figure 14.4 Synergizing 6G and edge computing.

maintenance, and remediation algorithms to increase efficiency, increase reliability, and reduce downtime in business processes.

Security and privacy issues: In the 6G IIoT environment, security and privacy issues should be a priority when using edge intelligence. Use access control, authentication and encryption technologies to protect confidential information and prevent unauthorized access. Make sure you comply with industry standards and regulations to reduce cyber security risks and prevent data breaches.

Integration with cloud services: Create a relationship for bi-directional data flow and centralized management and administration of edge devices and cloud services. Leverage cloud-based analytics tools and use edge analytics and machine learning algorithms on edge devices to instantly analyze streaming data and derive recommendations. Using technologies such as invisible sensing, predictive maintenance and optimization algorithms to increase efficiency, increase reliability and reduce downtime in the industry.

Security and privacy considerations: Prioritize security and privacy considerations when deploying edge technologies in the 6G IIoT environment [23]. Use encryption, authentication and control methods to protect sensitive data and prevent unauthorized access. Ensure compliance with industry standards and regulations to mitigate cyber security risks and prevent data breaches. Integration with cloud services: Seamlessly integrate edge devices with cloud services to enable bi-directional data flow and centralized management and control. Leverage cloud-based analytics and storage options to aid long-term data analysis and research, ease the burden of compute-intensive tasks, and enhance intelligence.

Continuous monitoring and optimization: Continuously evaluate and improve the capabilities of intelligent applications in the 6G IIoT environment. Set up remote diagnostics [24], troubleshooting, and system monitoring to instantly find and fix hardware failures, latency issues, and poor performance.

14.1.6.3 Implications and Advantages in IIoT

The internet of things has a positive impact, allowing businesses to improve the efficiency of the supply chain, increase operational efficiency, increase security, and comply with selected information, promote innovation and support Sustainable development– By leveraging IIoT technologies and their transformational resources, organizations can seize new opportunities for expansion, competition, and success in the digital world.

Operational Efficiency: Enhanced production and efficiency are the results of real-time monitoring and optimization.
Predictive maintenance: Being productive and efficient is the result of time management and optimization.
Security and Compliance: Improve monitoring to ensure better employee safety compliance.
Supply Chain Optimization: Improve logistics and inventory management with real-time tracking and analysis.
Data-driven decision-making: Enable strategic planning and informed decision-making through actionable data.
Business Model Development: Shifting to a business model can strengthen customer relationships and create new revenue streams. Bandwidth issues need to be addressed. Be careful when using 6G IIoT edge intelligence.

14.1.6.4 *Challenges and Solutions in Implementing Edge Intelligence for 6G IIoT*

14.1.6.4.1 Latency and Bandwidth Considerations

Localizing the edge helps reduce latency, which is important for instant response to edge applications. Reduce delays and ensure timely response to critical incidents by analyzing data and making decisions closer to the data source. Conversely, bandwidth limitations can hinder the performance of data transfers, resulting in interruptions and decreased performance. To solve this problem, bandwidth can be optimized using attractive data and compression technology to ensure the transmission of important data [24].

Quality service advisories and content delivery guidelines further improve network performance by monitoring traffic and caching resources closer to the end user, reducing latency and improving the orchestration of all responses. By overcoming these challenges, organizations can leverage the potential of edge intelligence in 6G IIoT to help make quick decisions and increase operational efficiency.

14.1.6.4.2 Security and Privacy Issues

Deployment of edge intelligence–6G IIoT is greatly affected by security and privacy issues. Security measures are in place to protect sensitive information from attackers. Since edge processes data and stores sensitive data locally, data privacy is a major concern. Unauthorized access and unauthorized access control of this information may compromise confidentiality and lead to unauthorized access. It also opens up new attack paths as the edge of the transmission. Therefore, secure communication and authentication tools are crucial to prevent data tampering and eavesdropping [25]. Additionally, since a lot of data generated by the device edge causes problems in terms of data availability and integrity, it must be monitored to protect against intrusions and intrusions on the network. Additionally, the growth of connected devices in the IIoT environment leads to attacks and increases the risk of distributed denial of service (DDoS) attacks, malware viruses, and other cyber security threats. Addressing these issues requires an approach that includes encryption, authentication, intrusion detection, and continuous monitoring to reduce risks and ensure security and privacy at the edge of the network. Smart in the 6G IIoT environment.

14.1.6.4.3 Integration with Existing Systems

Integrating the edge intelligence of 6G IIoT with existing systems requires a way to solve the problem of conflicting information. Using centralized solutions and compliance with industry standards is important to ensure the technology communicates effectively with the legacy system. Additionally, using an integrated system that focuses on the implementation of high-impact problems can reduce impact and promote better practices. Collaborating with suppliers and partners is required to continuously improve the integration process, using intelligence to accelerate deployment, and unlocking the potential of advanced skills to drive efficiency and innovation. Additionally, the importance of compatibility and enabling capabilities in integration is crucial to future-proofing IIoT deployment. This involves analyzing the scalability of existing systems and ensuring they can keep up with the large volumes of data generated by edge devices. Additionally, monitoring and maintenance procedures must be developed to address the issue of integration changes and maintain reliability over time. By taking an integrated and forward-thinking approach, organizations can combine capabilities with existing systems, unlock the potential for change, and take business even further in the 6G IIoT era.

14.1.6.4.4 Overcoming Technological Barriers

Defending Security Threats– Overcoming business disruption is the key to successfully use edge intelligence in 6G IIoT. The biggest challenge is that advanced technology is limited in terms of energy and storage capacity, affecting the execution of complex processes and analytical tasks. To solve this problem, advances in hardware capabilities and algorithm optimization are required to ensure efficient resource utilization and maximize performance in limited environments. Additionally, interoperability between end devices, 6G networks [26], and existing systems is also an important issue. Standardization efforts and the adoption of open protocols facilitate interrelationships between heterogeneous systems by supporting seamless communication and data exchange. Addressing business impacts through innovation, design, and security measures is critical to unlocking the potential of edge intelligence to increase operational efficiency and innovation in the 6G IIoT environment.

14.1.7 Digital Twins for Real-Time Monitoring

14.1.7.1 Digital Twins

A digital twin is a technology that combines both the real and the virtual representations. Any real-world object or device can be considered an asset to be represented in a digital twin. Data collected from sensors associated with any physical asset can be collected from the real world and processed at the edge level of data acquisition or stored in the cloud. The collected data is simulated as a virtual copy of the asset in a virtual environment. After simulating the environment, parameters are applied to real assets. This representation of physical assets and associated data in both the real and virtual worlds helps optimize the performance of real assets. Some of the use cases of digital twins are automotive, construction, manufacturing, healthcare, and many more. The digital twin is considered a major revolution in Industry 4.0. A digital twin captures all the data from the real world and in turn, represents it in the digital space. Virtual reality (VR) or artificial intelligence (AI) is used to simulate the effects of any change to an asset or its environment. Any change in real-time data is consequently reflected in the virtual environment as well. The study, which was suggested by [27], examines the idea of a "digital twin" as well as several significant digital twin framework models. It concludes that data, models, and services are the main components of digital twin implementation.

14.1.7.2 Integration of Digital Twin and IIoT

IIoT enables real-time collection of data and digital twin aids in virtual representation of real-time entities and provides a platform for simulation and testing. Integration of IIoT with digital twin facilitates decision-making by increasing productivity through predictive maintenance. This provides a data-driven approach to optimizing industrial productivity through smart manufacturing and automation. The advent of IPv6 and 5G has opened up the environment for rapid communication of real-time data from multiple IIoT systems while providing a responsive ecosystem for data-driven decision-making, preventive maintenance, and predictive analytics integrated with digital twin technology. [28], has proposed a methodology for the creation and deletion of a digital twin model. [29], has presented a federated learning-based digital twin 6G-enabled IIoT workflow.

14.1.7.3 Framework for Digital Twin in IIoT

Data synchronization between the actual physical assets and their digital counterparts is essential. [30], has proposed a digital twin framework for the detection of malware in IoT data. This can be accomplished with the help of various communication protocols. [31], proposes a blockchain-based virtual reality –digital twin network model to improve the quality of service parameters. A framework for seamless integration of both technologies should provide scalability; both operational and technical compatibility. To ensure this, it is suggested that IIoT data be converted and transmitted in a network format and re-converted to a host-specific format. To achieve interoperability between IIoT devices, standardization of data models and protocols is essential. Insights from the digital twin need to be translated into mandates for preventive maintenance or predictive analytics. This enables industries to adapt to dynamic challenges and take proactive measures. Figure 14.5, illustrates the framework for the integration of IIoT device with its digital twin. The digital data acquired from IIoT devices are aggregated and filtered at the edge or fog end and are communicated to the virtual digital twin; where the data is monitored, analyzed, and reported through the dashboard or alert messages for appropriate proactive action or preventive maintenance.

Digital Twin is the virtual replica of the physical assets of an IIoT system. A methodical and quantitative approach to make the spatial-temporal data of a digital twin analytically tractable has been put forth by [32]. Continuous exchange of real-time data between the IIoT system and its digital counterpart, monitoring and analyzing a physical system from a remote location is possible. The methodology required for this integration is,

1. Identify primary IIoT devices to be monitored using digital twin.
2. Replicate digital twin models of each of the identified IIoT devices to emulate its functionality, behavior, and actual characteristics.

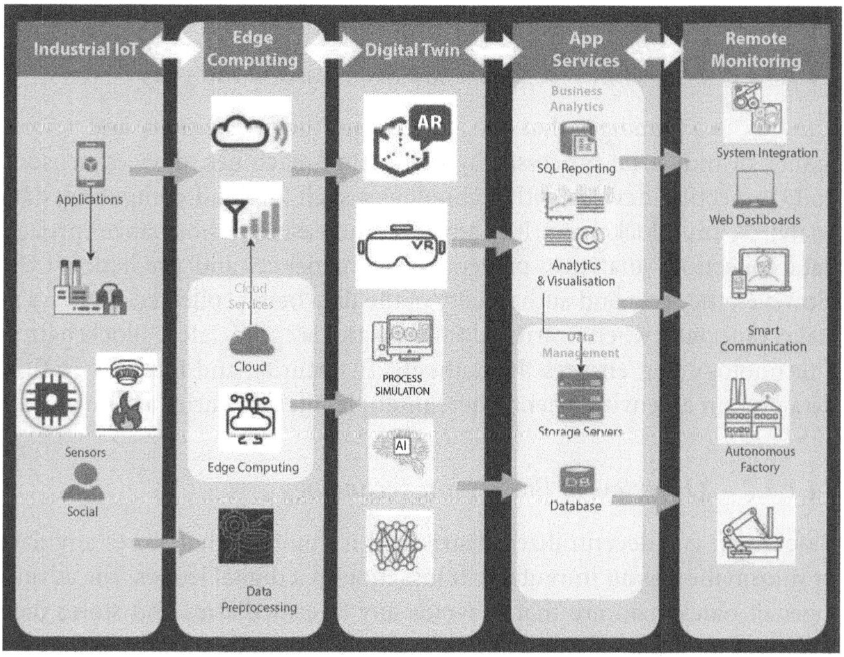

Figure 14.5 Framework for IIoT and digital twin.

3. Integrate the IIoT sensors with the digital data source to acquire real-time data and communicate the same to its digital twin.
4. Select the appropriate communication protocols to ensure appropriate data exchange format, high reliability and security, and low latency.
5. Select the appropriate computing and filtering paradigm such as edge or fog processing before sending the real-time data to its virtual twin.
6. Choose the appropriate monitoring and analysis tools to detect patterns from incoming data and detect anomalies.
7. A user-friendly monitoring and visualization dashboard is recommended for the user to analyze the performance of IIoT devices in real-time and make the appropriate decision on predictive maintenance, anomaly detection, and performance optimization.
8. Alerts and Notifications are to be sent to various stakeholders of the IIoT system based on the operational policy of the organization.

14.1.8 Blockchain for Data Security and Integrity

14.1.8.1 Blockchain for IIoT Data Security and Integrity

The IIoT is a paradigm that aims to enhance the productivity and performance of industrial processes by integrating machines, devices, sensors, and connecting devices with technologies such as cloud computing, data analytics, and blockchain. It is aimed at increasing performance through data collection, analytics, preventive maintenance, and prediction [33]. However, the trust and authenticity of the data being collected is always at stake, especially when untrusted third parties are associated. Blockchain is a technology that ensures the authenticity, security, and integrity of IIoT data even in an environment where multiple intermediaries are involved.

14.1.8.2 Overview of Blockchain Technology

Blockchain is a decentralized distributed technology that stores any data or information as an immutable transaction in a digital ledger. The advantages of blockchain are that it avoids any intermediaries and stores data with timestamps after validation by multiple peer nodes. It provides access control, pseudonymity, and transparency. A blockchain network can be either permissionless in the case of a public blockchain or permissioned in the case of a private blockchain. A permissionless blockchain allows anyone to participate in the network and the transactions are verified by any peer node in the blockchain. In the case of a private blockchain a participating node needs to be permitted by an authorized node. For storing data in the blockchain, the sender of the data must use his private key to sign and the data is broadcast to peer nodes in the blockchain network. The peer nodes validate the data. Such validated data are grouped to form blocks. The nodes called miners use consensus algorithms such as proof of work, proof stake, proof of activity, practical Byzantine fault tolerance, etc. [34], to choose a block to be added to the blockchain. The blocks are interconnected with each other to form a chain. The block header and data are given as input to a hash algorithm to generate a hash value. Every block stores the hash value of the previous block. Hence, any change in data stored will change the hash value and the block automatically gets removed from the blockchain. A Merkle tree is the data structure used to store the hash value of the data and is used to validate the data by traversing up the hierarchy until the root node.

14.1.8.3 Need for Blockchain in IIoT

Blockchain is a technology that addresses the vulnerabilities and challenges that are inherent in an IIoT system. Blockchain assures that the data stored in the blockchain are authenticated, validated, and can be verified at any time. It allows traceability at any point in time, as it is time-stamped and immutable. A few use cases of IIoT where blockchain can be used are supply chain and logistics, smart manufacturing, automotive sector, product management, e-commerce, and retail industry, etc. [35]. It provides a digital identity for various stakeholders that may be pseudonymous [36].

14.1.8.4 Smart Contract and DApp

In the blockchain, "The Code is Law". A smart contract is a digital agreement or contract between various stakeholders involved in an IIoT system to enter into an agreement about the data to be stored in blockchain. The hierarchy, authorization, and access control rights of various stakeholders involved are decided by the creators of the blockchain and are coded in a smart contract. The smart contract is a self-executing code that is triggered whenever a transaction is initiated. [37–39], have described the process of integration of Web3 and DApp to retrieve data from the blockchain. Figure 14.6, illustrates the integration of IIoT and blockchain frameworks. The sensor data from IIoT is aggregated either in edge or cloud end and is sent to the blockchain network. The nodes in the blockchain validate and verify the data using mining and consensus algorithms. Validated data is time-stamped and stored in the peer-to-peer blockchain nodes in a distributed

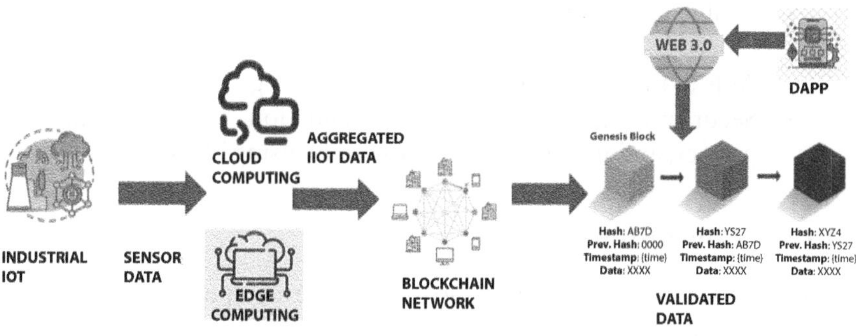

Figure 14.6 Integration of IIoT and blockchain framework.

fashion–in a secured, immutable manner. Distributed application (DApp) interacts through Web3 with the smart contract written in blockchain to retrieve the data. Access control policies written in smart contracts ensures trust, integrity, and authentication.

An IIoT system has interoperability and trust issues as different vendors are involved. Blockchain provides a trustable and interoperable platform for the exchange of data and communication. The shared distributed ledger can be used as a standard format for storing and retrieving data thereby alleviating any compatibility issues. Web 3.0 has paved the way to decentralize the web development framework by developing a decentralized application (DApp). The DApp interacts with the smart contract whenever data is stored or retrieved. The blockchain bridge or cross-chain enables interoperability across different blockchains used by different stakeholders of IIoT.

14.1.8.5 Benefits of the Use of Blockchain in IIoT

- Blockchain can provide device identification and authentication for various devices involved.
- It enables data confidentiality, integrity, nonrepudiation, and access control.
- It prevents the forging of IoT data as it is time-stamped and is immutable.
- It assures trust in an untrusted environment involving unknown stakeholders.
- Allows predictive maintenance of machines.
- Ensures regulatory compliance through smart contracts.
- Enables acquisition of real-time data within a short response time.
- Aids in monitoring IIoT assets and tracking.
- Security measures such as user validation, authorization, privacy, and integrity can be assured by using blockchain.

14.1.9 Conclusion

In summary, the integration of IIoT and edge computing represents a transformative synergy that meets the growing needs of our interconnected world. By bringing computing capabilities closer to data sources, edge computing reduces latency, improves real-time performance, and reduces bandwidth requirements. This creates more efficient and effective systems for applications ranging from smart cities and industrial automation to healthcare and autonomous vehicles.

14.1.9.1 Recapitulation of Key Findings

Ubiquitous Connectivity: IIoT enables seamless connection of devices and systems, fostering a highly interconnected environment.
Data Proliferation: The proliferation of IIoT devices generates massive amount of data. This data deluge presents both opportunities and challenges, requiring robust infrastructure, advanced analytics and effective management strategies to gain valuable insights. Industry transformation: IIoT is driving a paradigm shift across industries, from manufacturing and healthcare to transportation and agriculture. Edge Computing Integration: The integration of edge computing with IoT addresses latency issues by processing data closer to the source. This not only reduces real-time capabilities but also reduces the strain on centralized cloud infrastructure.
Proximity to the data source: Edge computing brings computational resources closer to the data source, reducing latency and enhancing real-time processing capabilities.
Decentralized processing: By distributing computing power to edge devices, edge computing decentralizes data processing.
Industry-specific applications: Edge computing finds various applications across industries such as manufacturing, healthcare, transportation and smart cities.

14.1.9.2 Future Trends and Emerging Technologies

6G networks: The proliferation of 5G and 6G networks is increasing the connectivity and communication capabilities of IIoT devices. The high-speed, low-latency 6G network enables more efficient data transmission that supports applications that require real-time sensing.
Edge AI: The integration of artificial intelligence (AI) at the edge of IoT networks enables the processing and analysis of device data. Blockchain for IIoT Security: Blockchain technology is explored to improve the security and reliability of IoT devices. Improved IIoT Security: With the increasing number of connected devices, the focus on IoT security is increasing. Future trends include the implementation of strong security measures, including better authentication, encryption and device management protocols. Human Augmentation: IIoT, integration with wearables and embedded technologies to enhance human capabilities, monitor health

and deliver personalized experiences, is expected to play an important role in human augmentation.

14.1.9.2.1 The Emerging Landscape of IoT

In 2024, the IIoT landscape is poised for dramatic change due to advances in cybersecurity, artificial intelligence (AI), and the increasing integration of IoT systems into critical infrastructure.

14.1.9.2.2 Anticipated Developments in Edge-to-Cloud Integration

The convergence of edge computing and cloud-native development offers a transformative approach to application development and deployment. Edge devices can act as distributed data processing and storage nodes, while cloud platforms provide centralized management and orchestration capabilities. Self-service: Organizations need the ability to easily and quickly spin up resources for new projects, such as new virtual machines (VM) or services for containers or MLOps. Point-and-click simplicity enables users to select and deploy the cloud services they need. A true edge-to-cloud platform should also provide a view of cost, usage and forecasting capabilities across the entire hybrid IT estate, including assets in the public cloud.

Rapidly scalable: To deliver on the cloud's promise of agility, the platform needs to include built-in buffer capacity; so when more capacity is needed, it's already installed and ready to go. Capacity reduction should also be facilitated, making it possible to more closely align infrastructure usage with business needs.

Pay as you go: Billing should be based on actual capacity used; so businesses can get new projects up and running without heavy upfront costs and procurement delays. This eliminates both the risk of disruptions caused by wasteful over-provisioning and under-provisioning.

14.1.9.2.3 Future of Edge-to-Cloud Synergy in IoT

The Dawn of Edge AI: In the rapidly advancing world of technology, edge AI stands as a transformative force, redefining the landscape of artificial intelligence (AI) and internet of things (IoT). This innovative approach involves using AI algorithms directly on local devices at the edge of the network, as opposed to processing data on a remote cloud server. This paradigm shift is not just a technological advance; it represents a fundamental change in data processing, analysis, and real-time applications.

The synergy between Edge AI and IoT is a match made technologically in heaven. IoT, constantly generating data through interconnected devices, benefits greatly from the edge.

AI disclosure statement: The author acknowledges the use of AI-based tools for minor language editing or grammatical correction. However, all intellectual contributions, analyses, and conclusions presented in this chapter are entirely the author's own.

References

1. Peter, O., Pradhan, A., Mbohwa, C., Industrial internet of things (IIoT): opportunities, challenges, and requirements in manufacturing businesses in emerging economies. *Procedia Comput. Sci., [Internet]*, 217, 3, 856–65, 2023 Jan 1.
2. Badarinath, R. and Prabhu, V.V., Advances in Internet of Things (IoT) in Manufacturing, in: *Advances in Production Management Systems The Path to Intelligent, Collaborative and Sustainable Manufacturing*, pp. 111–8, 2017.
3. Park, Y., Woo, J., Choi, S., A Cloud-based Digital Twin Manufacturing System based on an Interoperable Data Schema for Smart Manufacturing. *Int. J. Comput. Integr. Manuf.*, 33, 12, 1259–1276, 2020 Sep 15.
4. Khan, W.Z., Rehman, M.H., Zangoti, H.M., Afzal, M.K., Armi, N., Salah, K., Industrial internet of things: Recent advances, enabling technologies and open challenges. *Comput. Electr. Eng., [Internet]*, 81, 106522, 2020 Jan 1.
5. A A, Dahan, F., Alroobaea, R., Alghamdi, W.Y., Mohammed, M.K., Hajjej, F., *et al.*, A smart IoMT based architecture for E-healthcare patient monitoring system using artificial intelligence algorithms. *Front. Physiol.*, 14, 2023 Jan 30.
6. Walas, F. and Redchuk, A., IIoT/IoT and Artificial Intelligence/Machine Learning as a Process Optimization driver under industry 4.0 model. *J. Comput. Sci. Technol.*, 21, 2, e15, 2021 Oct 21.
7. Hazra, A., Adhikari, M., Amgoth, T., Srirama, S.N., A Comprehensive Survey on Interoperability for IIoT: Taxonomy, Standards, and Future Directions. *ACM Comput. Surv.*, 55, 1, 1–35, 2023 Jan 31.
8. Sengupta, J., Ruj, S., Bit, S.D., A Comprehensive Survey on Attacks, Security Issues and Blockchain Solutions for IoT and IIoT. *J. Netw. Comput. Appl.*, 149, 102481, 2020 Jan.
9. Boyes, H., Hallaq, B., Cunningham, J., Watson, T., The industrial internet of things (IIoT): An analysis framework. *Comput. Ind., [Internet]*, 101, 1, 1–12, 2018 Oct, Available from: https://www.sciencedirect.com/science/article/pii/S0166361517307285.

10. Shawish, A. and Salama, M., Cloud computing: paradigms and technologies, in: *Inter-cooperative collective intelligence: Techniques and applications*, pp. 39–67, Springer Berlin Heidelberg, Berlin, Heidelberg, 2013 Aug 14.
11. Chi, H.R., Wu, C.K., Huang, N.F., Tsang, K.F., Radwan, A., A Survey of Network Automation for Industrial Internet-of-Things Toward Industry 5.0. *IEEE Trans. Ind. Inf., [Internet]*, 19, 2, 2065–77, 2023 Feb 1.
12. Kumari, S., Tulshyan, V., Tewari, H., Cyber Security on the Edge: Efficient Enabling of Machine Learning on IoT Devices. *Information*, 15, 3, 126, 2024 Feb 23.
13. George, A.S., George, AS.H., Baskar, T., Edge Computing and the Future of Cloud Computing: A Survey of Industry Perspectives and Predictions. *Zenodo, (CERN European Organization Nuclear Research)*, 2, 2, 1–12, 2023 Jun 20.
14. Hamdan, S., Ayyash, M., Almajali, S., Edge-Computing Architectures for Internet of Things Applications: A Survey. *Sensors.*, 20, 22, 6441, 2020 Nov.
15. Ai, Y., Peng, M., Zhang, K., Edge computing technologies for Internet of Things: a primer. *Digital Commun. Netw., [Internet]*, 4, 2, 77–86, 2018 Apr.
16. Shuaib, M., Bhatia, S., Alam, S., Masih, R.K., Alqahtani, N., Basheer, S., Alam, M.S., An optimized, dynamic, and efficient load-balancing framework for resource management in the internet of things (IoT) environment. *Electronics.*, 12, 5, 1104, 2023 Feb 23.
17. Wang, T., Qiu, L., Sangaiah, A.K., Liu, A., Bhuiyan, M.Z.A., Ma, Y., Edge-Computing-Based Trustworthy Data Collection Model in the Internet of Things. *IEEE Internet Things J., [Internet]*, 7, 5, 4218–27, 2020 May 1, [cited 2021 Nov 15].
18. Singh, R. and Gill, S.S., Edge AI: a survey. *Internet Things Cyber-Phys. Syst.*, 3, 71–92, 2023 Jan 1.
19. Zhang, L., Wang, H., Xue, H., Zhang, H., Liu, Q., Niyato, D., *et al.*, Digital Twin-Assisted Edge Computation Offloading in Industrial Internet of Things With NOMA. *IEEE Trans. Veh. Technol.*, 72, 9, 11935–50, 2023 Sep 1.
20. Nguyen, D.C., Ding, M., Pathirana, P.N., Seneviratne, A., Li, J., Niyato, D., *et al.*, 6G Internet of Things: A Comprehensive Survey. *IEEE Internet Things J.*, 9, 1, 1–1, 2021.
21. Ahmed, I., Anisetti, M., Ahmad, A., Jeon, G., A Multilayer Deep Learning Approach for Malware Classification in 5G-Enabled IIoT. *IEEE Trans. Ind. Inf.*, 19, 2, 1495–503, 2023 Feb.
22. Gong, C., Lin, F., Gong, X., Lu, Y., Intelligent Cooperative Edge Computing in Internet of Things. *IEEE Internet Things J.*, 7, 10, 9372–82, 2020.
23. Hussain, F., Hussain, R., Hassan, S.A., Hossain, E., Machine Learning in IoT Security: Current Solutions and Future Challenges. *IEEE Commun. Surv. Tutor., [Internet]*, 22, 3, 1686–721, 2020.
24. Quy, V.K., Hau, N.V., Anh, D.V., Quy, N.M., Ban, N.T., Lanza, S., *et al.*, IoT-Enabled Smart Agriculture: Architecture, Applications, and Challenges. *Appl. Sci.*, 12, 7, 3396, 2022 Mar 27.

25. Akyildiz, I.F., Kak, A., Nie, S., 6G and Beyond: The Future of Wireless Communications Systems. *IEEE Access, [Internet]*, 8, 133995–4030, 2020.
26. Tariq, F., Khandaker, M., Wong, K.K., Imran, M., Bennis, M., Debbah, M., A Speculative Study on 6G [Internet], arXiv.org. 2019 [cited 2024 Jul 29].
27. Jiang, Z., Guo, Y., Wang, Z., Digital twin to improve the virtual-real integration of industrial IoT. *J. Ind. Inf. Integr.*, 22, 100196, 2021 Jun 1.
28. Jia, W., Wang, W., Zhang, Z., From simple digital twin to complex digital twin Part I: A novel modeling method for multi-scale and multi-scenario digital twin. *Adv. Eng. Inf.*, 53, 101706, 2022 Aug.
29. Qi, Y. and Hossain, M.S., Semi-supervised Federated Learning for Digital Twin 6G-enabled IIoT: A Bayesian Estimated Approach. *J. Adv. Res.*, 66, 47–57, 2024 Feb 1.
30. Cha, H.J., Yang, H.K., Song, Y.J., Kang, A.R., Intelligent Anomaly Detection System through Malware Image Augmentation in IIoT Environment Based on Digital Twin. *Appl. Sci.*, 13, 18, 10196–6, 2023 Sep 11.
31. Song, J., Kang, Y., Song, Q., Guo, L., Jamalipour, A., Distributed Resource Optimization With Blockchain Security for Immersive Digital Twin in IIoT. *IEEE Trans. Ind. Inf.*, 19, 5, 7258–67, 2023 May 1.
32. He, X., Ai, Q., Pan, B., Tang, L., Qiu, R., Spatial-temporal data analysis of digital twin. *Digit. Twin.*, 2, 7, 2022 Apr 19.
33. Tyagi, A.K., Dananjayan, S., Agarwal, D., Thariq Ahmed, H.F., Blockchain—Internet of Things Applications: Opportunities and Challenges for Industry 4.0 and Society 5.0. *Sensors*, 23, 2, 947, 2023 Jan 13.
34. Jayapal, C. and Sudhahar, C., Distributed Technologies and Consensus Algorithms for Blockchain. *Novel Res. Dev. Approaches Heterogen. Syst. Algorithms.*, 7, 100, 2023 Mar.
35. Alladi, T., Chamola, V., Parizi, R.M., Choo, K.K., Blockchain applications for industry 4.0 and industrial IoT: A review. *IEEE Access*, 7, 176935–51, 2019 Nov 29.
36. RLakshmana, K., Khan F, K.S., Rho, S., A Survey on blockchain for industrial Internet of Things. *Alexandria Eng. J.*, 61, 8, 6001–22, 2022 Aug.
37. Rupa, C., Midhunchakkaravarthy, D., Hasan, M.K., Alhumyani, H., Saeed, R.A., Industry 5.0: Ethereum blockchain technology based DApp smart contract. *Math. Biosci. Eng.*, 18, 5, 7010–27, 2021 Aug 23.
38. Kaur, J., Bhambri, P., Rani, S., Digital Twin Enabling Technologies, Applications, and Challenges, in: *AI-Driven Digital Twin and Industry 4.0: A Conceptual Framework with Applications*, 1st, S. Rani, P. Bhambri, S. Kumar, P.K. Pareek, A.A. Elngar (Eds.), pp. 90–104, CRC Press, 2024, https://doi.org/10.1201/9781003395416.
39. Bhambri, P., Rani, S., Kumar, S., Sinha, V.K., Big Data Analytics with Digital Twin for Industrial Applications, in: *AI-Driven Digital Twin and Industry 4.0: A Conceptual Framework with Applications*, 1st, S. Rani, P. Bhambri, S. Kumar, P.K. Pareek, A.A. Elngar (Eds.), pp. 105–26, CRC Press, 2024, https://doi.org/10.1201/9781003395416.

11. [illegible]

15

Advancing Industrial Intelligence: Leveraging Optimized Edge Devices With Large Language Model Concepts

S. Sathishkumar[1*], R. Devi Priya[2], K. Karthika[3] and A. Menaka[4]

[1]Department of Computer Science and Engineering, Kangeyam Institute of Technology, Kangeyam, Tiruppur, Tamilnadu, India
[2]Department of Computer Science and Engineering, KPR Institute of Engineering and Technology, Coimbatore, India
[3]Department of Computer Science and Engineering, Sri Sairam College of Engineering, Anekal, Bengaluru, India
[4]Department of Computer Science and Engineering, B.N.M. Institute of Technology, Bengaluru, India

Abstract

This chapter delves into the transformative potential of edge devices empowered by large language model (LLM) concepts in revolutionizing industrial intelligence. By amalgamating cutting-edge technologies like internet of things (IoT) and artificial intelligence (AI) with the prowess of LLMs, industrial enterprises can revolutionize their operational frameworks, driving efficiency and innovation to unprecedented levels. At the core of this discussion lies the concept of edge computing, which enables data processing at the source, mitigating latency and enhancing real-time analytics. By using LLMs, edge devices are able to enhance decision-making processes by processing data as well as interpreting and drawing conclusions from unstructured textual material. But, the integration of LLMs into edge devices poses unique challenges, including computational resource constraints and the need for efficient model deployment techniques. Strategies for addressing these challenges are explored, encompassing methodologies such as model distillation, quantization, and edge-native optimization frameworks tailored to accommodate LLMs. Moreover, this chapter delves into the symbiotic relationship between edge devices and LLMs in bolstering industrial applications,

**Corresponding author*: sathismecse@gmail.com

Sita Rani, Pankaj Bhambri, Balamurugan Balusamy, Rishabha Malviya and Seifedine Kadry (eds.) Edge Intelligence for 6G-Enabled Industrial Internet of Things, (321–338) © 2026 Scrivener Publishing LLC

ranging from predictive maintenance and quality control to demand forecasting and anomaly detection. Through illustrative case studies and practical examples, the efficacy of LLM-empowered edge computing in enhancing operational resilience and agility is demonstrated. The chapter concludes by highlighting the paradigm change that edge computing and LLMs in industrial settings have brought about, bringing in a new era of adaptive intelligence and data-driven decision-making. Industrial businesses can handle the complexity of contemporary operations with unmatched efficiency and foresight by embracing these technologies in concert.

Keywords: Edge computing, large language models, industrial intelligence, operational resilience, internet of things

15.1 Introduction

In the contemporary landscape of industrial operations, the convergence of cutting-edge technologies has ushered in a new era of optimization and efficiency. This introduction serves as a gateway to understanding the transformative potential of edge computing and its integration with advanced technologies such as the internet of things (IoT) and artificial intelligence (AI) in industrial settings. Through a comprehensive exploration of key concepts and methodologies, this section aims to elucidate the significance of optimized edge devices in driving industrial intelligence [1].

15.1.1 The Evolution of Industrial Intelligence

The evolution of industrial intelligence marks a significant shift from traditional manufacturing paradigms to the dynamic landscape of Industry 4.0. Historically, industrial operations relied on manual labor and rudimentary machinery, with decision-making processes largely based on human intuition and experience [2]. However, with the advent of digital technologies, the industrial sector has undergone a profound transformation, characterized by automation, data-driven insights, and interconnected systems.

Industry 4.0, often referred to as the fourth industrial revolution, represents the culmination of this transformation, heralding a new era of smart factories and intelligent manufacturing processes. At its core, Industry 4.0 emphasizes the integration of cyber-physical systems, IoT devices, and advanced analytics to optimize operations, enhance efficiency, and drive innovation.

The journey towards Industry 4.0 has been marked by several key milestones and technological advancements. The introduction of Computer-Aided Manufacturing (CAM) and Computer-Aided Design (CAD) systems in the late 20th century laid the foundation for digitizing industrial processes and streamlining production workflows. These technologies enabled manufacturers to design, simulate, and optimize products and processes in virtual environments, reducing time-to-market and enhancing product quality [3].

The proliferation of automation technologies further accelerated the pace of industrial transformation, enabling tasks traditionally performed by humans to be executed by machines. Robotics, for instance, revolutionized assembly lines and manufacturing operations, increasing productivity and precision while minimizing errors and safety risks.

15.1.1.1 From Traditional Manufacturing to Industry 4.0

From traditional manufacturing to Industry 4.0, the industrial landscape has undergone a profound transformation. Historically reliant on manual labor and basic machinery, Industry 4.0 integrates digital technologies like IoT, AI, and edge computing to create smart factories [4]. This evolution emphasizes automation, data-driven decision-making, and interconnected systems, revolutionizing production processes and efficiency.

15.1.2 Understanding Edge Computing

Understanding edge computing is pivotal in navigating the modern industrial landscape. At its core, edge computing involves processing data closer to its source, thereby reducing latency and enhancing real-time analytics. Unlike traditional cloud-based architectures, where data is transmitted to remote servers for processing, edge computing distributes computational tasks to local devices or "edge nodes." This decentralized approach offers several advantages, including improved response times, reduced network bandwidth usage, and enhanced privacy and security.

Key components of edge computing include edge devices, such as sensors, actuators, and embedded systems, as well as edge servers or gateways responsible for aggregating and processing data locally [5]. The architecture of edge computing systems varies depending on the specific use case and deployment scenario but typically involves a hierarchical structure with multiple layers of processing. In industrial contexts, edge computing plays a crucial role in enabling real-time monitoring, predictive maintenance, and autonomous decision-making.

15.1.2.1 Defining Edge Computing

Defining edge computing entails processing data near its source to minimize latency and enhance real-time analytics. Unlike traditional cloud-based models, edge computing distributes computational tasks to local devices or "edge nodes," offering faster response times and reduced network bandwidth usage [6]. This decentralized approach is vital in industrial settings, enabling real-time monitoring, predictive maintenance, and autonomous decision-making.

15.1.2.2 The Conceptual Framework

The conceptual framework of edge computing outlines its fundamental principles and architecture. At its core, edge computing aims to process data closer to its source, mitigating latency and improving response times compared to traditional cloud-based approaches. This framework involves deploying computational resources at the edge of the network, where data is generated, rather than relying solely on centralized data centers [7].

15.1.2.3 Key Components and Architecture

Key components and architecture of edge computing entail a distributed infrastructure designed to process data closer to its source, thereby reducing latency and enhancing real-time analytics. At its core, edge computing relies on several key components and architectural principles to achieve its objectives.

Firstly, edge devices serve as the entry point for data into the edge computing environment. These devices include sensors, actuators, and IoT endpoints capable of collecting and transmitting data from the physical world to the edge infrastructure [8].

Secondly, edge servers or gateways play a pivotal role in aggregating and processing data locally. These devices are responsible for executing computational tasks, running edge-specific applications, and facilitating communication between edge devices and central data repositories.

The architecture of edge computing typically follows a hierarchical structure, with multiple layers of processing distributed across the network [9]. At the edge, devices may perform initial data filtering, preprocessing, and analysis to extract relevant insights before transmitting summarized information to higher-level edge servers or the cloud for further processing.

15.1.3 Enabling Technologies

Enabling technologies in edge computing encompass internet of things (IoT) devices and advanced artificial intelligence (AI) algorithms. IoT

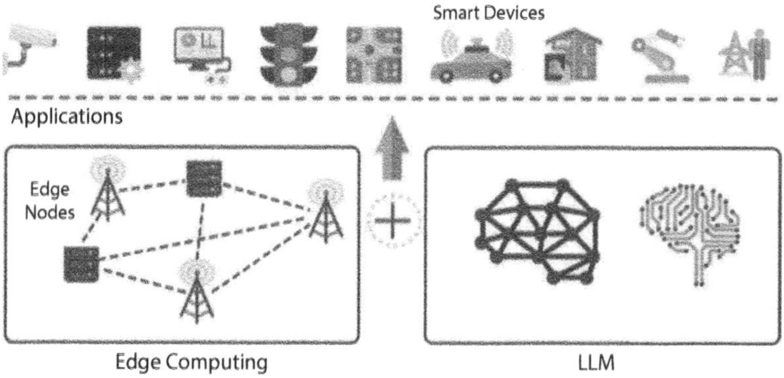

Figure 15.1 LLM enabled edge computing applications.

devices, equipped with sensors and actuators, facilitate data collection and transmission from physical assets to the edge infrastructure. Enabling technologies in edge computing encompass IoT devices and advanced artificial intelligence (AI) algorithms. IoT devices, equipped with sensors and actuators, facilitate data collection and transmission from physical assets to the edge infrastructure. Figure 15.1 illustrates the integration of LLM-enabled edge computing applications. These devices play a crucial role in capturing real-time data from industrial environments, enabling organizations to monitor equipment health, track production metrics, and optimize resource utilization [10].

Furthermore, AI algorithms empower edge devices to analyze and derive actionable insights from the collected data. Machine learning models, in particular, enable edge devices to recognize patterns, predict future outcomes, and make autonomous decisions in real-time. By combining IoT sensors with AI capabilities, organizations can unlock the full potential of edge computing, driving operational efficiency, predictive maintenance, and adaptive decision-making in industrial settings [11].

15.1.3.1 Internet of Things (IoT) in Industrial Context

In the industrial context, IoT revolutionizes operations by connecting devices and enabling data exchange. IoT devices equipped with sensors and actuators gather real-time data from machinery and processes, facilitating monitoring and optimization. This interconnected network empowers industries to enhance efficiency, reduce downtime, and improve decision-making through data-driven insights [12].

Integration of IoT with Edge Computing

The integration of IoT with edge computing revolutionizes data processing by enabling real-time analytics at the network's edge. IoT devices collect vast amounts of data from the physical environment, while edge computing facilitates local data processing and analysis. By processing data closer to its source, organizations reduce latency, conserve bandwidth, and enhance privacy and security. This seamless integration empowers industries to leverage the combined strengths of IoT and edge computing, driving efficiency, agility, and innovation in diverse applications such as predictive maintenance, quality control, and supply chain management [13].

IoT Sensors and Data Acquisition

IoT sensors play a pivotal role in data acquisition, enabling the collection of real-time information from various sources in industrial environments. These sensors are equipped with diverse functionalities, ranging from temperature and pressure monitoring to vibration analysis and image recognition. Through continuous data acquisition, IoT sensors provide insights into equipment performance, environmental conditions, and operational metrics, facilitating proactive maintenance, quality control, and process optimization. The seamless integration of IoT sensors with data acquisition systems empowers organizations to monitor assets, detect anomalies, and make informed decisions in dynamic industrial settings [13].

15.1.3.2 Artificial Intelligence (AI) Paradigms

Artificial Intelligence (AI) paradigms encompass a spectrum of techniques enabling machines to simulate human intelligence. In industrial contexts, AI algorithms play a pivotal role in processing and analyzing vast amounts of data collected by IoT sensors. Machine learning, a subset of AI, includes algorithms that enable systems to learn from data and make predictions or decisions without explicit programming. Deep learning, a sophisticated form of machine learning, employs neural networks with multiple layers to extract complex patterns and insights from raw data. Reinforcement learning, another AI paradigm, enables machines to learn through trial and error, optimizing decision-making processes over time. By harnessing AI paradigms, industrial enterprises can unlock actionable insights, automate repetitive tasks, and improve operational efficiency. These technologies empower organizations to achieve predictive maintenance, quality control, and supply chain optimization, driving innovation and competitive advantage in Industry 4.0 environments [14].

Machine Learning Algorithms for Edge Devices

Machine learning algorithms tailored for edge devices enable localized data processing and real-time decision-making, crucial in industrial settings. These algorithms, optimized for resource-constrained environments, include lightweight models capable of running efficiently on edge hardware. Common approaches include decision trees, support vector machines, and k-nearest neighbors, which require minimal computational resources while offering competitive performance. Additionally, techniques such as model compression and quantization further reduce the memory and processing requirements of machine learning models, making them suitable for deployment on edge devices with limited capabilities [15, 16]. By leveraging machine learning algorithms at the edge, industrial enterprises can achieve timely insights, optimize resource allocation, and enhance operational efficiency. These algorithms empower edge devices to autonomously analyze data streams, detect anomalies, and trigger appropriate responses, facilitating predictive maintenance, quality control, and process optimization in real-time [5].

Deep Learning Models and Their Application in Industrial Settings

Deep learning models, renowned for their ability to process complex data and extract intricate patterns, find significant application in industrial settings. These models, comprising multiple layers of interconnected neurons, excel at analyzing vast datasets collected from sensors and other sources in industrial environments. In manufacturing, deep learning facilitates predictive maintenance by identifying subtle equipment anomalies indicative of potential failures [6].

Quality control benefits from image classification algorithms capable of detecting defects in products with high accuracy. Supply chain optimization leverages deep learning for demand forecasting, inventory management, and route optimization. Moreover, anomaly detection algorithms powered by deep learning enhance cybersecurity by identifying unusual patterns in network traffic or system behavior. The versatility and adaptability of deep learning models make them indispensable tools for improving efficiency, reliability, and safety across various industrial domains, positioning them as key enablers of Industry 4.0 transformations. As depicted in Figure 15.2, the comprehensive guide to predictive maintenance implementation outlines the necessary steps for data acquisition, predictive modeling, real-time monitoring, and continuous improvement.

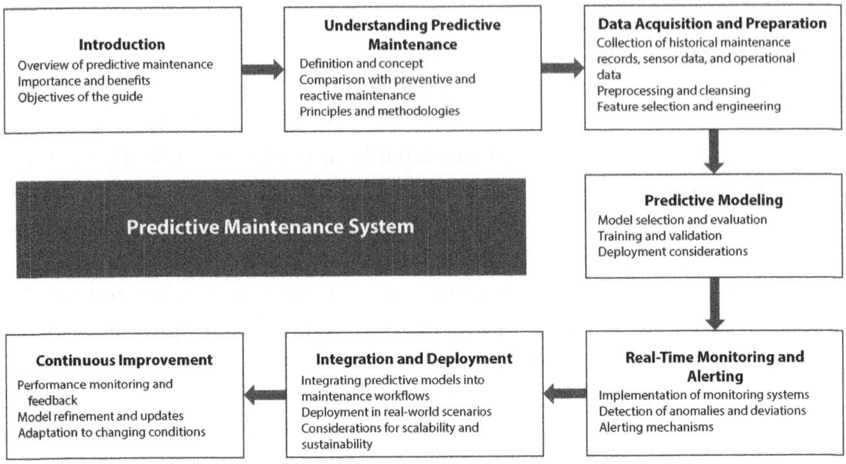

Figure 15.2 Comprehensive guide to predictive maintenance implementation.

15.1.4 Challenges and Opportunities

Challenges and opportunities abound in the realm of edge computing within industrial contexts. Computational resource constraints pose a significant challenge, requiring optimization techniques to ensure efficient operation of edge devices with limited processing power and memory. Additionally, reducing latency to meet real-time processing requirements remains a priority, necessitating the development of efficient data transmission and processing strategies. Security concerns surrounding edge devices, such as vulnerabilities to cyberattacks and unauthorized access, require robust authentication and encryption mechanisms to safeguard sensitive data [7].

However, amidst these challenges lie ample opportunities for innovation and advancement. Edge computing offers the potential to unlock new levels of operational efficiency, agility, and responsiveness in industrial operations. By harnessing the power of edge devices and decentralized data processing, organizations can achieve real-time insights, predictive analytics, and autonomous decision-making, driving transformative changes across diverse applications such as predictive maintenance, quality control, and supply chain optimization [5].

15.1.4.1 Computational Resource Constraints

Computational resource constraints pose significant challenges in the deployment of edge computing solutions within industrial environments.

Edge devices, often characterized by limited processing power, memory, and energy resources, must contend with the complexities of executing computational tasks efficiently. These constraints necessitate the optimization of algorithms and software architectures to minimize resource utilization while maintaining performance levels. Techniques such as model compression, quantization, and lightweight algorithm design help mitigate the impact of resource limitations, enabling edge devices to execute machine learning and AI algorithms effectively. Furthermore, advancements in hardware acceleration technologies, such as specialized processing units and accelerators, offer promising avenues for enhancing computational capabilities at the edge while conserving energy. By addressing computational resource constraints through innovative strategies and technologies, industrial enterprises can unlock the full potential of edge computing, driving efficiency, scalability, and agility in their operations [7].

Optimization Techniques for Edge Devices

Optimization techniques tailored for edge devices are pivotal in overcoming computational constraints and maximizing performance within industrial contexts. These techniques encompass a range of strategies aimed at minimizing resource usage while preserving functionality and efficiency. Model compression techniques reduce the size of machine learning models, enabling them to fit within the limited memory capacity of edge devices without sacrificing accuracy [11]. Quantization further reduces computational overhead by representing model parameters with lower precision, thereby conserving memory and processing resources.

Lightweight Machine Learning Algorithms

Lightweight machine learning algorithms are essential for efficient data processing on resource-constrained edge devices in industrial settings. These algorithms are characterized by their ability to deliver accurate results while minimizing computational and memory requirements. Techniques such as decision trees, k-nearest neighbors, and linear models are commonly employed due to their simplicity and low computational overhead. Additionally, ensemble methods like random forests and gradient boosting provide enhanced predictive performance without significantly increasing resource usage. Furthermore, model pruning and feature selection techniques help streamline algorithms by removing redundant or irrelevant components, further reducing computational burden. By leveraging lightweight machine learning algorithms, industrial enterprises can achieve real-time analytics, predictive maintenance, and anomaly detection on edge devices with limited processing power and memory, unlocking the full potential of edge computing for optimizing operations and driving innovation [13].

15.1.4.2 Security Considerations

Security considerations are paramount in the deployment of edge computing solutions within industrial environments. Edge devices, often dispersed across geographically diverse locations, are susceptible to various security threats, including unauthorized access, data breaches, and malware attacks. Robust authentication mechanisms, such as multi-factor authentication and digital certificates, are essential for verifying the identity of users and devices accessing the edge network. Encryption techniques safeguard data transmission and storage, ensuring confidentiality and integrity. Additionally, access control mechanisms restrict unauthorized access to sensitive resources and functionalities, mitigating the risk of insider threats. Continuous monitoring and threat detection mechanisms enable prompt identification and response to security incidents, minimizing potential damage [10].

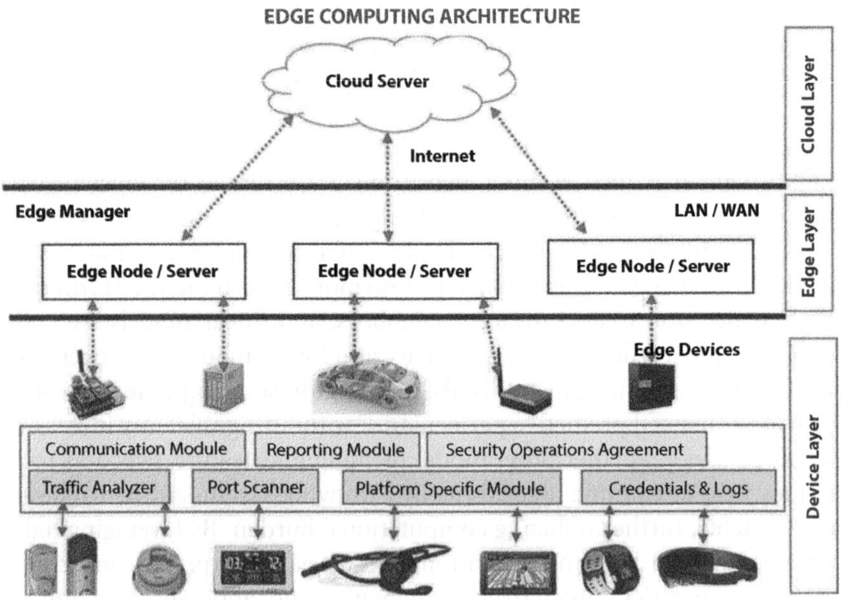

Figure 15.3 Edge computing architecture.

Secure Edge-to-Cloud Communication Protocols ensure the confidentiality and integrity of data transmitted between edge devices and cloud platforms. These protocols, such as transport layer security (TLS) and datagram transport layer security (DTLS), encrypt data during transmission, preventing unauthorized interception or tampering. The edge computing architecture, as illustrated in Figure 15.3, highlights the integration of edge devices, edge servers, and cloud infrastructure in the system design.

Robust Authentication and Access Control Mechanisms are essential for verifying the identity of users and devices accessing edge computing systems. Multi-factor authentication, digital certificates, and role-based access control (RBAC) are commonly employed to authenticate users and restrict access to authorized personnel only. These mechanisms help prevent unauthorized access and protect sensitive data from malicious actors [13].

15.1.5 Industrial Applications

Industrial applications of edge computing encompass a wide range of use cases, revolutionizing operational efficiency and decision-making processes. One key application is predictive maintenance, where edge devices analyze equipment data in real-time to detect potential failures before they occur, minimizing downtime and maintenance costs. Quality control benefits from edge computing through real-time inspection and defect detection, ensuring product quality and reducing waste. Supply chain management is optimized by leveraging edge devices for inventory tracking, demand forecasting, and logistics optimization, enhancing efficiency and responsiveness. Furthermore, edge computing enables real-time monitoring of environmental conditions and process parameters, facilitating compliance with regulatory standards and ensuring workplace safety. Overall, industrial applications of edge computing empower organizations to achieve agility, resilience, and innovation in their operations, driving competitive advantage in today's dynamic market landscape [3].

15.1.5.1 Predictive Maintenance

Predictive maintenance encompasses early fault detection systems and condition monitoring techniques, revolutionizing industrial maintenance practices. By analyzing sensor data in real-time, predictive maintenance systems detect anomalies indicative of potential equipment failures before they occur. Early fault detection systems leverage machine learning algorithms to identify subtle deviations in performance metrics, triggering timely interventions to prevent downtime and costly repairs. Additionally, condition monitoring techniques continuously assess equipment health, tracking parameters such as temperature, vibration, and lubricant levels to detect signs of wear or deterioration. By implementing predictive maintenance strategies, industrial enterprises can optimize maintenance schedules, extend asset lifespan, and minimize unplanned downtime, enhancing operational efficiency and reliability [5].

15.1.5.2 Quality Control and Assurance

Quality control and assurance are critical aspects of industrial operations, ensuring product integrity and customer satisfaction. Real-time quality inspection utilizes advanced sensing technologies and machine learning algorithms to assess product quality during the manufacturing process. By analyzing data from sensors and cameras in real-time, manufacturers can detect defects and deviations from quality standards promptly. Defect detection algorithms leverage image processing techniques and pattern recognition to identify anomalies such as cracks, scratches, or irregularities in manufactured goods. These algorithms enable automated inspection systems to classify and reject defective products, maintaining quality standards and reducing waste. By integrating real-time quality inspection and defect detection algorithms into production workflows, industrial enterprises can achieve consistent product quality, minimize rework and recall, and enhance customer trust and loyalty. These quality control measures drive efficiency and competitiveness in the marketplace, positioning organizations for success in today's demanding industrial landscape [6].

15.1.5.3 Supply Chain Management

Supply chain management plays a pivotal role in optimizing operational efficiency and meeting customer demands. Inventory optimization strategies aim to strike a balance between maintaining sufficient stock levels and minimizing excess inventory costs. By leveraging data analytics and optimization algorithms, organizations can accurately forecast demand, identify optimal reorder points, and dynamically adjust inventory levels to align with fluctuating demand patterns. Demand forecasting models utilize historical sales data, market trends, and external factors to predict future demand for products or services. These models enable proactive decision-making, helping organizations anticipate market shifts, optimize production schedules, and allocate resources effectively. By integrating inventory optimization and demand forecasting models into supply chain management processes, industrial enterprises can achieve leaner, more agile operations, reduce carrying costs, and enhance customer satisfaction through timely product availability and fulfillment. This proactive approach to supply chain management fosters resilience and competitiveness in today's dynamic business landscape [8].

15.2 Proposed Architecture/System for Industrial Edge Computing

15.2.1 Introduction

In the field of industrial operations, the adoption of edge computing is increasingly widespread, providing the ability to transform in improving efficiency, reliability, and agility. This proposed architecture/system aims to provide a comprehensive framework for implementing edge computing solutions tailored to the unique needs of industrial environments. By leveraging advanced technologies and innovative design principles, this architecture/system seeks to address the challenges inherent in industrial fringe computing, while increasing opportunities for optimization and innovation [10, 14].

Key components of the conceptual framework include edge devices, which include sensors, actuators, and other IoT devices capable of collecting and transmitting data. These devices act as an entry point for data in an edge computing environment. Additionally, edge servers or gateways play a key role in aggregating and processing data locally before sending relevant insights to the cloud or central data repositories.

15.2.2 Key Components and Architecture

Conceptual Framework: Definition of Industrial Edge Computing

- Define the key principles and objectives of industrial edge computing in the context of industrial operations.
- Highlights the importance of proximity to data sources, real-time analytics and decentralized processing in industrial settings.

Key Components and Architecture: Edge Device Layer

- Description of edge devices including sensors, actuators and embedded systems used at the edge of the network.
- Explanation of the role of edge devices in data collection, pre-processing and local decision making.

Edge Computing Infrastructure

- Overview of edge computing infrastructure, which includes edge servers, gateways, and edge computing nodes.
- A discussion of the hierarchical architecture and distributed processing capabilities of edge computing infrastructure.

Optimization Techniques: Data Processing and Analytics

- Introduction to optimization techniques for data processing and analytics at the edge, including data aggregation, compression and filtering.
- Discussion of edge-native optimization frameworks and lightweight machine learning algorithms suitable for edge devices.

Security Considerations: Authentication and Access Control

- Overview of authentication mechanisms such as digital certificates and multi-factor authentication to verify the identity of users and devices accessing the edge network.
- Description of access control mechanisms to limit unauthorized access to sensitive resources and functions. The security framework for industrial edge computing, shown in Figure 15.4, illustrates the various layers and security protocols critical for safeguarding edge computing environments.

Data Encryption and Privacy:

- Discussion of encryption techniques to protect data transmission and storage, ensuring confidentiality and integrity.
- Description of privacy-protection techniques, such as differential privacy and data anonymization, to protect sensitive information.

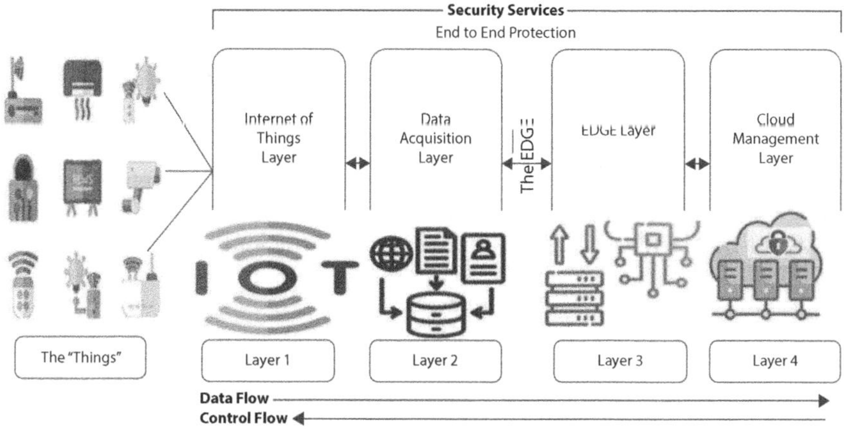

Figure 15.4 Security framework for industrial edge computing.

15.3 Conclusion

In conclusion, implementing a comprehensive predictive maintenance strategy holds enormous promise for industrial organizations seeking to improve operational efficiency, reduce downtime, and improve asset performance. Through the systematic integration of advanced technologies, data-driven methods and proactive maintenance practices, predictive maintenance provides a proactive approach to asset management that transcends the limitations of traditional preventive and reactive maintenance paradigms.

The journey toward predictive maintenance begins with a clear understanding of organizational objectives and maintenance goals, ensuring alignment with broader business strategies. By leveraging historical maintenance records, sensor data, and operational insights, organizations can build predictive models capable of predicting equipment failures and performance degradation with greater accuracy. Deployment of real-time monitoring systems enables timely detection of anomalies and deviations, enabling proactive intervention before critical failures occur.

Integrating and deploying predictive maintenance solutions into existing workflows is a key step in realizing their full potential. Organizations must consider scalability, consistency, and interoperability when integrating predictive models into maintenance processes. Furthermore, continuous improvement and adaptation is necessary to ensure the effectiveness and relevance of predictive maintenance strategies over time. Performance monitoring, model refinement, and feedback mechanisms enable organizations to iterate and improve their predictive maintenance approaches based on evolving operational requirements and changing environmental conditions.

AI disclosure statement: The author confirms that no artificial intelligence (AI)-generated content or AI-assisted writing tools were used in the preparation of this chapter (including summaries and the abstract). All text, analysis, and conclusions are the result of the author's original work.

References

1. Smith, A., Advancements in Predictive Maintenance Techniques. *Ind. Eng. J., Springer*, 12, 3, 45–56, 2023.
2. Patel, R., Machine Learning Approaches for Predictive Maintenance. *IEEE Trans. Ind. Electron.*, IEEE, 67, 5, 789–802, 2022.
3. Garcia, M., Real-Time Monitoring Systems for Predictive Maintenance. *Sens. Actuators A Phys.*, Elsevier, 410, 123–135, 2021.
4. Kim, Y., Cloud-Based Predictive Maintenance Solutions for Industry 4.0. *J. Manuf. Syst.*, Elsevier, 48, 102–115, 2020.
5. Wang, Q., Data-Driven Predictive Maintenance Strategies. *J. Oper. Manage.*, Wiley, 31, 2, 278–291, 2023.
6. Lee, J., Predictive Maintenance Frameworks for Railway Systems. *Transp. Res. Part C Emerging Technol.*, Elsevier, 55, 78–91, 2022.
7. Chen, L., Wireless Sensor Networks for Predictive Maintenance in Smart Manufacturing. *J. Manuf. Processes*, Elsevier, 40, Part A, 234–245, 2020.
8. Rodriguez, E., Smart Sensors for Predictive Maintenance Applications. *IEEE Sens. J.*, IEEE, 19, 8, 3456–3467, 2021.
9. Gupta, S., Predictive Maintenance and Asset Management in the Oil and Gas Industry. *Oil Gas Sci. Technol.*, EDP Sciences, 78, 4, 567–580, 2023.
10. Wilson, K., Cost-Benefit Analysis of Predictive Maintenance Implementations. *J. Bus. Res.*, Elsevier, 75, 98–111, 2020.
11. Martinez, F., Predictive Maintenance in Aerospace: Challenges and Future Directions. *Aerosp. Sci. Technol.*, Elsevier, 101, 102345, 2021.
12. Brown, S., Machine Learning Applications in Predictive Maintenance: A Review. *Expert Syst. Appl.*, Elsevier, 93, 212–225, 2022.
13. Yang, G., Predictive Maintenance for Energy Systems: Challenges and Opportunities. *Energy Rep.*, Elsevier, 6, 789–802, 2020.
14. Li, H., Predictive Maintenance Frameworks for Industrial IoT Systems. *J. Ind. Inf. Integr.*, Elsevier, 45, 234–247, 2021.

15. Johnson, A., Predictive Maintenance Strategies for Sustainable Manufacturing. *Sustain. Prod. Consumption*, Elsevier, 34, 567–580, 2022.
16. Rani, S., Bhambri, P., Kumar, S., Pareek, P.K., Elngar, A.A. (Eds.), AI-Driven Digital Twin and Industry 4.0: A Conceptual Framework with Applications (1st ed.). CRC Press, 2024. https://doi.org/10.1201/9781003395416.

16

Advancing Edge Intelligence: The Role and Future in 6G Networks

L. Maria Suganthi*, P. Senthamizh Pavai, K. Geetha and J. Vigneshwari

Faculty of Education, Dr. M.G.R. Educational and Research Institute, Chennai, Tamil Nadu, India

Abstract

This paper explores the pivotal role of edge intelligence in shaping the evolution of 6G networks and beyond. It delves into the foundational principles of edge intelligence, its integration within the context of 6G networks, and its future prospects in revolutionizing telecommunications. The paper encompasses three main areas: the evolution of 6G networks, the emergence of edge intelligence within the framework, and the anticipated advancements in future edge intelligence capabilities. Through collaboration among researchers, industry leaders, policymakers, and stakeholders, edge intelligence is poised to become a transformative force, driving innovation, standardization, and interoperability. Ultimately, edge intelligence holds the potential to transcend its role as a mere technological advancement, emerging as a societal asset that empowers individuals and organizations worldwide.

***Keywords*:** Edge intelligence, edge AI, edge computing, 6G networks, security and privacy, telecommunication evolution

**Corresponding author*: mariasuganthi.bed@drmgrdu.ac.in; ORCID: 0000-0002-7323-8306

P. Senthamizh Pavai: ORCID: 0000-0003-0468-6188

K. Geetha: ORCID: 0000-0002-2121-3916

J. Vigneshwari: ORCID: 0000-0003-2874-7360

Sita Rani, Pankaj Bhambri, Balamurugan Balusamy, Rishabha Malviya and Seifedine Kadry (eds.) Edge Intelligence for 6G-Enabled Industrial Internet of Things, (339–364) © 2026 Scrivener Publishing LLC

16.1 Introduction

An enormous increase in connectivity, ultra-reliable low latency communication, and formerly unprecedented data speeds are all anticipated in the rapidly approaching 6G era, which is expected to revolutionize the telecom industry. Within this burgeoning landscape, the concept of edge intelligence emerges as a cornerstone, heralding a new phase of smart, efficient, and highly responsive network systems. "Advancing Edge Intelligence: The Role and Future in 6G Networks" delves into the symbiotic relationship between the next-generation mobile networks and the intelligent edge, exploring how this integration is pivotal to realizing the full spectrum of 6G's potential.

16.2 What is 6G Networks?

It is anticipated that 6G networks—the sixth generation of wireless communications technologies supporting cellular data networks—will replace the existing 5G networks [18]. While still in the early stages of research and development, with commercial deployment anticipated to begin around 2030, the vision for 6G is to significantly enhance the capabilities offered by its predecessor, 5G.

Building upon the foundation laid by 5G, 6G aims to deliver unprecedented data rates, potentially reaching up to 1 terabit per second, and ultra-low latency in the range of microseconds. With effortless and instantaneous interactions, these developments will pave the way for a new era of immersive experiences, like augmented reality (AR), virtual reality (VR), and extended reality (XR). Furthermore, 6G is anticipated to enable the rapid expansion of connected devices, promoting the creation of smart environments and the broad adoption of the internet of things (IoT) [10].

Another key aspect of 6G networks is their emphasis on energy efficiency and sustainability. By incorporating advanced AI and machine learning (ML) algorithms, 6G networks will optimize resource allocation, reduce power consumption, and enhance network management. This focus on sustainability is crucial in addressing the growing environmental concerns associated with the proliferation of digital technologies.

Moreover, 6G is set to revolutionize communication security and privacy [5]. 6G networks will provide a strong defense against cyberattacks by combining quantum computing and cryptography techniques, guaranteeing the integrity and confidentiality of data transfer. Supporting vital applications in industries like healthcare, finance, and national defense requires increased security.

By giving underserved and remote areas access to high-speed internet, the development of 6G networks also holds promise for closing the digital divide. Through advanced satellite and aerial communication technologies, 6G aims to deliver reliable connectivity to every corner of the globe, fostering digital inclusion and enabling socio-economic development.

As research and development efforts continue, collaborations between academia, industry, and governments will be pivotal in realizing the full potential of 6G networks. The transformative impact of 6G will not only enhance our daily lives but also drive innovation and economic growth, shaping the future of global communication [3].

16.3 Key Characteristics of 6G Networks

- **Higher Data Rates:** 6G aims to provide substantially higher data rates than 5G, potentially reaching speeds of 1 terabit per second (Tbps) or more. This would enable ultra-fast downloads and uploads, transforming the user experience with high-speed internet services.
- **Ultra-Low Latency:** 6G networks are anticipated to have latency down to microseconds (μs), which will greatly enhance response times and allow real-time applications like tactile internet, VR, AR, and autonomous driving.
- **Massive Connectivity:** Massive machine-type communications (mMTC) will be supported by 6G, which will increase 5G's mMTC capacity and support even more devices concurrently. With billions of devices connected, this is essential for the IoT, automated industries, and smart cities.
- **Advanced Antenna Technologies:** Utilizing higher frequency bands, including terahertz (THz) frequencies and advanced antenna technologies for improved capacity and energy efficiency. This will support the transmission of large amounts of data at very high speeds.
- **Artificial Intelligence Integration:** AI will be deeply integrated into the network to improve operational efficiency, network management, and the personalization of services. AI will be crucial to controlling the complexity of 6G networks, allocating resources optimally, and boosting security.

- **Sustainability:** It's a focus on energy efficiency and reduced carbon footprint, aiming for more sustainable network operations. This covers advancements in software and hardware to reduce energy usage and increase the application of renewable energy sources.
- **Enhanced Security and Privacy:** Advanced cryptographic techniques and security protocols ensure user privacy and data protection, addressing the increasingly sophisticated cybersecurity threats.

16.4 Technological Innovations Driving 6G

A new era of connectivity, propelled by numerous ground-breaking technological advancements, is anticipated with the introduction of 6G networks. These advancements are set to revolutionize how we communicate, interact with our environment, and utilize digital services [3]. Here are some of the key technological innovations propelling the development of 6G:

- **1. Terahertz (THz) Frequency Bands:** 6G networks will leverage the terahertz frequency spectrum, which lies between the microwave and infrared regions. This higher frequency range will enable ultra-high-speed data transfer rates, potentially reaching up to 1 terabit per second. Ultra-high-definition video streaming and holographic communication are two examples of applications that will benefit from the use of THz frequencies, which will enable the real-time transmission of massive amounts of data.
- **2. Advanced AI and Machine Learning:** AI and machine learning will play a major role in 6G network optimization. These technologies will enable intelligent network management, automated decision-making, and predictive maintenance. AI can analyze vast volumes of data in realtime, optimize resource allocation, enhance network performance, and boost energy efficiency. ML algorithms will also be used to forecast network congestion and dynamically adjust network parameters to maintain optimal performance.
- **3. Quantum Communication:** To offer previously unheard levels of security, 6G networks will incorporate quantum

communication technologies. By utilizing the ideas of quantum mechanics, quantum key distribution (QKD) provides secure data transmission and renders it nearly impossible for malicious actors to intercept communications. This quantum-based security will be essential for protecting sensitive information in sectors such as finance, healthcare, and national defense.

- **4. Intelligent Reflecting Surfaces (IRS):** Intelligent reflecting surfaces, also known as smart surfaces, will enhance signal propagation and coverage in 6G networks. These surfaces can dynamically control the reflection and refraction of electromagnetic waves, improving signal strength and reducing interference. By deploying IRS in urban environments and indoor spaces, 6G networks can provide seamless and reliable connectivity, even in challenging conditions.
- **5. Holographic Beamforming:** Holographic beamforming is a cutting-edge technique that allows precise control of the direction and shape of radio waves. This innovation will enable 6G networks to focus signals more accurately on specific users or devices, reducing interference and increasing spectral efficiency. Holographic beamforming will be particularly beneficial in densely populated areas, where efficient use of the spectrum is critical.
- **6. Integrated Sensing and Communication (ISAC):** 6G will merge communication and sensing capabilities into a unified framework. ISAC will not only allow networks to transmit data but also sense and interpret the surrounding environment. This integration will enable applications such as environmental monitoring, gesture recognition, and location-based services. For instance, 6G-enabled cars will be able to sense road conditions and communicate with one another, improving safety and enabling autonomous driving.
- **7. Enhanced MIMO (Multiple Input, Multiple Output) Technology:** MIMO technology, which involves employing multiple antennas to transmit as well as receive data, will be significantly enhanced in 6G networks. Massive MIMO, with a large number of antennas, will improve spectral efficiency and increase network capacity. With this development, a vast array of devices will have dependable connectivity and will be able to meet the increasing demand for high-speed data.

- **8. Reconfigurable Intelligent Surfaces (RIS):** RIS technology will allow dynamic control of the wireless environment. These surfaces can be programmed to change their electromagnetic properties, optimizing signal propagation and enhancing network coverage. By deploying RIS in various locations, 6G networks can adapt to changing conditions and provide consistent, high-quality connectivity.

The convergence of these technological innovations will make 6G networks a cornerstone of the future digital landscape. As research and development efforts continue, the realization of these advancements will drive unprecedented connectivity, transform industries, and enhance our everyday lives.

16.5 Challenges and Opportunities in 6G Development

The future of international communications will be formed by the opportunities and challenges that come with developing 6G networks. The requirement for large investments in infrastructure and research to investigate and deploy the cutting-edge technologies needed for 6G, like intelligent reflecting surfaces, quantum computing, and terahertz communication, is one of the main obstacles [20]. Additionally, ensuring global standardization and interoperability of 6G networks poses a significant hurdle, requiring collaboration across international regulatory bodies, industry leaders, and academic institutions.

With its unprecedented data speeds, ultra-low latency, and seamless connectivity, 6G offers the potential to completely transform a number of industries. Innovation in fields such as driverless cars, smart cities, and fully immersive augmented reality experiences will now have more opportunities [10]. Additionally, 6G can promote digital inclusion by bridging the digital divide, promoting socioeconomic development, and offering high-speed internet access to underserved and remote areas. As these issues are resolved, there will be more and more chances to have revolutionary effects on society and industry, which will make 6G a crucial development in the history of wireless communication [8, 12].

16.6 Applications and Implications of 6G Networks

6G networks will enable a host of futuristic applications and technologies, including immersive AR and VR experiences, holographic communications, highly autonomous vehicles, and smart ecosystems. These networks will facilitate seamless connectivity and interaction between humans, machines, and everything in between, marking a significant step towards the realization of the internet of everything (IoE).

The implications of 6G networks extend far beyond enhanced connectivity and faster speeds. These networks are poised to revolutionize numerous industries by enabling unprecedented levels of data collection, analysis, and real-time responsiveness [5]. For instance, in healthcare, 6G could support remote surgeries with robotic precision, enabled by ultra-low latency and high reliability [4]. With the use of advanced sensor networks and AI-driven analytics, smart cities may be able to maximize traffic flow, lower energy use, and enhance public safety.

The financial sector might benefit from enhanced security protocols and faster transaction processing, while education could see the rise of fully immersive virtual classrooms, breaking down geographical barriers to learning. The pervasive, high-capacity nature of 6G networks will also drive innovation in fields like entertainment, agriculture, and manufacturing, creating new opportunities and transforming existing paradigms.

16.7 The Role of AI in 6G Networks

As the world anticipates the rollout of 5G technology, researchers and industry leaders are already looking ahead to the next generation: 6G networks, predicted to be operational by 2030, promise to revolutionize telecommunications with unprecedented speed, capacity, and versatility. A crucial component driving this innovation will be AI, [5]. AI is anticipated to be crucial to the creation and functionality of 6G networks.

- **Enhancing Network Efficiency**
  AI's ability to analyze vast amounts of data and make real-time decisions will be central to optimizing 6G networks. Unlike previous generations, 6G will need to handle a massive increase in connected devices, each demanding low latency and high-speed communication. AI can manage this complexity by dynamically allocating resources, predicting

network congestion, and optimizing traffic flow. By adjusting operations to maintain optimal performance based on patterns of network usage, machine learning algorithms can decrease latency and boost overall efficiency.

- **Intelligent Resource Management**
  In 6G networks, resource management will become more sophisticated with AI. Machine learning models can predict demand and allocate bandwidth accordingly, ensuring that resources are used efficiently. For example, AI can prioritize emergency communications over less critical data transfers in real time. Applications like autonomous vehicles and remote surgery that require ultra-reliable low-latency communications (URLLC) will depend on this intelligent resource management.
- **Enhanced Security**
  There is a greater chance of security flaws as the number of connected devices rises. AI will be essential in defending 6G networks against online attacks. Artificial intelligence (AI) can detect and respond to security breaches more quickly than traditional methods by continuously monitoring network traffic and identifying unusual patterns. AI-driven security systems offer a more resilient defense against complex cyberattacks since they can also adjust to changing threats.
- **Facilitating Edge Computing**
  A major component of 6G networks will be edge computing, which processes data closer to its source rather than depending on centralized data centers. AI will make edge computing more effective by intelligently allocating computational tasks throughout the network. This will guarantee seamless operation of real-time processing-demanding applications like VR and AR and reduce latency.
- **Enabling Autonomous Networks**
  One of the most transformative aspects of AI in 6G will be the development of autonomous networks. These self-optimizing networks will use AI to manage and maintain themselves with minimal human intervention. AI will monitor network health, predict potential issues, and take corrective actions automatically. This level of autonomy will significantly reduce operational costs and enhance network reliability.

- **Supporting Advanced Applications**
  To fully utilize the sophisticated applications that 6G networks will enable, AI will be crucial. AI will offer the required intelligence to manage the complicated data processing and decision-making required for everything from smart cities and the IoT to immersive VR experiences. To optimize energy consumption in a smart city and increase efficiency and sustainability, AI algorithms, for example, can analyze data from millions of IoT sensors.

As we look towards the future of 6G networks, it is clear that AI will be at the forefront of this technological revolution. By enhancing network efficiency, enabling intelligent resource management, bolstering security, facilitating edge computing, and supporting advanced applications, AI will be the driving force behind the next generation of telecommunications. Artificial intelligence (AI) in 6G will change not only how we connect, but also how we live, work, and engage with our surroundings (5). The future of connectivity appears incredibly promising with AI and 6G working together to enable innovations that were previously only found in science fiction [19].

16.8 Security and Privacy Enhancements in 6G Networks

As the world stands on the brink of the 6G era, the promise of unprecedented speed, connectivity, and innovation comes with significant challenges in security and privacy. As the number of connected devices rises and our dependence on digital infrastructure grows, it is critical that 6G networks have strong security and privacy protocols. 6G network security and privacy will be shaped by innovations and strategies [17].

- **Advanced Encryption Techniques**
  Encryption will remain a cornerstone of network security in the 6G era. However, traditional encryption methods will evolve to meet the demands of faster and more complex data exchanges. Quantum-resistant encryption algorithms will become essential as quantum computing advances, posing new threats to current cryptographic techniques. These advanced algorithms will protect sensitive data from being

deciphered by quantum computers, ensuring long-term security.

- **AI-Driven Threat Detection**
  The improvement of 6G network security will be greatly aided by artificial intelligence (AI). In comparison to conventional techniques, AI-powered threat detection systems can identify and mitigate possible threats more quickly by analyzing enormous volumes of network traffic in realtime. Proactive defense mechanisms such as cyberattack prediction and prevention can be achieved by machine learning algorithms through the use of historical data. AI provides a dynamic and responsive security solution by adapting to new and evolving threats.
- **Zero Trust Architecture**
  Securing 6G networks will heavily depend on the move to a Zero Trust Architecture (ZTA). ZTA implements the "never trust, always verify" tenet, in contrast to traditional security models that presume everything on the network can be trusted. No matter where a device is located within the network, this method necessitates constant user identity and device integrity verification. An important way to lower the risk of illegal access and data breaches in 6G networks is to implement ZTA.
- **Secure Edge Computing**
  6G networks will be built around edge computing, which will move data processing closer to the source [6]. This lowers latency and boosts efficiency, but it also presents new security risks. Strong security measures will be needed to protect data at the edge to stop illegal access and guarantee data integrity [11]. Sensitive data can be protected at edge nodes by deploying AI-driven security measures that can monitor and react to threats instantly.
- **Blockchain for Data Integrity**
  Blockchain technology will be leveraged to enhance data integrity and transparency in 6G networks. By creating an immutable ledger of transactions, blockchain can ensure that data has not been tampered with, providing a reliable method for verifying data authenticity. This is particularly relevant for supply chain management applications, where data integrity is crucial. Blockchain also makes it possible for

peer-to-peer communication to be secure, which eliminates the need for centralized servers and the likelihood of failure points.

- **Privacy-Preserving Technologies**
  6G networks will include privacy-preserving technologies to safeguard user data as data privacy concerns increase. Sensitive data can be kept private by using methods like homomorphic encryption, which enables calculations to be done on encrypted data without first decrypting it. Another method for protecting user privacy while enhancing AI capabilities is federated learning, which allows machine learning models to be trained on decentralized data sources without exchanging raw data [6].
- **Robust Authentication Mechanisms**
  Strengthening authentication mechanisms will be essential to prevent unauthorized access to 6G networks. As multi-factor authentication (MFA) becomes standard practice, users will have to use a variety of identityverification techniques, including passwords, biometrics, and security tokens. Furthermore, methods for continuous authentication, which keep an eye on user behavior and device patterns, can offer continuous verification and spot anomalies that might lead to a security risk.
- **Regulatory Compliance and Standards**
  Ensuring security and privacy in 6G networks will also involve adhering to regulatory standards and compliance requirements. Governments and industry bodies will need to collaborate to establish clear guidelines and frameworks for 6G security. Compliance with these standards will ensure that networks are built and operated with robust security measures in place, protecting users and their data.

The transition to 6G networks promises to revolutionize connectivity, but it also brings new challenges in security and privacy. Advanced encryption techniques, AI-driven threat detection, zero trust architecture, secure edge computing, blockchain technology, privacy-preserving methods, robust authentication mechanisms, and regulatory compliance will be essential components of a secure 6G ecosystem. By prioritizing these enhancements, we can build a 6G network that not only delivers exceptional performance but also ensures the highest levels of security and privacy for all users. To fully utilize this revolutionary technology and protect our digital future as we approach the 6G era, security, and privacy must be given the greatest importance [23, 24].

16.9 What is Edge Intelligence?

The combination of edge computing and artificial intelligence (AI) is known as Edge Intelligence or Edge AI. This novel combination enables machine learning algorithms to be performed directly on edge devices, the source of the data. By doing this, edge intelligence has the potential to make accessible artificial intelligence, enabling anyone and any organization, wherever they may be, to use it [1].

16.10 AI Chips for Edge Devices - Transforming Localized Processing and Intelligence

AI chips for edge devices are becoming an essential technology as the need for low-latency applications and real-time data processing increases. These specialized processors enable edge devices, such as smartphones, IoT gadgets, and autonomous vehicles, to perform complex AI computations locally, without relying on cloud-based systems. This feature addresses important concerns about data security and privacy in addition to improving processing speed and efficiency. AI chips make intelligent features more dependable and accessible by bringing AI capabilities right into the device, thereby reducing reliance on cloud resources and constant internet connectivity [16].

Consequently, industries ranging from healthcare to smart cities are experiencing a transformative impact, with AI chips at the forefront of this on-device intelligence revolution. In healthcare, AI chips facilitate real-time patient monitoring and diagnostics, enabling rapid and accurate decision-making that can save lives. In the automotive sector, these chips are integral to the development of autonomous driving systems, providing the necessary computational power to process vast amounts of sensor data instantaneously. Smart cities leverage AI chips to enhance infrastructure, manage resources efficiently, and improve the quality of life for their inhabitants. Furthermore, industrial applications benefit from predictive maintenance and optimized operations, driven by the edge AI capabilities that these chips provide. As AI technology continues to advance, the proliferation of AI chips in edge devices is set to drive innovation and efficiency across various sectors, heralding a new era of intelligent, interconnected systems [2].

16.11 Edge Intelligence in 6G Networks

Edge Intelligence in the context of 6G networks signifies a transformative approach to network design and operation, blending the capabilities of AI and edge computing with the advanced features of 6G technology. With this integration, we hope to push the limits of speed, dependability, and efficiency in the way that data is processed, analyzed, and utilized throughout the network. Anticipated to represent the next generation of wireless networks, 6G networks should offer ultra low latency, massive device connectivity, extremely high data rates, and highly dependable communication links.

6G networks can process and analyze data closer to the source by integrating edge intelligence, which reduces the amount of data that needs to travel to centralized cloud servers. This proximity not only reduces latency but also enhances data security and privacy, as sensitive information remains within the local network environment. Additionally, the implementation of AI at the edge facilitates predictive analytics and real-time decision-making, both of which are essential for applications like advanced healthcare systems, smart cities, and autonomous cars.

Edge intelligence in 6G also supports the seamless integration of IoT devices, allowing for efficient management and operation of a vast array of connected devices. This capability is essential for the realization of fully autonomous and interconnected ecosystems, where devices can communicate and coordinate actions without human intervention. Additionally, edge intelligence can optimize network resources and manage traffic dynamically, ensuring that the high performance and reliability standards of 6G networks are consistently met.

As we move towards a more connected and data-driven world, the synergy between AI, edge computing, and 6G technology is set to unlock unprecedented opportunities and drive innovation across various sectors. From enhancing user experiences to enabling new business models, edge intelligence in 6G networks is poised to be a cornerstone of the next generation of wireless communication.

16.12 Key Components of Edge Intelligence in 6G Networks

Figure 16.1 illustrates the key foundational components of edge intelligence, including distributed AI, advanced data processing, enhanced privacy and security, efficient network management, and energy efficiency [15].

- **Distributed AI:** Edge Intelligence disperses AI algorithms over the network, particularly at the edge, nearer to the locations where data is generated and gathered, in contrast to conventional centralized AI models that concentrate on cloud computing. This approach significantly reduces latency by minimizing the distance that data must travel for processing and action, which is crucial for time-sensitive applications.
- **Advanced Data Processing:** Edge Intelligence enables real-time data processing and prompt decision-making and action by utilizing the computational power at the network's edge. Applications that demand quick responses, like emergency response systems, remote surgery, and autonomous car navigation, should pay particular consideration to this.
- **Enhanced Privacy and Security:** Processing data locally at the edge reduces the need to transmit sensitive information over the network to a central server for analysis, thereby enhancing data privacy and security – a critical aspect in an era where data breaches and privacy concerns are rampant [15].
- **Efficient Network Management:** Edge Intelligence enables smarter network management strategies, including dynamic resource allocation, predictive maintenance, and congestion

Figure 16.1 Key components of edge intelligence in 6G networks.

management. By understanding and anticipating network conditions and user demands in realtime, 6G networks can optimize performance and resource utilization, ensuring a seamless user experience.

- **Energy Efficiency:** AI deployed at the edge minimizes energy consumption by minimizing the need for long-distance data transmission for processing. This is increasingly important as the number of connected devices skyrockets and sustainability becomes a central concern.

Edge Intelligence in 6G networks is about embedding smart. Autonomous capabilities throughout the network infrastructure enable not only faster and more reliable communications but also smarter and more efficient operations.

16.13 The Role of Edge Intelligence in 6G Networks

By bringing processing power closer to the data source, edge intelligence significantly lowers latency, which is essential for real-time applications.

- **Ultra-Reliable and Low-Latency Communication (URLLC):** 6G's goal to achieve even lower latency and higher reliability than 5G will be underpinned by edge intelligence [15]. By processing data where it is generated, decisions can be made swiftly, ensuring a level of responsiveness and reliability that centralized processing could never achieve.
- **Massive Machine Type Communications (mMTC):** Edge Intelligence will enable the massive connectivity ambitions of 6G by efficiently managing the data generated by billions of IoT devices [5]. Decreasing network congestion and enhancing overall system efficiency, intelligent edge nodes can make decisions locally and eliminate the need for continuous communication with a central cloud.
- **Elevated Security and Privacy:**
  By processing and storing data closer to the user, edge intelligence improves data security and privacy by default [15]. Reducing the quantity of data that must be transmitted across networks considerably lowers the likelihood of interception or compromise.

16.14 Security and Privacy in Edge Intelligence

As the integration of edge intelligence into 6G networks becomes more prevalent, ensuring robust security and privacy measures is paramount. Edge intelligence, which combines edge computing with artificial intelligence (AI), processes data closer to the source, reducing latency and improving efficiency [4]. To preserve user confidence and safeguard sensitive data, decentralization also brings up new security and privacy issues that need to be resolved.

16.14.1 Introduction to Security and Privacy in Edge Intelligence

By processing and analyzing data locally at the network's edge, edge intelligence makes use of AI. Although there are many advantages to this, such as decreased latency and improved real-time decision-making, it also creates new vulnerabilities [9]. The effective implementation of edge intelligence in 6G networks depends on the protection of edge devices and the data they manage [13].

16.14.2 Threat Landscape for Edge Intelligence

The edge environment is inherently more vulnerable to security threats compared to centralized systems. Common threats include:

- **Device Tampering**: Physical access to edge devices can lead to tampering or theft.
- **Data Breaches**: Sensitive data processed at the edge is at risk of being intercepted or stolen.
- **Distributed Denial of Service (DDoS) Attacks**: Edge devices can be targeted to disrupt network operations.
- **Malware and Ransomware**: Malicious software can infiltrate edge devices, compromising data and functionality.

16.14.3 AI-Driven Security Solutions for Edge Intelligence

AI can improve edge security by offering real-time threat detection and reaction. Among the AI-powered security solutions are:

- **Real-Time Threat Detection and Response**: Machine learning algorithms can monitor network traffic and detect anomalies, enabling rapid response to potential threats.
- **Predictive Analytics for Threat Prevention**: AI can analyze historical data to predict and prevent future attacks, enhancing proactive security measures.
- **Adaptive Security Models**: AI systems can adapt to evolving threats, continually updating their defenses to protect against new vulnerabilities.

16.14.4 Data Privacy Concerns and Solutions

With edge intelligence processing sensitive data closer to the user, ensuring data privacy is critical. Key strategies include:

- **Protecting Sensitive Information at the Edge**: Using robust encryption methods to protect data while it's being transmitted and stored.
- **Privacy-Preserving Techniques**: Employing techniques to secure data while permitting analysis, such as homomorphic encryption and differential privacy.
- **Compliance with Data Privacy Regulations**: Ensuring that edge intelligence systems adhere to relevant data protection laws and regulations, such as GDPR and CCPA.

16.14.5 Secure Edge Device Management

To stop illegal access and tampering, edge device security management is essential. Among the best practices are:

- **Authentication and Authorization Mechanisms**: Enforcing role-based access control and strong multi-factor authentication to confirm user identities.
- **Secure Boot and Firmware Integrity**: Ensuring that edge devices start-up securely and that their firmware is protected from tampering.
- **Remote Management and Updates**: Providing secure remote management capabilities to update and patch devices, maintaining their security posture.

16.14.6 Encryption and Data Integrity

Advanced encryption techniques are essential to protect data in edge intelligence systems. Strategies include:

- **Advanced Encryption Techniques**: Employing end-to-end encryption to protect data during transmission and storage.
- **Ensuring Data Integrity in Edge Communications**: Using cryptographic methods to verify the integrity of data, preventing unauthorized modifications.
- **Quantum-Resistant Encryption**: Preparing for future threats posed by quantum computing by adopting quantum-resistant cryptographic algorithms.

16.14.7 Zero Trust Architecture in Edge Networks

Zero Trust Architecture (ZTA) is crucial for securing edge intelligence. Key principles and implementation strategies include:

- **Principles of Zero Trust for Edge Intelligence**: Adopting a "never trust, always verify" approach, continuously validating the identities of users and devices.
- **Implementation Strategies**: Deploying micro-segmentation, continuous monitoring, and robust identity management to enforce Zero Trust principles.
- **Benefits and Challenges**: Enhancing security by reducing the attack surface, while addressing the complexity of implementing ZTA in distributed edge environments.

16.14.8 Blockchain for Enhanced Security and Privacy

The following are some ways that blockchain technology can improve edge intelligence security and privacy:

- **Use Cases of Blockchain in Edge Intelligence**: Ensuring data integrity and transparency through immutable ledgers.
- **Ensuring Data Integrity and Transparency**: Verifying the authenticity of data and transactions, preventing tampering.
- **Peer-to-Peer Security Solutions**: Reducing reliance on centralized servers, minimizing potential points of failure.

16.14.9 Federated Learning and Collaborative AI

With federated learning, AI models can be trained without requiring raw data sharing across a number of decentralized devices [14]. This improves AI capabilities while maintaining privacy:

- **Ensuring Privacy in Distributed AI Models**: Keeping data localized on edge devices, minimizing exposure.
- **Secure Data Sharing Mechanisms**: Using secure aggregation techniques to combine model updates without revealing individual data points.
- **Advantages of Federated Learning**: Enhancing privacy, reducing data transfer, and enabling collaborative AI development.

16.14.10 Case Studies: Security and Privacy Best Practices

Examining real-world implementations of edge intelligence can provide valuable insights:

- **Industry Examples of Secured Edge Intelligence**: Demonstrating effective implementations across a range of industries, including manufacturing, smart cities, and healthcare.
- **Lessons Learned from Real-World Implementations**: Understanding common challenges and effective solutions.
- **Impact on User Trust and Adoption**: Demonstrating how robust security and privacy measures can enhance user confidence and drive adoption.

16.14.11 Future Directions in Security and Privacy for Edge Intelligence

In the future, new developments in technology and privacy protection will continue to influence the field: [7]

- **Emerging Technologies and Innovations**: Exploring advancements such as AI-driven autonomous security, quantum cryptography, and enhanced privacy-preserving techniques.

- **Anticipating Future Threats**: Preparing for new vulnerabilities and threat vectors as 6G networks evolve.
- **Building Resilient and Secure Edge Networks**: Fostering collaboration between industry, academia, and regulatory bodies to develop comprehensive security frameworks.

As 6G networks integrate edge intelligence, ensuring robust security, as well as privacy measures, is essential. By leveraging advanced encryption techniques, AI-driven security solutions, zero trust architecture, blockchain technology, and federated learning, we can build secure and resilient edge intelligence systems. These measures will not only protect sensitive data but also foster user trust and drive the adoption of edge intelligence in the 6G era.

16.15 The Future of Edge Intelligence in 6G Networks

Figure 16.2 illustrates the advanced dimensions of edge intelligence, including AI-driven network optimization, federated learning and distribution of AI, and quantum edge computing with AI [7].

- **AI-Driven Network Optimization:** Future 6G networks will leverage AI not just for data processing at the edge but also for optimizing network operations [7]. AI algorithms will predict network loads, detect potential failures before

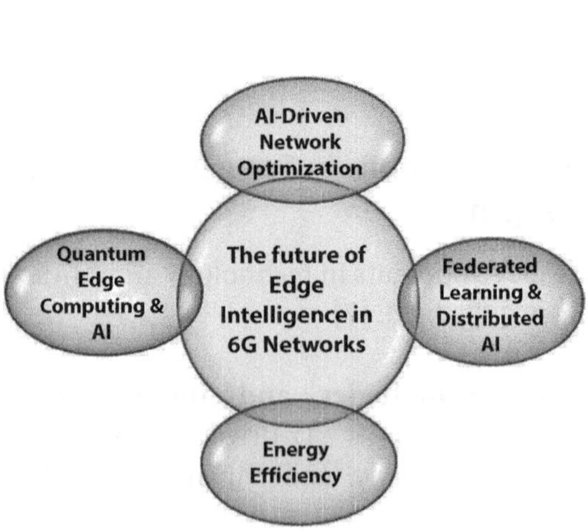

Figure 16.2 The future of edge intelligence in 6G networks.

they occur, and dynamically allocate resources, ensuring optimal performances across the network.

- **Federated Learning and Distribution AI:** To further heighten privacy and efficiency, federated learning - a form of distributed AI, will become a key component of Edge Intelligence in 6G networks. Federated learning allows for collaborative learning without risking user privacy. AI models are trained locally on devices, and only model updates are shared instead of raw data.
- **Energy Efficiency:** With the exponential growth of connected devices, energy efficiency is becoming an increasingly important issue. Edge intelligence in 6G networks will focus on minimizing energy consumption through optimized data processing and AI algorithms that can smartly manage power use in edge devices and network infrastructure.
- **Quantum Edge Computing and AI:** Looking further into the future, the integration of quantum computing technologies with Edge AI could open up new frontiers in processing capabilities, security and efficiency. Although this is still a developing area, it represents a potential quantum leap for edge intelligence capabilities in 6G networks.

16.16 Advantages of Edge Intelligence

Figure 16.3 shows the key advantages of edge intelligence across various domains, including improved latency, enhanced data privacy, efficient

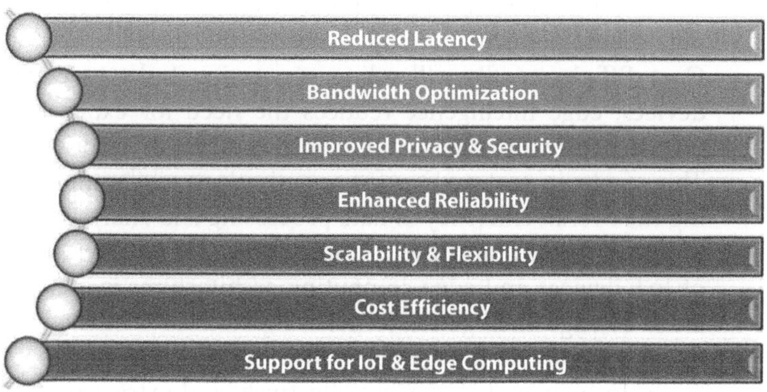

Figure 16.3 Advantages of edge intelligence.

resource utilization, and real-time decision-making [21]. Edge Intelligence offers a multitude of benefits across various domains, revolutionizing how data is processed, analyzed and utilized at the network edge. Some key advantages include,

- **Reduced Latency:** Edge intelligence significantly decreases latency by processing data closer to its sources, allowing for real-time responses and improving the efficiency of time-sensitive applications.
- **Bandwidth Optimization:** Edge intelligence optimizes bandwidth utilization and relieves network congestion by reducing the need to send massive amounts of data to centralized servers for processing.
- **Improved Privacy and Security:** By lowering the possibility of sensitive data being sent over large distances and stored on distant servers, edge data processing improves privacy and security. This decentralized approach mitigates potential vulnerabilities associated with centralized data processing and storage.
- **Enhanced Reliability:** Edge intelligence enhances the reliability of networked systems by enabling localized decision-making and autonomous operation at the edge. This reduces dependence on centralized infrastructure, making systems more resilient to network outages and disruptions.
- **Scalability and Flexibility:** Edge intelligence offers scalable and flexible solutions that can adapt to dynamic network conditions and evolving user requirements [21]. Edge devices can dynamically adjust their processing capabilities and resource allocations based on changing demand, ensuring optimal performance and resource utilization.
- **Cost Efficiency:** By offloading processing tasks to edge devices, edge intelligence reduces the need for expensive infrastructure upgrades and cloud computing resources. This results in cost savings for organizations while improving the overall efficiency of data processing and analysis.
- **Support for IoT and Edge Computing:** The proliferation of IoT devices and edge computing architectures is greatly aided by edge intelligence. It makes it possible for intelligent data processing and edge decision-making, which makes it easier to manage IoT devices effectively and extract useful insights from sensor data.

16.17 Challenges in Edge Intelligence

Although edge intelligence has many advantages, there are also some issues that must be resolved before it can be successfully implemented and adopted [9]. Among the principal difficulties are:

- Resource Constraints
- Data Privacy and Security
- Network Connectivity and Reliability
- Edge-Cloud Coordination
- Edge Device Management and Maintenance
- Edge AI Model Optimization
- Regulatory and Ethical Considerations

Collaboration between various stakeholders, such as technology providers, policymakers, industry consortia, and standardization bodies, is necessary for addressing these challenges. It will be essential to overcome these obstacles to fully utilize edge intelligence and reap its advantages across a range of industries [22].

16.18 Conclusion

The evolution of edge intelligence stands as a pivotal force in shaping the trajectory of 6G networks and beyond. The combination of edge computing and AI is emerging as a key to telecommunications' full potential as humanity struggles to make sense of an increasingly interconnected world. Moreover, maximizing the transformative potential of edge intelligence will require the cooperative efforts of researchers, business executives, legislators, and interested parties. By fostering innovation, standardization and interoperability, edge intelligence can ensure that it becomes not just a technological advancement, but a societal asset that benefits individuals and organizations worldwide.

AI disclosure statement: The author acknowledges the use of AI-based tools for minor language editing or grammatical correction. However, all intellectual contributions, analyses, and conclusions presented in this chapter are entirely the author's own.

References

1. Vermesan, O. and Marples, D., *Advancing Edge Artificial Intelligence: System Contexts*, 1st, River Publishers, 2024, https://doi.org/10.1201/9781003478713.
2. Raj, P., Akilandeswari, J., Marimuthu, M., The edge AI paradigm: Technologies, platforms and use cases. *Adv. Comput.*, *127*, 139–182, 2021, https://doi.org/10.1016/bs.adcom.2022.02.003.
3. Seppo Yrjölä, S., Ahokangas, P., Matinmikko-Blue, M., Value Creation and Capture From Technology Innovation in the 6G Era. *IEEE Access*, 10, 16299–16319, 2022, doi:10.1109/ACCESS.2022.3149590.
4. Rajendran, S., Mathivanan, S.K., Jayagopal, P., Purushothaman, J., Emphasizing privacy and security of edge intelligence with machine learning for healthcare. *Int. J. Intell. Comput. Cybern.*, ahead-of-print, ahead-of-print, 92–109, 2022, doi: 10.1108/IJICC-05-2021-0099.
5. Chataut, R., Nankya, M., Akl, R., 6G Networks and the AI Revolution—Exploring Technologies, Applications, and Emerging Challenges. *Sensors*, *24*, 6, 1888, 2023, https://doi.org/10.3390/s24061888.
6. Nguyen, V.-L., Lin, P.-C., Cheng, B.-C., Hwang, R.-H., Lin, Y.-D., Security and Privacy for 6G: A Survey on Prospective Technologies and Challenges. *IEEE Commun. Surv. Tutor.*, 23, 4, 2384–2428, Fourthquarter 2021, doi: 10.1109/COMST.2021.3108618.
7. Mendez, J., Bierzynski, K., Cuéllar, M.P., Morales, D.P., Edge intelligence: concepts, architectures, applications, and future directions. *ACM Trans. Embedded Comput. Syst. (TECS)*, *21*, 5, 1–41, 2022, https://doi.org/10.1145/3486674.
8. Xu, D., Li, T., Li, Y., Su, X., Tarkoma, S., Hui, P., A survey on edge intelligence, *arXiv preprint arXiv:2003.12172,* 2020, https://d1wqtxts1xzle7.cloudfront.net/94551941/2003.12172v1-libre.pdf?1668952359=&response-content-disposition=inline%3B+filename%3DA_Survey_on_Edge_Intelligence.pdf&Expires=1722584600&Signature=D14eCOj1xPBhOt8HH1WxL7jXytpGjPzd1vsGdXSK~m3moHWYfK4gEicdQ~jKQGRILy2zDBxijexAV0uzHW1AZNbPpHZs0DNgo2gwUxmJuUNRa34SZlj2elR49v-AS~~6Wyh83pr3ATHmXcvDUkleZz4vYTT~YGhXa4895QTZ8RbZfb~KLxgLVVksr9dqbMfB89m7WMnv4NAqOnDoq0cR5iRjwuJ9eu7CQmavU2HqMqietmcr4493TTGnucT76y-nR2HuY251tCIuqnLi3Enyj~lDIhhAXfQk7EPkpnyOLZ5J9H3bjcK22ysHBbEg7–hc7XRkdggCev0uM61u6mL5w__&Key-Pair-Id=APKAJLOHF5GGSLRBV4ZA.
9. Li, Y., Yu, Y., Susilo, W., Hong, Z., Guizani, M., Security and privacy for edge intelligence in 5G and beyond networks: Challenges and solutions. *IEEE Wireless Commun.*, *28*, 2, 63–69, 2021, Doi: 10.1109/MWC.001.2000318.
10. Tomkos, I., Klonidis, D., Pikasis, E., Theodoridis, S., Toward the 6G Network Era: Opportunities and Challenges. *IT Prof.*, 22, 1, 34–38, 1 Jan.-Feb. 2020, doi: 10.1109/MITP.2019.2963491.

11. Ferrag, M.A., Friha, O., Kantarci, B., Tihanyi, N., Cordeiro, L., Debbah, M., Hamouda, D., Al-Hawawreh, M., Choo, K.-K.R., Edge learning for 6G-enabled Internet of Things: A comprehensive survey of vulnerabilities, datasets, and defenses. *IEEE Commun. Surv. Tutor.*, 25, 4, 3052–3078, 2023. https://doi.org/10.1109/COMST.2023.3317242.
12. Raivi, A.M. and Moh, S., A comprehensive survey on data aggregation techniques in UAV-enabled Internet of Things. *Comput. Sci. Rev.*, 50, 100599, 2023. https://doi.org/10.1016/j.cosrev.2023.100599.
13. https://www.sciencedirect.com/topics/computer-science/edge-intelligence.
14. https://www.run.ai/guides/machine-learning-operations/edge-ai.
15. Letaief, K.B., Shi, Y., Lu, J., Lu, J., Edge Artificial Intelligence for 6G: Vision, Enabling Technologies, and Applications, in: *IEEE Journal on Selected Areas in Communications*, vol. 40, no. 1, pp. 5–36, Jan. 2022, doi: 10.1109/JSAC.2021.3126076.
16. John, A., 6G Technology. *SlideShare*. 2017, January 28. https://www.slideshare.net/slideshow/6-g/40755855.
17. Kranz, G. and Christensen, G., What is 6G? Overview of 6G networks & technology. *TechTarget*, 2023, November 20. https://www.techtarget.com/searchnetworking/definition/6G.
18. Kitanov, S. and Nikolikj, V., The Role of Edge Artificial Intelligence in 6G Networks, 2022 57th International Scientific Conference on Information. *Commun. Energy Syst. Technol. (ICEST)*, 1–4, Ohrid, North Macedonia, 2022. doi: 10.1109/ICEST55168.2022.9828567.
19. https://ieeexplore.ieee.org/document/9828567.
20. https://www.linkedin.com/advice/1/what-main-challenges-deploying-6g-networks.
21. Aftab, How to overcome the top 5 challenges of edge computing. ASB Resources, 2023, July 31. https://asbresources.com/how-to-overcome-the-top-5-challenges-of-edge-computing.
22. Moozakis, C. and Gittlen, S., Enterprise 5G: Guide to planning, architecture and benefits. *TechTarget*, 2023, December 8. https://www.techtarget.com/searchnetworking/Enterprise-5G-Guide-to-planning-architecture-and-benefits.
23. Bhambri, P., Rani, S., Kumar, S., Sinha, V.K., Big Data Analytics with Digital Twin for Industrial Applications, in: *AI-Driven Digital Twin and Industry 4.0: A Conceptual Framework with Applications*, 1st, S. Rani, P. Bhambri, S. Kumar, P.K. Pareek, A.A. Elngar (Eds.), pp. 105–26, CRC Press, 2024, https://doi.org/10.1201/9781003395416.
24. Bhambri, P., Rani, S., Pareek, P.K., Paperless Paradigm: Intelligent Automation in Document and Record Management, in: *Generating Entrepreneurial Ideas with AI*, D. Darwish (Ed.), pp. 164–83, IGI Global, 2024, https://www.igi-global.com/book/hyperautomation-business-society/335477.

17

Optimizing Edge Devices for Industrial Intelligence

Tharun Satla[1], Srikanth Jannu[1*], Pankaj Bhambri[2] and Chaitanya Thuppari[1]

[1]Vaagdevi Engineering College, Bollikunta, Warangal, Telangana, India
[2]Guru Nanak Dev Engineering College, Ludhiana, Punjab, India

Abstract

The Industrial Internet of Things became the most promising research topic in many applications, such as health-care monitoring, battle field monitoring, agriculture, and so on, due to its self-organizing nature and low cost. The IIoT edge nodes are meant to sense local information from the target area. However, the nodes suffer from a major problem: a limited battery. Moreover, it is difficult to recharge or replace the batteries of nodes in critical environments like underground coal mines. Clustering the nodes is proven to be an efficient way to preserve the battery of the nodes. However, clustering IIoT nodes is a NP hard problem. Edge intelligence (EI) is an innovative technology that employs EI algorithms on edge nodes which has the ability to handle and analyze data in real time. Encompassing EI in industrial IIoT devices can produce best results for NP hard problems. Moreover, EI develops the performance of 6G based industrial IIoT. Therefore, in this chapter, we introduce an energy-efficient clustering algorithm using the osprey optimization technique. For energy efficiency, we considered various fitness functions such as residual energy, sink and intra-cluster distance. Moreover, the proposed algorithm is simulated against various case scenarios; i.e., in first case we have taken the base station location at (50, 50) and in second case, the base station location is at (50, 100), and the simulation results of our algorithm show superior efficacy in terms of residual energy, network lifetime, and number of alive nodes when compared to other existing algorithms. The results of the proposed algorithm exhibit 96% efficiency in terms of network lifetime over traditional approaches.

**Corresponding author*: j.srikanth@live.com

Sita Rani, Pankaj Bhambri, Balamurugan Balusamy, Rishabha Malviya and Seifedine Kadry (eds.) Edge Intelligence for 6G-Enabled Industrial Internet of Things, (365–386) © 2026 Scrivener Publishing LLC

Keywords: 6G Internet of Things, artificial intelligence, Osprey optimization technique, cluster-head selection, meta heuristic optimization

17.1 Introduction

In the past few decades, the progression of the industrial internet of things (IIoT) has been driven by the merging of various applications such as edge computing, wireless sensor networks (WSNs), enhanced embedded systems, and the rise of advanced machine learning capabilities. The modern research community is attracting attention towards the applications of sixth generation (6G) based IIoT networks such as forest fire detection [1], healthcare monitoring [2], battle field monitoring [3], tsunamis, thunderstorms, including underground coal mines [4] (UCMs), etc. The sixth generation (6G) sustainable networks are evolving to become energy-efficient solutions that are going to focus on saving energy in the network of IIoT. 6G with its low bandwidth as well as high data rates will enable IIoT devices to transmit data and converse with one another instantaneously with almost no delays. This will enhance the efficiency and reliability of various IIoT applications. The 6G based IIoT network is a collection of many nodes that are deployed in the target area. The IIoT nodes are meant for sensing local information like temperature, humidity, CO_2, etc. However, these nodes suffer from holding limited energy because they generate a large quantity of information by sensing the local parameters consistently, so that the energy of the nodes depletes very quickly. Moreover, it is difficult to replace or recharge the batteries in harsh environments like UCMs, etc. Hence, preserving the energy of IIoT nodes is still a challenging task for the researchers involved in the development of the IIoT network. One of the most prominent ways to preserve the energy of IIoT nodes is by clustering the nodes. Clustering is a resource optimization strategy that involves grouping IIoT nodes into clusters. Every cluster comprises a number of nodes and a leader, i.e., the CH node. Initially, all the IIoT nodes collect local information from target region and send the information to the nearby CH. Then, the CH nodes aggregate that data and transmit it to the base station (BS). In the aggregation process, the CH avoids the redundant data sent by nodes to conserve energy and improve network life. A cluster-based communication between nodes and the BS is represented in Figure 17.1.

Since clustering IIoT nodes optimization technique is a NP hard problem, edge intelligence (EI) is an innovative technology that can produce solutions for NP hard problems. Moreover, EI enables the development of

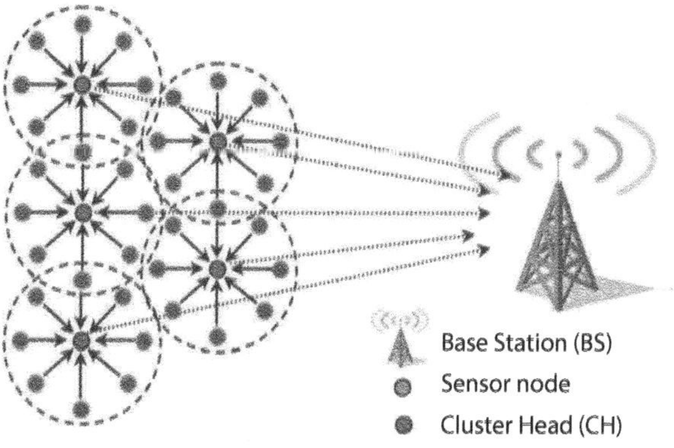

Figure 17.1 Cluster-based communication between nodes and the base station.

6G based industrial IIoT. In this chapter, we developed a nature-inspired algorithm; i.e., the Osprey optimization algorithm, for clustering nodes to reduce the energy-draining problem of nodes and improve network life in the 6G enabled IIoT. Therefore, the main contributions of our chapter are as follows:

- Efficient CH selection algorithm using Osprey member/agent as EI agents
- Derivation of energy efficient fitness functions for CH selection using Osprey optimization
- Formation of optimal number clusters
- Extensive simulations of the proposed algorithm over other algorithms, conducted to compare its efficacy.

17.1.1 Overview of OOA

The Osprey optimization algorithm (OOA) is a meta-heuristic optimization algorithm motivated by the social behavior of osprey birds [21], which is also termed the sea hawk or water hawk. In OOA, Osprey bird is a basic computational agent that computes optimal solutions for given optimization problems. An osprey is 0.9-2.1kg in weight, has a length of 50-66cm, and a wingspan of 127-180cm. The osprey generally eats fish from hunting, which weighs up to 2 kilograms. Ospreys have exceptional vision and can identify fish underwater. Ospreys possess the capacity to detect subaqueous fish while traversing at an elevation of 40m above the surface of the water. Later, they capture prey (fish) using their feet, dive into the water, and carry them to a safe place to eat. The design of a new optimization algorithm is inspired by the hunting and eating strategy of osprey. Hence, the intelligent behaviors exhibited by osprey are translated into computational representations, serving as the foundation for the development of the proposed Osprey optimization algorithm, which is elucidated further.

17.1.2 Organization

The remaining chapter is explained as follows: Section 17.2 describes the related works; the system models are explained in Section 17.3, followed by proposed work in Section 17.4. Then, the simulation results are explained in Section 17.5. Finally, the chapter concludes in Section 17.6.

17.2 Related Work

In recent years, numerous heuristic and meta-heuristic techniques have been developed for clustering IIoT nodes. Padmaa *et al.* [5], presented an EEC-SDTP approach for electing optimal CH nodes and most effective routing paths for data transmission in network. For efficient cluster head selection and formation, they incorporated oppositional chaos game optimization-based clustering. Dogra *et al.* [6], developed a novel approach for data collection in intelligent transaction systems considering various heuristic factors and they specifically addressed the energy hole issue in network clustering reduce the time to first node death (FDT) and increase the amount of time all nodes are alive (ADT). Jana *et al.* [7], utilized PSO for developing an energy-efficient clustering algorithm that considers intra-cluster and sink distances, as well as node residual energy as fitness functions. Jaiswal and Anand [8], proposed a clustering method based on Gray Wolf Optimization (GWO). They also employ a quality of service (QoS)-aware routing method to select reliable relay nodes for data transfer between cluster heads (CHs) and base stations (BSs), ensuring efficiency and reliability. Sankar *et al.* [9], developed a Sandpiper optimization algorithm 4 (SOA) that considers distance and residual energy parameters to build clusters and decide the best cluster head node. Its primary goal is to prolong the network's lifespan by fine-tuning the formation of clusters processes and increasing cluster head selection efficiency. Rajasekaran *et al.* [10], created the CBACO method for cluster-based wireless networks of sensors, which uses ant colony optimization. It finds the shortest path among each sensing node and the BS using clever the enhancement inspired by ant behavior. In [11], the authors have suggested a hybrid technique, integrating the Improved Cuckoo Optimization Algorithm

(ICOA) with the Improved Jumping Levy Flight Algorithm (IJLFA), to improve energy usage and network longevity. Adumbabu *et al.*'s [12], suggested HACO-ABC-CHS algorithm optimizes cluster head selection in WSNs. This technique tries to enhance the efficiency of cluster head selection processes by overcoming limitations observed in both ACO and ABC optimization algorithms. Senthil *et al.* [13], developed an optimized OrphanLEACH (O-LEACH) approach that improves clustering in WSNs. O-LEACH is a pioneering technique to clustering that optimizes overall network efficiency by reducing energy usage and increasing network lifetime. Natesan *et al.* [14], introduced the MFA-AOA optimal approach for enhancing lifespan and energy stability in wireless sensor networks. By integrating MFA global optimization with AOA local optimization, it provides a balanced CH selection for improved energy stability. Somula *et al.* [15], proposed the osprey optimization algorithm (SWARAM) in determining optimal cluster heads (CH) in wireless sensor networks. SWARAM computes the fitness function using the distance and residual energy ratio (RER) parameters, with an objective to increase CH selection efficiency. K. Kousalya *et al.* [16], designed an Artificial Bee Colony (ABC) technique to efficiently choose CHs and multipath routing in WSNs. The goal is to provide efficient data transfer to the BS while reducing the usage of energy. Rodriguez *et al.* [17], developed YSGAP, a clustered routing protocol that optimizes network design to reduce energy consumption in each cycle and extend network lifetime. Sharma *et al.* [18], introduced the PRESEP (Priority-Based Residual Energy and Shortest Path) algorithm for large heterogeneous WSNs, which enhances network lifetime and scalability for IIoT applications. Sahoo *et al.* [19], developed NCOGA (Optimized Cluster Head Selection Method Using Genetic Algorithm), which uses adaptive crossover and binary tournament selection approaches to optimize cluster head (CH) 5 selection in a heterogeneous WSNs. The goal is to significantly extend the network's lifetime.

17.3 System Models

17.3.1 Network Models

In this network model, we have considered a homogeneous model in which we use IIoT nodes and CHs nodes. Initially, all the nodes are placed arbitrarily within the intended region, and the nodes are immovable after their installation in sensing field. Each node deployed within the target area will gather the local environmental parameters and transmit that data to the nearby CH. Therefore, the CH collects the data from nearby sensor nodes, removes redundant data by using the data aggregation method, and then transmit it to the BS. However, the selection of CHs and cluster formation will be explained in Section 17.4.

17.3.2 Energy Models

The energy model utilized in this chapter is as same as the radio model used in [20]. Assuming that the energy required to transmit t-bits of data over the distance d, the energy consumption for transmitting data is

$$E_{trans}(t,d) = E_{elec} \times k + e_{amp} \times t \times d^2 \tag{17.1}$$

$$E_{trans}(t,d) = E_{elec} \times k + e_{amp} \times t \times d^4 \tag{17.2}$$

the energy required for receiving data,

$$E_{rec}(t) = E_{elec} \times t \tag{17.3}$$

where,

- E_{trans} is the energy usage for the transmitting data.
- E_{elec} is the energy consumed by the circuit.
- e_{amp} is the energy required by the amplifier.
- E_{rec} is the receiving energy.
- d is the distance between the CH and node.

17.4 Proposed Work

This section presents the proposed osprey optimization algorithm. The algorithm consists of two main phases, i.e., cluster head selection and cluster formation. Initially, we define some terminologies that are helpful to demonstrate the suggested osprey optimization algorithm. Table 17.1 shows the terminology used in the proposed Osprey Optimization Algorithm.

Table 17.1 Terminology used in the Algorithm.

Notation	Depiction
X_i	i^{th} Osprey
n	Total number of Osprey's population
m	Problem variables
$X_{i,j}$	*ith* Osprey within the *jth* dimensions
UB_j, LB_j	Upper and lower limits for the *jth* problem variable
$r_{i,j}$	Random integer in the range [0,1]
O_i	The fitness function of ith osprey value
FP_i	The set of prey positions for i^{th} osprey
$I_{i,j}$	Random number from the set [1,2]
X_{best}	best candidate solution
X_i^{P1}	The new location of ith osprey during phase 1
$X_{i,j}^{P1}$	i^{th} Osprey birds j^{th} dimension during phase two
$XF_{i,j}$	The chosen fish for i^{th} osprey
X_i^{P2}	The updated location of ith osprey at during 2
$X_{i,j}^{P2}$	i^{th} osprey's j^{th} dimesion at phase 2

17.4.1 OOA Based Cluster Head Selection

17.4.1.1 Initialization

The proposed OOA employs a population-based method to identify a feasible solution in the area of problem-solving by using a repetition-based procedure. The osprey population is represented mathematically by using a vector. Therefore, every osprey is a feasible solution to the problem. In general, all ospreys gather together to form an osprey population, which can be computed as follows:

$$X = \begin{bmatrix} X_1 \\ \vdots \\ X_i \\ \vdots \\ X_n \end{bmatrix} = \begin{bmatrix} X_{1,1} \cdots X_{1,j} \cdots X_{1,m} \\ \vdots \\ X_{i,1} \cdots X_{i,j} \cdots X_{i,m} \\ \vdots \\ X_{n,1} \cdots X_{n,j} \cdots X_{n,m} \end{bmatrix} \tag{17.4}$$

Each osprey's location is initialized randomly according to the following equation:

$$X_{i,j} = LB_j + r_{i,j}.(LB_j - UB_j), \quad i = 1,2,....n, \quad j = 1,2,....n \tag{17.5}$$

Since every osprey indicates a potential solution to the problem, every individual osprey can undergo evaluation by the objective function. These assessed values for the problem's objective function are described as vectors using the following equation:

$$O = \begin{bmatrix} O_1 \\ \vdots \\ O_i \\ \vdots \\ O_n \end{bmatrix}_{n\times 1} = \begin{bmatrix} O(X_1) \\ \vdots \\ O(X_i) \\ \vdots \\ O(X_n) \end{bmatrix}_{n\times 1} \tag{17.6}$$

The values assessed by the objective function act as the principal metrics for assessing the efficacy of potential solutions. Consequently, the poorest candidate solution, referred to as the worst member, corresponds to the objective function's lowest value, while the optimal candidate solution aligns with its highest value. In every iteration of the algorithm, the location of the ospreys is updated along with the best solution.

17.4.1.2 Phase 1: Exploration

Ospreys are skilled predators with powerful eyesight that enables them to locate fish underwater with high accuracy. Once the osprey identifies the fish's location, it hunts the prey by diving under water. The initial phase of population update in the algorithm is designed by simulating the natural behavior of ospreys. The location of osprey changes within the search area due to modeling of fish hunting behavior, which strengthens exploration power in finding optimal area.

In the osprey optimization algorithm design, for every osprey bird, the locations of other osprey birds with the best fitness function in the search space. The set of prey (fish) for every osprey is computed as follows:

$$FP_i = \{X_k \mid k \in \{1,2,...N\} \cap O_k < O_i\} \cup \{X_{best}\} \tag{17.7}$$

The osprey bird randomly identifies one of these fish's positions and initiates an attack. A new location for the corresponding osprey is evaluated depending on the simulation of the osprey bird movement towards the prey using the following equations:

$$X_{i,j}^{P_1} = X_{i,j} + r_{i,j}.(XF_{i,j} - I_{i,j}.X_{i,j}) \tag{17.8}$$

$$X_{i,j}^{P_1} = \begin{cases} X_{i,j}^{P_1}, & LB_j \le X_{i,j}^{P_1} \le UB_j; \\ LB_j, X_{i,j}^{P_1} < LB_j; \\ UB_j, X_{i,j}^{P_1} > UB_j; \end{cases} \tag{17.9}$$

$$X_i^1 = \begin{cases} X_i^{P_1}, & O_i^{P_1} < O_i; \\ X_i, & O_i^{P_1} \ge O_i; \end{cases} \tag{17.10}$$

17.4.1.3 Phase 2: Exploitation

The osprey carries the fish to a safest location to eat after hunting it. In OOA, the second phase of population update is designed by simulating the natural strategy of ospreys. The design of bringing the fish to the appropriate area causes minor changes in the location of the osprey within the search area, hence increasing the exploitation potential of OOA in local search and convergence towards optimal solutions.

To evaluate the natural behavior of ospreys in OOA, initially, for every osprey within the search space, a new location is computed as a preferred spot for eating prey using the following equations:

$$X_{i,j}^{P_1} = X_{i,j} + \frac{LB_j + r_{i,j}.(LB_j - UB_j)}{t} \tag{17.11}$$

where, i ranges from 1 to N, j ranges from 1 to m and t varies from 1 to T

$$X_{i,j}^{P_2} = \begin{cases} X_{i,j}^{P_2}, & LB_j \le X_{i,j}^{P_2} \le UB_j; \\ LB_j, X_{i,j}^{P_2} < LB_j; \\ UB_j, X_{i,j}^{P_2} > UB_j; \end{cases} \tag{17.12}$$

$$X_i^2 = \begin{cases} X_i^{P_2}, & O_i^{P_2} < O_i; \\ X_i, & O_i^{P_2} \ge O_i; \end{cases} \tag{17.13}$$

After the above two phases, the OOA updates all osprey positions and iteratively calculates the population until the optimal solution or maximum number of iterations is achieved.

17.4.1.4 OOA Representation

In this algorithm, each osprey represents a collection of IIoT nodes that serve as cluster heads among all IIoT nodes. The cluster heads are updates based on the exploration and exploitation phases until the stopping criteria is reached. Therefore, the best osprey's nodes are considered as CH nodes and the detailed procedure is explained in Algorithm 17.1.

17.4.2 Derivation of Fitness Functions

The fitness function for cluster head selection uses following parameters:

17.4.2.1 Sink Distance

It can be calculated as the distance between each node and BS. This metric is crucial in evaluating the efficiency and performance of the network, particularly in terms of transmission overhead, energy usage, and data transmission latency. Hence, to preserve the energy of the network, we need to reduce the distance between the node to BS.

$$f_1 = \sum_{i=1}^{N} dist(S_i, BS) \tag{17.14}$$

17.4.2.2 Residual Energy

It can be evaluated as the ratio of each node's energy that remains to total energy of the node.

$$f_2 = \frac{E_{res}(S_i)}{\sum E_{res}(S_n)} \tag{17.15}$$

17.4.2.3 Intra-Cluster Distance

It is computed as the average sum of distances between all nodes and their respective selected CH. In general, every node requires some amount of energy to send data to the selected CH. To decrease energy usage in the network, it is important to reduce the average distance of intra-cluster communication. Therefore, the intra-cluster distance is calculated as follows:

$$f_3 = \sum_{i=1}^{N} dist(S_i, C_j) \tag{17.16}$$

$$minimize\ F = \alpha_1 \times f_1 + \alpha_2 \times \frac{1}{f_2} + \alpha_3 \times f_3 \tag{17.17}$$

where $\alpha_1, \alpha_2, \alpha_3$ are random values and $\alpha_1 + \alpha_2 + \alpha_3 = 1$

Algorithm 17.1 Proposed Algorithm for Selection of Cluster Heads

```
Input: Set of Sensor nodes S = {S_1, S_2, S_3..., S_n}, Max no. of iterations t = {1,2,3,...T}
Output: Set of Cluster-Heads CH = {CH_1, CH_2, CH_3..., CH_n}
Initialize network population randomly using eq. (5) X_i,j = LB_j + r_i,j.(UB_j - LB_j)
for t=1 to T do
    Phase 1 : Exploration
    for i=0 to n do
        Update the positions of fish for the i^th member of the OOA using the eq. (7).
        FP_i = {X_k|k ∈ {1, 2, ..., N} ∩ O_k < O_i} ∪ {X_best}
        Randomly select the fish i.e., SF determined by the i^th Osprey.
```

Compute the new position of the ith member of the OOA using the initial phase of OOA
using eq. (8) $X^{P1}_{i,j} = Xi,j + r_{i,j}, (XF_{i,j} - I_{i,j}, XF_{i,j})$
Verify boundary criteria for the updated locations of population members using eq. (9)
Update the ith member of the OOA using the eq. (10)
Phase 2 : Exploitation Phase
for *i=0 to n* **do**
Compute the new position of the ith member of the OOA using second phase of OOA
using eq. (11) $X^{P2}_{i,j} = Xi,j + \frac{LB_j + r_{i,j}, UB_j - LB_j)}{t}$
Verify the boundary conditions for the updated positions of OOA members using equation (12)
Update the ith member of the OOA utilizing equation (13).
Best osprey act as CH

17.4.3 Cluster Formation

The cluster formation is crucial after the selection of CH among the nodes. In cluster formation, to conserve energy, a node S_i, should connect with the closest CH_j within its transmission range. The lesser the distance, the lower the energy required. Hence, clusters are formed based on intra-cluster distance.

17.4.4 An Illustration

Let us consider a target area of 10 × 10 m_2, and we also assume that there are 3 ospreys each selecting 3 cluster heads among the set of nodes, and the CH nodes are selected using the fitness function in which the best osprey's solution is considered as cluster heads.

Initially, we randomly deployed nine nodes and a base station in the target area, as shown in Figure 17.2. The positions of all nodes are given in Table 17.2. Three ospreys (X_1, X_2, X_3) are initialized for selecting three cluster heads. Here, randomly three cluster heads are selected for each osprey; i.e., (X_1 = {S_1, S_4, S_6}, X_2 = S_2, S_5, S_8}, X_3 = {S_3, S_7, S_9}). The distance between all nodes is evaluated, and it is shown in Table 17.3.

$$X = \begin{bmatrix} X_1 \\ X_2 \\ X_3 \end{bmatrix} = \begin{bmatrix} (1,1)(3,2)(2,4) \\ (3,7)(5,5)(8,6) \\ (8,9)\ (9,4)\ \ (3,9) \end{bmatrix} \tag{17.18}$$

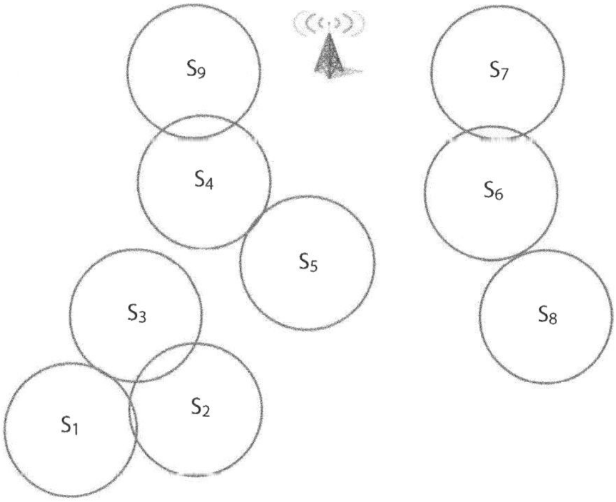

Figure 17.2 Illustration of node deployment in the target area.

Table 17.2 Positions of nodes.

Node	Position
S_1	(1,1)
S_2	(3,2)
S_3	(2,4)
S_4	(3,7)
S_5	(5,5)
S_6	(8,6)
S_7	(8,9)
S_8	(9,4)
S_9	(3,9)
BS	(5,10)

The fitness function of each osprey is evaluated using equation (17.17) as follows:

$$O = \begin{bmatrix} O(X_1) \\ O(X_2) \\ O(X_3) \end{bmatrix} = \begin{bmatrix} 11.98 \\ 13.97 \\ 11.38 \end{bmatrix} \tag{17.19}$$

Table 17.3 Distance table for nodes.

	S_1	S_2	S_3	S_4	S_5	S_6	S_7	S_8	S_9	BS
S_1	0.00	2.20	3.16	6.32	5.65	8.60	10.95	8.54	8.24	9.84
S_2	2.20	0.00	2.23	5.00	3.60	6.40	8.60	6.32	7.00	8.24
S_3	3.16	2.23	0.00	3.16	3.16	6.32	7.81	7.00	5.09	6.70
S_4	6.32	5.00	3.16	0.00	2.82	5.09	5.38	6.70	2.00	3.60
S_5	5.65	3.60	3.16	2.82	0.00	3.16	5.00	4.12	4.4	5.00
S_6	8.60	6.40	6.32	5.09	3.16	0.00	3.00	2.20	5.80	5.00
S_7	10.95	8.60	7.81	5.38	5.00	3.00	0.00	5.09	5.00	3.16
S_8	8.54	6.32	7.00	6.70	4.12	2.20	5.09	0.00	7.81	7.21
S_9	8.24	7.00	5.09	2.00	4.40	5.80	5.00	7.81	0.00	2.23

Here, we are considering the least fitness value as the best solution, i.e., X_3. Then, the prey positions of ospreys are updated using equation (17.6). The prey positions are $XF_1 = \{X_3\}$.

The X_1 osprey attacks the X_3 osprey, i.e., selected from SF_1. Then, the positions of osprey are updated after hunting prey using equation (17.7). The updated position for X_1 is for S_1.

$$X_1^{pos_1}(S_1) = (1,1) + 0.2((2,4) - 1(1,1)$$

Therefore, the updated position of $X_1(S_1)$ is

$$X_1^{pos_1}(S_1) = \{1.2, 1.6\} \sim \{1,1\}$$

Similarly, the updated location of X_1 after phase 1 is $X_1^{pos_1} = \{\{1,1\}, \{3,7\}, \{5,5\}\} = \{S_1, S_4, S_5\}$ and the fitness value for the updated position is 13.68. Here, the fitness value of the updated position is not better than the initial fitness value, i.e., (11.94 < 13.68). The osprey has now hunted the prey, and then it has to bring that prey to a safe location to eat, i.e., the exploitation phase. Hence, the updated position for X_1 is computed using eq. (17.10), so for S_1,

$$X_1^{pos_2}(S_1) = (1,1) + 0 + 0.1(10 - 0)$$

Hence, the updated position of $X_1(S_1)$ is

$$X_1^{pos_2}(S_1) = \{2, 2\} \sim \{3, 2\}$$

Similarly, the updated position for X_1 after phase 2 is $X_1^{pos_2}(S_1) = \{3, 2\}, \{8, 9\}, \{8, 6\} = \{S_2, S_7, S_6\}$, and the fitness value of the updated position is 12.79. Therefore, the updated position fitness value is not better than the fitness value of X_1 after phase 1, i.e., (11.3 < 12.79). After computing the positions and fitness values of all ospreys, the updated positions are as follows:

$$X = \begin{bmatrix} X_1 \\ X_2 \\ X_3 \end{bmatrix} = \begin{bmatrix} (3,2)(8,9)(8,6) \\ (3,2)(5,5)(8,6) \\ (2,4)\ (8,9)\ \ (3,9) \end{bmatrix}$$

The fitness values are

$$O = \begin{bmatrix} O(X_1) \\ O(X_2) \\ O(X_3) \end{bmatrix} = \begin{bmatrix} 11.98 \\ 12.51 \\ 11.38 \end{bmatrix}$$

Hence, we can consider X_3 as the best solution because it has a better fitness value when compared to other ospreys, and $\{S_3, S_7, S_9\}$ are considered cluster heads among the 9 sensor nodes. The cluster formation is based on the average intra-cluster distance; then, the cluster members for $S_3 = \{S_1, S_2, S_5\}$, $S_7 = \{S_6, S_8\}$, and $S_9 = \{S_4\}$.

17.5 Simulation Results

In this section, we show the simulation results of our suggested approach. The proposed algorithm is developed using Python programming on the Windows 10 platform. The proposed algorithm is compared with four traditional approaches, such as ABC [22], WO [23], GWO [24], and ECRP

Table 17.4 Simulation parameters.

Parameter	Value
Target area	$100 \times 100m^2$
BS Location	(50, 50) & (50, 100)
Number of nodes	100
Initial Energy	$0.5J$
Packet length	2000 bits
α_1, α_2 and α_3	0.3, 0.3 and 0.4
E_{elec}	50 nJ/bit
E_{amp}	$10pJ/bit/m^2$

[25–27], to show the efficacy of our algorithm. Table 17.4 provides the simulation parameters.

For simulation, we considered two scenarios, where in the first scenario, the sink is positioned at (50, 50), and in the second scenario, it is at (50, 100), with a target area of 100×100 m_2. In the target area, we randomly deployed 100 nodes, with each node having 0.5J initial energy. The suggested approach is compared with existing algorithms in terms of residual energy, network lifetime, and the number of nodes alive.

17.5.1 Residual Energy

The simulation outcomes of the proposed approach is compared with [22–25] in terms of residual energy, as shown in Figure 17.3. In the proposed optimization algorithm, the energy usage is lower compared to existing algorithms. In the existing algorithms, in ABC, only residual energy and intra-cluster distance are considered for fitness functions; in WO, the CH node energy and neighbor node's residual energy are considered for fitness values; in GWO, only the distance between the CH node and BS is considered for fitness values; in ECRP, only the nodes with the maximum energy are considered cluster heads. Our proposed algorithm evenly distributes nodes to reduce individual CH loads, reducing energy needs for data transmission. Therefore, the proposed algorithm demonstrates its effectiveness by preserving residual energy levels across the network.

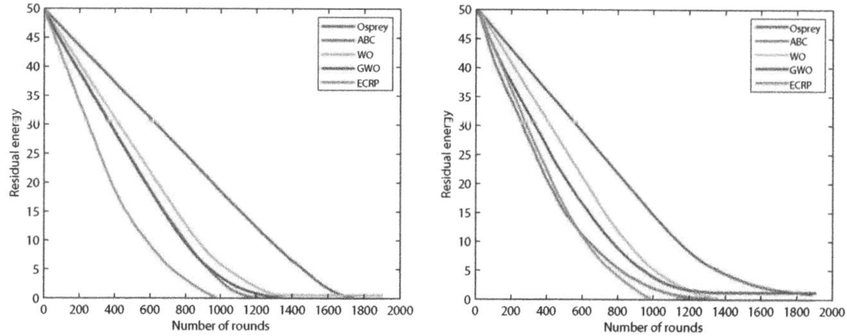

(a) Base Station location at: (50, 50)

(b) Base Station location at: (50, 100)

Figure 17.3 Comparison in terms of residual energy over a number of rounds.

17.5.2 Network Lifetime

The simulation results of various algorithms in terms of network lifetime is depicted in Figure 17.4. In Figure 17.4, the first graph is plotted with the base station at (50, 50), and the second graph is plotted with the base station at (50, 100). Our proposed algorithm demonstrates superior performance compared to existing ones such as [22–25]. The reason behind this is that in the proposed approach, the distance between BS and CH is reduced, which leads to efficient energy usage by the CH for sending the data to base station.

17.5.3 Number of Alive Nodes

The performance of various algorithms can be observed by comparing the number of alive nodes across the number of rounds, as illustrated in Figure 17.5. Our proposed algorithm consistently maintains a greater number of

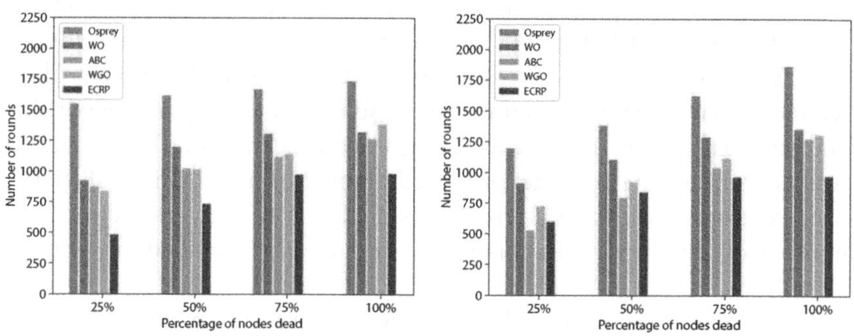

(a) Base Station at (50, 50)

(b) Base Station at (50, 100)

Figure 17.4 Comparison in terms of network lifetime over a number of rounds.

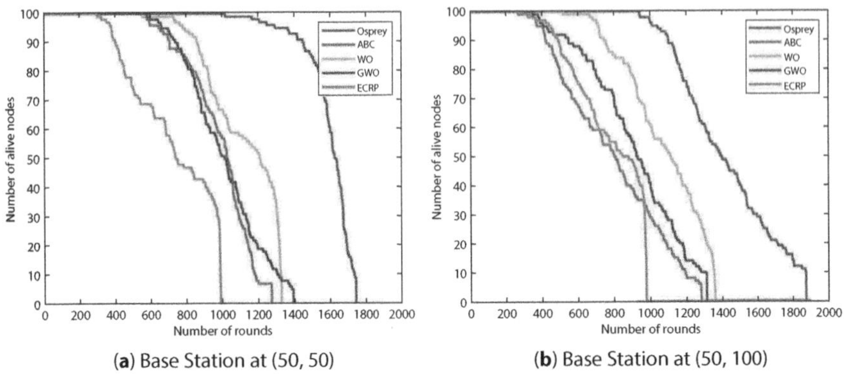

Figure 17.5 Comparison in terms of number of alive nodes over number of rounds.

active nodes throughout the rounds compared to existing algorithms such as [22–25]. This is achieved by optimizing residual energy, minimizing intra-cluster distance, and reducing the average distance between the BS and nodes.

17.6 Conclusion

In this chapter, we mainly focused on maximization of network lifetime of 6G enabled industrial internet of things. To achieve this, we have developed an energy-efficient clustering algorithm using edge intelligence (EI) i.e., Osprey optimization technique. For extending the network lifetime of 6G IIoT nodes, we have considered various fitness functions such as residual energy, average sink and intra-cluster distance. Then, after selecting CH, we formed clusters using intra-cluster distance. In addition, the proposed algorithm is simulated against various case studies, in the first case, the BS is situated at (50, 50) and in the second, the base station is located at (50, 100) for a given number of 6G enabled IIoT nodes. Then, we have shown extensive simulation results of the proposed algorithm and various existing approaches using various scenarios. The simulation results demonstrate that our proposed algorithm has superior efficiency over existing algorithms in terms of residual energy, network lifetime, and number of alive nodes. In this work, we have not included any routing algorithms.

In the future, our work will aim to design a routing method for maximizing network lifetime using meta-heuristic techniques. Additionally, we aim to develop a clustering algorithm for both homogeneous and heterogeneous nodes.

Acknowledgement

Partial funding for this research was provided by the Science and Engineering Research Board and the Department of Science and Technology, Government of India, under grant number EEQ/2021/000456.

AI disclosure statement: The author confirms that no artificial intelligence (AI)-generated content or AI-assisted writing tools were used in the preparation of this chapter (including summaries and the abstract). All text, analysis, and conclusions are the result of the author's original work.

References

1. Grari, M.O., Yandouzi, M.I., Idrissi, I.D., Boukabous, M.O., Moussaoui, O.M., Azizi, M., Moussaoui, M., Using IoT and ML for forest fire detection, monitoring, and prediction: a literature review. *J. Theor. Appl. Inf. Technol.*, 100, 19, 5445–61, 2022 Oct 15.
2. Alshamrani, M., IoT and artificial intelligence implementations for remote healthcare monitoring systems: A survey. *J. King Saud Univ. Comput. Inf. Sci.*, 34, 8, 4687–701, 2022 Sep 1.
3. Bera, B., Das, A.K., Garg, S., Piran, M.J., Hossain, M.S., Access control protocol for battlefield surveillance in drone-assisted IoT environment. *IEEE Internet Things J.*, 9, 4, 2708–21, 2021 Jan 4.
4. Muduli, L., Mishra, D.P., Jana, P.K., Application of wireless sensor network for environmental monitoring in underground coal mines: A systematic review. *J. Netw. Comput. Appl.*, 106, 48–67, 2018 Mar 15.
5. Padmaa, M., Jayasankar, T., Venkatraman, S., Dutta, A.K., Gupta, D., Shamshirband, S., Rodrigues, J.J., Oppositional chaos game optimization based clustering with trust based data transmission protocol for intelligent IoT edge systems. *J. Parallel Distrib. Comput.*, 164, 142–51, 2022 Jun 1.
6. Dogra, R., Rani, S., Babbar, H., Verma, S., Verma, K., Rodrigues, J.J., DCGCR: Dynamic clustering green communication routing for intelligent transportation systems. *IEEE Trans. Intell. Transp. Syst.*, 23, 9, 16197–205, 2022 Feb 16.
7. Rao, P.S., Jana, P.K., Banka, H., A particle swarm optimization based energy efficient cluster head selection algorithm for wireless sensor networks. *Wirel. Netw.*, 23, 2005–20, 2017 Oct.

8. Jaiswal, K. and Anand, V., A Grey-Wolf based Optimized Clustering approach to improve QoS in wireless sensor networks for IoT applications. *Peer-to-Peer Netw. Appl.*, 14, 4, 1943–62, 2021 Jul.
9. Sankar, S., Ramasubbareddy, S., Dhanaraj, R.K., Balusamy, B., Gupta, P., Ibrahim, W., Verma, R., Cluster head selection for the internet of things using a sandpiper optimization algorithm (SOA). *J. Sens.*, 2023, 1, 3507600, 2023.
10. Rajasekaran, A. and Nagarajan, V., Cluster-based wireless sensor networks using ant colony optimization. *International Conference on Intelligent Data Communication Technologies and Internet of Things (ICICI) 2018*, Springer International Publishing, pp. 42–55, 2019.
11. Adumbabu, I. and Selvakumar, K., Energy efficient routing and dynamic cluster head selection using enhanced optimization algorithms for wireless sensor networks. *Energies*, 15, 21, 8016, 2022 Oct 28.
12. Janakiraman, S., A hybrid ant colony and artificial bee colony optimization algorithm-based cluster head selection for IoT. *Procedia Comput. Sci.*, 143, 360–6, 2018 Jan 1.
13. Senthil, G.A., Raaza, A., Kumar, N., Internet of things energy efficient cluster-based routing using hybrid particle swarm optimization for wireless sensor network. *Wirel. Pers. Commun.*, 122, 3, 2603–19, 2022 Feb.
14. Natesan, G., Konda, S., de Prado, R.P., Wozniak, M., A hybrid mayfly-Aquila optimization algorithm based energy-efficient clustering routing protocol for wireless sensor networks. *Sensors*, 22, 17, 6405, 2022 Aug 25.
15. Somula, R., Cho, Y., Mohanta, B.K., SWARAM: Osprey Optimization Algorithm-Based Energy-Efficient Cluster Head Selection for Wireless Sensor Network-Based Internet of Things. *Sensors*, 24, 2, 521, 2024.
16. Shanmugapriya, T. and Kousalya, K., Cluster Head Selection and Multipath Routing Based Energy Efficient Wireless Sensor Network. *Intell. Autom. Soft Comput.*, 36, 1, 111–123, 2023.
17. Rodríguez, A., Del-Valle-Soto, C., Velázquez, R., Energy-efficient clustering routing protocol for wireless sensor networks based on yellow saddle goatfish algorithm. *Mathematics*, 8, 9, 1515, 2020 Sep 4.
18. Sharma, S.K. and Chawla, M., PRESEP: Cluster based metaheuristic algorithm for energy-efficient wireless sensor network application in internet of things. *Wirel. Pers. Commun.*, 133, 2, 1243–63, 2023 Nov.
19. Sahoo, B.M., Pandey, H.M., Amgoth, T., A genetic algorithm inspired optimized cluster head selection method in wireless sensor networks. *Swarm Evol. Comput.*, 75, 101151, 2022 Dec 1.
20. Heinzelman, W.R., Chandrakasan, A., Balakrishnan, H., Energy-efficient communication protocol for wireless microsensor networks, in: *Proceedings of the 33rd annual Hawaii international conference on system sciences*, p. 10, IEEE, 2000 Jan 7.

21. Dehghani, M. and Trojovský, P., Osprey optimization algorithm: A new bio-inspired metaheuristic algorithm for solving engineering optimization problems. *Front. Mech. Eng.*, 8, 1126450, 2023 Jan 20.
22. Ahmad, T., Haque, M., Khan, A.M., An energy-efficient cluster head selection using artificial bees colony optimization for wireless sensor networks, in: *Advances in nature-inspired computing and applications*, pp. 189–203, 2019.
23. Jadhav, A.R. and Shankar, T., Whale optimization based energy-efficient cluster head selection algorithm for wireless sensor networks, *arXiv preprint arXiv:1711.09389*, 2017 Nov 26.
24. Sekaran, K., Rajakumar, R., Dinesh, K., Rajkumar, Y., Latchoumi, T.P., Kadry, S., Lim, S., An energy-efficient cluster head selection in wireless sensor network using grey wolf optimization algorithm. *TELKOMNIKA (Telecommun. Comput. Electron. Control)*, 18, 6, 2822–33, 2020 Dec 1.
25. Moussa, N., Hamidi-Alaoui, Z., El Belrhiti El Alaoui, A., ECRP: an energy-aware cluster-based routing protocol for wireless sensor networks. *Wirel. Netw.*, 26, 2915–28, 2020 May.
26. Bhambri, P., Rani, S., Kumar, S., Sinha, V.K., Big Data Analytics with Digital Twin for Industrial Applications, in: *AI-Driven Digital Twin and Industry 4.0: A Conceptual Framework with Applications*, 1st, S. Rani, P. Bhambri, S. Kumar, P.K. Pareek, A.A. Elngar (Eds.), pp. 105–26, CRC Press, Boca Raton, FL, USA, 2024, https://doi.org/10.1201/9781003395416.
27. Bhambri, P., Rani, S., Pareek, P.K., Paperless Paradigm: Intelligent Automation in Document and Record Management, in: *Generating Entrepreneurial Ideas with AI*, D. Darwish (Ed.), pp. 164–83, IGI Global, Hershey, PA, USA, 2024, https://www.igi-global.com/book/hyperautomation-business-society/335477.

18

6G Enabled Industrial Internet of Medical Things: Prospective, Development and Challenges

Meetali Chauhan and Sita Rani*

Department of Computer Science and Engineering, Guru Nanak Dev Engineering College, Ludhiana, Punjab, India

Abstract

The sixth generation (6G) technology will bring revolution in medical domain supporting remote healthcare for all ages of people in three-dimensional space (3D). Time and distance are major constraints in healthcare which can be overcome by 6G. Future healthcare will be a collaboration of 6G and internet of things (IoT) which will address certain limitations such as network performance, cellular coverage and security issues. The next generation 6G network aims to provide link between intelligent machines and humans through wireless network. Quality of life (QOL), Intelligent Wearable Devices (IWD), Industrial Internet of Medical Things (IIOMT) and Hospital to Home Services (H2H) are new business models which must be implemented for improving healthcare domain. 6G communication technology will be used in telesurgery and pandemics. This paper discusses and highlights various prospects, challenges, and future directions of 6G Technology.

Keywords: 6G, IOT, healthcare, industrial internet of medical things, communication, sensors

**Corresponding author*: sitasaini80@gmail.com; ORCID: 0000-0003-2778-0214
Meetali Chauhan: ORCID: 0000-0002-3403-9929

Sita Rani, Pankaj Bhambri, Balamurugan Balusamy, Rishabha Malviya and Seifedine Kadry (eds.) Edge Intelligence for 6G-Enabled Industrial Internet of Things, (387–406) © 2026 Scrivener Publishing LLC

18.1 Introduction

The generations with advancement of technology have major impact on development due to the automation system which is based on demands of users. Due to network-based technologies, enormous amount of data is shared at high speed, where transition can be seen from 1G to 6G in terms of faster communication, digitization, enabling text messages, data services, mobility, integration of devices, mobile internet, video calling and connectivity. Figure 18.1 shows the conversion from of 1G-6G network technologies comprising advancements over a period of time.

Technology plays most important role in various provinces like as transportation, education, farming as well as hospitals for bringing upgradation in services provided to users. The need of the hour is to improvise the most important domain for society— that is, healthcare. To reduce health risk, enhanced healthcare system is required. There is need to upgrade medical domain with better approaches for providing immediate medical care to patients with emerging technologies such as AI, IOT and cloud computing [1]. IOT consists of physical items, sensors as well as other components to shared network. IOT devices are used to monitor body parameters of patient in medical domain and data is shared over network to analyze the measured parameters. This has been made possible with radio frequency classification, big data analytics, technological advancement and spectrum sharing. To retrieve necessary information, investigate the data, devices can be connected over network [2]. Most of the IOT devices are equipped with actuators, micro controllers' chip, sensors, communication network, and protocol stacks. In addition to this, various devices are anticipated to detect control and process models for improving the implementation of applications based on cyber physical IOT [3].

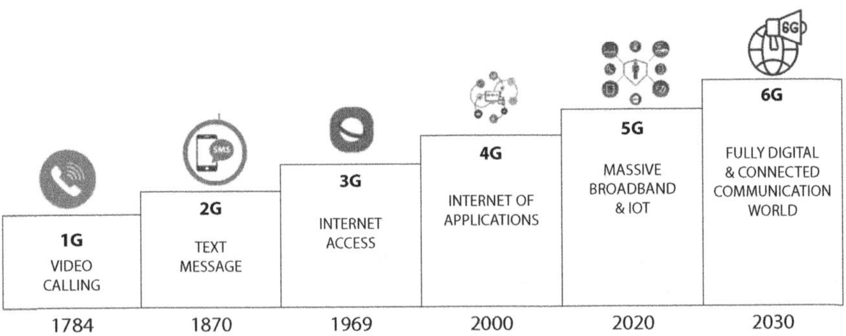

Figure 18.1 Conversion from 1G to 6G network technologies.

Advanced IOT framework has been exemplified as IOMT which has been integrated with wireless protocols, smartphones and various devices providing seamless connection between medical professionals, various equipment patients, and healthcare centers. IOT based wearable devices that comprise smart watches, medical sensors, fitness trackers, smart shoes, smart band within IOMT landscape, facilitate patient monitoring, health data acquisition and remote health services. IOMT infrastructure includes healthcare system to take leverage of various technologies for elevation of patient care, diagnostic accuracy, and analyzing parameters using IOT sensor-based wearables. The reason for IOT devices gaining popularity is due to increasing demand of communication using wireless networks. Wireless sensor network is used for effective communication to collect patients' information.

In current times, sensors are deployed in operating rooms, intensive care unit (ICU), emergency departments to capture critical patient parameters. In addition to this, wearables sensors-based health devices capture parameters enabling real-time patient monitoring, reducing medical expenses and improvising patient health. This demands enhancement of wireless network for next generation. Although 5G network is effective to provide efficient services, using IOT devices is not sufficient to accomplish requirements of latest smart applications. So, researchers have a vision to launch 6G wireless communication system for improving existing 5G based network system. 6G technology is effective for communication. 6G communication technology also attracts many researchers to bring revolution in upcoming years. 6G will use terahertz (THz) for signal transmission. This increases data rate and bandwidth [1]. Table 18.1 shows comparative analysis of 5G and 6G technology in terms of performance over network [4].

The goal of the high bandwidth is to provide a signal that is three times stronger than 5G. Furthermore, 6G intends to provide 3D services while using cutting-edge technology like blockchain, artificial intelligence, cloud computing, and the internet of things. Device-to-device and satellite communication coverage will be deeper and wider, thanks to the integrated and pervasive communication network.Computation, sensing and navigation will be interconnected in 6G communication network [5]. In 6G network, various operations such as data processing, service-based communication and resource management are driven by AI. The objective of this paper is to provide an overview of how 6G technology will enhance IOMT in the future by considering various aspects of healthcare domain [6].

Table 18.1 Comparison analysis of 5G and 6G.

Performance attributes	5G	6G
Application Types	URLLC	mURLLC
Interoperable Devices	Smartphones, Sensors, Drones	Sensors, DLT Devices, XR
Mobility Support	500 Km/h	1000 Km/h
Artificial Intelligence	Limited	Yes
Maximum Frequency	90 GHz	10 THz
Satellite Integration	No	Yes
Peak Data Rate	10 Gb/s	1 Tb/s
Channel Bandwidth	100 MHz	500-1000 MHz
Wavelength	3mm	1mm
Time Buffer	Not Real time	Real time
Smart City Components	Separate	Integrated
Bio Sensors	Limited	Yes
Automation	Micro Second	Nano Second
Centre of Gravity	User Centric	Service Centric
Architecture	Massive MIMO	Intelligent Surface
Spectral Efficiency	30 Hz	100 Hz
Autonomous Vehicles	Limited	Yes

18.2 Literature Survey

A medical professional's top priority is speedy and trouble-free usage of healthcare data to develop a successful healthcare system and prevent disastrous situations [26]. Death rates have grown in recent years owing to life expectancy. This suggests that the number of senior persons falling sick is growing every year. People of all ages are most typically afflicted by

Table 18.2 Related work.

Author	Year	Objective
Saad *et al.* [7]	2019	Discusses performance requirement and trends of 6G technology
Letaief *et al.* [8]	2019	AI based 6G applications and optimized networking-based architecture
Yang *et al.* [9]	2019	6G future trends and techniques are analysed for scope of improvement
Giordani *et al.* [10]	2020	6G requirements and use case are presented
Tariq *et al.* [11]	2020	Extension of vision from 5G to enable 6G effectively
Dang *et al.* [12]	2020	Focused on future challenges associated with deployment of 6G technology
Tomkos *et al.* [13]	2020	Presented review on IOT technology based on 6G network
Zhang *et al.* [14]	2019	Considering main technological aspects such as IOT, and AI
Guiet *et al.* [15]	2020	Survey on machine learning techniques for communication, network, and security of 6G vehicular technology
Y. Al-Eryani *et al.* [16]	2019	Multiple access method for massive access using 6G network is proposed
L Loven *et al.* [17]	2019	Role of edge AI in 6G communication network has been discussed
Prafulla *et al.* [18]	2021	The synthesis of 6G, IoT, IoE, industrial internet of everything (IIoE)
Shafin *et al.* [19]	2020	Review on challenges, applications, and future scope for B5G as well as 6G network
Chowdhury *et al.* [20]	2019	Detailed review of 6G based wireless communication using AI
L Tomkos *et al.* [21]	2020	Convergence and transformation of 5G and IOT technologies towards 6G network

chronic lifestyle problems. Numerous research initiatives have focused on enhancing the healthcare sectors. Some of them are covered in this section. In recent years, various studies and research projects have been done to promote and develop healthcare for people. Table 18.2 represents detailed analysis of work carried out by various researchers and studies highlighted by various authors for using 6G technology in healthcare.

Various researches have focused on 6G network-based skills, architecture, and research tasks in recent years [22]. For instance, in [23], the author has portrayed review of 6G wireless communication-based security and privacy perspective using blockchain technology. The author further discusses architecture failure of security system. The author in [24], discusses in depth the role of 6G based communication for IOT applications in healthcare, vehicles and satellite communication using UAV's. The author [25], has analysed various parameters like latency, network mobility, and energy consumption. The limitations of 5G technology have been highlighted which can be rectified using advancement of 6G technology-based communication.

18.3 6G Technology

6G is 6th generation wireless cellular technology. It uses higher frequencies than previously available networks. It is expected that 6G will be able to facilitate context aware digital services, location services and sensory experience towards extended reality including holograms. There is a possibility that real-time communication using wearable sensors will be possible where users might experience physical sensation of next person they are interacting with through virtual connection. 6G will enhance IOT to expand and provide more services with efficient management of data. The 6G network relies much on IOT to process data. The next generation 6G network aims to provide link between intelligent machines and humans through wireless network. 6G will allow effective communication anywhere. Table 18.3 shows various 6G technology-based communication standards used for providing services in healthcare domain [26, 27].

To implement 6G technology in real-world certain requirements need to be taken care of, such as high coverage, network flexibility, end-to-end communication, cognitive networks, diversified embedded networks, trusted systems and devices, network computing. Hence, 6G based technology can be used in multiple domains smart production, smart life, smart society, smart education, and smart healthcare.

Table 18.3 6G based communication standards.

Technology	Application	Challenges
OCC	• Monitor oxygen pulse • Monitor health in ICU • Central hub for communication and emotion checking	• Low data rate due to limited bandwidth • Noise problem from sources
FSO	• Telemedicine • Broadband service for communication of health report • Lastmile technology	• ML based switching between RF and FSO
Haptic Communication	• Telesurgery • Support mental health • Rehabilitation robots • Social assistance to blind	• Patient location is difficult to access
Lifi	• MRI medical equipment • Lifi wearables	• Expensive to use
VLC	• Tracking of blind, wheelchair, medical equipment's • Anomaly detection • Surgery • Health monitoring • Ambulance to ambulance communication • Health data security	• Shadow effect during surgery • Noise and flickering effects
WBCI Wet	• Brain implants • Control computing devices • Wireless power E-Band • Healthcare device and gadgets wearables	• Intrinsic neurophysiological instability of brain dynami • Frequency problem
Tactile Internet	• Communication of patient and medical staff	• Performance issues

(*Continued*)

Table 18.3 6G based communication standards. (*Continued*)

Technology	Application	Challenges
Thz Communication	• Communication of robot and doctor using 3D healthcare connectivity services	• Upgradation of devices
Satellite Communication	• Signal amplification • Surgery over SC channel • Diagnosis and treatment of disease	• High power consumption

18.4 Role of 6G Technology towards Healthcare

6G will capture healthcare system with effective communication in various domains such as quality of life, hospital to home services, IIOMT, intelligent wearable devices, and blood sample reader. To secure and provide efficient services in medical domain, it is important to reduce health risk globally. This can be achieved by facilitating basic requirement of people. 6G communication technology in medical industry aims to provide efficiency in various services such as telesurgery using holographic communication. The current healthcare system provides basic facilities. Some of the services still need to be focused; for example, ambulance equipped with oxygen facility and priority to drive on road among traffic. But still, if patient is critical and is unable to reach the hospital and dies on the way, there is no alternative to resolve such extreme level of emergency case. In addition to this, accident detection system is missing which is another example of extreme emergency where sometimes, a patient dies on the spot due to unapproachable medical aid at that point of time. So, there is a need to develop intelligent healthcare system [5].

6G is a ray of hope in medical field which aims to fulfil certain requirements such as high data rate, high mobility, wavelength for efficient communication. Like telesurgery requires real-time communication, 6G technology focuses more on virtual and augmented reality. Another aspect for 6G technology is rural connectivity, as it is still a challenge for 5G technology in terms of healthcare domain. The rural people are not able to get medical facilities and on time services [28]. The effective communication technology aims to boost up health services performance and healthcare system.

This includes improvement of ambulance services, redefining IOT based medical wearable devices, improving e-healthcare services [29].

6G robotics will be used for remote surgery where physicians will guide robotic devices without any latency. The physician will provide instructions to robots for following surgery procedure. Telemedicine services and AAL technology to monitor people and provide on-time treatment would assist 6G based intelligent network. As healthcare domain is not only confined to individual patient with illness, it aims to provide medical services and enhance living standards. IOT based medical devices are very useful for providing patient parameters, for example, in measuring cardiac rate, blood test, body weight, blood pressure, sugar level, temperature, number of steps, calories intake, health issues etc. This makes patient life easier and minimizes hospital visit for patients as parameters can be controlled at home with in-depth analysis using IOT medical devices. 6G will enhance network communication for IIOMT based devices [6]. Wireless body area network improves device performance and enhances speedy transfer of data and information. So 6G is most suitable for healthcare networks. As enhanced spectrum, integrated intelligence, inbuilt optimization capability, ultra-low latency, reduced operational cost will ensure effective communication removing time and space constraints from IOMT based devices [30].

Wearable devices, smart watches, medical sensors and fitness trackers serve as IOMT real-time patient monitoring devices. Sensors are deployed in emergency departments, or in the ICU to capture patient state [31]. 6G technology will also be innovative in the commercial sector. Nowadays, the hospital is paid directly by the patient for their care, either by a family member or *via* their health insurance. Many organizations operate the medical insurance coverage as a kind of commercial establishment. Additionally, this medical center accepts cashless payments, which are taken straight out of the insurance company. But insurance policies also have exceptions as many diseases covered under medical insurance services. This is inconvenient for patients to pay cost to the hospitals even after covered under insurance policy. In such cases neither hospitals nor insurance companies are reliable sources for all types of situations [32].

6G technology will help to reframe policies where insurance policies will be premium based to pay directly to hospitals. Policies will include telesurgery, aged care, personalization, pregnancy, vaccinations and serious illness diseases like neurological, flu and mishaps. There will be no cost limit for patient to get number of treatments. Figure 18.2 shows 6G based healthcare system [33].

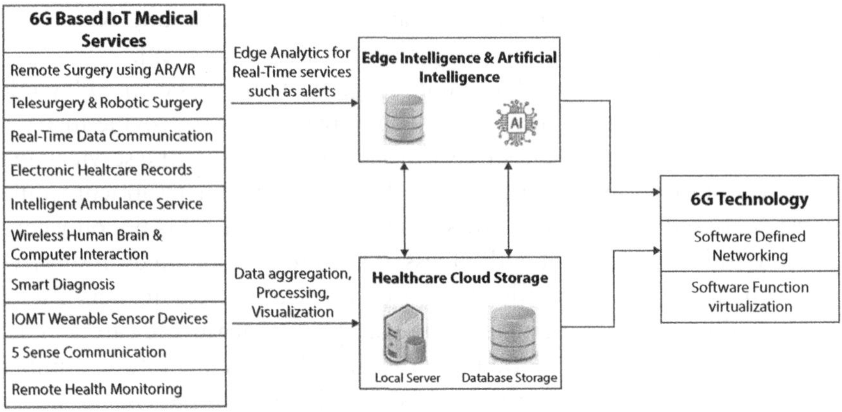

Figure 18.2 6G based healthcare system.

18.5 6G Based IIoMT Applications

The intelligent internet of medical things (IIoMT) will contribute to human well-being in the context of 6G connection. IIoMTs are intelligent, AI-driven devices employ communication technology to make choices on their own. Medical gadgets will be able to connect to the internet as IoE and IIoMT evolve. For instance, CT and MRI scans. Using 6G technology, the scanner will scan the devices and communicate the data to faraway locations. The pathologist may review the data in real time. Nearly every medical gadget will be able to connect to the internet, enabling for speedy decision-making. Consequently, time, money, and space will not be an issue for IIoMT. Several IIOMT-based applications are mentioned below.

18.5.1 Holographic Communication

Hologram is physical recording that employs diffraction to provide 3D vision. The picture formed includes parallax, depth as well as other features of original item. For such 3D picture generation, communication is conceivable utilizing cameras from multiple angles to build a hologram of an item. It utilizes eMBB and URLLC. But this demands high data rate to deliver decent quality of video. Very low latency is required for real-time voice as well as immediate control response. 6G network technology will help people to connect using holographic communication. In medical domain, this will bring revolution as in case of emergency–doctors sometimes having to wait for specialized doctors for diagnosis and guidance for treatment. But it is risk taking for patient health. Using holographic communication, experts can diagnose patient virtually and can supervise medical team. In addition to this, sometimes patients have to travel to different countries or different cities for appropriate treatment and medical checkup. This causes inconvenience to patient. But using holographic, doctors can be consulted remotely for correct diagnosis. Holographic communication will also help to connect globally in healthcare and rural areas. It is best possible approach where various doctors around the world can collaborate for complex and critical medical cases [5].

18.5.2 Augmented Reality and Virtual Reality

Virtual Reality refers to present imagination and virtual world and augmented reality to deploy virtuality into real- world objects. It is collaboration of sensory ability using audio, haptic, somato sensory etc. AR presents 3D images and real-time interaction of virtuality and real-world objects. 6G network technology is required for AR and VR as high data transfer rate is required. It is a useful component for healthcare devices. AR will permit the patient's body to be observed without any incisions. For medical diagnosis, clinicians may undertake accurate body component analysis. For enhanced visibility and study of the patient's health condition, the specific bodily component could be increased. Holographic communication and AR can even work together to deliver an accurate diagnosis. With the use of IOT-based technology linked to 6G internet, UR allows surgeons to undertake high-risk, complicated surgical operations.

18.5.3 Haptic Internet

Virtual touch employing haptic internet causes the user to move and vibrate. Virtual touch may be conveyed to humans or robots *via* the tactile internet. However, this requires for ERLLC and quick communication. This technology is used for one of the most important aspects of medical domain that is telesurgery. This also provides medical diagnosis of patient using IOT based sensor touch without physical presence of doctors. Haptic based interaction (HCI) of human and computer is further classified as desktop, wearable, and surface. In desktop HCI, remote doctor will use virtual tool for diagnosis and surgery. In surface type of HCI, movement will be based on 2D, but the command given will be using mobile or tablet. This will help to give command to robot to interact with patient. In wearable type of HCI, IOT based wearable medical devices can be used by doctors such as haptic gloves.

18.5.4 Sample Reader Sensors

Traditional method comprises of physical presence of human being where he is injected to take blood sample from the body. But 6G based smart healthcare will introduce sample reader sensors (SRS) needle free method for diabetic patients to monitor glucose level. SRS has potential to revolutionize health domain from blood that is WBC, RBC etc. But SRS implementation requires 6G internet connectivity for taking sample using sensor. The blood tests can be conducted periodically using this approach. This type of sensor can be useful to read not only blood but also various other body parameters such as thyroid, wine sample, stools etc. Thus, SRS will be the most demanded medical device for healthcare [6].

18.5.5 Intelligent Wearable Devices

IOT devices are connected to the internet which convey data to health monitoring centers. The devices are effective to measure various parameters of the body like blood pressure, heart beat, blood tests, body weights, and nutrition. It helps human being to study body parameter and analyze health status which can advise them the required action like walk or running. Even if a person has nutrition deficiency, person will come to know based on health parameters measured using IOT devices. Person can make necessary changes in his life style and diet to stay healthy. This reduces the frequency of human beings to visit hospitals.

18.5.6 Hospital to Home Services

In current times, ambulance services is just a means of transport to take patient from home to hospital with availability of oxygen supply for patients. Priority to drive is given during road traffic so that patient can reach the hospital as soon as possible. But there is no provision of emergency services to patient as soon as some cases urgent treatment is required and approaching towards hospitals might lead to death of patient. So advanced ambulance services is required. With the help of 6G based communication technology, emergency situations can be tackled safely. Future vehicles will be fully AI based. For example, in case of road accident, the patient can be given immediate treatment on the spot instead of taking him to the hospital. Medical team can reach and treat the patient before reaching the hospital.

18.5.7 Telesurgery

Telesurgery is remote surgery conducted by a doctor. It requires robots, nurses, and source of medium to connect with doctors. Effective 6G communication is an important aspect for telesurgery. In addition to this, it requires URLLC and high data rate. These requirements cannot be provided using 5G and B5G due to lack of virtual reality. Hence, 6G technology is required for support of virtual reality. The doctor can provide teleassistance and guidance to perform surgery. Holographic communication is an effective source of medium for guidance. AR and VR are used for telestration. Hence, 6G will prove surgery can be performed beyond boundaries [34].

18.6 Challenges and Future Perspective

18.6.1 Challenges for 6G Technology

- **Security and Privacy issues.** The integration of 6G based IOT devices is prone to wireless attacks such as denial of service, unauthorized data access, hacking, hijacking, eavesdropping, spoofing etc. This can cause major loss to healthcare data centers and apps. As the number of connections increases, threat to security also increases. Patient medical parameters can be changed from data retrieved from IOT based medical devices. This can compromise patient health. Blockchain based approach can be suitable in era of 6G for security and privacy purpose [35].
- **Low Power and Communication.** IOT medical devices are connected to various servers. But some of the devices require maintenance cost and power battery on regular basis. This causes serious problem. So, devices must be of low power consumption. Efficient energy techniques are required for devices to communicate with less energy. There is a need for development in the field of wireless communication, energy harvesting, and microelectronics [36].
- **Location and Precise Positioning.** Some indoor as well as outdoor locations might not be accessible during emergency. GPS is required for tracing such outside locations.

But GPS is not effective in case of inside locations. Like, when hospitals become overloaded with patients due to any pandemic, then locating specialists, patients, and medical staff becomes difficult, especially if the hospital is huge. So, in case of emergency in real-time environment, there is a requirement of possible fast response and easily locatable medical staff which is possible with efficient implementation of 6G technology [6].

- **Healthcare Data Analytics.** Smart healthcare generates a huge amount of data. The data is comprised of personal information of patients as well. So, to examine such sensitive data, intelligent algorithms are required.
- **Intelligent Spectrum Sharing.** Device-to-device communication, non-orthogonal multiple access and full duplex communication are few spectrum sharing technologies deployed in 6G IOT networks. So, there is a need to improve the system performance to manage a large number of connections in 6G technology [30].

18.6.2 Future Perspective

6G technology will enable wireless facilities and internet of bio nano things in healthcare which will enable every individual to become part of network communication motivating them to lead a better lifestyle. Humans will be able to self-monitor health parameters using sensors to inculcate timely medical prescriptions, dietary changes and get on time medical treatments keeping themselves fit and healthy. Healthcare system will grow effectively than conventional system using 6G. 6G technology aims to combine multiple intelligent devices over AI based network expectations for efficient implementation of IOMT over edge/fog/cloud computing technology. A case study is presented to better understand the future perspectives [6, 37–39].

Case Study

Remote surgery is an advanced level surgery procedure which would be carried out by robotic machines. This would consist of medical team and patient connected over strong network communication geographically as it is a sensitive task. Remote surgery also called as telesurgery is performed without surgeons through robots. The surgeons could collaborate as a team using holographic communication; and instructions will be given to the robot to carry out operation. Recent analysis confirms that 5G technology has been used to perform various robotic operations [39]. But 6G technology aims to provide strong communication over network without any interruption. Figure 18.3 shows collaboration of surgeons located at different places to perform a surgery. The process also highlights that the medical team is accessing information about previous health records of patient to make necessary decisions. Hospitals are connected to cellular tower over 6G network for data exchange. The tower is further in connection with satellite communication. The surgery is performed by controlling robotic arms remotely. The general physician will start the treatment with some preparations and an anesthesiologist would join to initiate the process by giving anesthesia to patient. The radiologist would localize the area of interest on the patient's body for treatment. The surgeon along with his team will perform surgery. Then after the surgery, the radiologist will stitch back the body and the anesthesiologist will get back the patient to his senses. But all these operations will be implemented remotely by the medical team using holographic approach. The actual implementation would be carried out by robots based on the instructions given by the team.

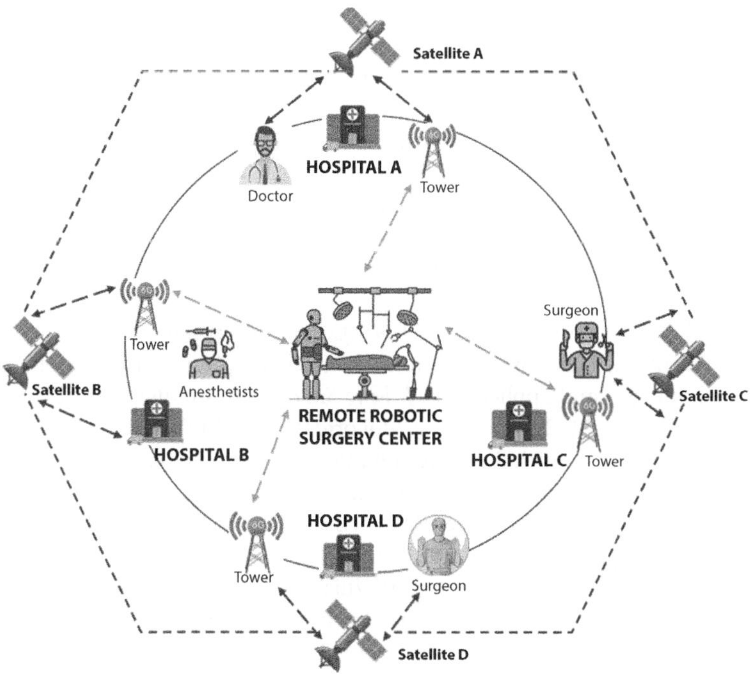

Figure 18.3 Layout of 6G based remote robotic surgery.

18.7 Conclusion

Future healthcare will enable medical experts to connect electronically and do remote robotic surgery. The patient's ailment will be diagnosed by the physicians effectively based on bodily characteristics utilizing IOT. Existing communication systems are complicated and cannot match dynamic demands of broad variety of smart healthcare applications. The 6G-IOT based network and apps are still in early phases of development. But if they are launched efficiently, it will change the current IOT infrastructure and raise the levels of services as well as the quality of life in healthcare. This research has analysed the extent of revolution employing 6G technology in different healthcare applications.

AI disclosure statement: The author confirms that no artificial intelligence (AI)-generated content or AI-assisted writing tools were used in the preparation of this chapter (including summaries and the abstract). All text, analysis, and conclusions are the result of the author's original work.

References

1. Gargish, S., Chauhan, S., Gupta, M., Obaid, A., 6G-Enabled IoT Wearable Devices for Elderly Healthcare, in: *6G-Enabled IoT and AI for Smart Healthcare*, pp. 157–169, 2023.
2. Padhi, P.K. and Charrua-Santos, F., 6G enabled industrial internet of everything: Towards a theoretical framework. *Appl. Syst. Innov.*, 4, 1, Article 11, 2021. https://doi.org/10.3390/asi4010011.
3. Wang, W., Liu, F., Zhi, X., Zhang, T., Huang, C., An integrated deep learning algorithm for detecting lung nodules with low-dose CT and its application in 6G-enabled Internet of Medical Things. *IEEE Internet Things J.*, 8, 7, 5274–5284, 2021. https://doi.org/10.1109/JIOT.2020.3023436.
4. Hakeem, S., Hussein, H., Vision, H., Kim, H., Research directions of 6G technologies and applications. *J. King Saud Univ.-Comput. Inf. Sci.*, Science Direct, 2419–2442, 2022, https://doi.org/10.1109/JIOT.2020.3023436.
5. Nayak, S. and Patgiri, R., 6G communication technology: A vision on intelligent healthcare. in: *Health informatics: A computational perspective in healthcare*, R. Patgiri, A. Biswas, & P. Roy (Eds.), Springer, Singapore, 1–22, 2021. https://doi.org/10.1007/978-981-15-9735-0_1.
6. Srinivasu, P.N., Ijaz, M.F., Shafi, J., Woźniak, M., Sujatha, R., 6G driven fast computational networking framework for healthcare applications. *IEEE Access*, 10, 94235–94248, 2022. https://doi.org/10.1109/ACCESS.2022.3203061.

7. Saad, W., Bennis, M., Chen, M., A vision of 6G wireless systems: Applications, trends, technologies, and open research problems. *IEEE Netw.*, 34, 3, 134–142, 2020. https://doi.org/10.1109/MNET.001.1900287.
8. Letaief, K.B., Chen, W., Shi, Y., *et al.*, The roadmap to 6G: AI empowered wireless networks. *Commun. Mag.*, IEEE, 57, 8, 84–90, 2019.
9. Yang, P., Xiao, Y., Xiao, M., Li, S., 6G wireless communications: Vision and potential techniques. *IEEE Netw.*, 33, 4, 70–75, 2019. https://doi.org/10.1109/MNET.2019.1800418.
10. Giordani, M., Polese, M., Mezzavilla, M., Toward 6G networks: Use cases and technologies. *Commun. Mag.*, IEEE, 58, 3, 55–61, 2020.
11. Tariq, F., Khandaker, M.R., Wong, K.-K., A speculative study on 6G. *J. Wireless Commun.*, IEEE, 27, 4, 118–125, 2020.
12. Dang, S., Amin, O., Shihada, B., From a human-centric perspective: What might 6G be, 2019.
13. Tomkos, I., Klonidis, D., Pikasis, E., Toward the 6G network era: Opportunities and challenges. *IT Prof.*, 22, 1, 34–38, 2020.
14. Zhang, Z., Xiao, Y., Ma, Z., 6G wireless networks: Vision, requirements, architecture and key technologies. *Mag. Veh. Technol.*, IEEE, 14, 3, 28–41, 2019.
15. Gui, G., Liu, M., Tang, F., 6G: Opening new horizons for integration of comfort, security and intelligence. *J. Wireless Commun.*, IEEE, 27, 5, 126–132, 2020.
16. Agiwal, M., Roy, A., Saxena, N., Next generation 5G wireless networks: A comprehensive survey. *J. Commun. Surv. Tutor.*, IEEE, 18, 3, 1617–1655, 2016.
17. Zong, B., Fan, C., Wang, X., 6G technologies: Key drivers, core requirements, system architectures and enabling technologies. *Veh. Technol. Mag.*, IEEE, 14, 3, 18–27, 2019.
18. Bhambri, P. Rani, S., Advancements in educational technology: Navigating the landscape of user experience in Web 3.0, in: *Architecting the Digital Future: Platforms, Design, and Application*, J.-É. Pelet (Ed.) IGI Global, 365–396, 2025. doi: 10.4018/979-8-3693-2973-3.ch014.
19. Shafin, R., Liu, L., Chandrasekhar, V., Chen, H., Reed, J., Zhang, J., Artificial intelligence-enabled cellular networks: A critical path to beyond-5G and 6G. arXiv, 2019. http://arxiv.org/abs/1907.07862v1.
20. Chowdhury, M.Z., Hossan, M.T., Hasan, M.K., Integrated RF/optical wireless networks for improving QoS in indoor and transportation applications. Springer, 107, 3, 1401–1430, 2019.
21. Saeed, N., Naffouri, T., Alouini, M.-S., Around the world of IoT/climate monitoring using internet of X-things. *Mag. Internet Things*, IEEE, 3, 2, 82–83, 2020.
22. Quadir, Z., Le, K.N., Saeed, N., Munawar, H., Towards 6G Internet of Things: Recent advances, use cases, and open challenges. *ICT Express*, 9, 3, 296–312, 2023. https://doi.org/10.1016/j.icte.2022.06.006.

23. Nguyen, V.-L., Lin, P.-C., Cheng, B.-C., Hwang, R.-H., Lin, Y.-D., Security and privacy for 6G: A survey on prospective technologies and challenges. *IEEE Commun. Surv. Tutor.*, 23, 4, 2384–2428, 2021, https://doi.org/10.1109/COMST.2021.3108618.
24. Nguyen, D.C., Ding, M., Pathirana, P.N., Seneviratne, A., Li, J., Niyato, D., Dobre, O., Poor, H.V., 6G Internet of Things: A comprehensive survey. *IEEE Internet of Things J.*, 9, 1, 359–383, 2021. https://doi.org/10.1109/JIOT.2021.3103320.
25. Dao, N.-N., Pham, Q.-V., Tu, N.H., Thanh, T.T., Bao, V.N.Q., Lakew, D.S., Cho, S., Survey on aerial radio access networks: Toward a comprehensive 6G access infrastructure. IEEE, 23, 2, 1193–1225, 2021.
26. Gupta, M., Jha, R., Jain, S., Tactile Based Intelligence Touch Technology in IoT Configured WCN in B5G/6G-A Survey. *IEEE Access*, 11, 30639–30689, 2023.
27. Kharche, S. and Kharche, J., 6G Intelligent Healthcare Framework: A Review on Role of Technologies, Challenges and Future Directions. *J. Mob. Multimedia*, 19, 603–644, 2023.
28. Bajpai, A. and Balodi, A., Role of 6G Networks: Use Cases and Research Directions, in: *Bangalore Humanitarian Technology Conference*, IEEE Explore, 2020.
29. Bin Ahammed, T. and Patgiri, R., 6G and AI: The emergence of future forefront technology, in: *2020 Advanced Communication Technologies and Signal Processing (ACTS)*, IEEE, 1–6, 2020. https://doi.org/10.1109/ACTS49415.2020.9350396.
30. Nasralla, M., Khattak, S., Rehman, I., Iqbal, M., Exploring the Role of 6G Technology in Enhancing Quality of Experience for m-Health Multimedia Applications: A Comprehensive Survey. *J. Edge Comput. Networked Sens. 6G Netw.*, MDPI, 23, 2023.
31. A Review on the Application of Internet of Medical Things in Wearable Personal Health Monitoring: A Cloud-Edge Artificial Intelligence Approach. *IEEE Access*, 12, 21437–21452, 2024.
32. khan, I., Ullah, F., Salam, A., Amin, F., Tabrez, S., Faisal, S., Choi, G., Big Data Analytics Model Using Artificial Intelligence (AI) and 6G Technologies for Healthcare. *IEEE Access*, 12, 97924–97937, 2024.
33. Nayak, S. and Patgiri, R., 6G communication technology: A vision on intelligent healthcare, in: *Health informatics: A computational perspective in healthcare*, R. Patgiri, A. Biswas, & P. Roy (Eds.). Springer, 1–18, 2021. https://doi.org/10.1007/978-981-15-9735-0_1.
34. Zaman, M., Ahmed, S., Shahjalal, M., Jang, Y., 6G Wireless Communication Systems: Applications, Requirements, Technologies, Challenges, and Research Directions. *J. Commun. Soc.*, IEEE Explore, 1, 957–975, 2020.
35. Ahad, A. and Tahir, M., Perspective—6G and IoT for Intelligent Healthcare: Challenges and Future Research Directions. *J. Electrochem. Soc.*, IOP, 2022.

36. Koren, A. and Prasad, R., IoT Health Data in Electronic Health Records (EHR): Security and Privacy Issues in Era of 6G. *J. ICT Stand.*, 10, 63–84, 2022.
37. Mucchi, L., Jayousi, S., Caputo, S., Paoletti, E., Zoppi, P., Geli, S., Dioniso, P., How 6G Technology Can Change the Future Wireless Healthcare, in: *Conference of 2nd 6G wireless summit*, IEEE Explore, 2020.
38. Bhambri, P., Rani, S., Kumar, S., Sinha, V.K., Big Data Analytics with Digital Twin for Industrial Applications, in: *AI-Driven Digital Twin and Industry 4.0: A Conceptual Framework with Applications*, 1st, S. Rani, P. Bhambri, S. Kumar, P.K. Pareek, A.A. Elngar (Eds.), pp. 105–26, CRC Press, 2024, https://doi.org/10.1201/9781003395416.
39. Bhambri, P., Rani, S., Pareek, P.K., Paperless Paradigm: Intelligent Automation in Document and Record Management, in: *Generating Entrepreneurial Ideas with AI*, D. Darwish (Ed.), pp. 164–83, IGI Global, 2024, https://www.igi-global.com/book/hyperautomation-business-society/335477.

Index

Printed and bound by CPI Group (UK) Ltd, Croydon, CR0 4YY
17/09/2026
14964263-0006